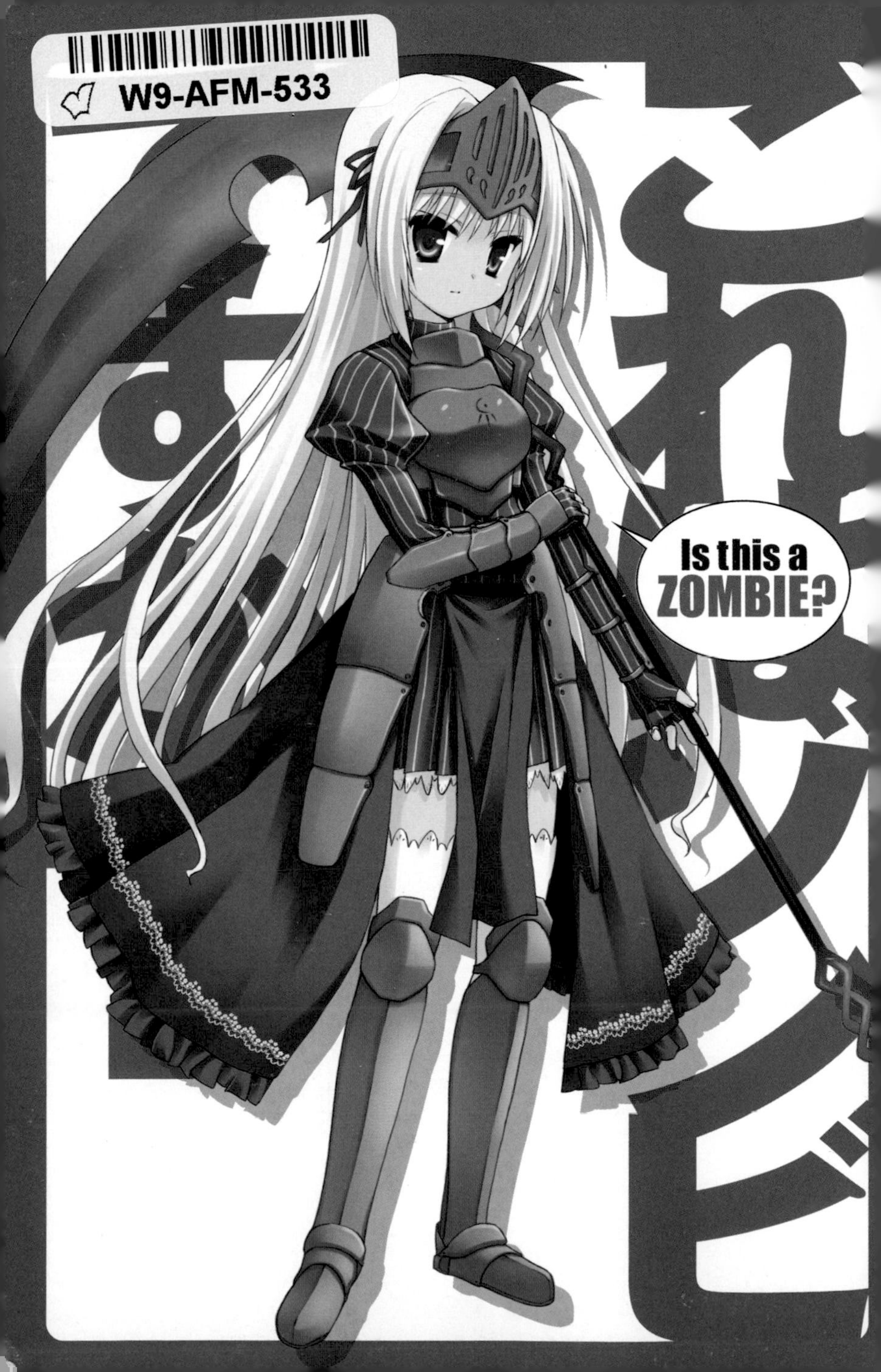
Is this a
ZOMBIE?

CONTENTS

Is this a ZOMBIE?

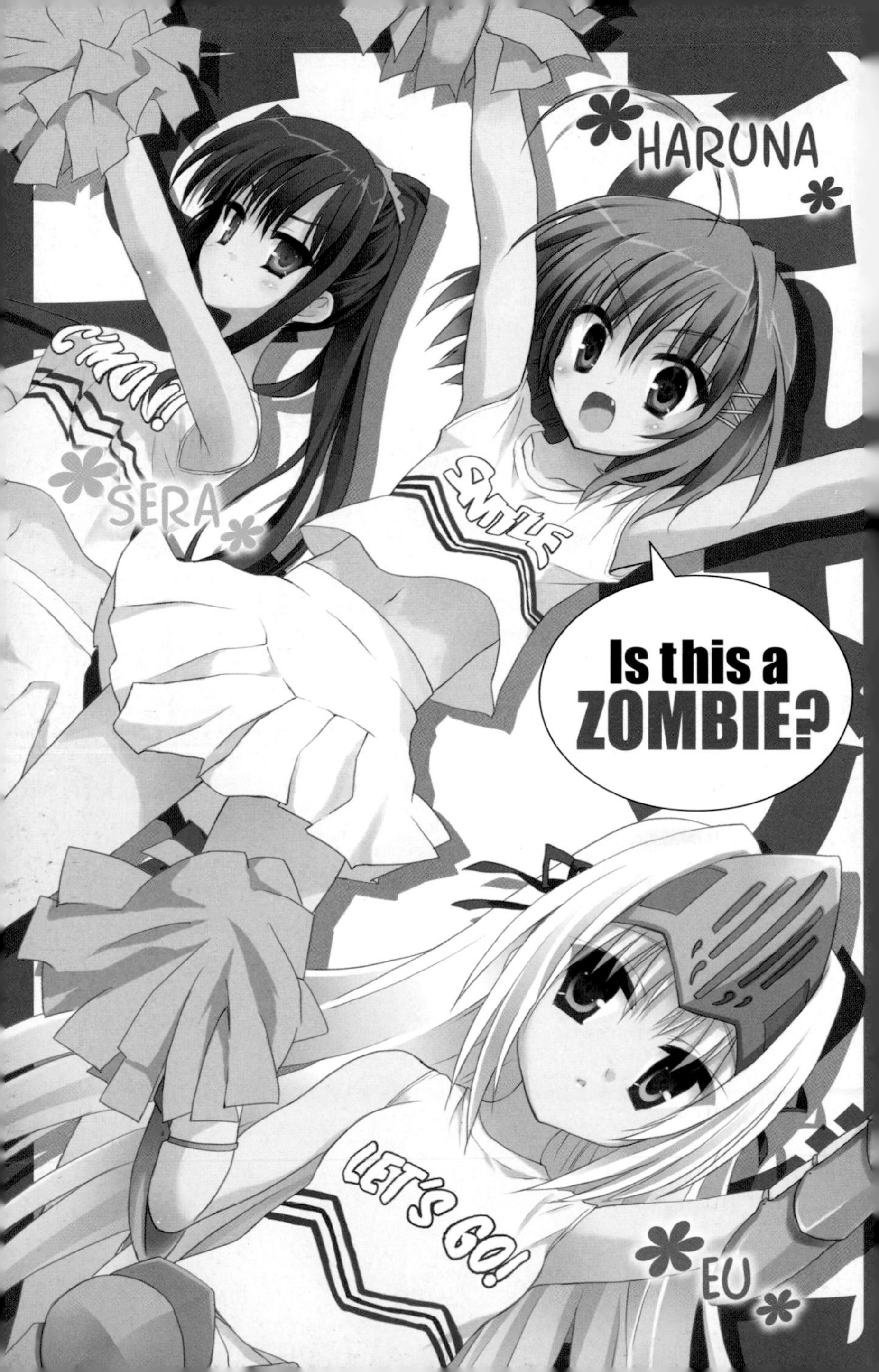
HARUNA
C'MON!!
SERA
SMILE
Is this a ZOMBIE?
LET'S GO!
EU

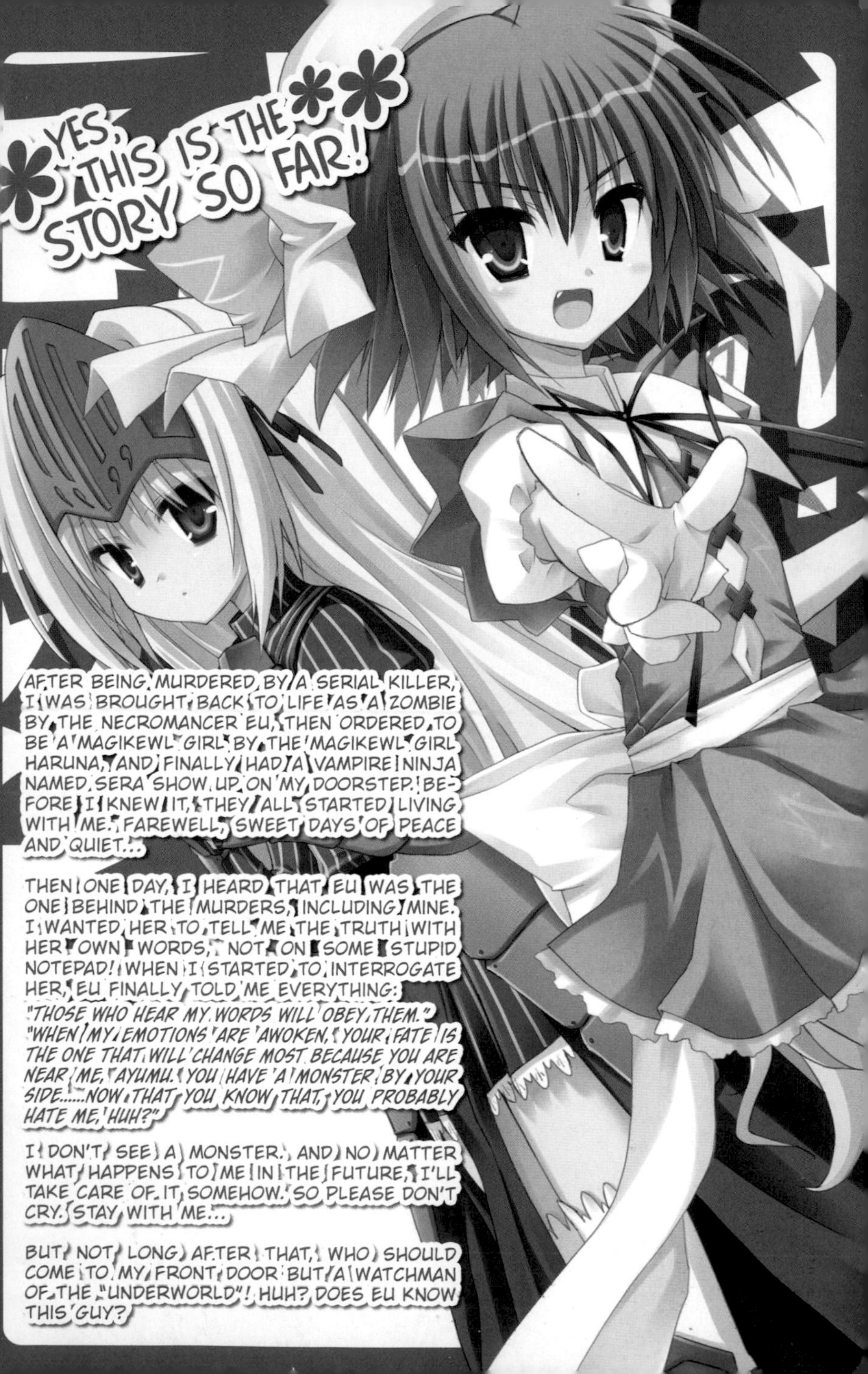

YES, THIS IS THE STORY SO FAR!

AFTER BEING MURDERED BY A SERIAL KILLER, I WAS BROUGHT BACK TO LIFE AS A ZOMBIE BY THE NECROMANCER EU, THEN ORDERED TO BE A MAGIKEWL GIRL BY THE MAGIKEWL GIRL HARUNA, AND FINALLY HAD A VAMPIRE NINJA NAMED SERA SHOW UP ON MY DOORSTEP. BEFORE I KNEW IT, THEY ALL STARTED LIVING WITH ME. FAREWELL, SWEET DAYS OF PEACE AND QUIET...

THEN ONE DAY, I HEARD THAT EU WAS THE ONE BEHIND THE MURDERS, INCLUDING MINE. I WANTED HER TO TELL ME THE TRUTH WITH HER OWN WORDS, NOT ON SOME STUPID NOTEPAD! WHEN I STARTED TO INTERROGATE HER, EU FINALLY TOLD ME EVERYTHING:
"THOSE WHO HEAR MY WORDS WILL OBEY THEM."
"WHEN MY EMOTIONS ARE AWOKEN, YOUR FATE IS THE ONE THAT WILL CHANGE MOST BECAUSE YOU ARE NEAR ME, AYUMU. YOU HAVE A MONSTER BY YOUR SIDE......NOW THAT YOU KNOW THAT, YOU PROBABLY HATE ME, HUH?"

I DON'T SEE A MONSTER. AND NO MATTER WHAT HAPPENS TO ME IN THE FUTURE, I'LL TAKE CARE OF IT SOMEHOW. SO PLEASE DON'T CRY. STAY WITH ME...

BUT NOT LONG AFTER THAT, WHO SHOULD COME TO MY FRONT DOOR BUT A WATCHMAN OF THE "UNDERWORLD"! HUH? DOES EU KNOW THIS GUY?

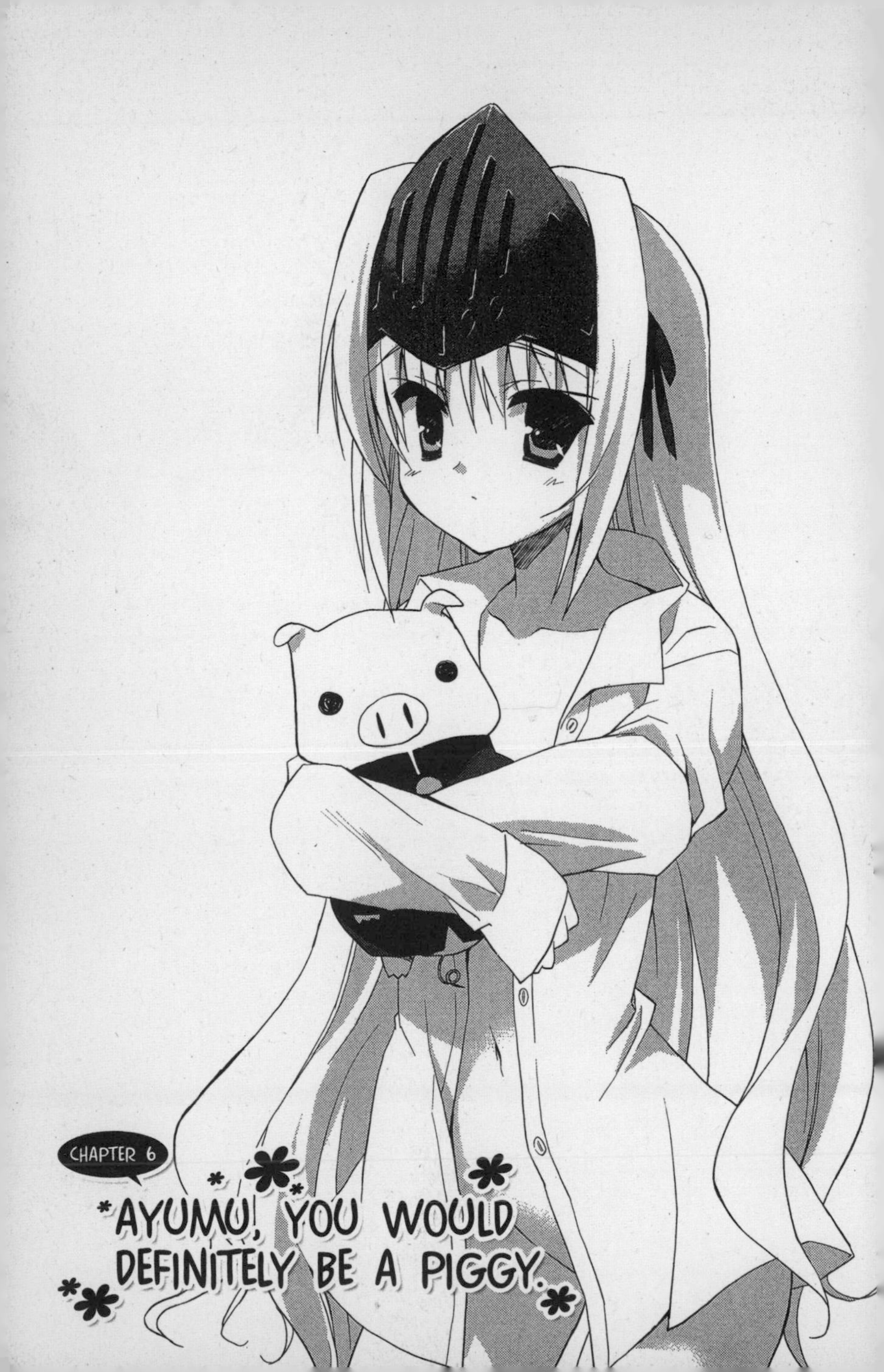
CHAPTER 6
AYUMU, YOU WOULD DEFINITELY BE A PIGGY.

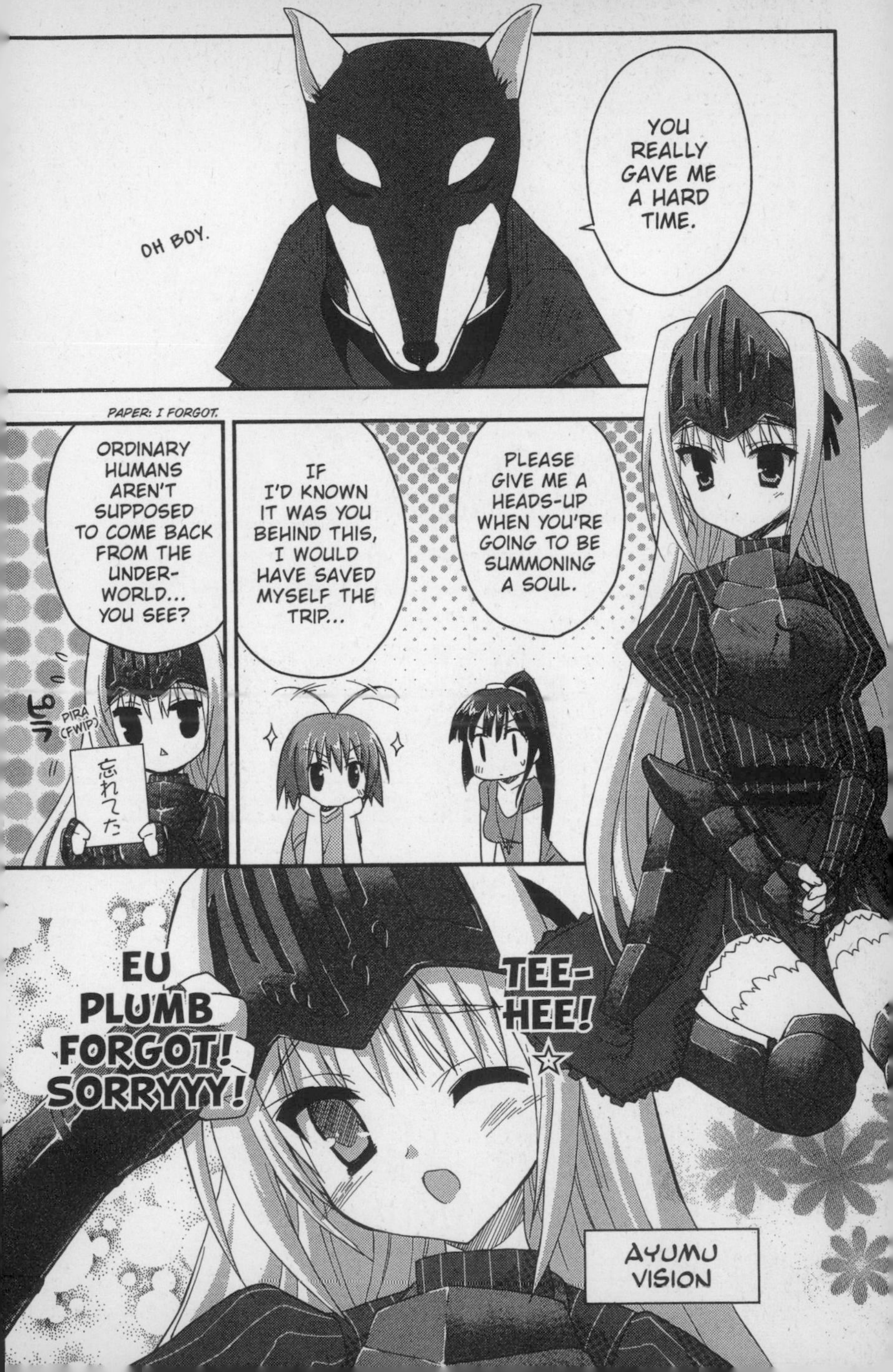
YOU REALLY GAVE ME A HARD TIME.
OH BOY.
PLEASE GIVE ME A HEADS-UP WHEN YOU'RE GOING TO BE SUMMONING A SOUL.
IF I'D KNOWN IT WAS YOU BEHIND THIS, I WOULD HAVE SAVED MYSELF THE TRIP...
ORDINARY HUMANS AREN'T SUPPOSED TO COME BACK FROM THE UNDER-WORLD... YOU SEE?
PAPER: I FORGOT.
ピラ
PIRA (FWIP)
忘れてた
TEE-HEE! ☆
EU PLUMB FORGOT! SORRYYY!
AYUMU VISION

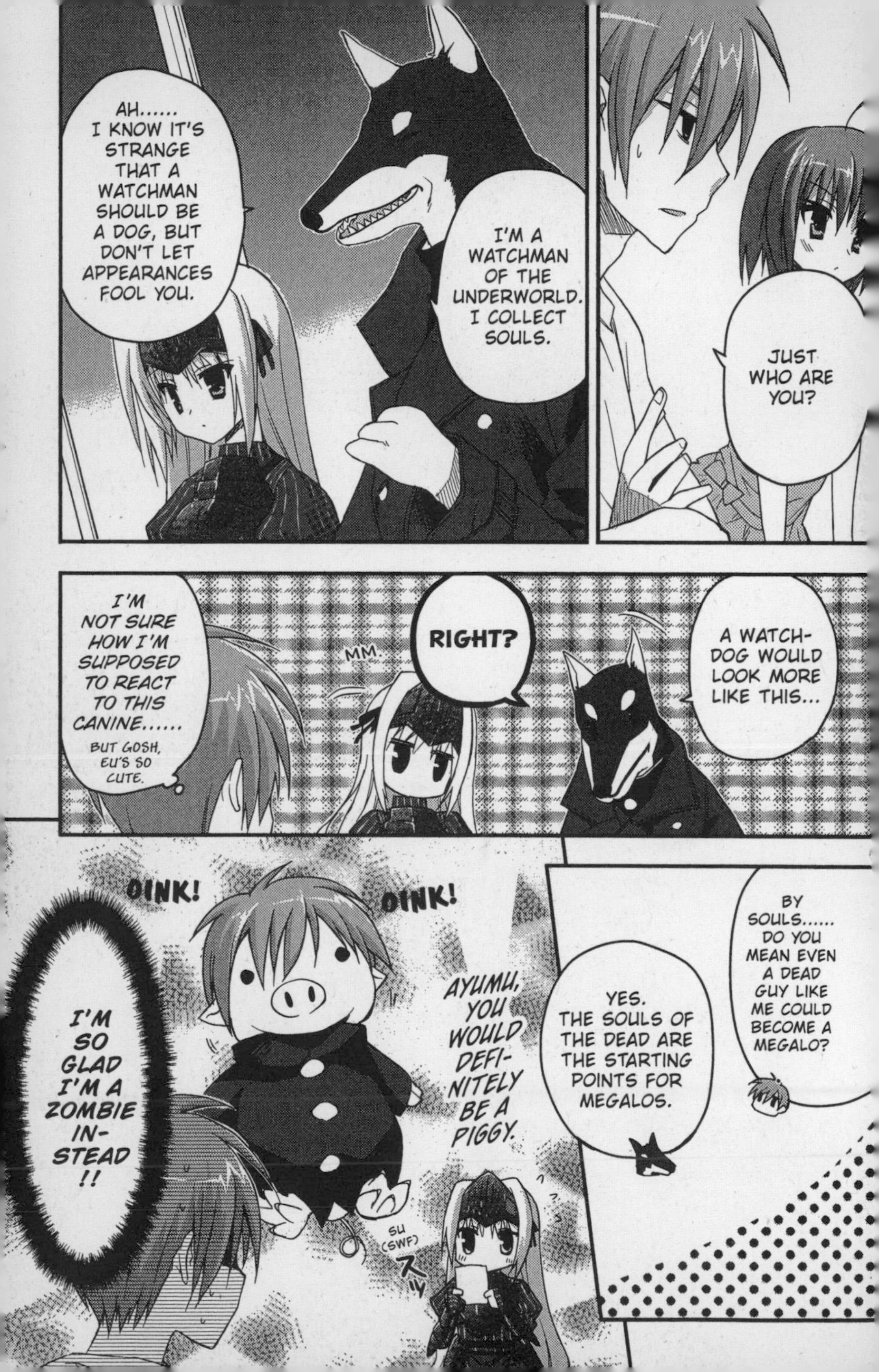
JUST WHO ARE YOU?
I'M A WATCHMAN OF THE UNDERWORLD. I COLLECT SOULS.
AH...... I KNOW IT'S STRANGE THAT A WATCHMAN SHOULD BE A DOG, BUT DON'T LET APPEARANCES FOOL YOU.
A WATCH-DOG WOULD LOOK MORE LIKE THIS...
RIGHT?
MM.
I'M NOT SURE HOW I'M SUPPOSED TO REACT TO THIS CANINE......
BUT GOSH, EU'S SO CUTE.
BY SOULS...... DO YOU MEAN EVEN A DEAD GUY LIKE ME COULD BECOME A MEGALO?
YES. THE SOULS OF THE DEAD ARE THE STARTING POINTS FOR MEGALOS.
AYUMU, YOU WOULD DEFI-NITELY BE A PIGGY.
SU (SWF)
OINK!
OINK!
I'M SO GLAD I'M A ZOMBIE IN-STEAD !!

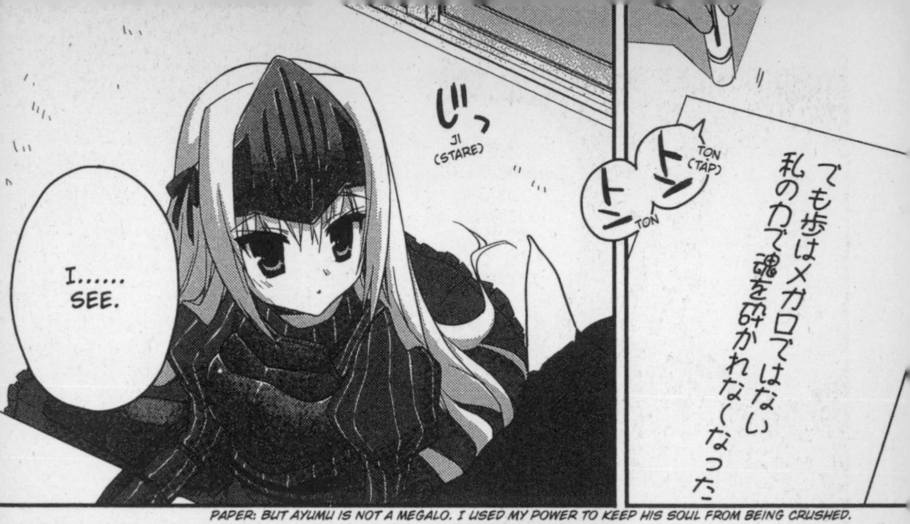
でも歩はメガロではない
私の力で魂を砕かれなくなった
トン TON (TAP)
トン TON
じっ JI (STARE)
I...... SEE.

PAPER: BUT AYUMU IS NOT A MEGALO. I USED MY POWER TO KEEP HIS SOUL FROM BEING CRUSHED.

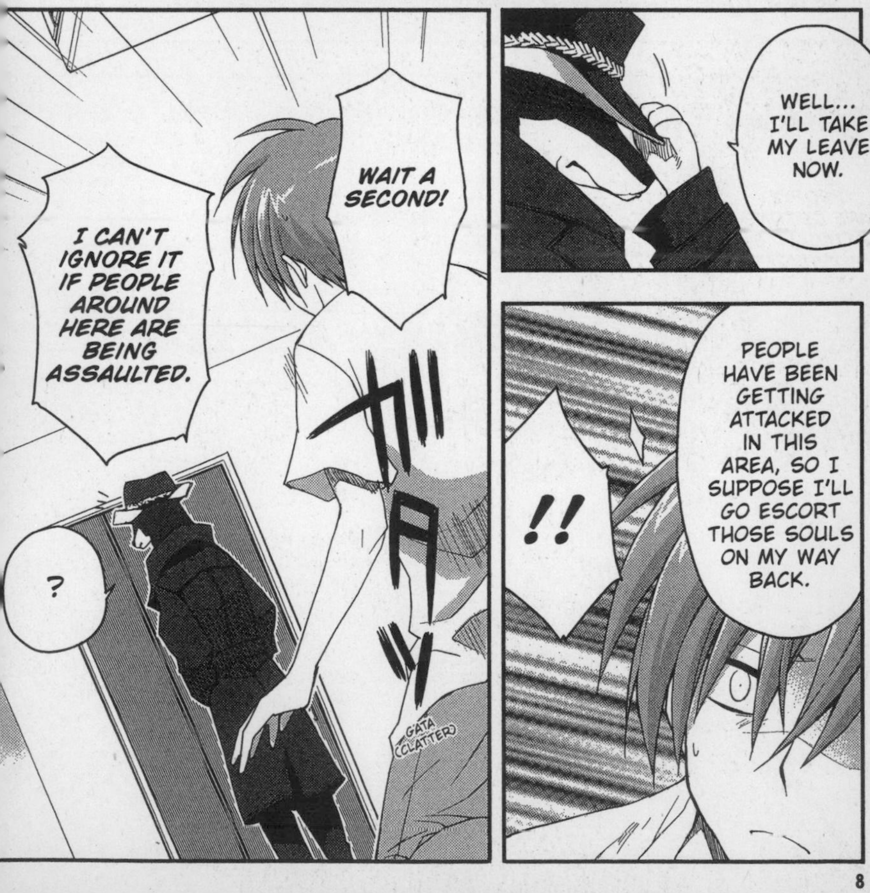
WELL... I'LL TAKE MY LEAVE NOW.
PEOPLE HAVE BEEN GETTING ATTACKED IN THIS AREA, SO I SUPPOSE I'LL GO ESCORT THOSE SOULS ON MY WAY BACK.
!!
WAIT A SECOND!
I CAN'T IGNORE IT IF PEOPLE AROUND HERE ARE BEING ASSAULTED.
?
ガタッ
GATA (CLATTER)

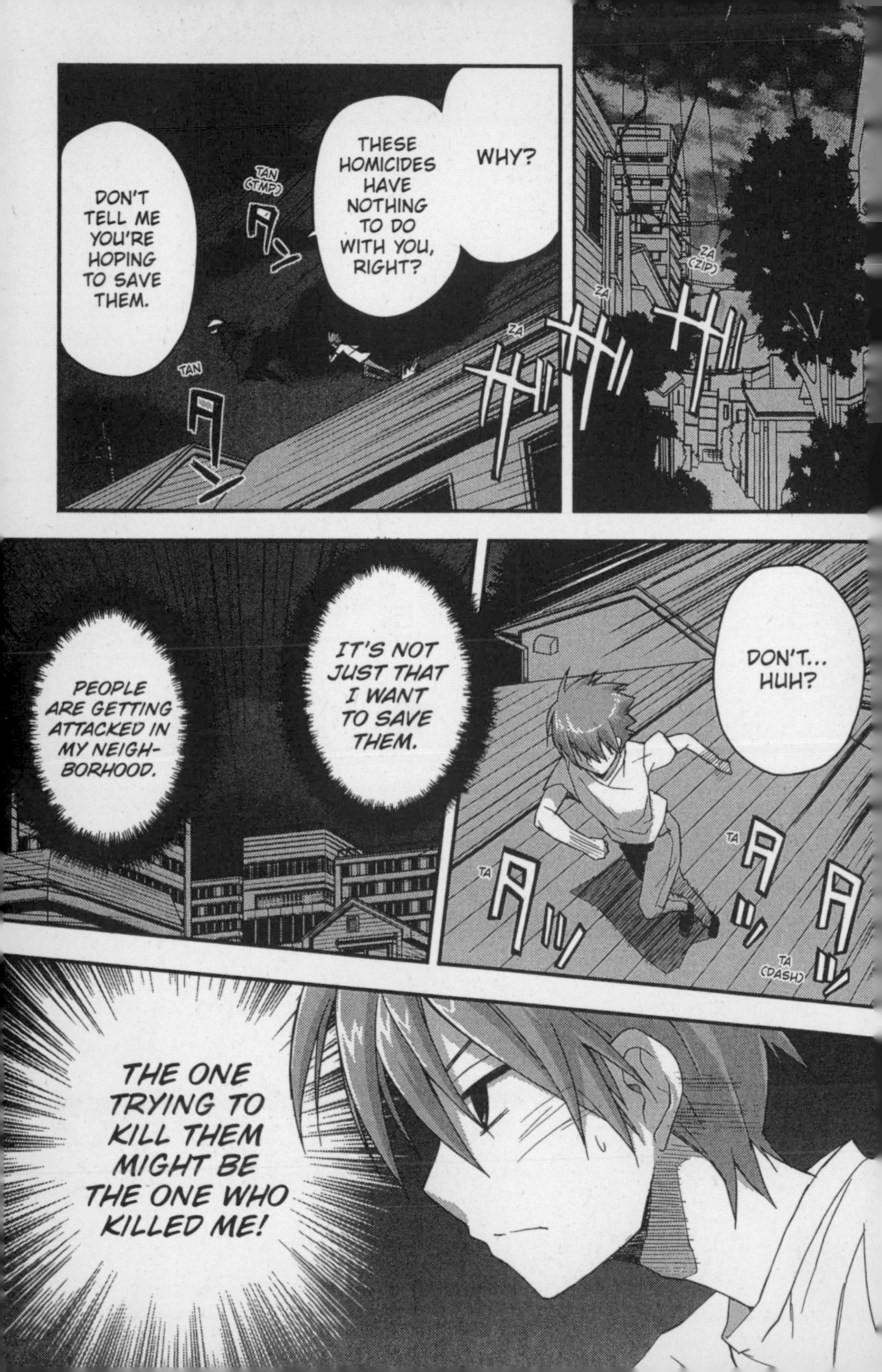
ZA (ZIP)
ZA
ZA
WHY?
THESE HOMICIDES HAVE NOTHING TO DO WITH YOU, RIGHT?
TAN (TMP)
DON'T TELL ME YOU'RE HOPING TO SAVE THEM.
TAN
DON'T... HUH?
TA
TA
TA (DASH)
IT'S NOT JUST THAT I WANT TO SAVE THEM.
PEOPLE ARE GETTING ATTACKED IN MY NEIGH-BORHOOD.
THE ONE TRYING TO KILL THEM MIGHT BE THE ONE WHO KILLED ME!

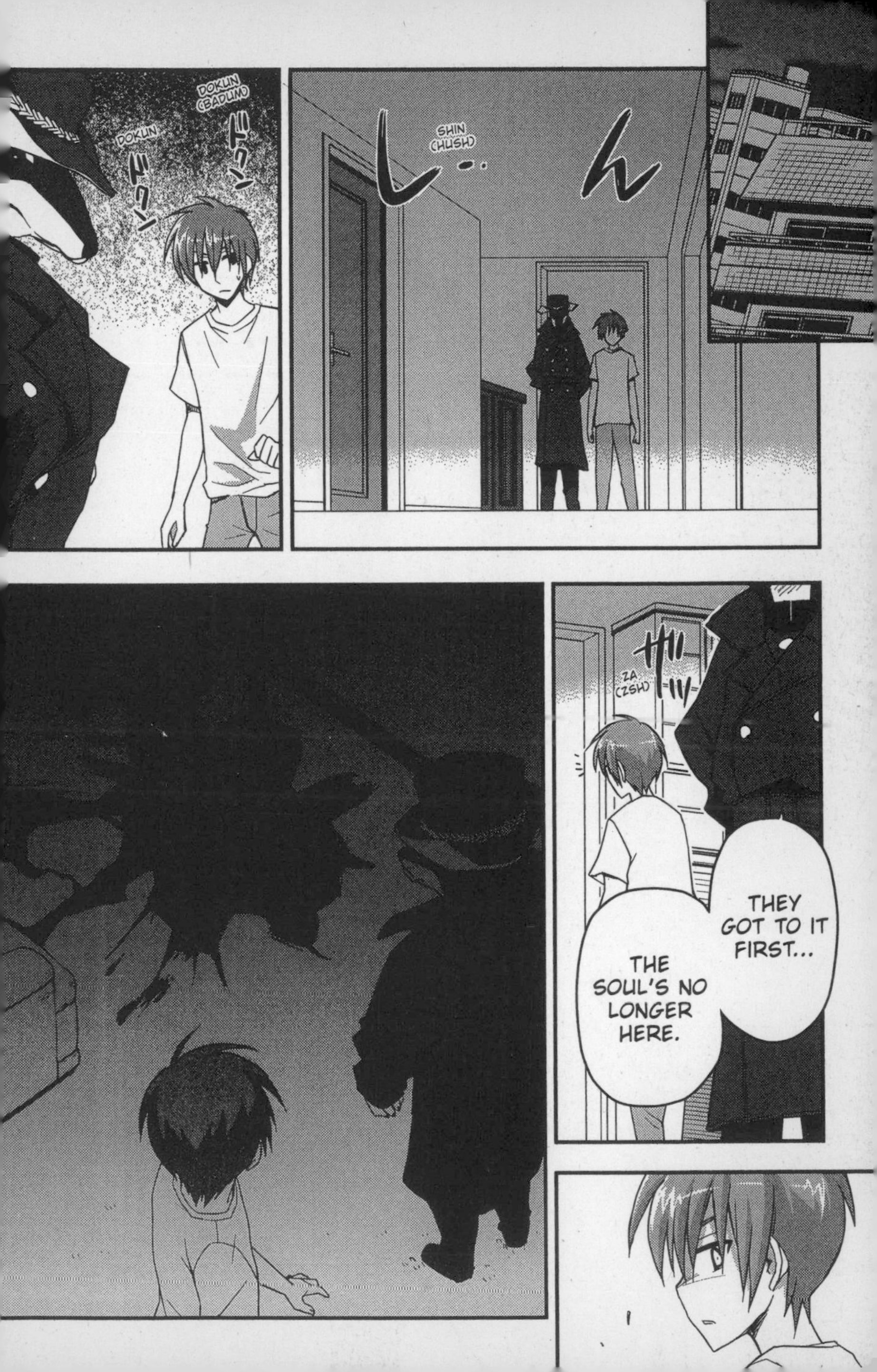
SHIN (HUSH)
しーん
DOKUN (BADUM)
ドクン
DOKUN
ドクン
ZA (ZSH)
ザッ
THEY GOT TO IT FIRST...
THE SOUL'S NO LONGER HERE.

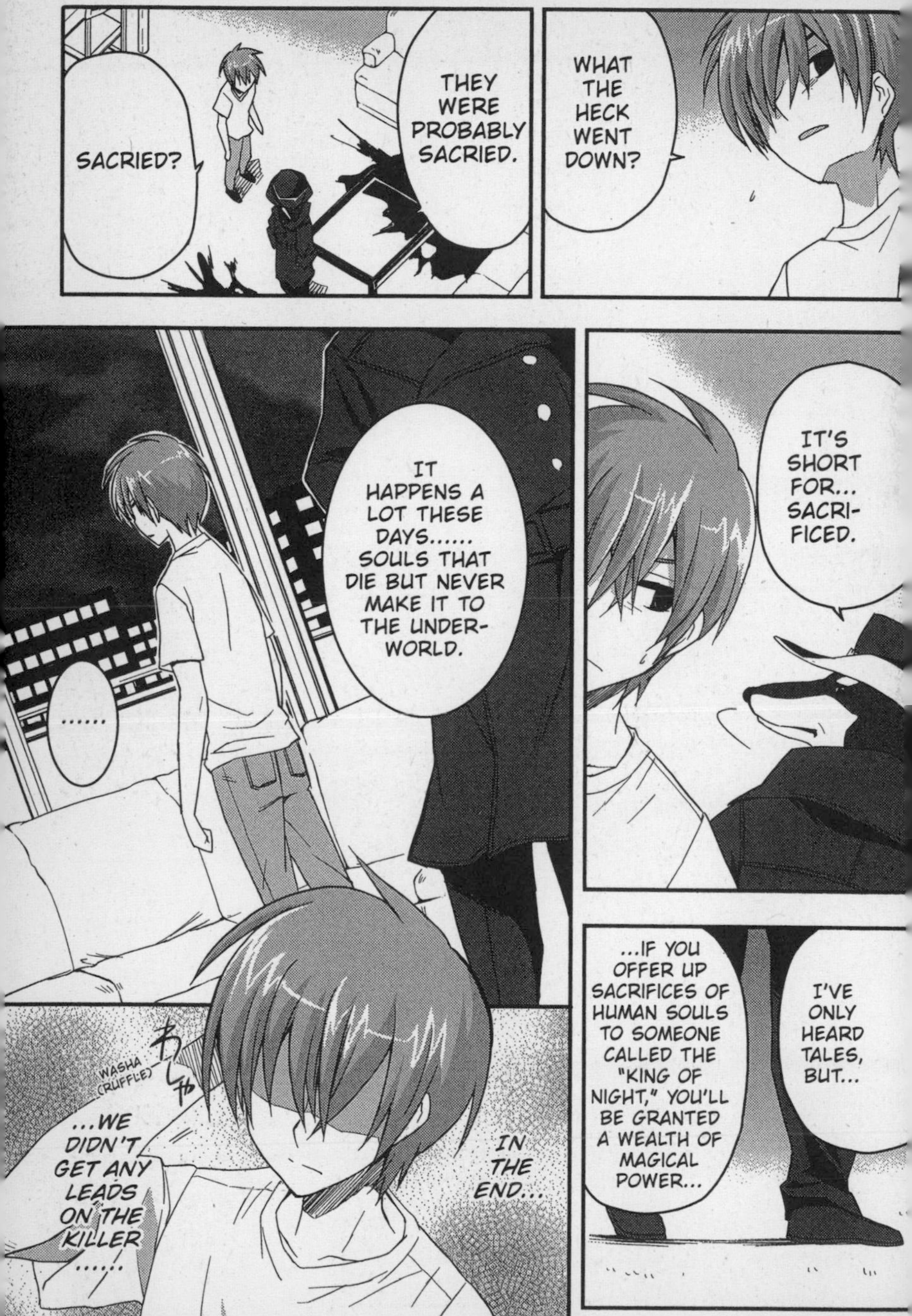
WHAT THE HECK WENT DOWN?
THEY WERE PROBABLY SACRIED.
SACRIED?
IT'S SHORT FOR... SACRI-FICED.
IT HAPPENS A LOT THESE DAYS...... SOULS THAT DIE BUT NEVER MAKE IT TO THE UNDER-WORLD.
......
I'VE ONLY HEARD TALES, BUT...
...IF YOU OFFER UP SACRIFICES OF HUMAN SOULS TO SOMEONE CALLED THE "KING OF NIGHT," YOU'LL BE GRANTED A WEALTH OF MAGICAL POWER...
IN THE END...
WASHA (RUFFLE)
...WE DIDN'T GET ANY LEADS ON THE KILLER ......

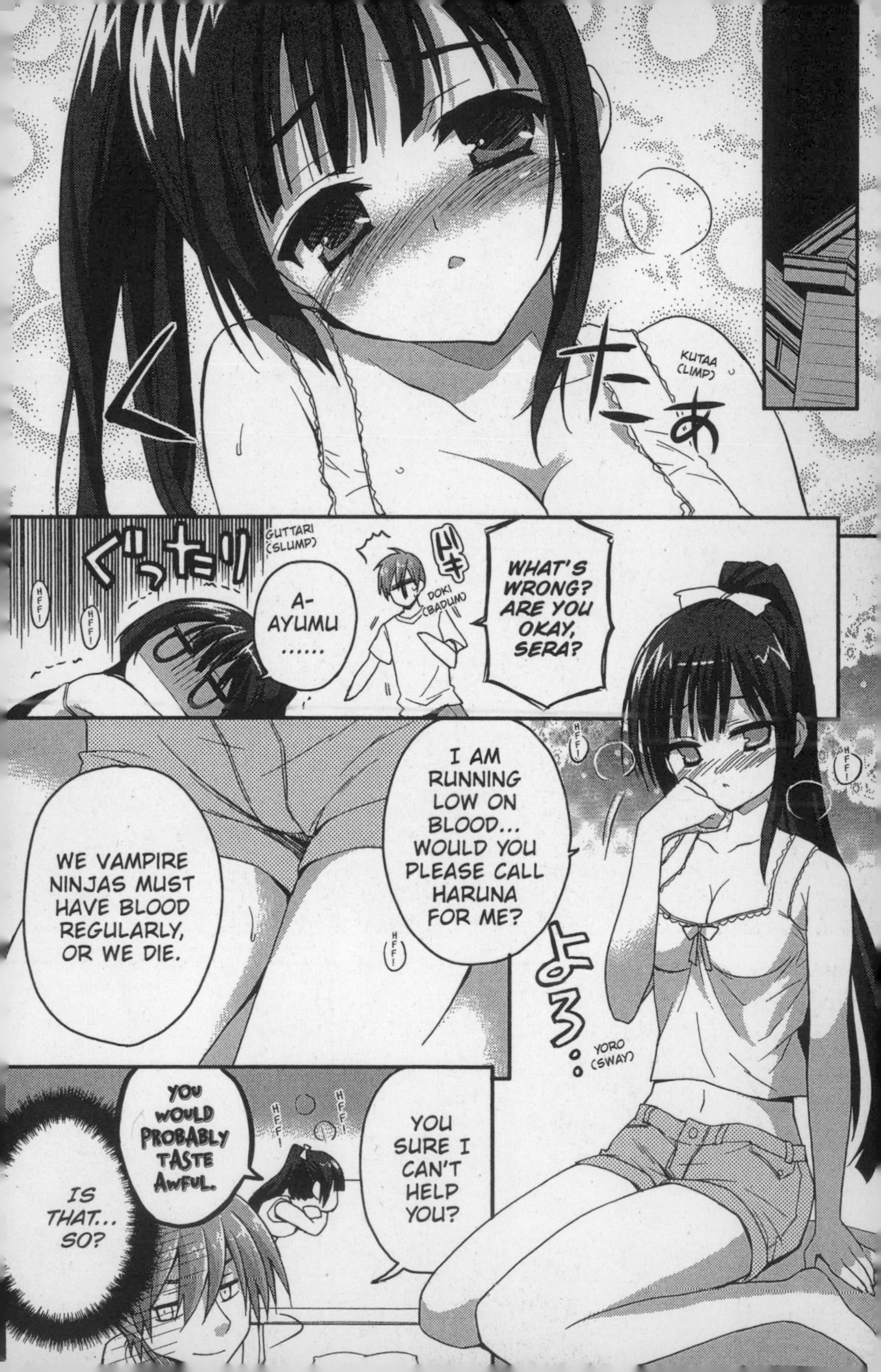
たーあ
KUTAA (LIMP)
ぐったり
GUTTARI (SLUMP)
HFF! HFF!
ドキ
DOKI (BADUMP)
WHAT'S WRONG? ARE YOU OKAY, SERA?
A-AYUMU......
HFF! HFF!
I AM RUNNING LOW ON BLOOD... WOULD YOU PLEASE CALL HARUNA FOR ME?
WE VAMPIRE NINJAS MUST HAVE BLOOD REGULARLY, OR WE DIE.
HFF!
よろ。
YORO (SWAY)
YOU SURE I CAN'T HELP YOU?
HFF! HFF!
YOU WOULD PROBABLY TASTE AWFUL.
IS THAT... SO?

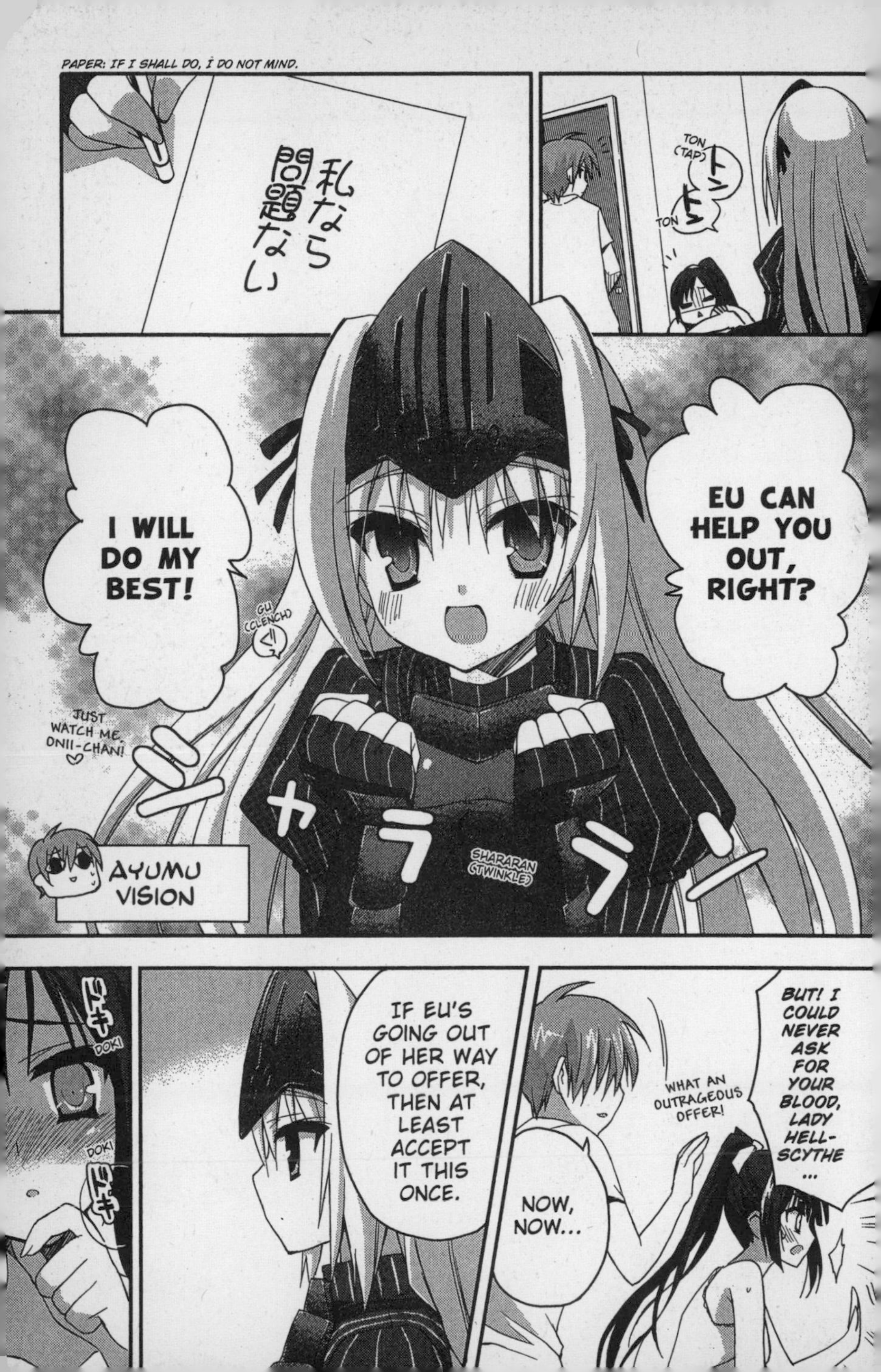

PAPER: IF I SHALL DO, I DO NOT MIND.
私なら問題ない
TON (TAP)
トン
TON
トン
EU CAN HELP YOU OUT, RIGHT?
I WILL DO MY BEST!
GU (CLENCH)
ぐ
JUST WATCH ME, ONII-CHAN!
AYUMU VISION
SHARARAN (TWINKLE)
BUT! I COULD NEVER ASK FOR YOUR BLOOD, LADY HELLSCYTHE...
WHAT AN OUTRAGEOUS OFFER!
IF EU'S GOING OUT OF HER WAY TO OFFER, THEN AT LEAST ACCEPT IT THIS ONCE.
NOW, NOW...
DOKI
DOKI

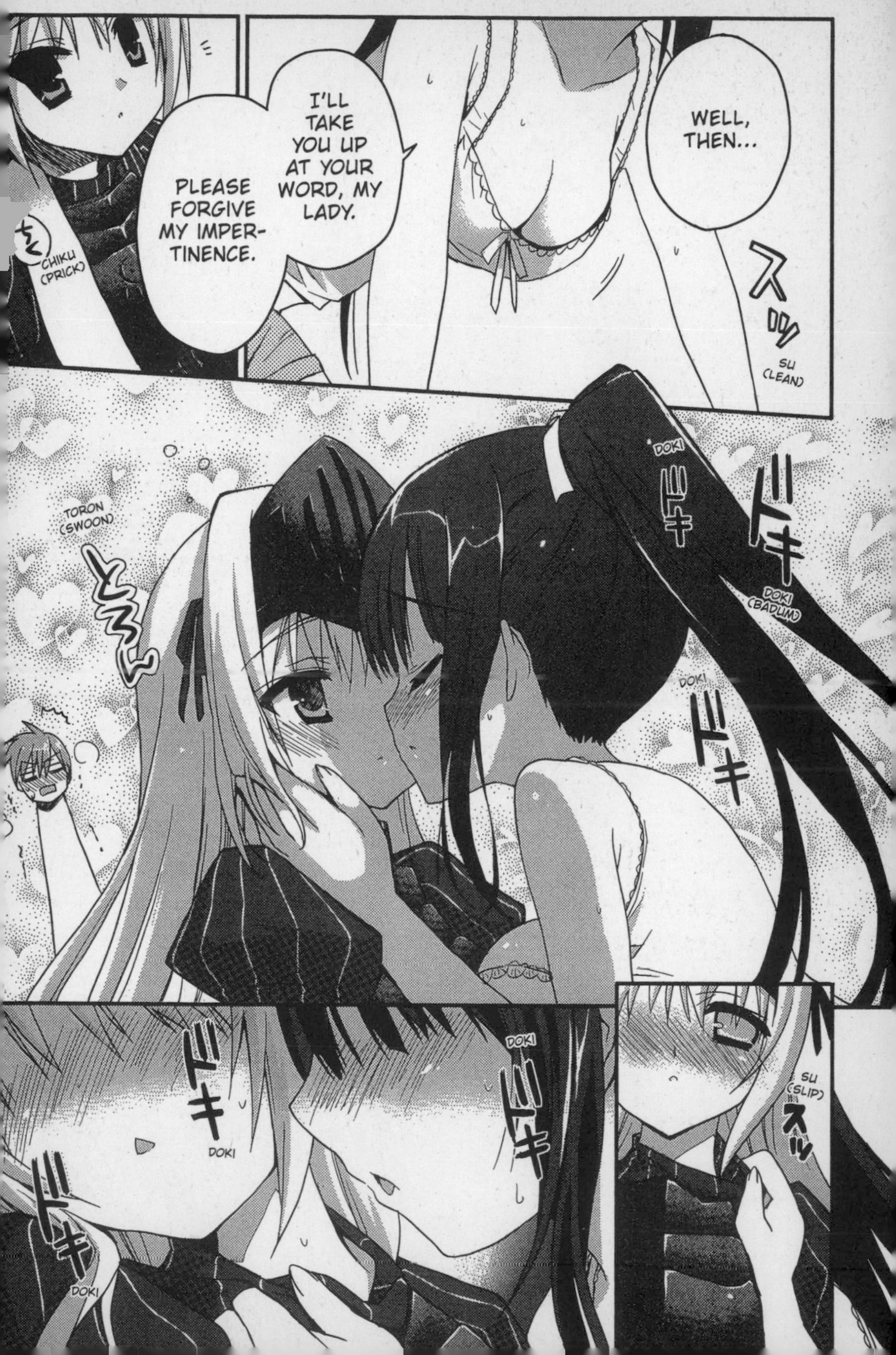
WELL, THEN...
スッ
SU (LEAN)
I'LL TAKE YOU UP AT YOUR WORD, MY LADY.
PLEASE FORGIVE MY IMPERTINENCE.
ちく
CHIKU (PRICK)
ドキ
DOKI (BADUM)
DOKI
DOKI
とろん
TORON (SWOON)
SU (SLIP)
スッ
DOKI
ドキ
DOKI
ドキ
DOKI

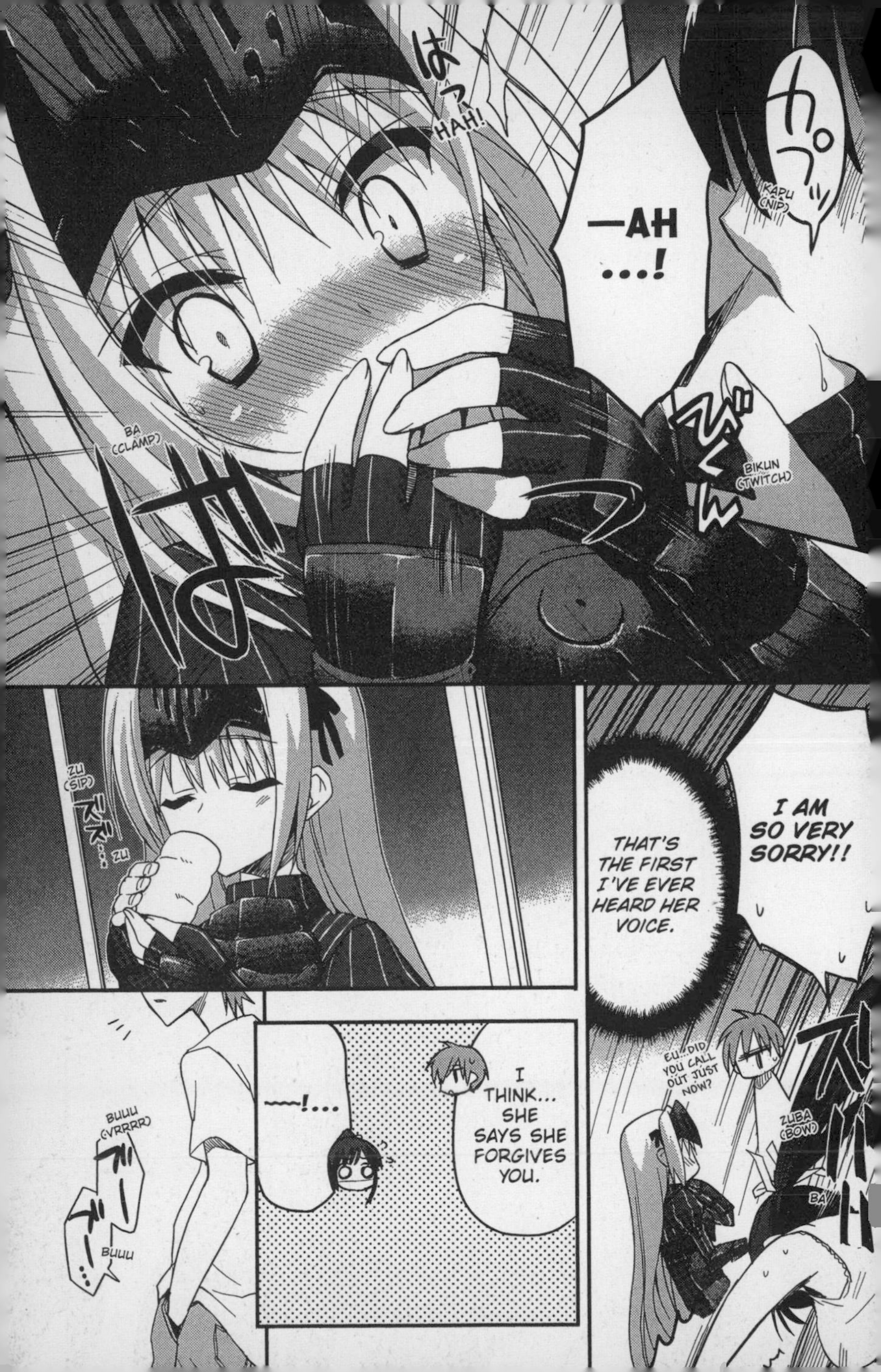

かぷッ
KAPU (NIP)
—AH ...!
はっ
HAH!
びくん
BIKUN (TWITCH)
ばっ
BA (CLAMP)
I AM SO VERY SORRY!!
THAT'S THE FIRST I'VE EVER HEARD HER VOICE.
ズズ...
ZU (SIP)
ZU
ズバッ
ZUBA (BOW)
BA
EU...DID YOU CALL OUT JUST NOW?
I THINK... SHE SAYS SHE FORGIVES YOU.
~~!...
ブー
BUUU (VRRRR)
ブー...
BUUU

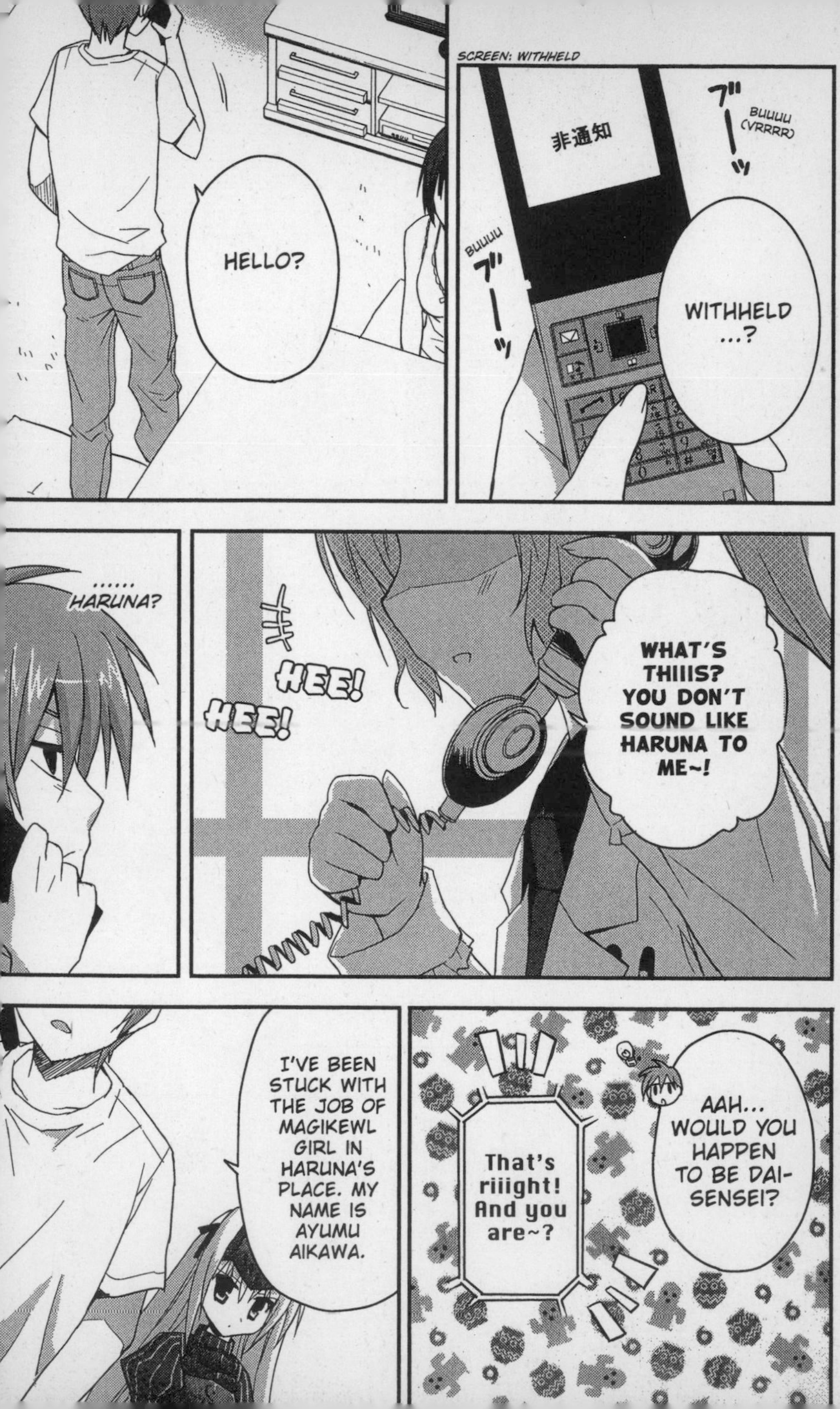
SCREEN: WITHHELD
非通知
Buuuu (VRRRR)
Buuuu
WITHHELD ...?
HELLO?
WHAT'S THIIIS? YOU DON'T SOUND LIKE HARUNA TO ME~!
HEE! HEE!
...... HARUNA?
AAH... WOULD YOU HAPPEN TO BE DAI-SENSEI?
That's riiight! And you are~?
I'VE BEEN STUCK WITH THE JOB OF MAGIKEWL GIRL IN HARUNA'S PLACE. MY NAME IS AYUMU AIKAWA.

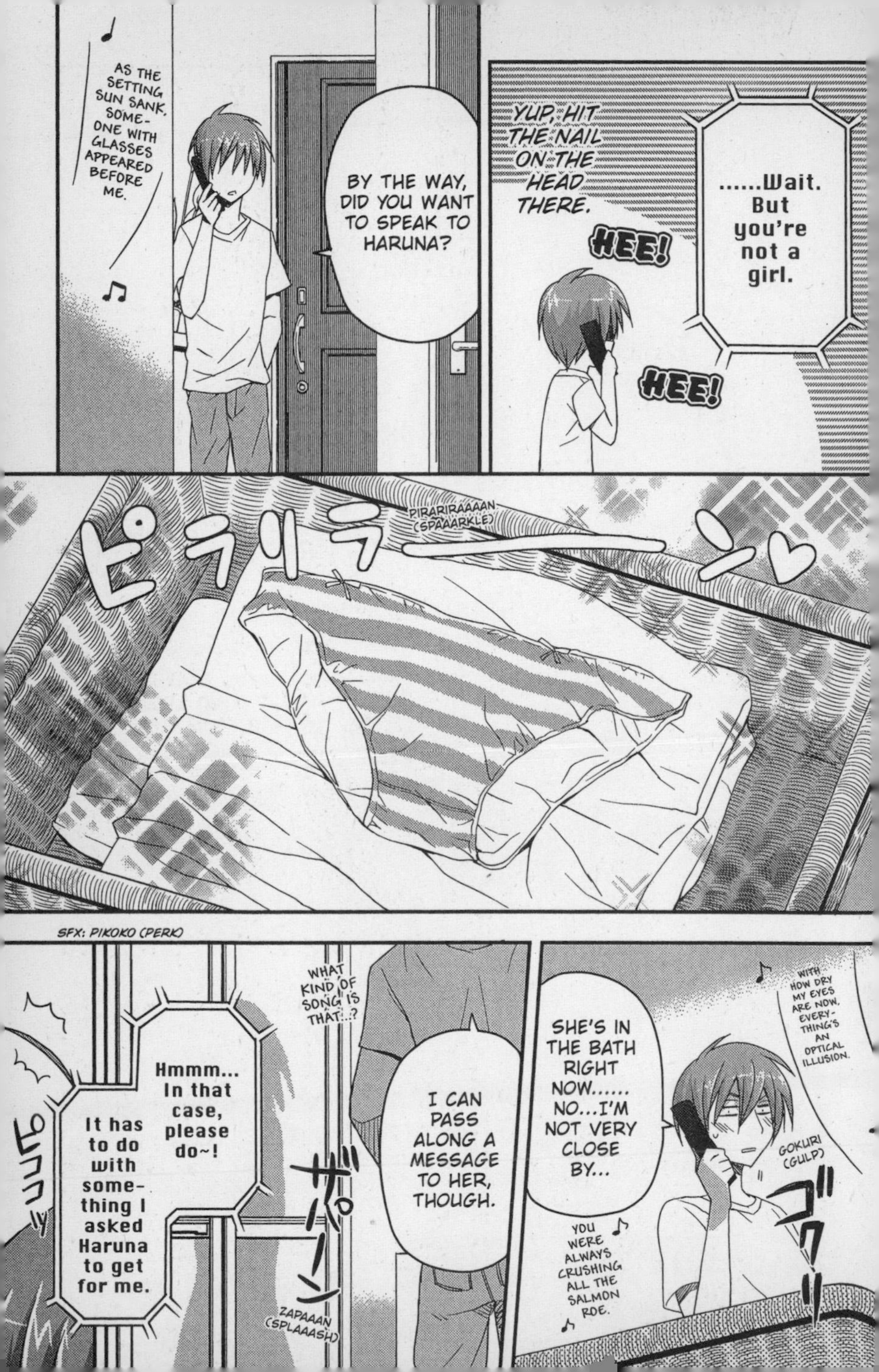
...Wait. But you're not a girl.
YUP, HIT THE NAIL ON THE HEAD THERE.
HEE!
HEE!
BY THE WAY, DID YOU WANT TO SPEAK TO HARUNA?
AS THE SETTING SUN SANK, SOME-ONE WITH GLASSES APPEARED BEFORE ME.
ピラリラーーン
PIRARIRAAAAN (SPAAARKLE)
SFX: PIKOKO (PERK)
WITH HOW DRY MY EYES ARE NOW, EVERY-THING'S AN OPTICAL ILLUSION.
SHE'S IN THE BATH RIGHT NOW...... NO...I'M NOT VERY CLOSE BY...
GOKURI (GULP)
ゴクリ
YOU WERE ALWAYS CRUSHING ALL THE SALMON ROE.
I CAN PASS ALONG A MESSAGE TO HER, THOUGH.
WHAT KIND OF SONG IS THAT...?
ザパーン
ZAPAAAN (SPLAAASH)
Hmmm... In that case, please do~!
It has to do with some-thing I asked Haruna to get for me.

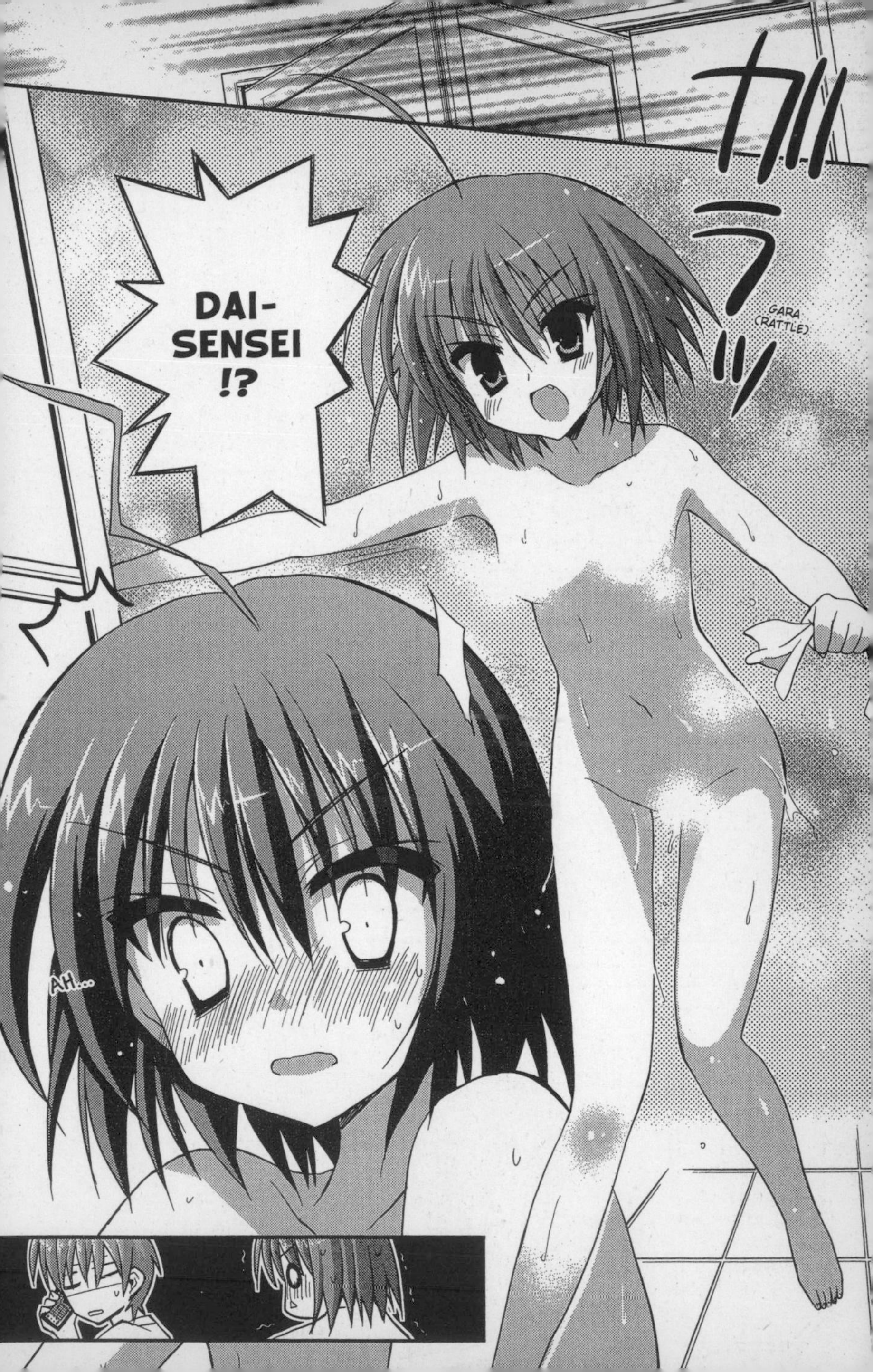
GARA (RATTLE)
DAI-SENSEI !?
AH...

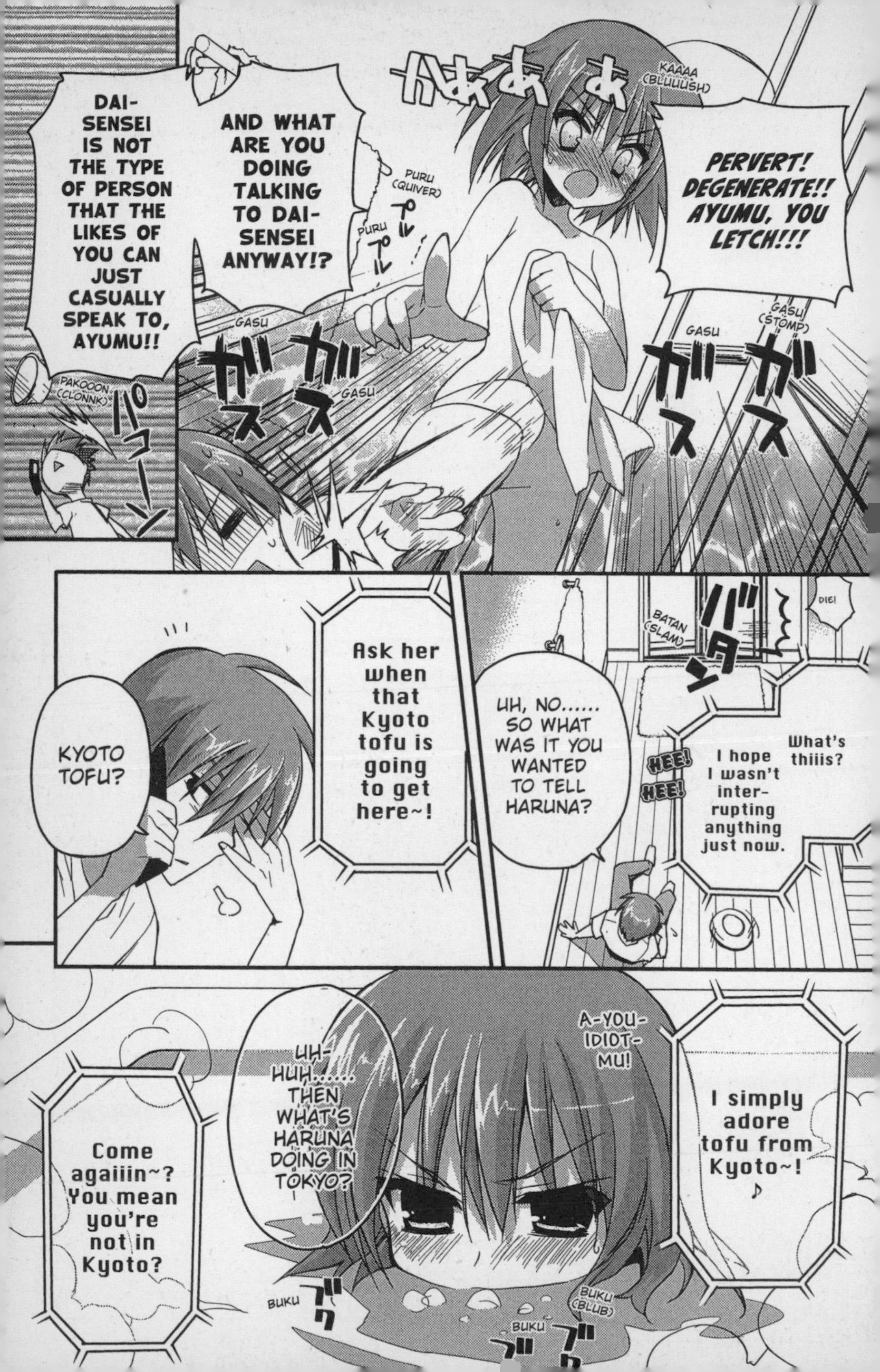

KAAAA (BLUUUSH)
PERVERT! DEGENERATE!! AYUMU, YOU LETCH!!!
PURU (QUIVER)
PURU
AND WHAT ARE YOU DOING TALKING TO DAI-SENSEI ANYWAY!?
DAI-SENSEI IS NOT THE TYPE OF PERSON THAT THE LIKES OF YOU CAN JUST CASUALLY SPEAK TO, AYUMU!!
GASU (STOMP)
GASU
GASU
GASU
PAKOOON (CLONNK)
BATAN (SLAM)
DIE!
What's thiiis?
I hope I wasn't interrupting anything just now.
HEE! HEE!
UH, NO...... SO WHAT WAS IT YOU WANTED TO TELL HARUNA?
Ask her when that Kyoto tofu is going to get here~!
KYOTO TOFU?
I simply adore tofu from Kyoto~! ♪
A-YOU-IDIOT-MU!
UH-HUH...... THEN WHAT'S HARUNA DOING IN TOKYO?
Come agaiiin~? You mean you're not in Kyoto?
BUKU (BLUB)
BUKU
BUKU

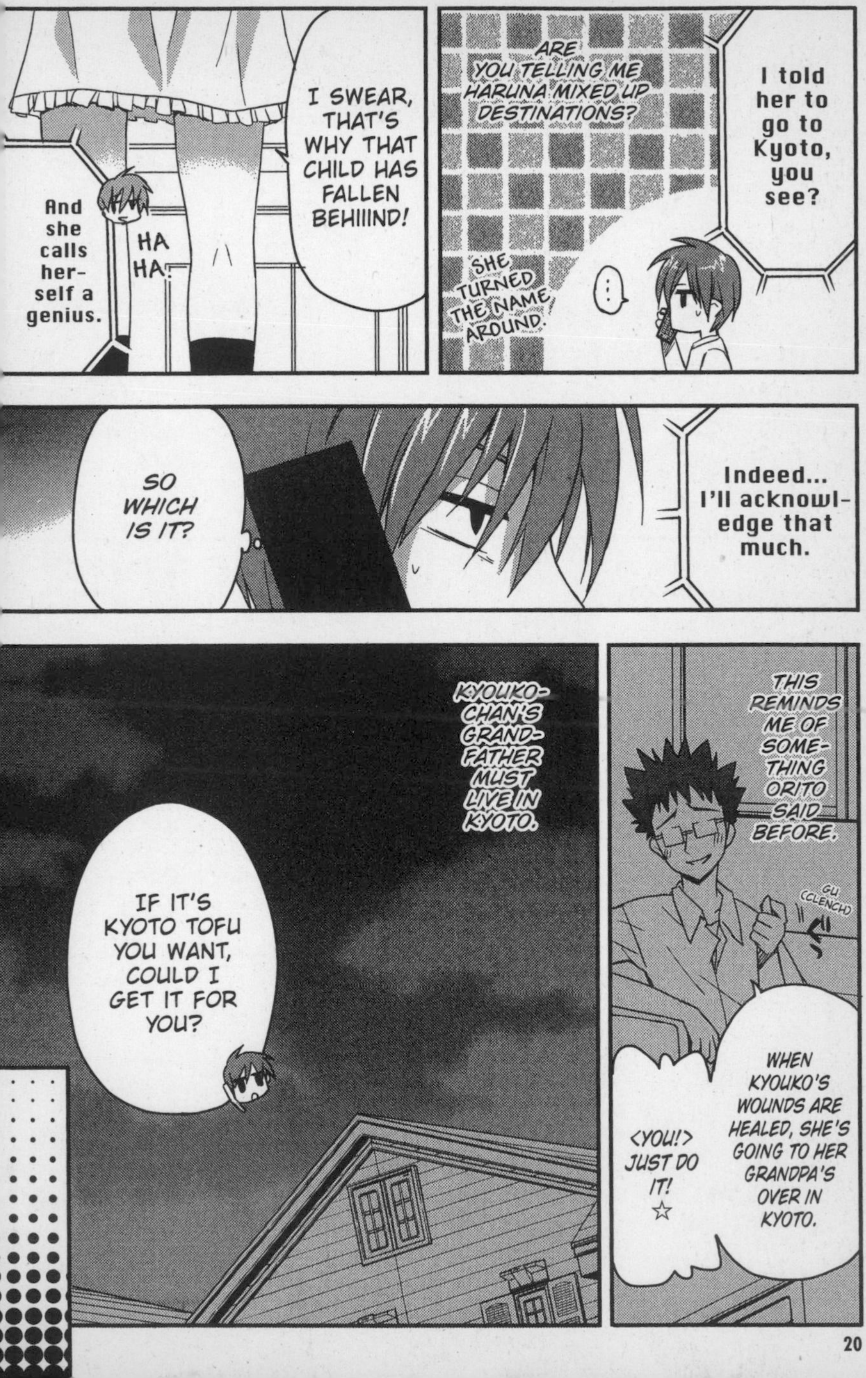
I told her to go to Kyoto, you see?
ARE YOU TELLING ME HARUNA MIXED UP DESTINATIONS?
SHE TURNED THE NAME AROUND.
...
I SWEAR, THAT'S WHY THAT CHILD HAS FALLEN BEHIIIIND!
HA HA.
And she calls herself a genius.
Indeed... I'll acknowledge that much.
SO WHICH IS IT?
THIS REMINDS ME OF SOMETHING ORITO SAID BEFORE.
GU (CLENCH)
WHEN KYOUKO'S WOUNDS ARE HEALED, SHE'S GOING TO HER GRANDPA'S OVER IN KYOTO.
<YOU!> JUST DO IT! ☆
KYOUKO-CHAN'S GRANDFATHER MUST LIVE IN KYOTO.
IF IT'S KYOTO TOFU YOU WANT, COULD I GET IT FOR YOU?

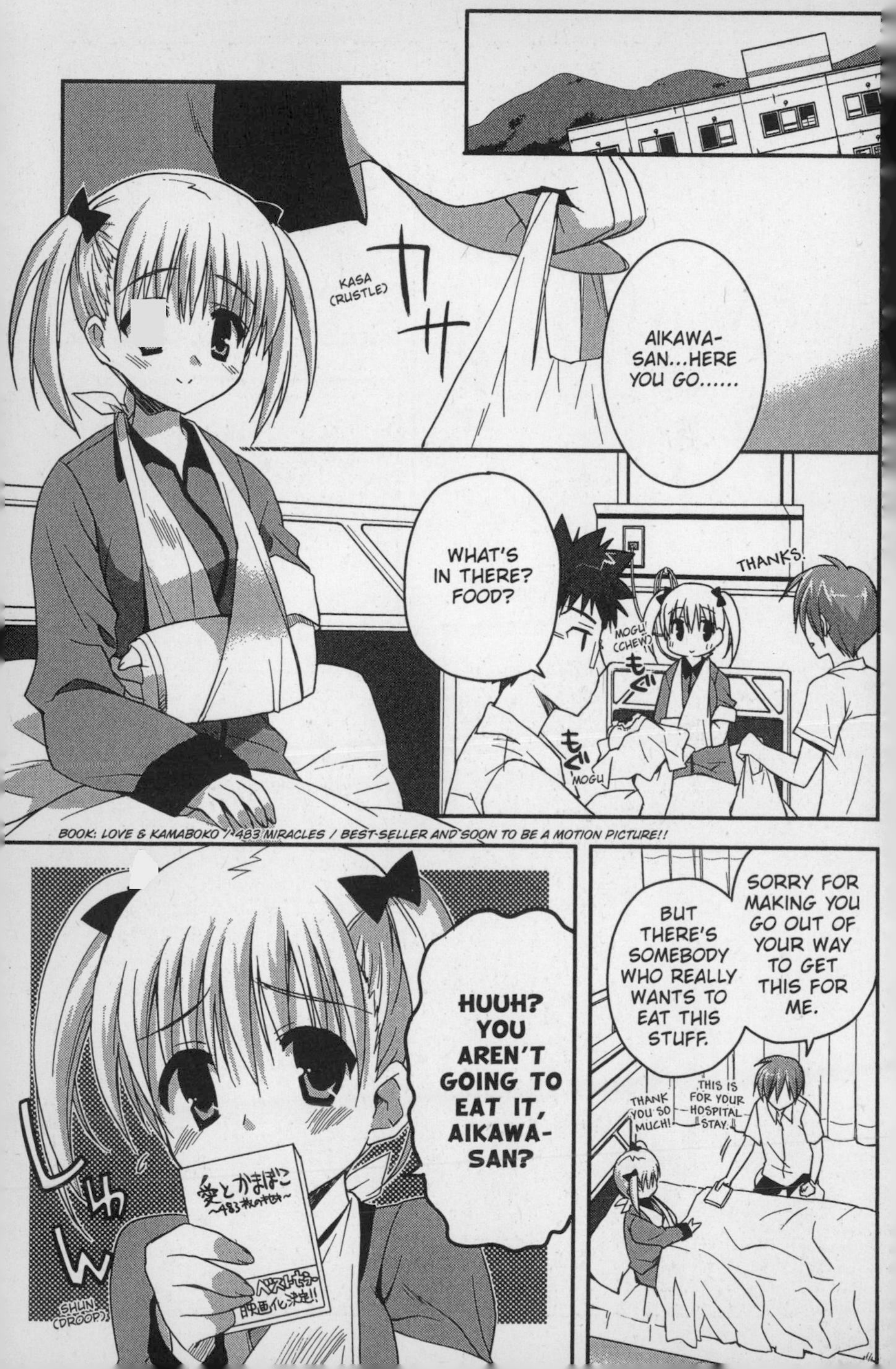
KASA (RUSTLE)
AIKAWA-SAN...HERE YOU GO......
THANKS.
WHAT'S IN THERE? FOOD?
MOGU (CHEW)
MOGU
BOOK: LOVE & KAMABOKO / 483 MIRACLES / BEST-SELLER AND SOON TO BE A MOTION PICTURE!!
SORRY FOR MAKING YOU GO OUT OF YOUR WAY TO GET THIS FOR ME.
BUT THERE'S SOMEBODY WHO REALLY WANTS TO EAT THIS STUFF.
THIS IS FOR YOUR HOSPITAL STAY.
THANK YOU SO MUCH!
HUUH? YOU AREN'T GOING TO EAT IT, AIKAWA-SAN?
愛とかまぼこ
SHUN (DROOP)

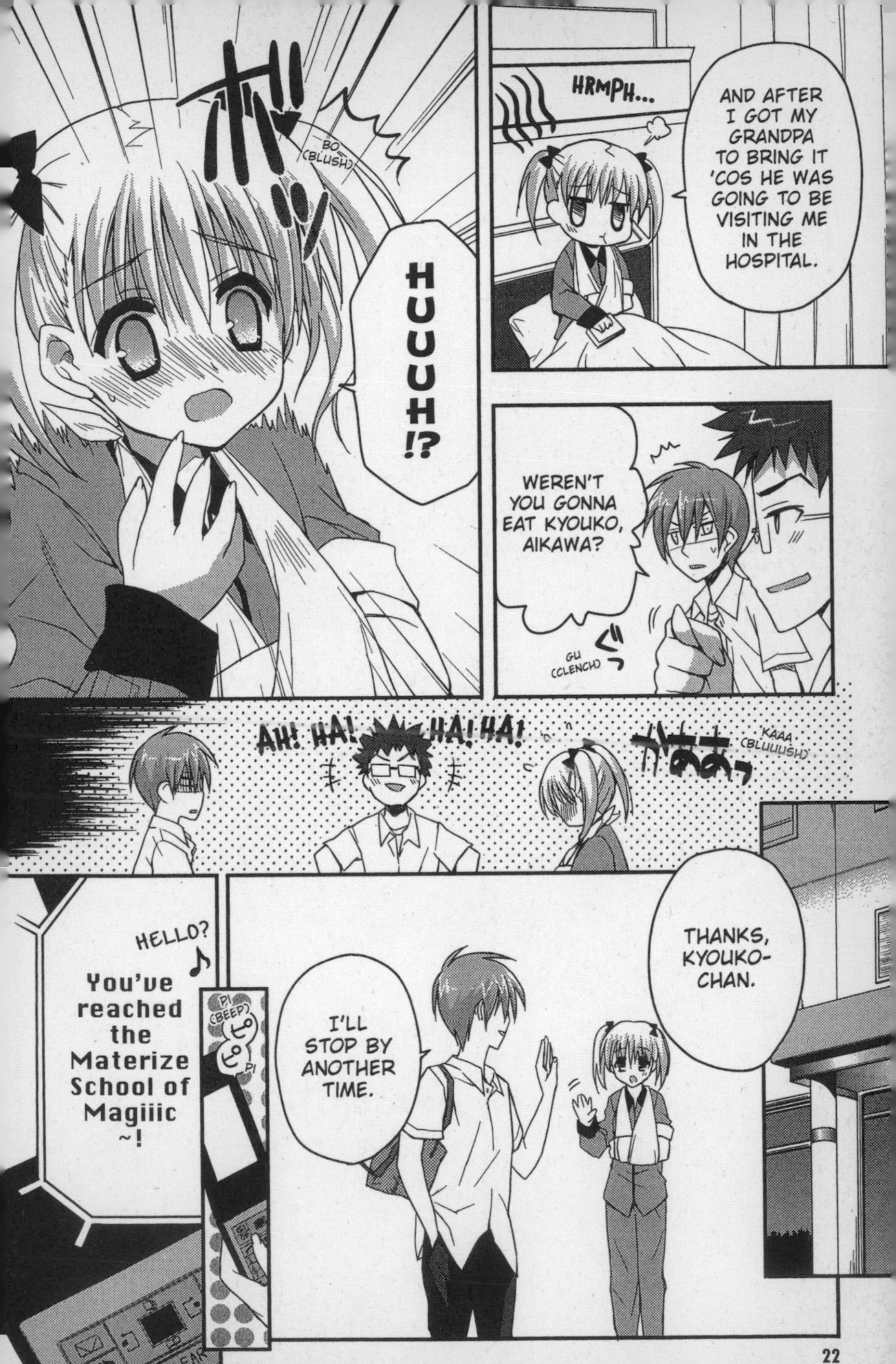
HRMPH...
AND AFTER I GOT MY GRANDPA TO BRING IT 'COS HE WAS GOING TO BE VISITING ME IN THE HOSPITAL.
WEREN'T YOU GONNA EAT KYOUKO, AIKAWA?
GU (CLENCH)
BO (BLUSH)
HUUUH!?
KAAA (BLUUUSH)
AH! HA! HA! HA!
THANKS, KYOUKO-CHAN.
I'LL STOP BY ANOTHER TIME.
PI (BEEP) PI
HELLO? ♪
You've reached the Materize School of Magiiic ~!
CLEAR

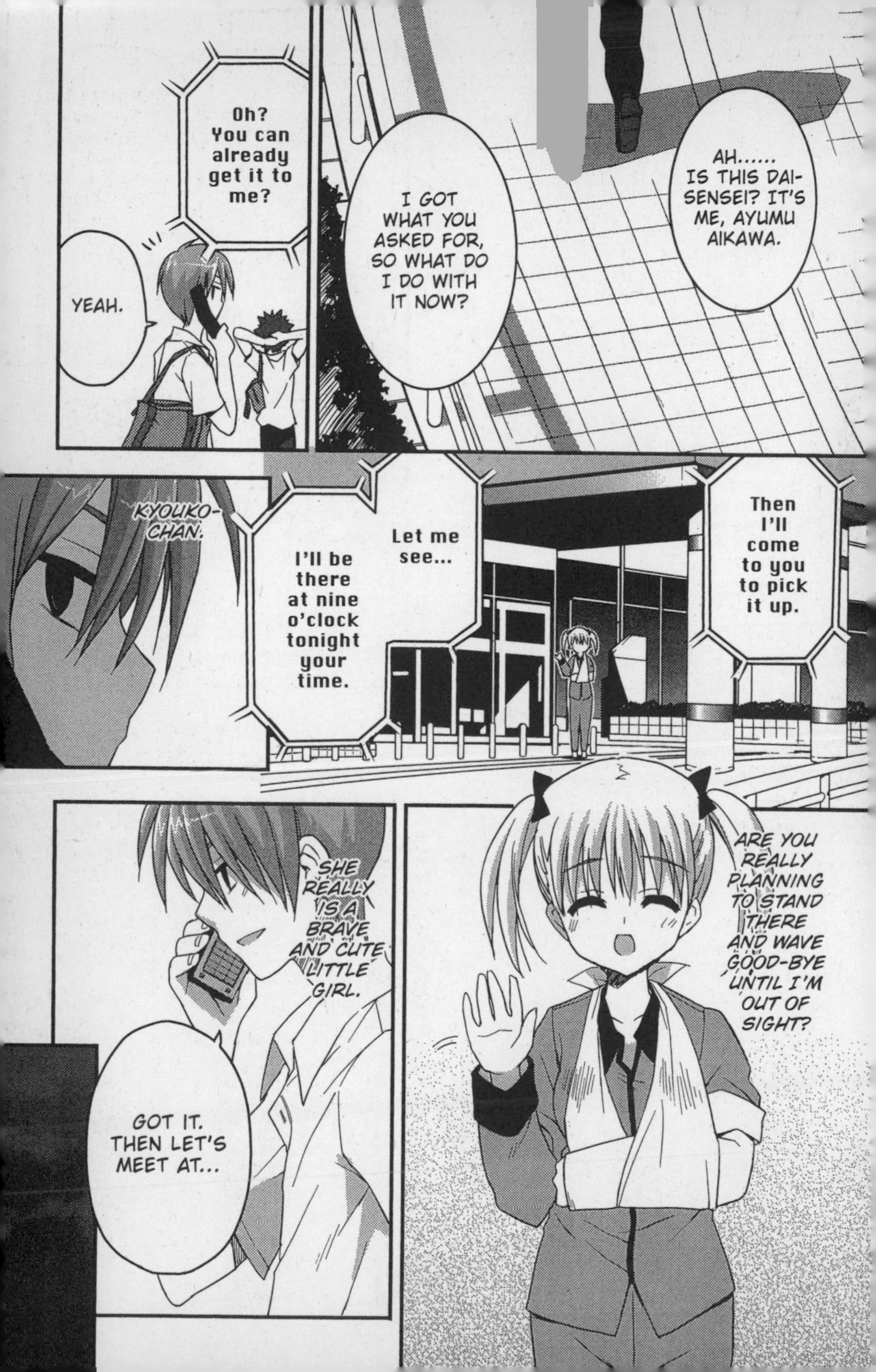
AH...... IS THIS DAI-SENSEI? IT'S ME, AYUMU AIKAWA.
I GOT WHAT YOU ASKED FOR, SO WHAT DO I DO WITH IT NOW?
Oh? You can already get it to me?
YEAH.
Then I'll come to you to pick it up.
Let me see...
I'll be there at nine o'clock tonight your time.
KYOUKO-CHAN.
ARE YOU REALLY PLANNING TO STAND THERE AND WAVE GOOD-BYE UNTIL I'M OUT OF SIGHT?
SHE REALLY IS A BRAVE AND CUTE LITTLE GIRL.
GOT IT. THEN LET'S MEET AT...

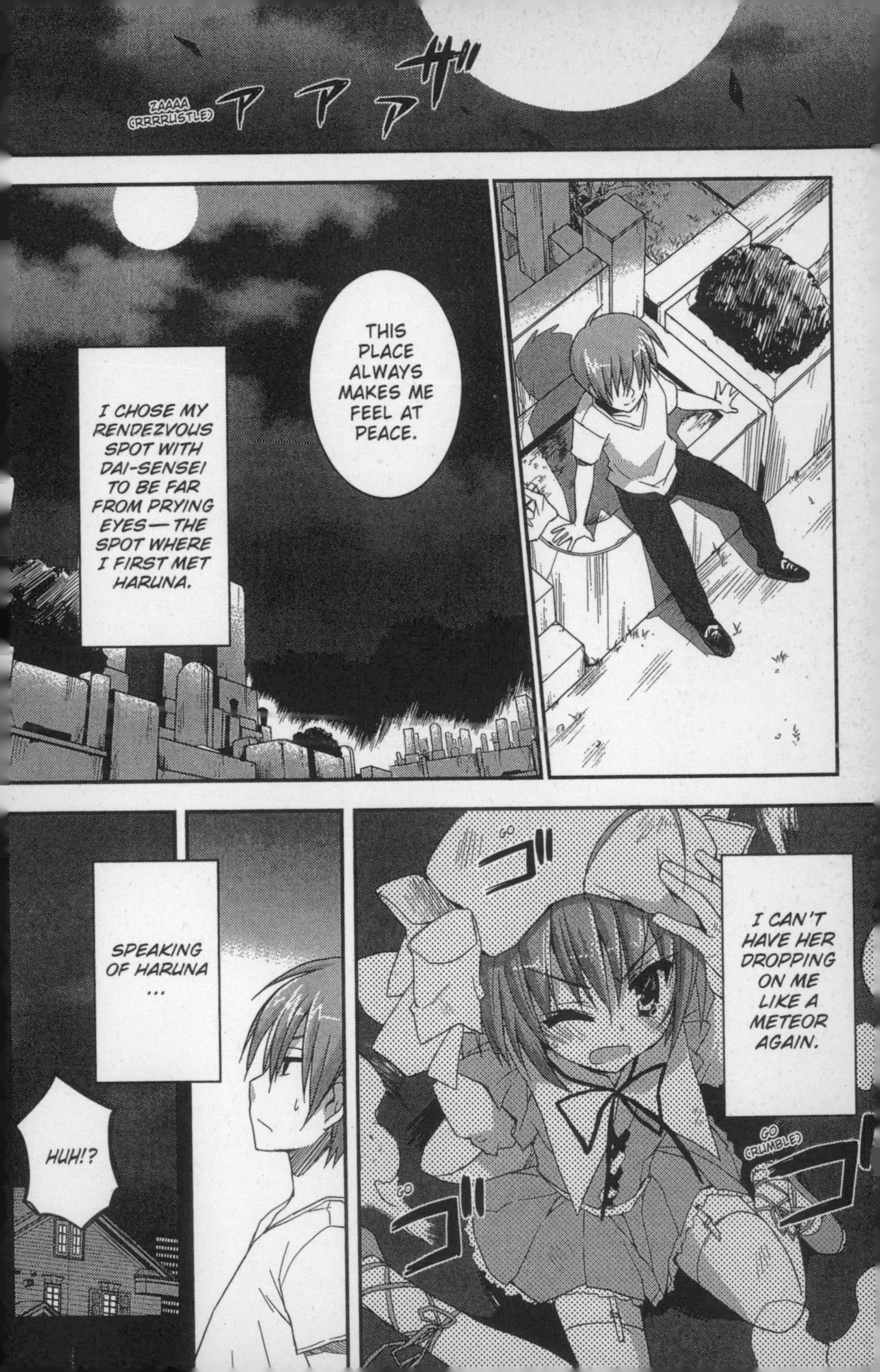

ZAAAA (RRRRUSTLE)
THIS PLACE ALWAYS MAKES ME FEEL AT PEACE.
I CHOSE MY RENDEZVOUS SPOT WITH DAI-SENSEI TO BE FAR FROM PRYING EYES—THE SPOT WHERE I FIRST MET HARUNA.
GO
I CAN'T HAVE HER DROPPING ON ME LIKE A METEOR AGAIN.
SPEAKING OF HARUNA ...
GO (RUMBLE)
GO
HUH!?

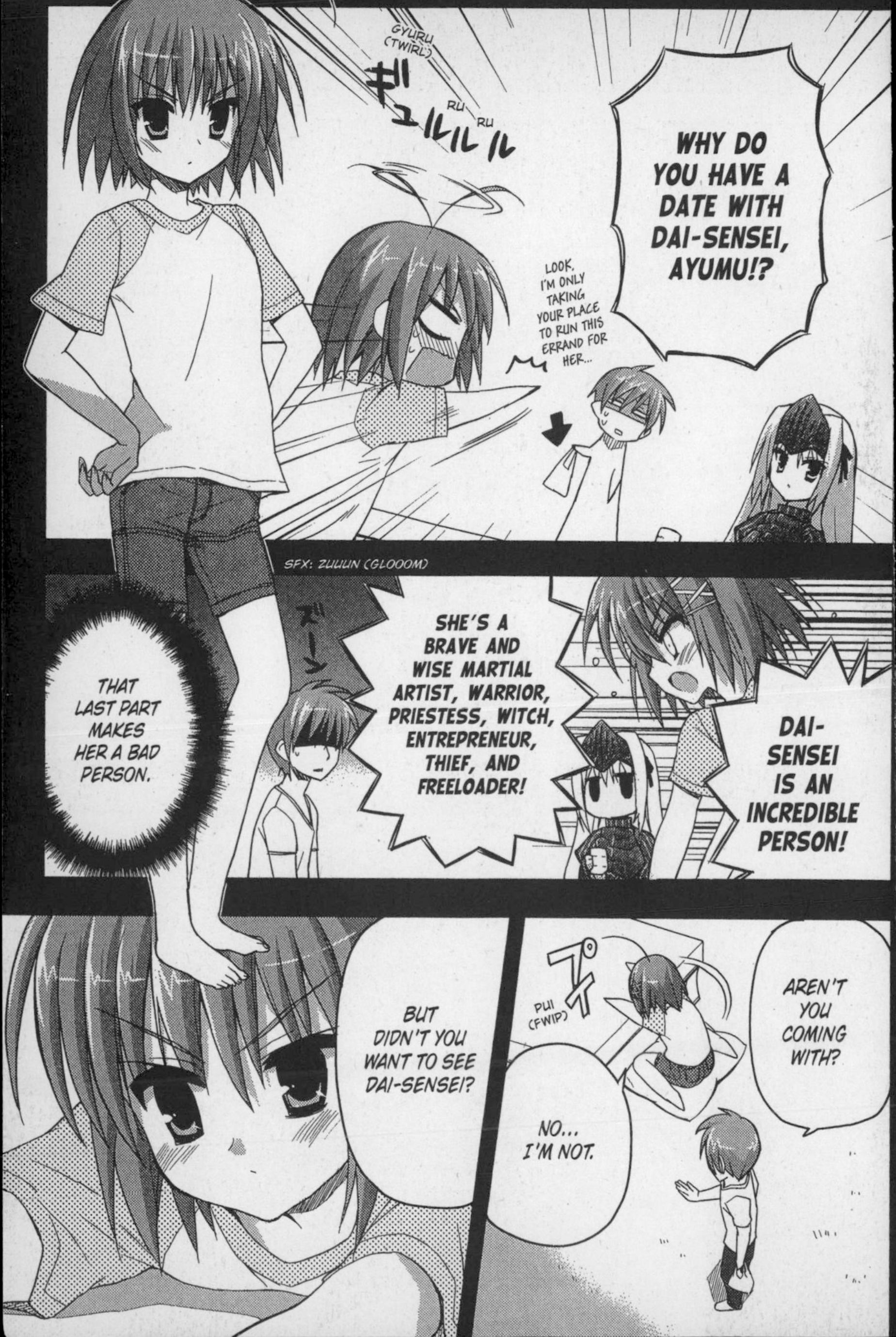
WHY DO YOU HAVE A DATE WITH DAI-SENSEI, AYUMU!?
GYURU (TWIRL)
ギュルルル
RU RU
LOOK, I'M ONLY TAKING YOUR PLACE TO RUN THIS ERRAND FOR HER...
SFX: ZUUUN (GLOOOM)
DAI-SENSEI IS AN INCREDIBLE PERSON!
SHE'S A BRAVE AND WISE MARTIAL ARTIST, WARRIOR, PRIESTESS, WITCH, ENTREPRENEUR, THIEF, AND FREELOADER!
ズーン
THAT LAST PART MAKES HER A BAD PERSON.
AREN'T YOU COMING WITH?
プイ
PUI (FWIP)
NO... I'M NOT.
BUT DIDN'T YOU WANT TO SEE DAI-SENSEI?

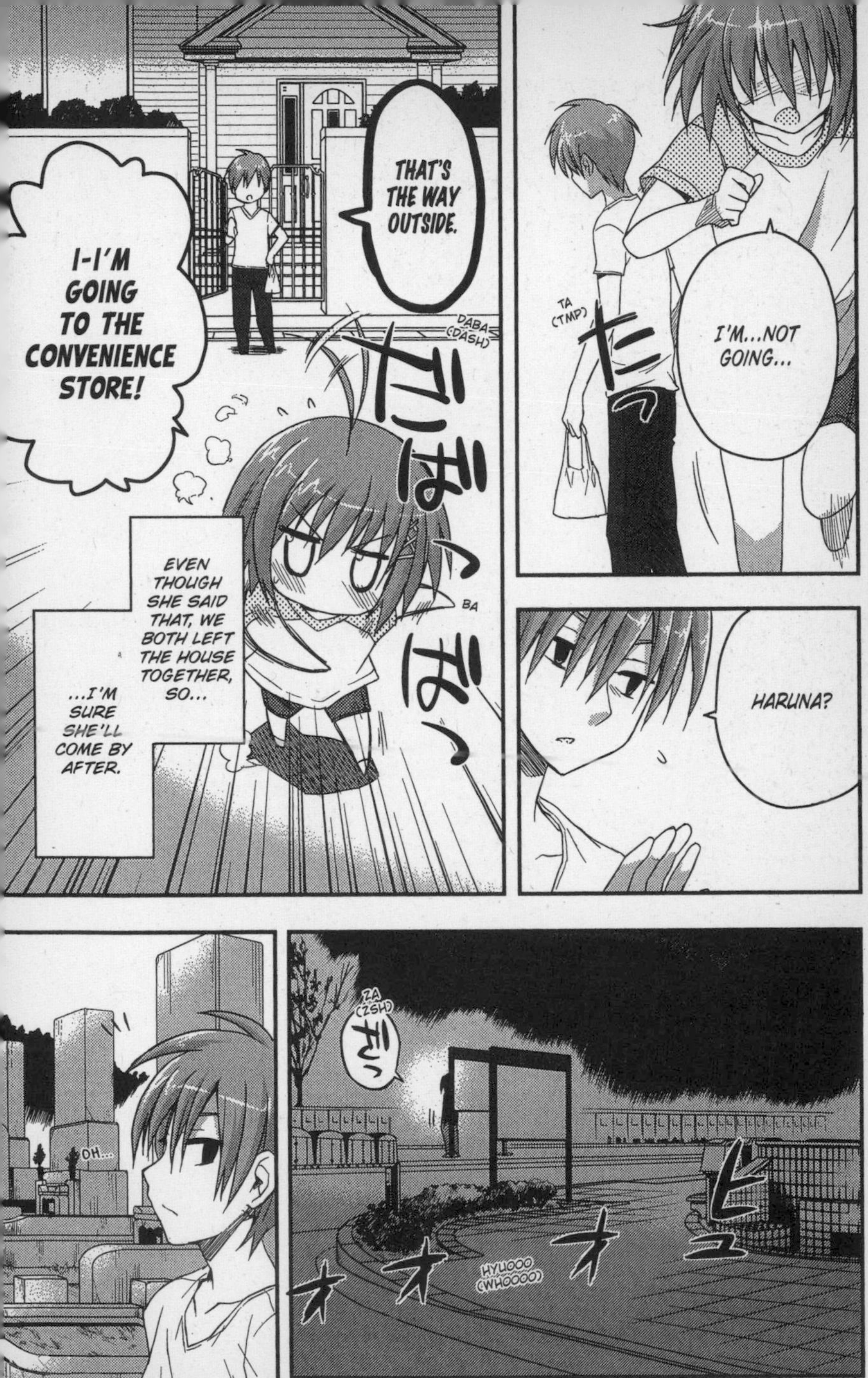
TA (TMP)
I'M...NOT GOING...
THAT'S THE WAY OUTSIDE.
I-I'M GOING TO THE CONVENIENCE STORE!
DABA (DASH)
BA
HARUNA?
EVEN THOUGH SHE SAID THAT, WE BOTH LEFT THE HOUSE TOGETHER, SO...
...I'M SURE SHE'LL COME BY AFTER.
ZA (ZSH)
HYUOOO (WHOOOO)
OH...

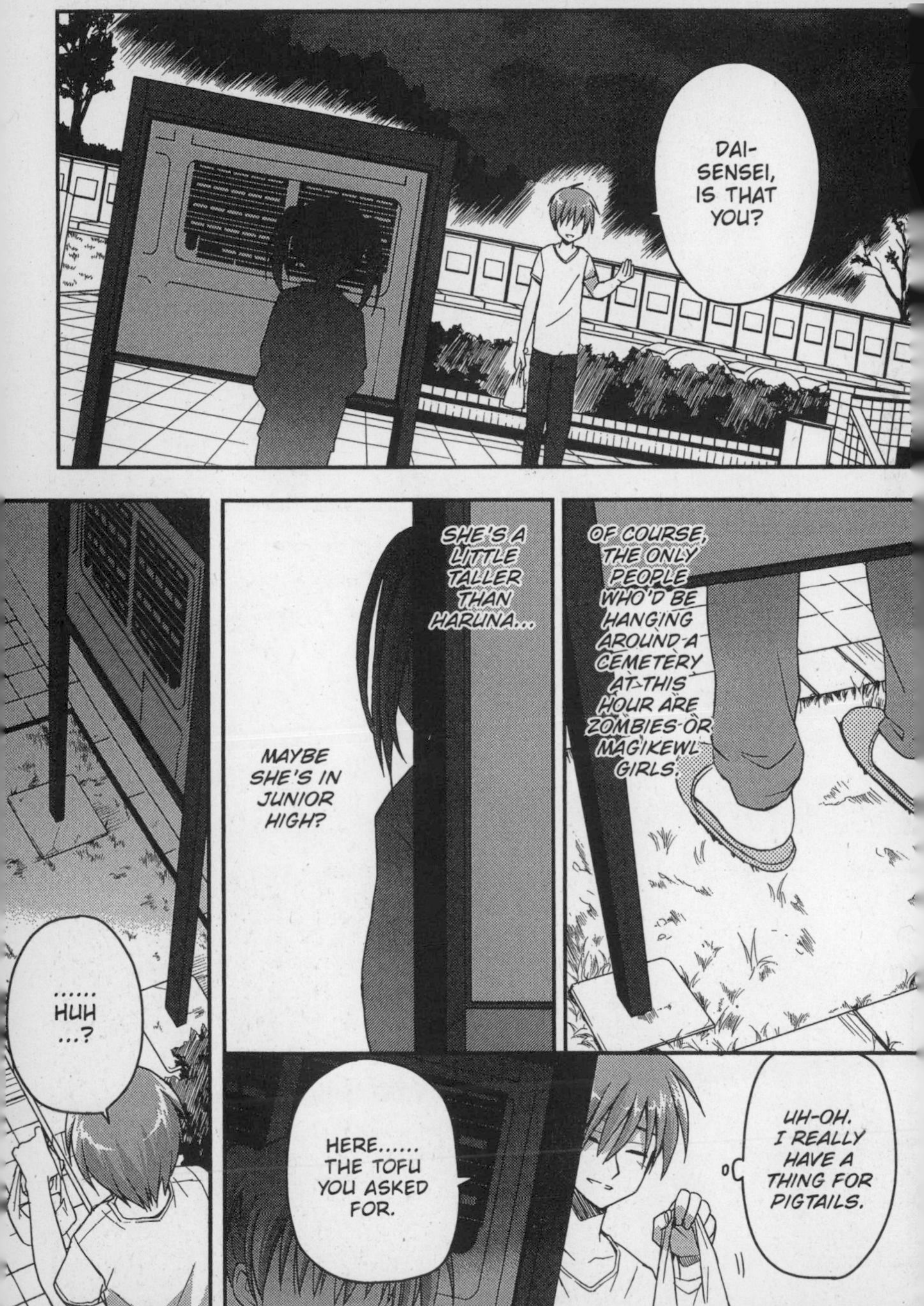
DAI-SENSEI, IS THAT YOU?
OF COURSE, THE ONLY PEOPLE WHO'D BE HANGING AROUND A CEMETERY AT THIS HOUR ARE ZOMBIES OR MAGIKEWL GIRLS.
SHE'S A LITTLE TALLER THAN HARUNA...
MAYBE SHE'S IN JUNIOR HIGH?
......HUH ...?
UH-OH. I REALLY HAVE A THING FOR PIGTAILS.
HERE...... THE TOFU YOU ASKED FOR.

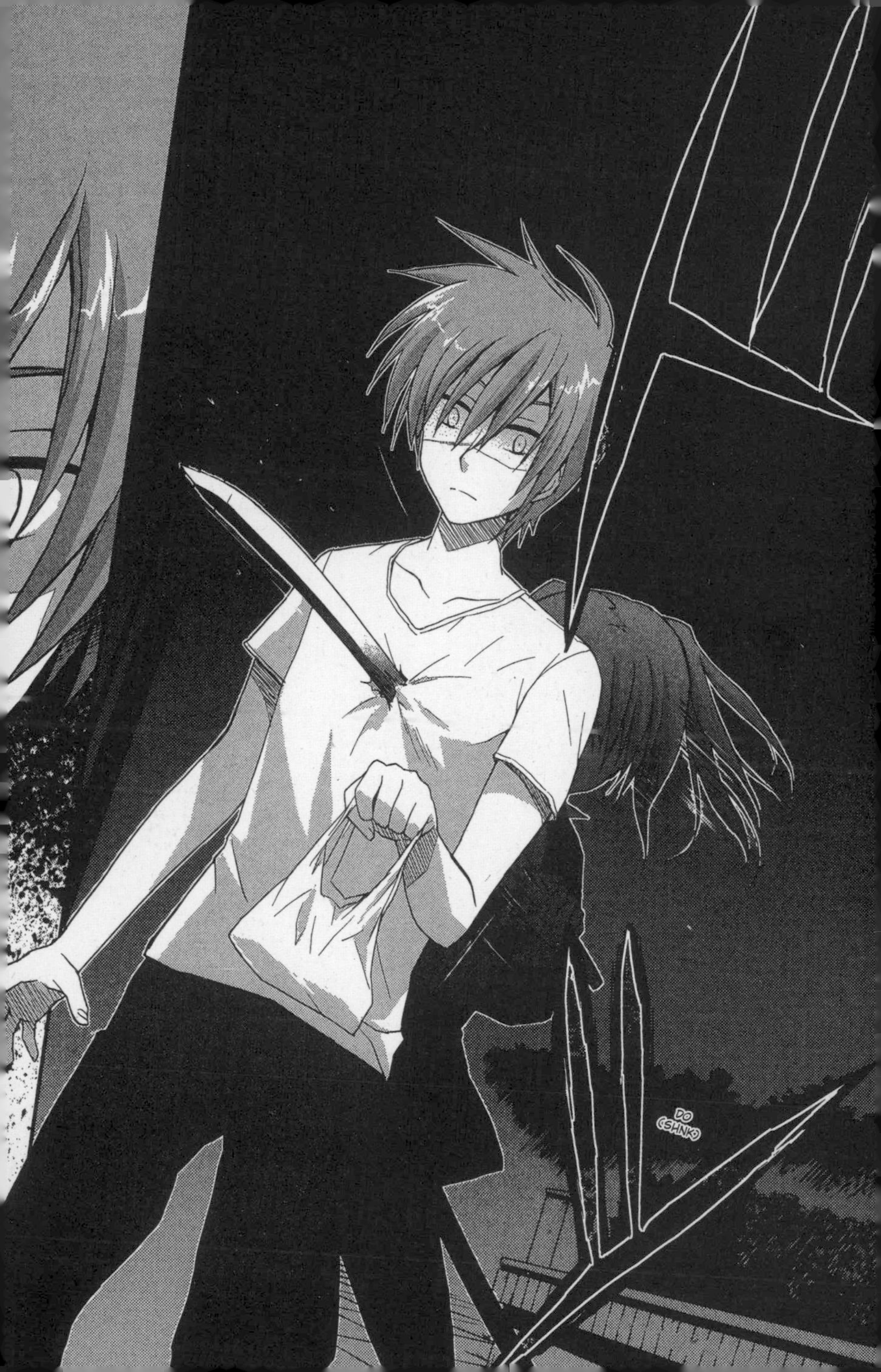
DO
(SHNK)

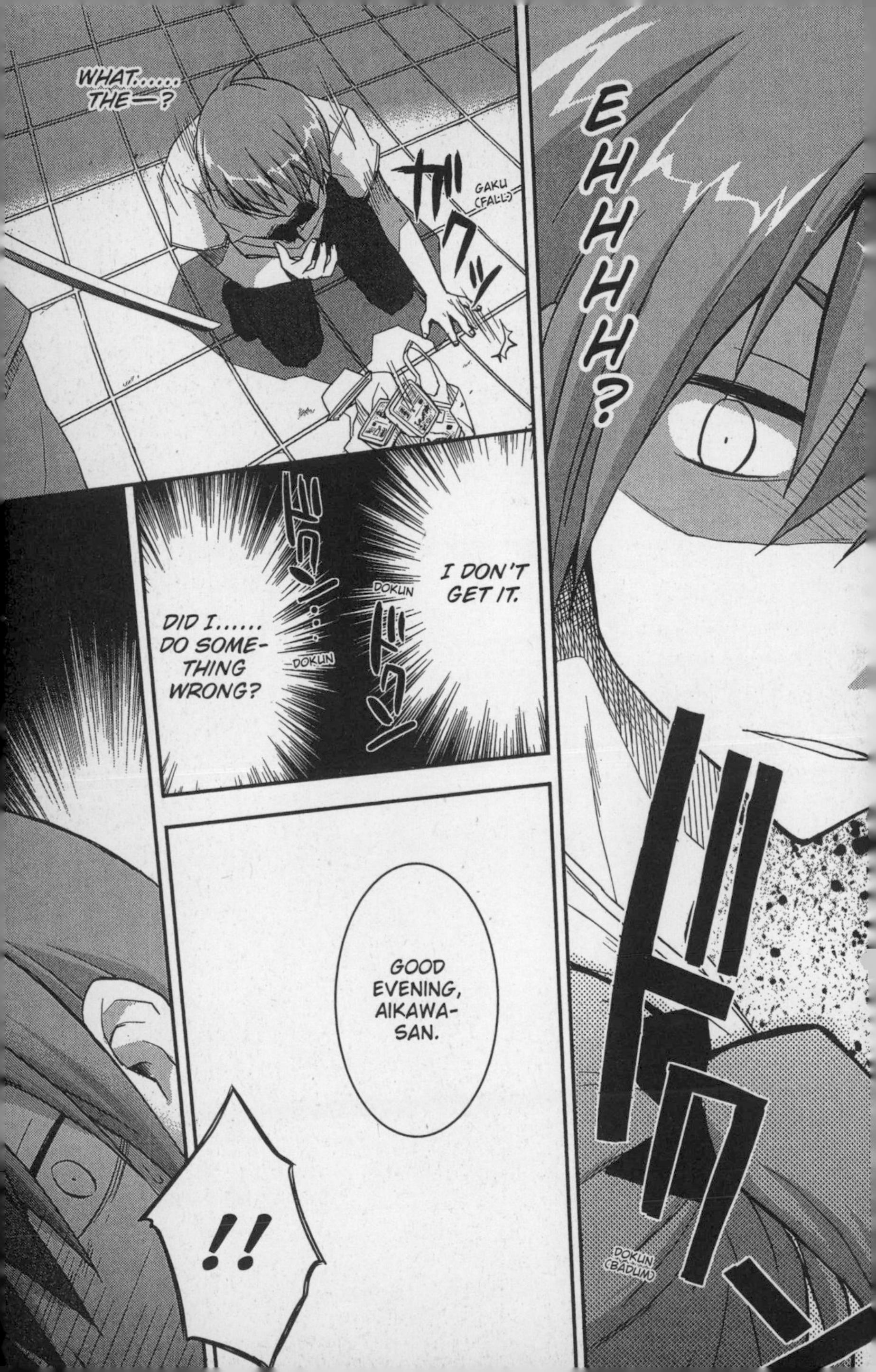
EHHHHH?
WHAT...... THE—?
GAKU (FALL)
I DON'T GET IT.
DOKUN
DOKUN
DID I...... DO SOME-THING WRONG?
DOKUN (BADUM)
GOOD EVENING, AIKAWA-SAN.
!!

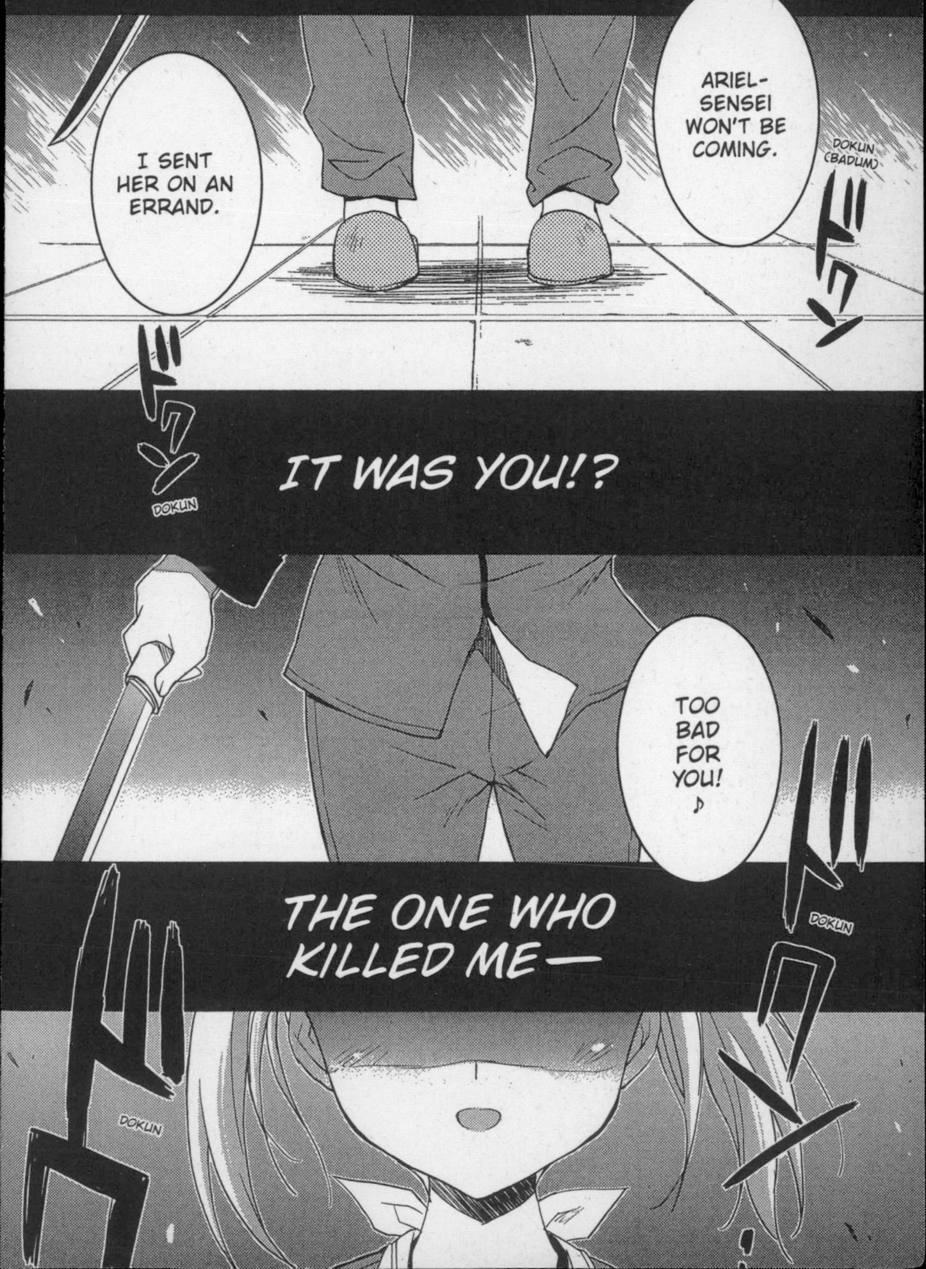
ARIEL-SENSEI WON'T BE COMING.
DOKUN (BADUM)
I SENT HER ON AN ERRAND.
DOKUN
IT WAS YOU!?
TOO BAD FOR YOU! ♪
DOKUN
THE ONE WHO KILLED ME—
DOKUN

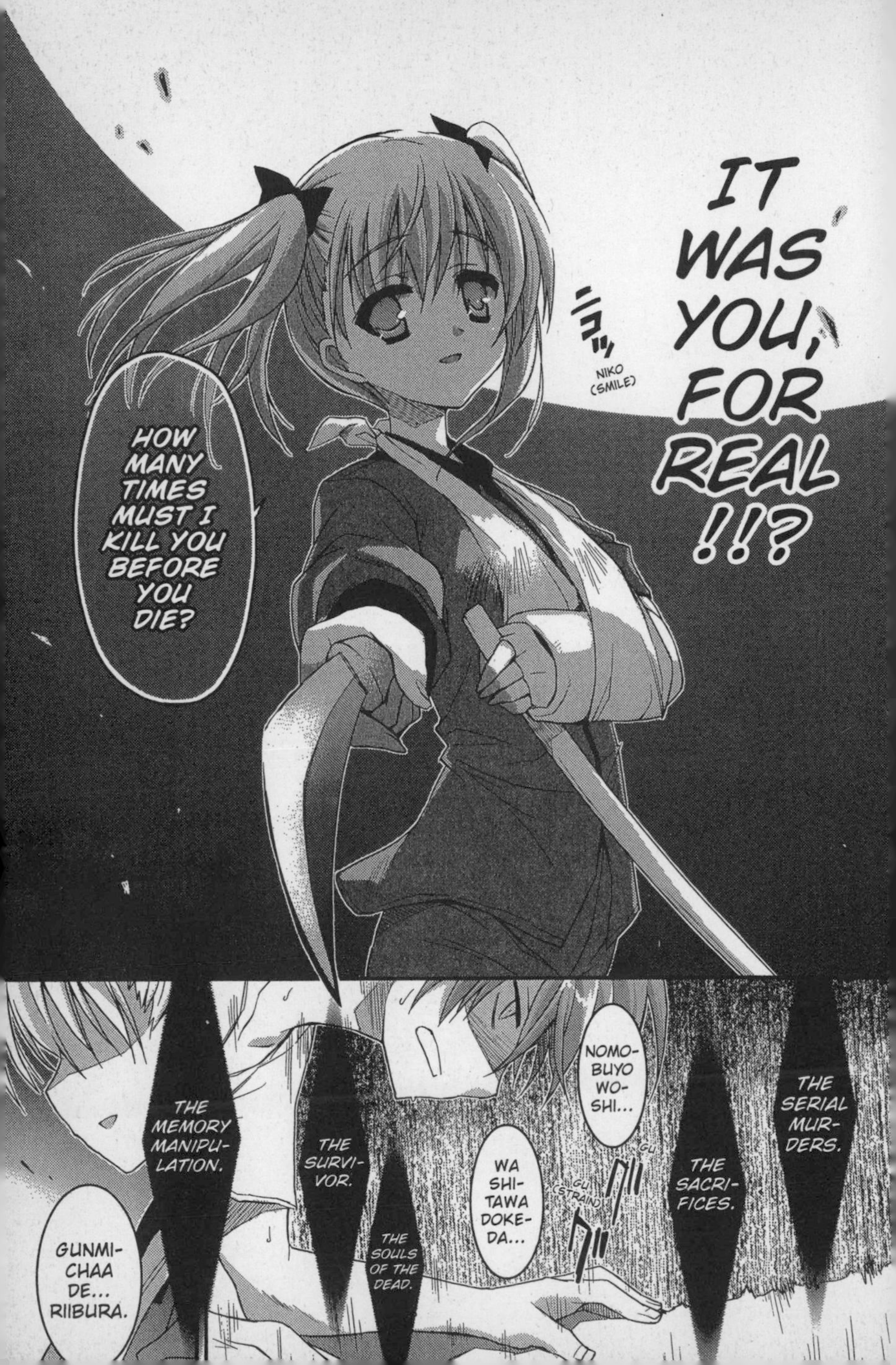
IT WAS YOU, FOR REAL!!?
ニコッ
NIKO (SMILE)
HOW MANY TIMES MUST I KILL YOU BEFORE YOU DIE?
THE SERIAL MURDERS.
THE SACRIFICES.
GU GU (STRAIN)
NOMOBUYO WOSHI...
WA SHITAWA DOKEDA...
THE SOULS OF THE DEAD.
THE SURVIVOR.
THE MEMORY MANIPULATION.
GUNMICHAA DE... RIIBURA.

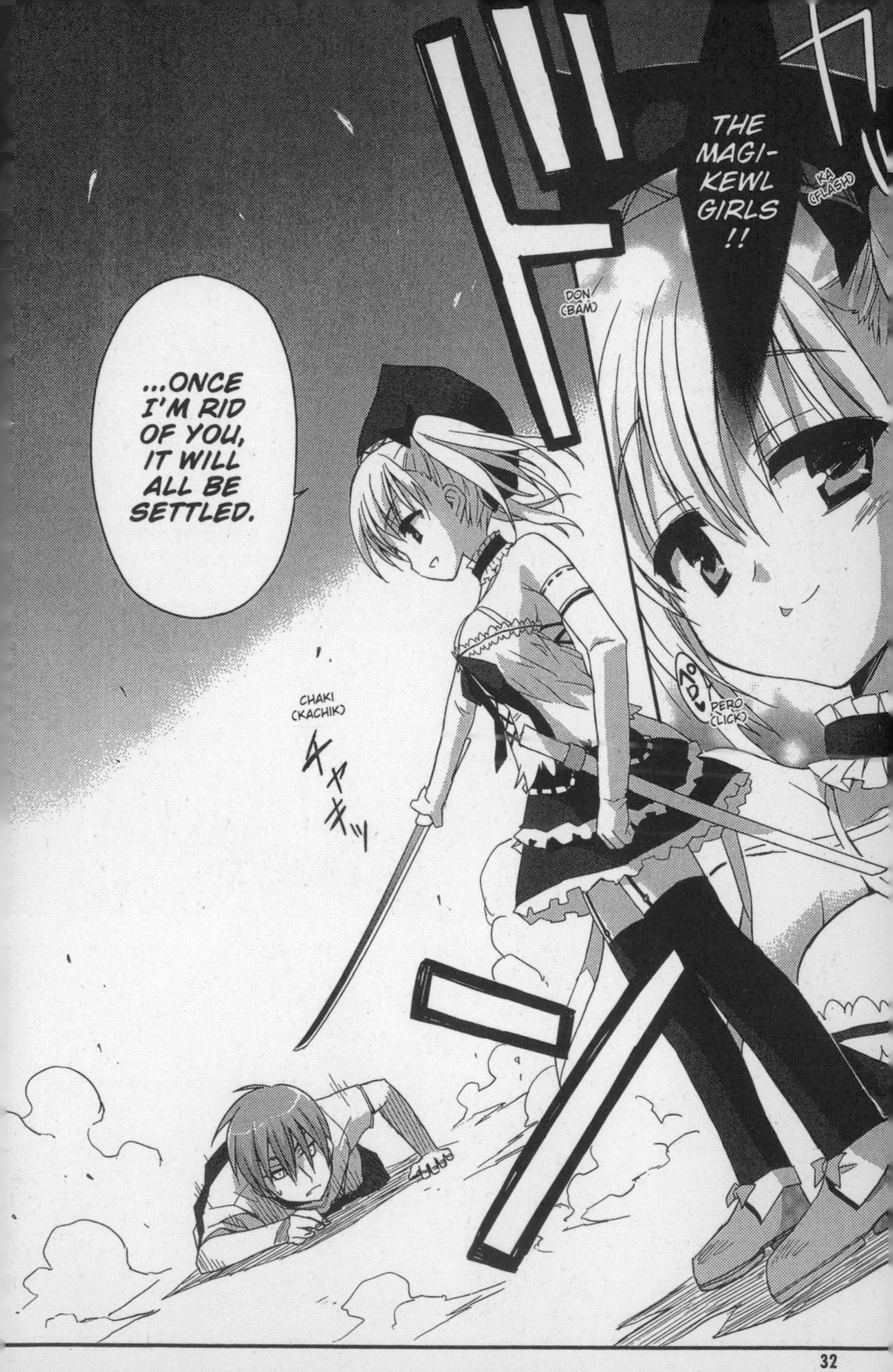
THE MAGI-KEWL GIRLS !!
KA (FLASH)
DON (BAM)
...ONCE I'M RID OF YOU, IT WILL ALL BE SETTLED.
PERO (LICK)
CHAKI (KACHIK)

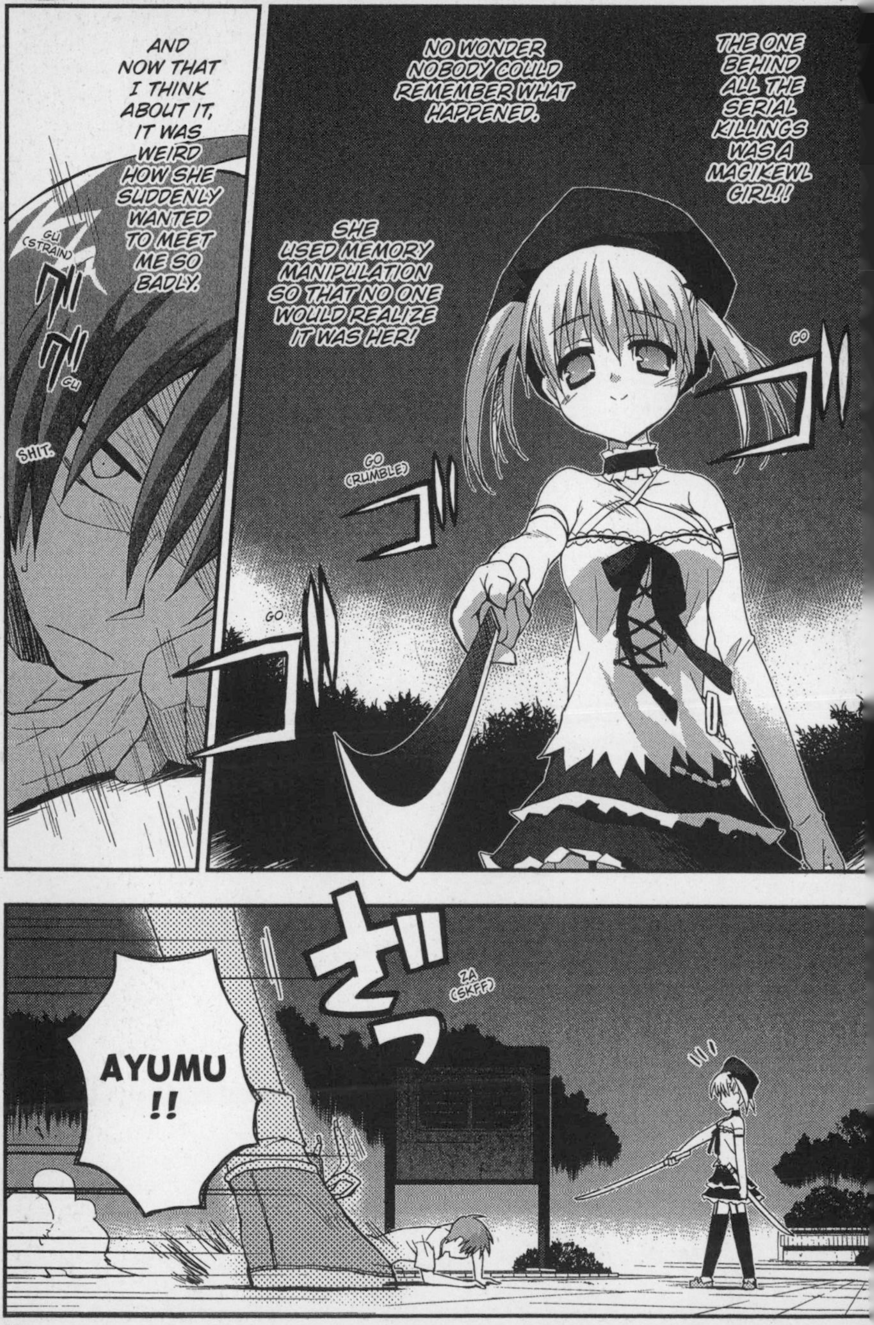
THE ONE BEHIND ALL THE SERIAL KILLINGS WAS A MAGIKEWL GIRL!!
NO WONDER NOBODY COULD REMEMBER WHAT HAPPENED.
SHE USED MEMORY MANIPULATION SO THAT NO ONE WOULD REALIZE IT WAS HER!
GO
GO (RUMBLE)
GO
AND NOW THAT I THINK ABOUT IT, IT WAS WEIRD HOW SHE SUDDENLY WANTED TO MEET ME SO BADLY.
GU (STRAIN)
GU
SHIT.
ZA (SKFF)
AYUMU !!

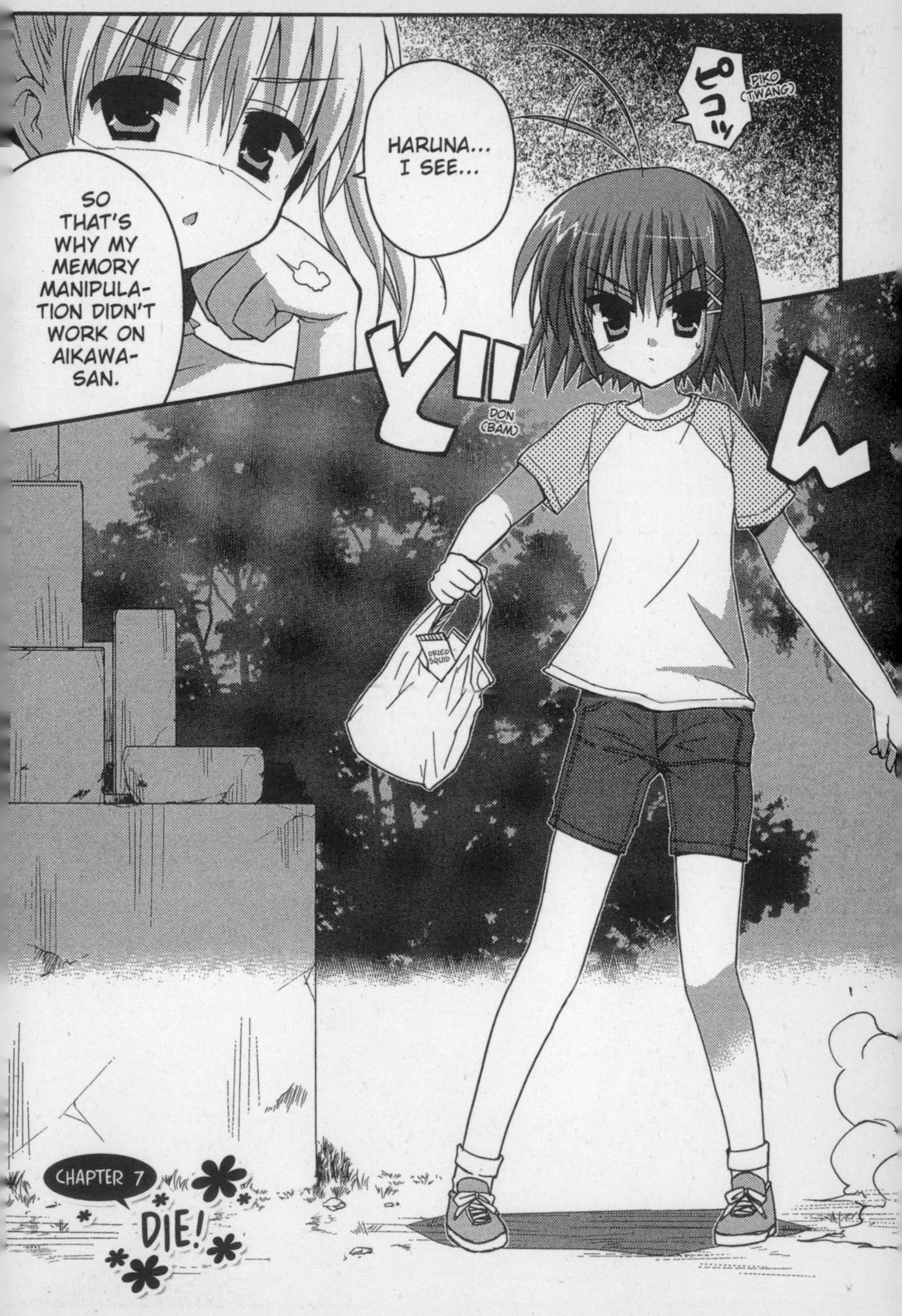
ピコッ
PIKO (TWANG)
HARUNA... I SEE...
SO THAT'S WHY MY MEMORY MANIPULATION DIDN'T WORK ON AIKAWA-SAN.
ドーん
DON (BAM)
DRIED SQUID
CHAPTER 7
DIE!

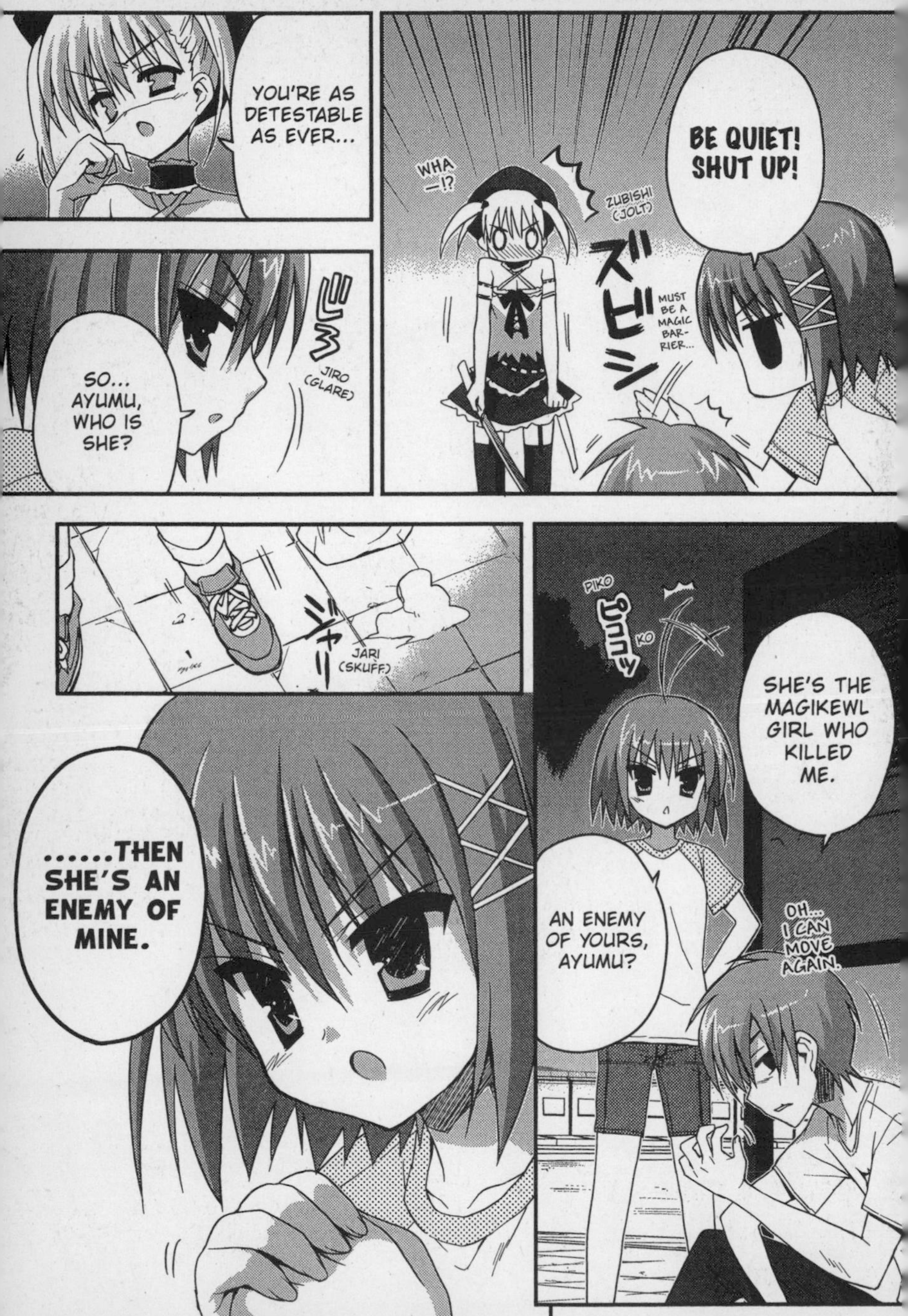
BE QUIET! SHUT UP!
WHA—!?
ZUBISHI (JOLT)
MUST BE A MAGIC BAR-RIER...
YOU'RE AS DETESTABLE AS EVER...
JIRO (GLARE)
SO... AYUMU, WHO IS SHE?
PIKO
KO
SHE'S THE MAGIKEWL GIRL WHO KILLED ME.
AN ENEMY OF YOURS, AYUMU?
OH... I CAN MOVE AGAIN.
JARI (SKUFF)
......THEN SHE'S AN ENEMY OF MINE.

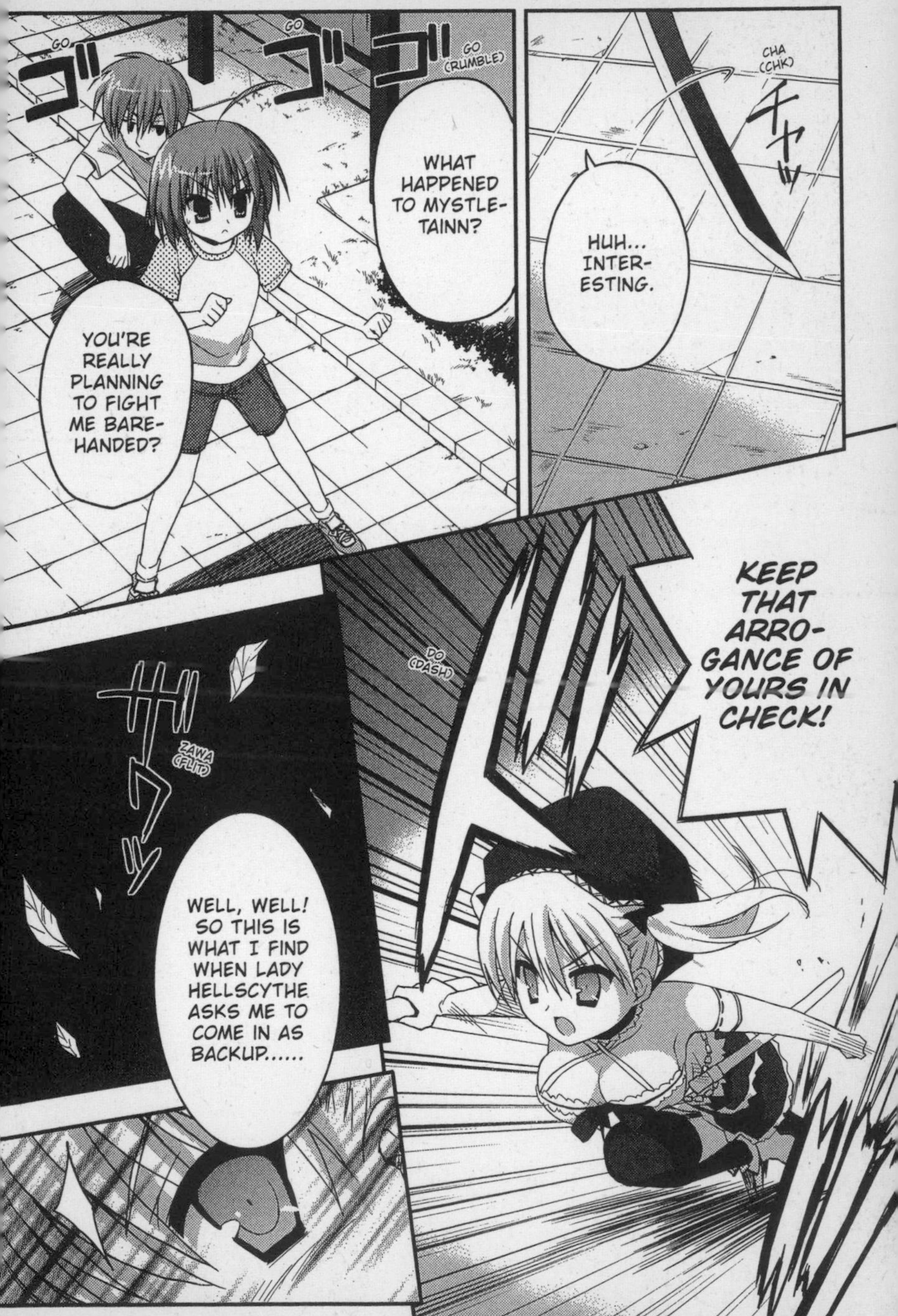
CHA (CHK)
HUH... INTER-ESTING.
GO GO GO (RUMBLE)
WHAT HAPPENED TO MYSTLE-TAINN?
YOU'RE REALLY PLANNING TO FIGHT ME BARE-HANDED?
DO (DASH)
KEEP THAT ARRO-GANCE OF YOURS IN CHECK!
ZAWA (FLIT)
WELL, WELL! SO THIS IS WHAT I FIND WHEN LADY HELLSCYTHE ASKS ME TO COME IN AS BACKUP......

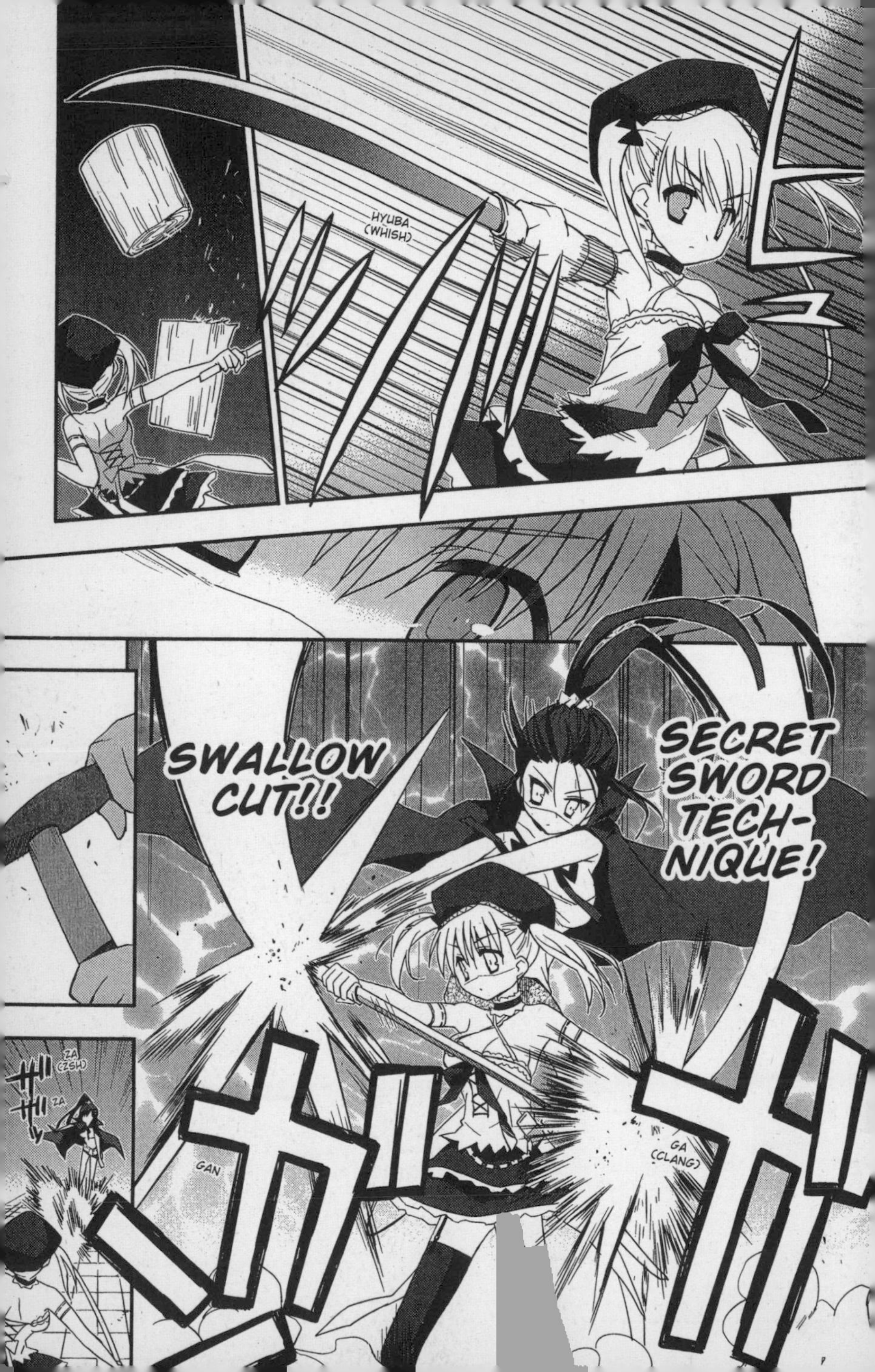
HYUBA (WHISH)
SECRET SWORD TECH-NIQUE!
SWALLOW CUT!!
GA (CLANG)
GAN
ZA (ZSH)
ZA

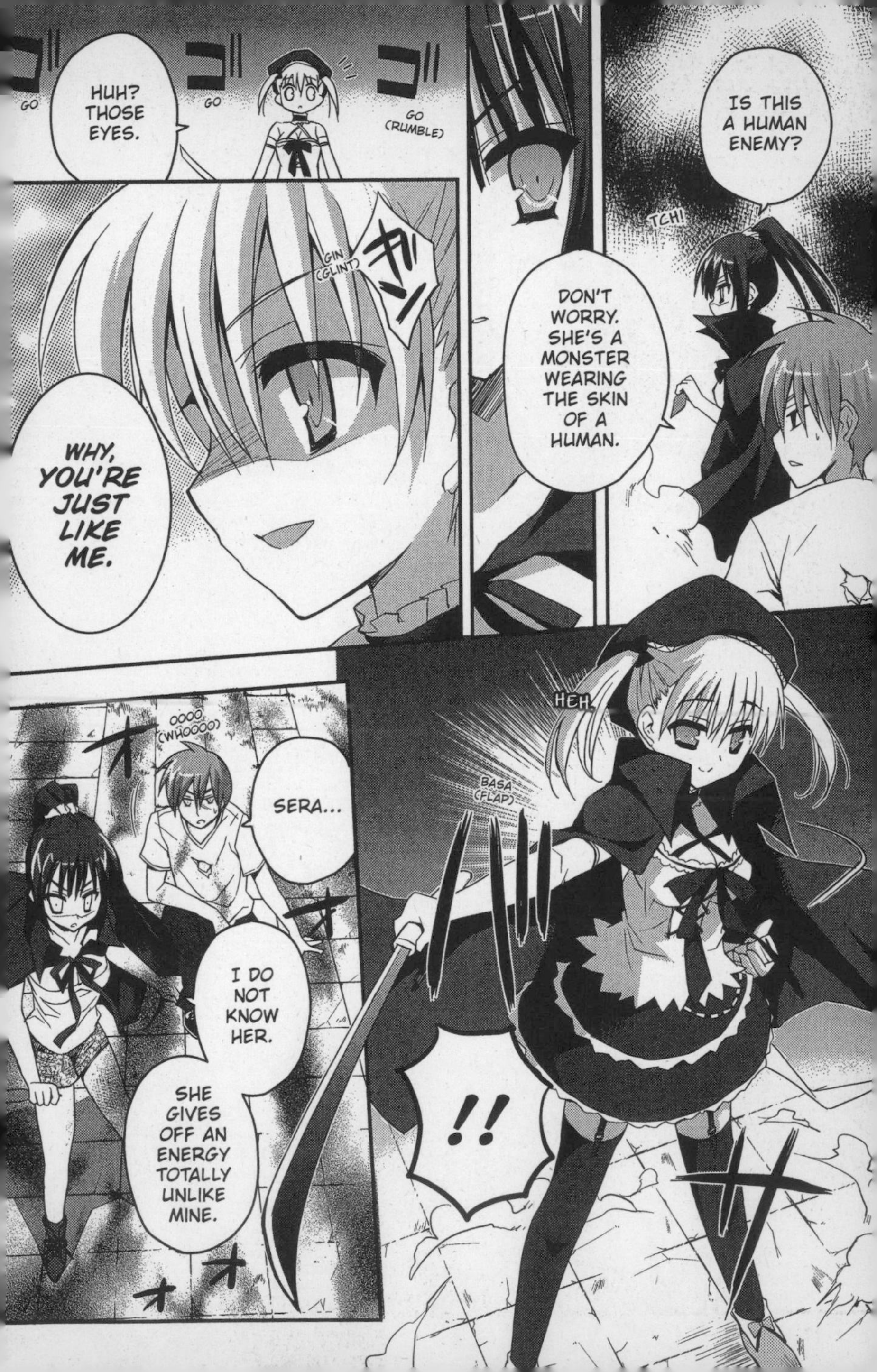

IS THIS A HUMAN ENEMY?
TCH!
DON'T WORRY. SHE'S A MONSTER WEARING THE SKIN OF A HUMAN.
GO
GO
GO (RUMBLE)
HUH? THOSE EYES.
GIN (GLINT)
WHY, YOU'RE JUST LIKE ME.
HEH.
BASA (FLAP)
!!
OOOO (WHOOOO)
SERA...
I DO NOT KNOW HER.
SHE GIVES OFF AN ENERGY TOTALLY UNLIKE MINE.

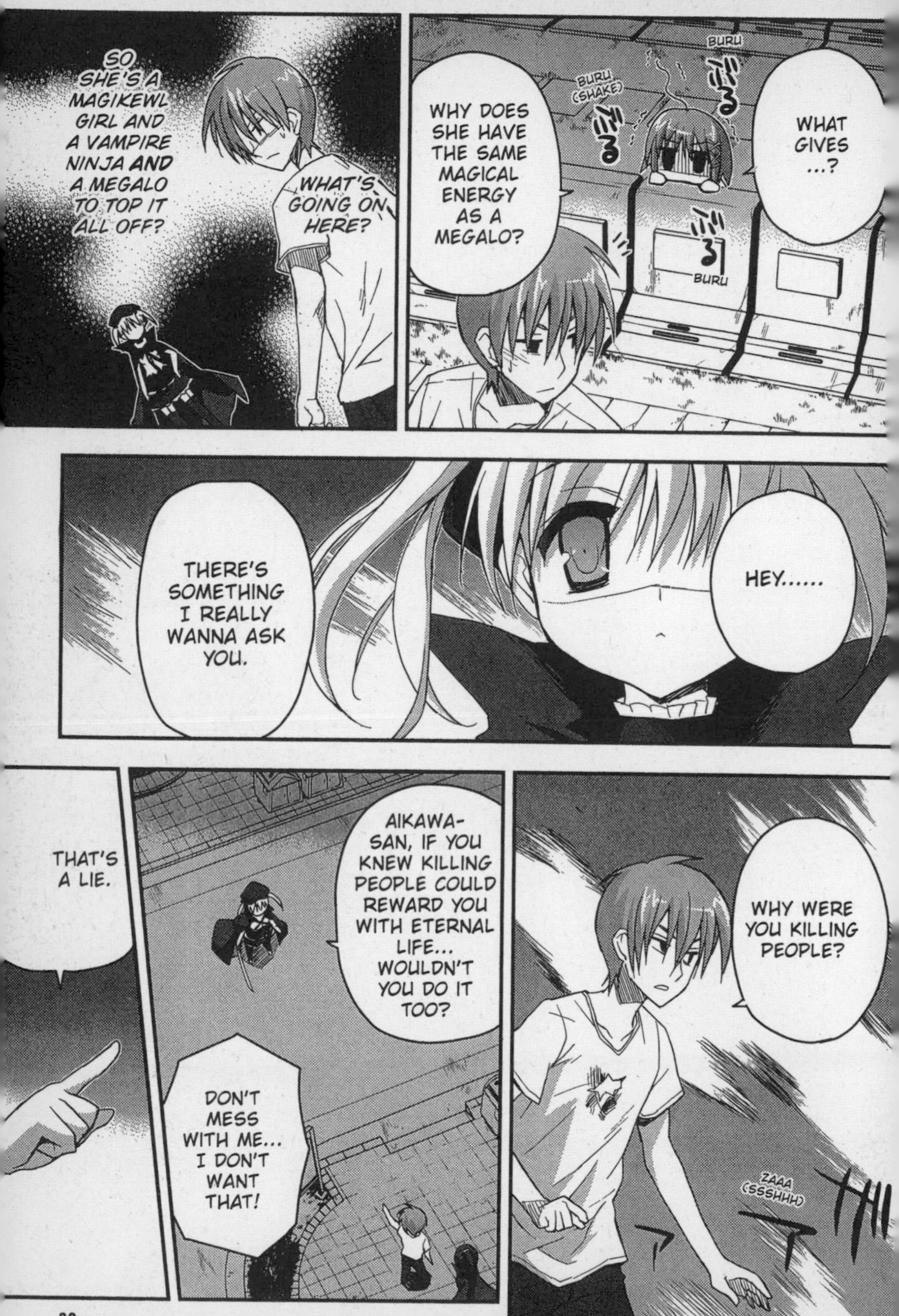
BURU
BURU (SHAKE)
WHAT GIVES ...?
BURU
WHY DOES SHE HAVE THE SAME MAGICAL ENERGY AS A MEGALO?
WHAT'S GOING ON HERE?
SO SHE'S A MAGIKEWL GIRL AND A VAMPIRE NINJA AND A MEGALO TO TOP IT ALL OFF?
HEY......
THERE'S SOMETHING I REALLY WANNA ASK YOU.
WHY WERE YOU KILLING PEOPLE?
ZAAA (SSSHHH)
AIKAWA-SAN, IF YOU KNEW KILLING PEOPLE COULD REWARD YOU WITH ETERNAL LIFE... WOULDN'T YOU DO IT TOO?
DON'T MESS WITH ME... I DON'T WANT THAT!
THAT'S A LIE.

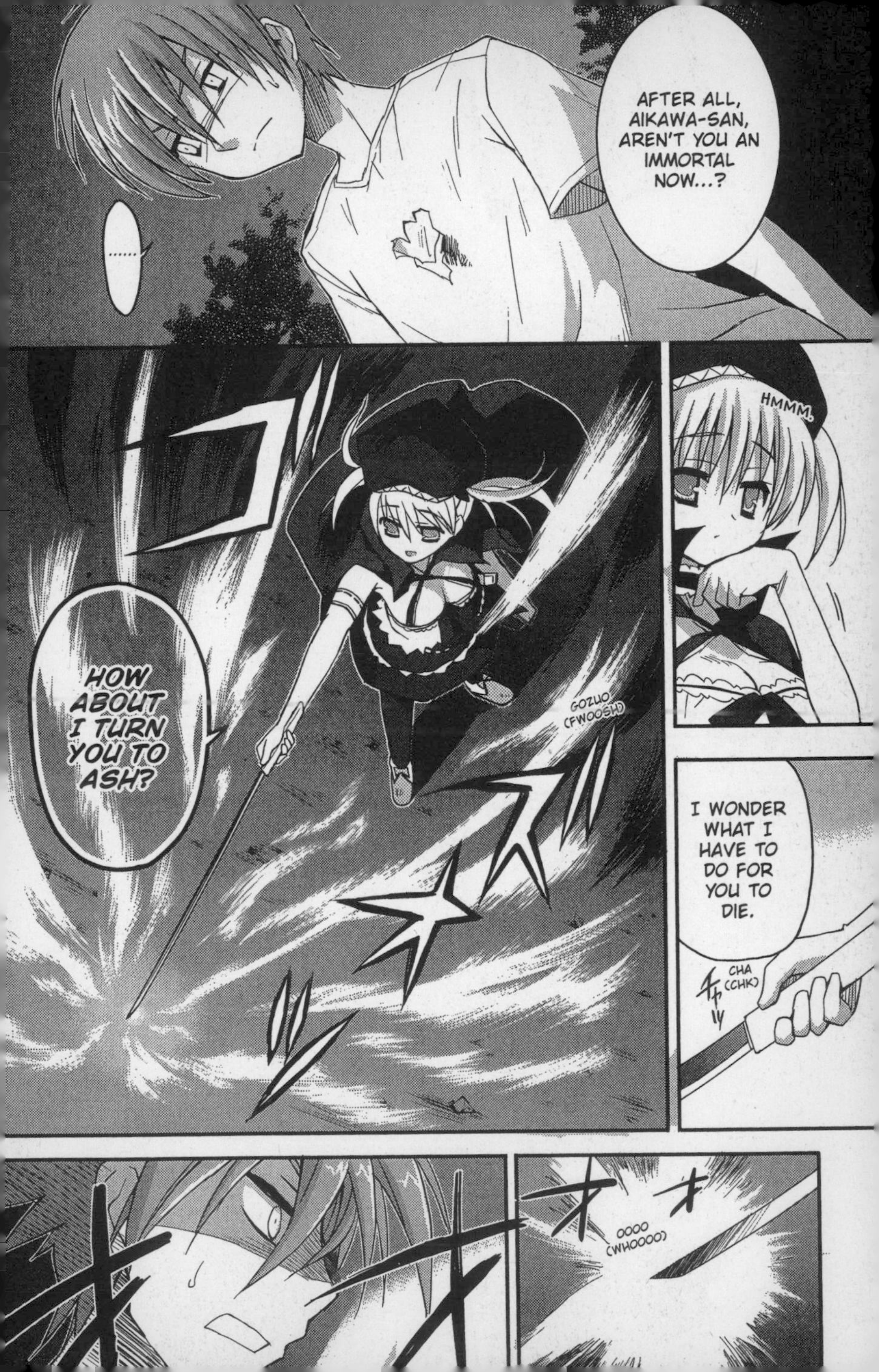
AFTER ALL, AIKAWA-SAN, AREN'T YOU AN IMMORTAL NOW...?
......
HMMM.
I WONDER WHAT I HAVE TO DO FOR YOU TO DIE.
CHA (CHK)
HOW ABOUT I TURN YOU TO ASH?
GOZUO (FWOOSH)
OOOO (WHOOOO)

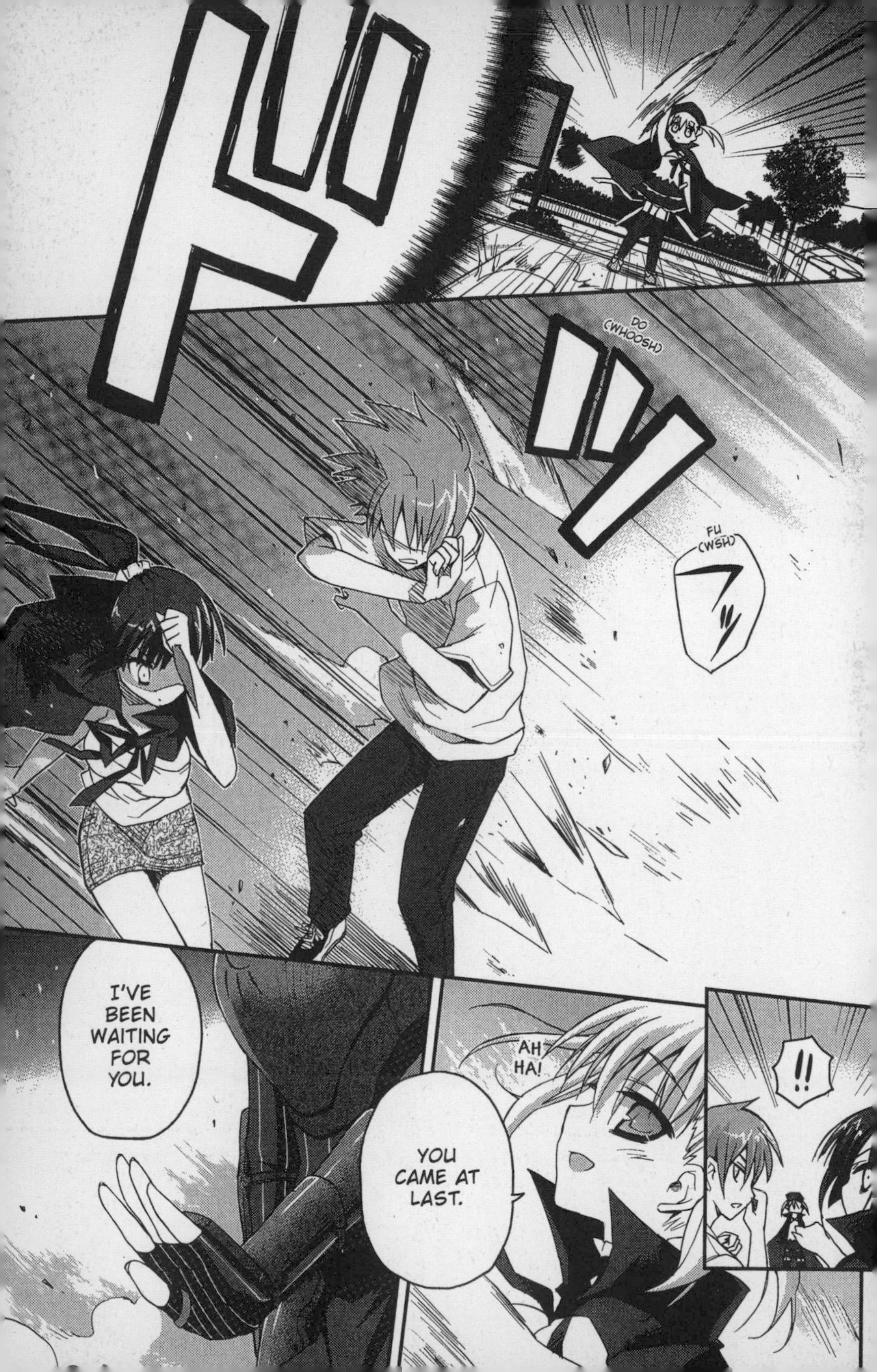
DO
(WHOOSH)
FU
(WSH)
I'VE BEEN WAITING FOR YOU.
!!
AH HA!
YOU CAME AT LAST.

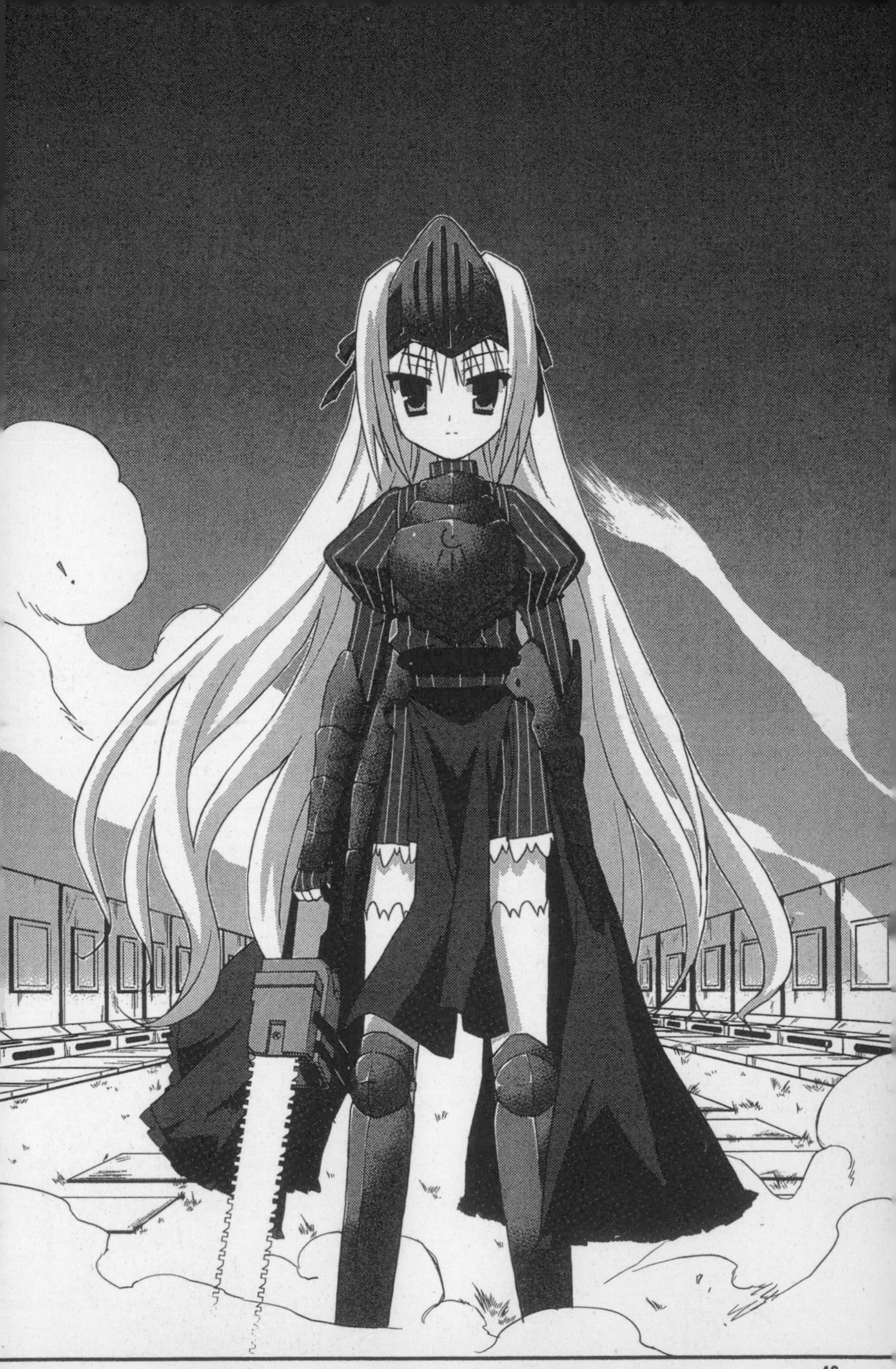

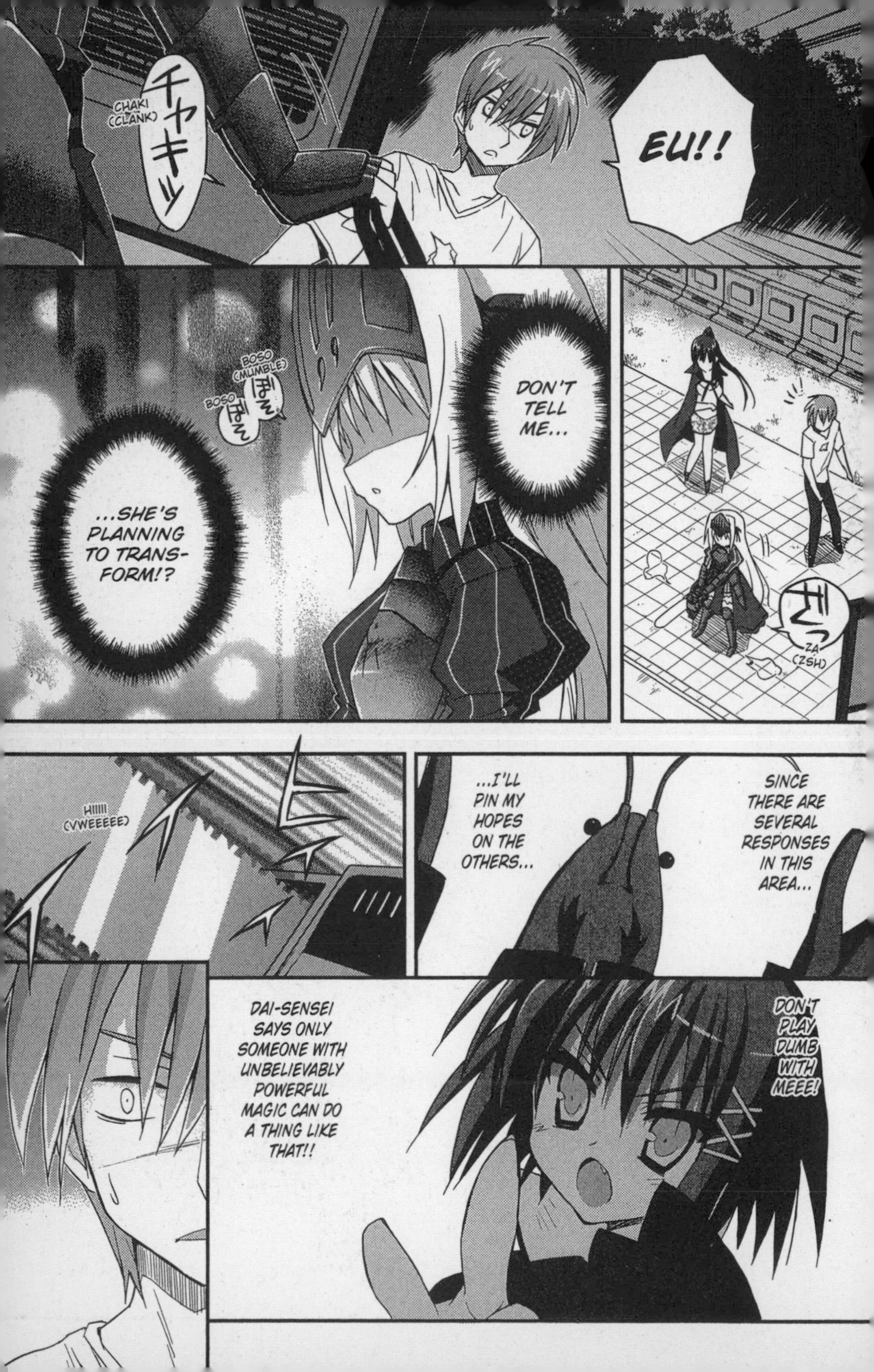
EU!!
チャキッ
CHAKI (CLANK)
DON'T TELL ME...
...SHE'S PLANNING TO TRANS-FORM!?
ぼそ
BOSO (MUMBLE)
ぼそ
BOSO
ざっ
ZA (ZSH)
SINCE THERE ARE SEVERAL RESPONSES IN THIS AREA...
...I'LL PIN MY HOPES ON THE OTHERS...
HIIIII (VWEEEEE)
DON'T PLAY DUMB WITH MEEE!
DAI-SENSEI SAYS ONLY SOMEONE WITH UNBELIEVABLY POWERFUL MAGIC CAN DO A THING LIKE THAT!!

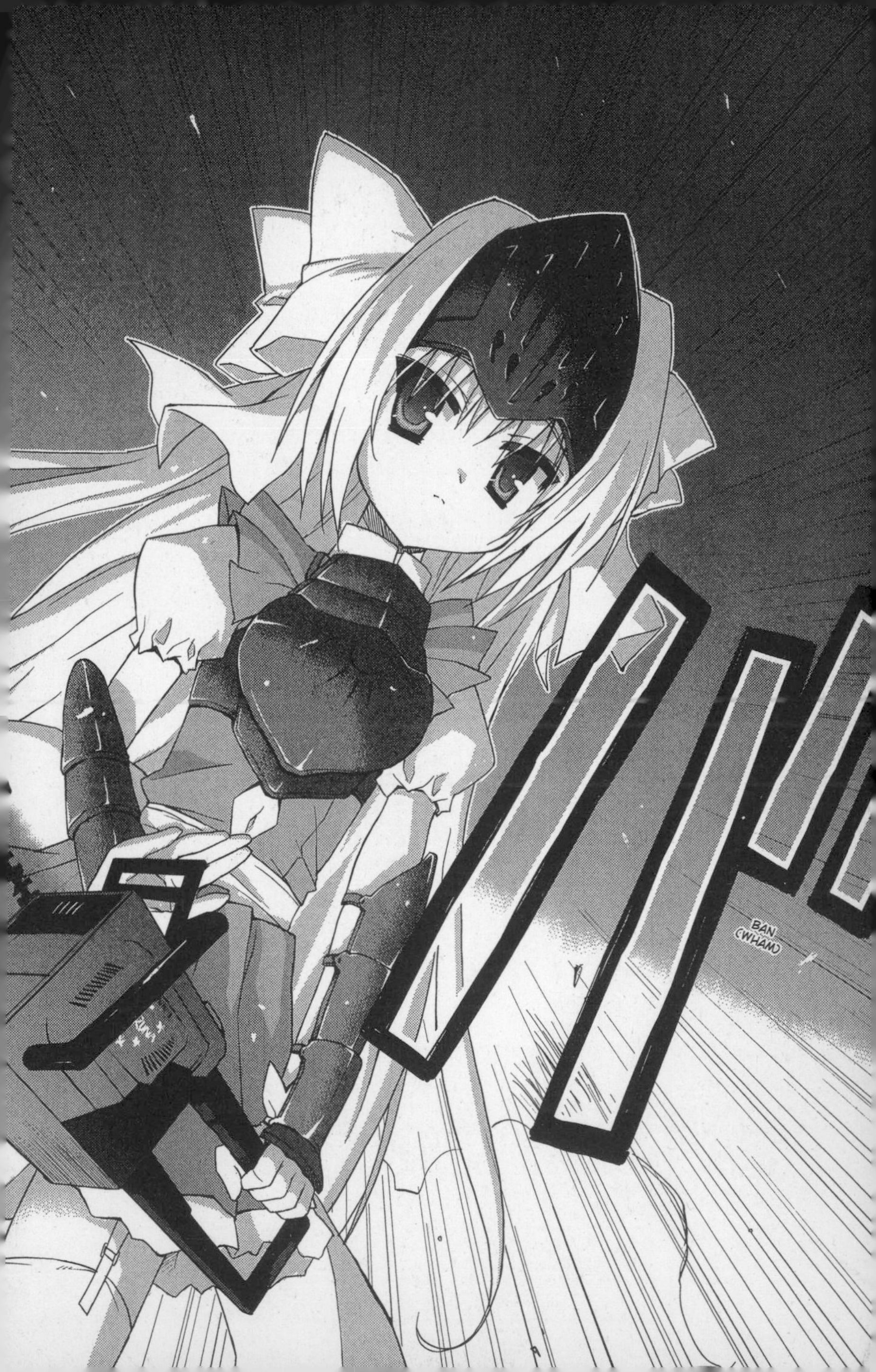
BAN
(WHAM)

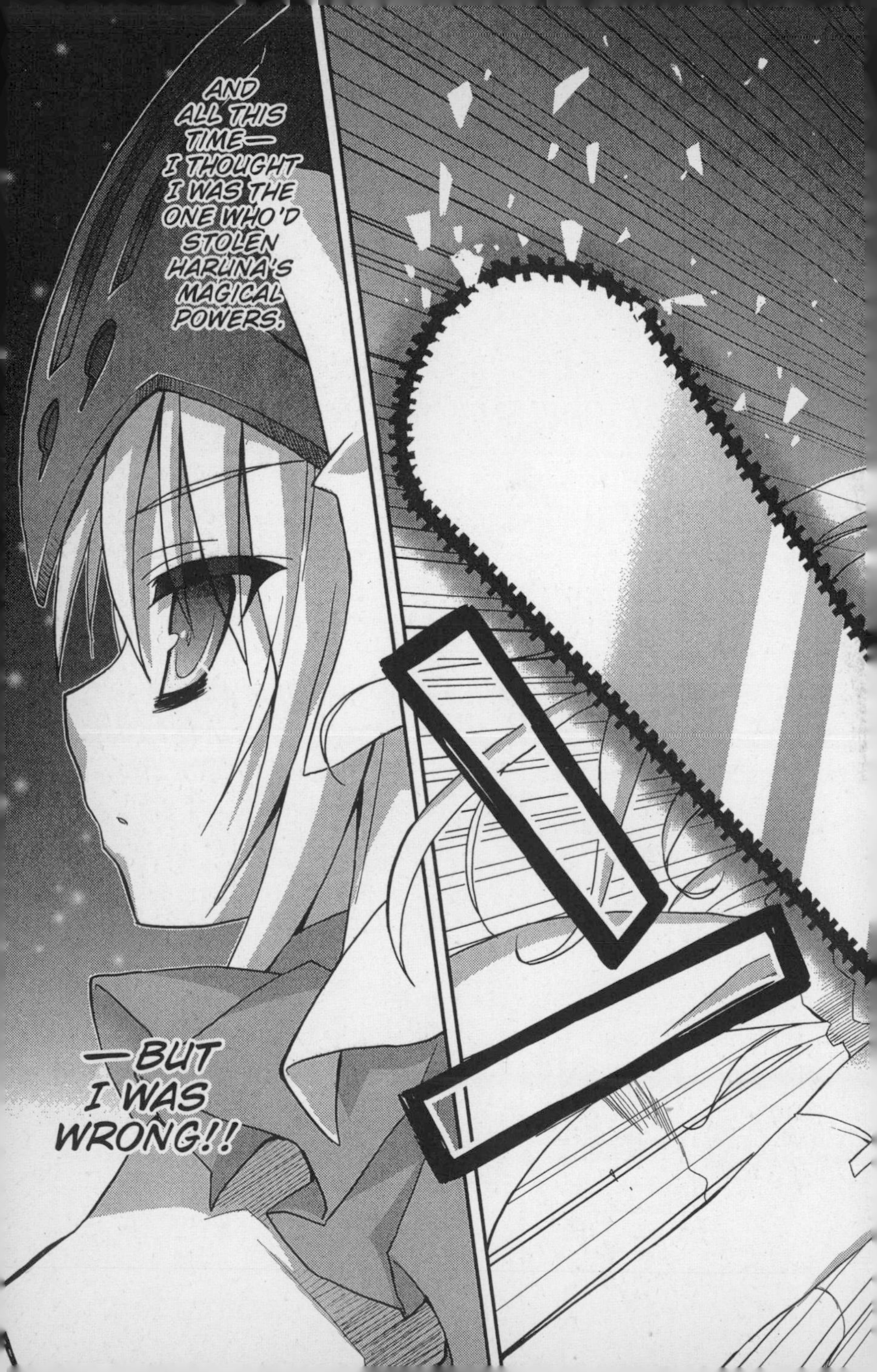
AND ALL THIS TIME— I THOUGHT I WAS THE ONE WHO'D STOLEN HARUNA'S MAGICAL POWERS.
—BUT I WAS WRONG!!

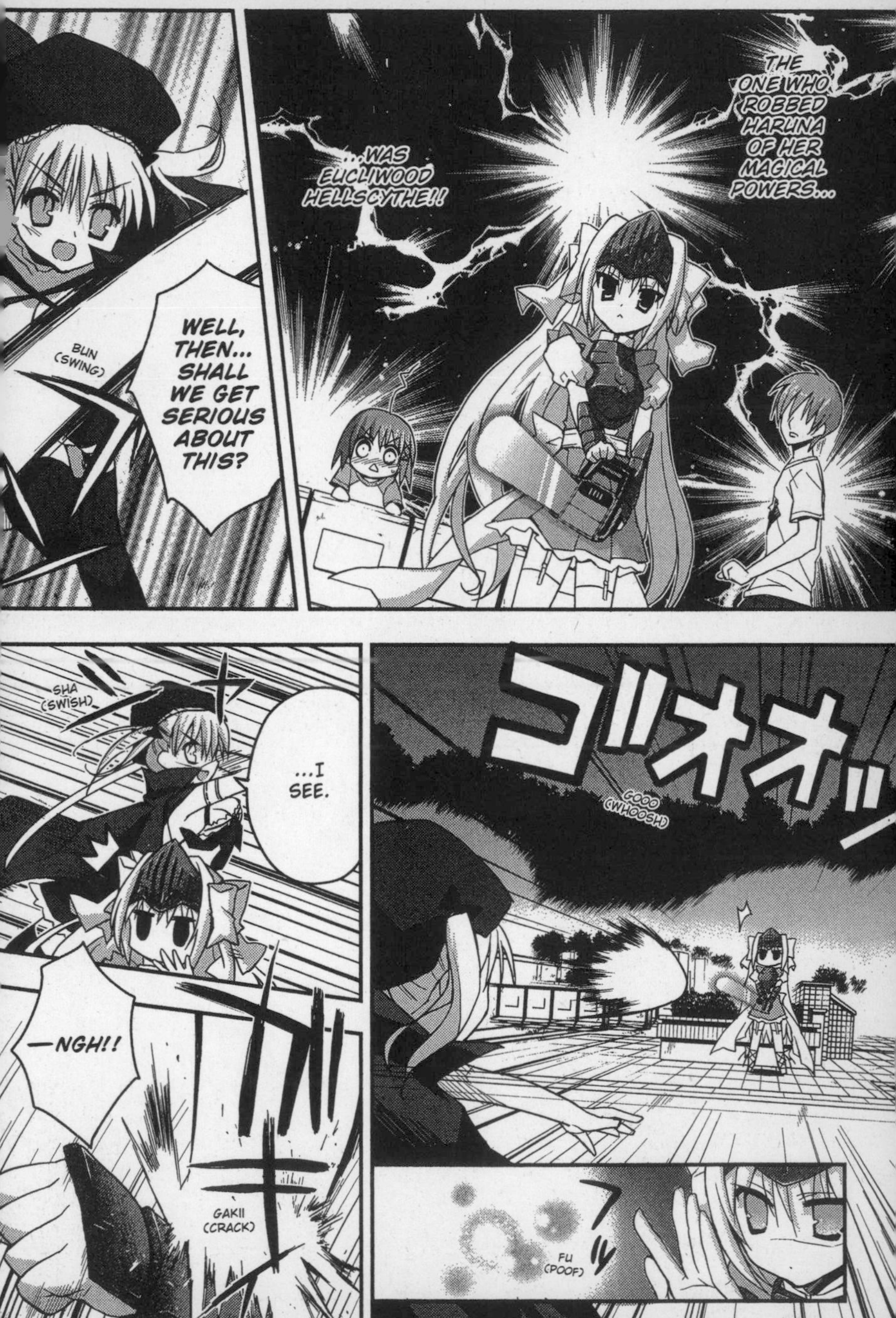
THE ONE WHO ROBBED HARUNA OF HER MAGICAL POWERS...
...WAS EUCLIWOOD HELLSCYTHE!!
WELL, THEN... SHALL WE GET SERIOUS ABOUT THIS?
BUN (SWING)
ゴオオッ
GOOO (WHOOSH)
SHA (SWISH)
...I SEE.
—NGH!!
GAKII (CRACK)
FU (POOF)

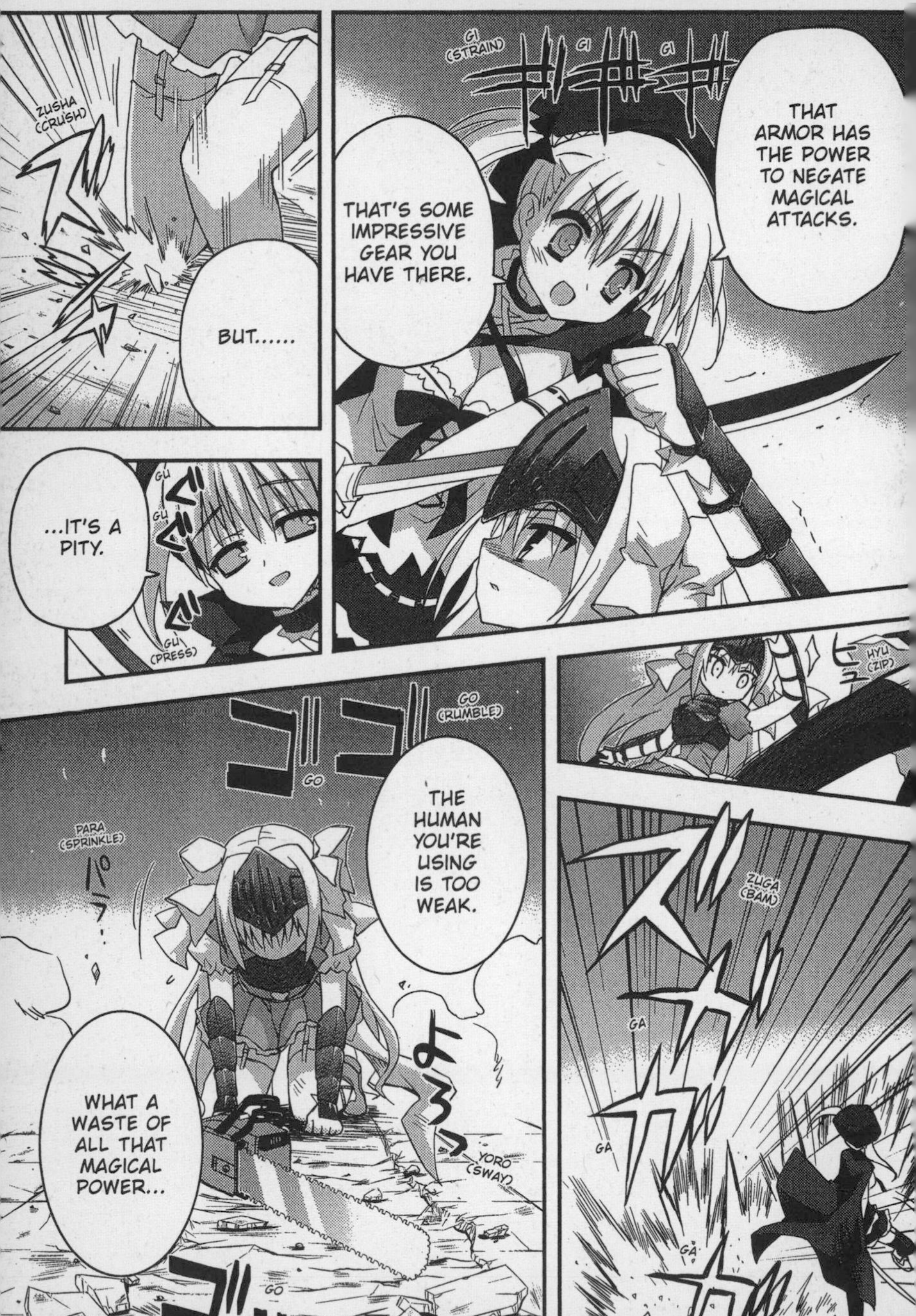
GI (STRAIN)
GI
GI
THAT ARMOR HAS THE POWER TO NEGATE MAGICAL ATTACKS.
THAT'S SOME IMPRESSIVE GEAR YOU HAVE THERE.
ZUSHA (CRUSH)
BUT......
GU
GU
...IT'S A PITY.
GU (PRESS)
HYU (ZIP)
ZUGA (BAM)
GA
GA
GA
GO (RUMBLE)
GO
THE HUMAN YOU'RE USING IS TOO WEAK.
PARA (SPRINKLE)
YORO (SWAY)
WHAT A WASTE OF ALL THAT MAGICAL POWER...
GO

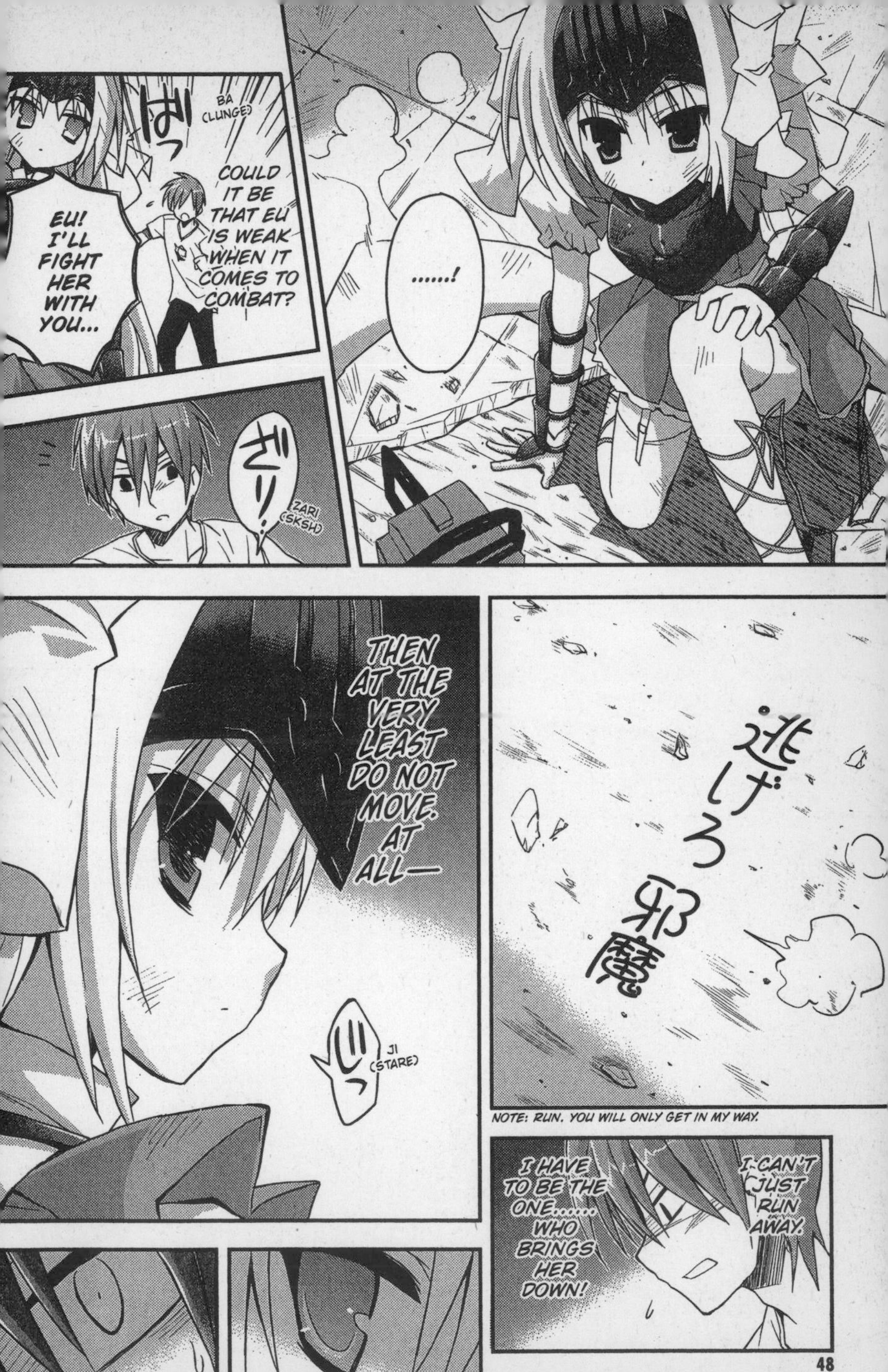
......!
ばっ
BA (LUNGE)
COULD IT BE THAT EU IS WEAK WHEN IT COMES TO COMBAT?
EU! I'LL FIGHT HER WITH YOU...
ざりっ
ZARI (SKSH)
逃げろ 邪魔
THEN AT THE VERY LEAST DO NOT MOVE. AT ALL—
じっ
JI (STARE)
I CAN'T JUST RUN AWAY.
I HAVE TO BE THE ONE...... WHO BRINGS HER DOWN!

NOTE: RUN. YOU WILL ONLY GET IN MY WAY.

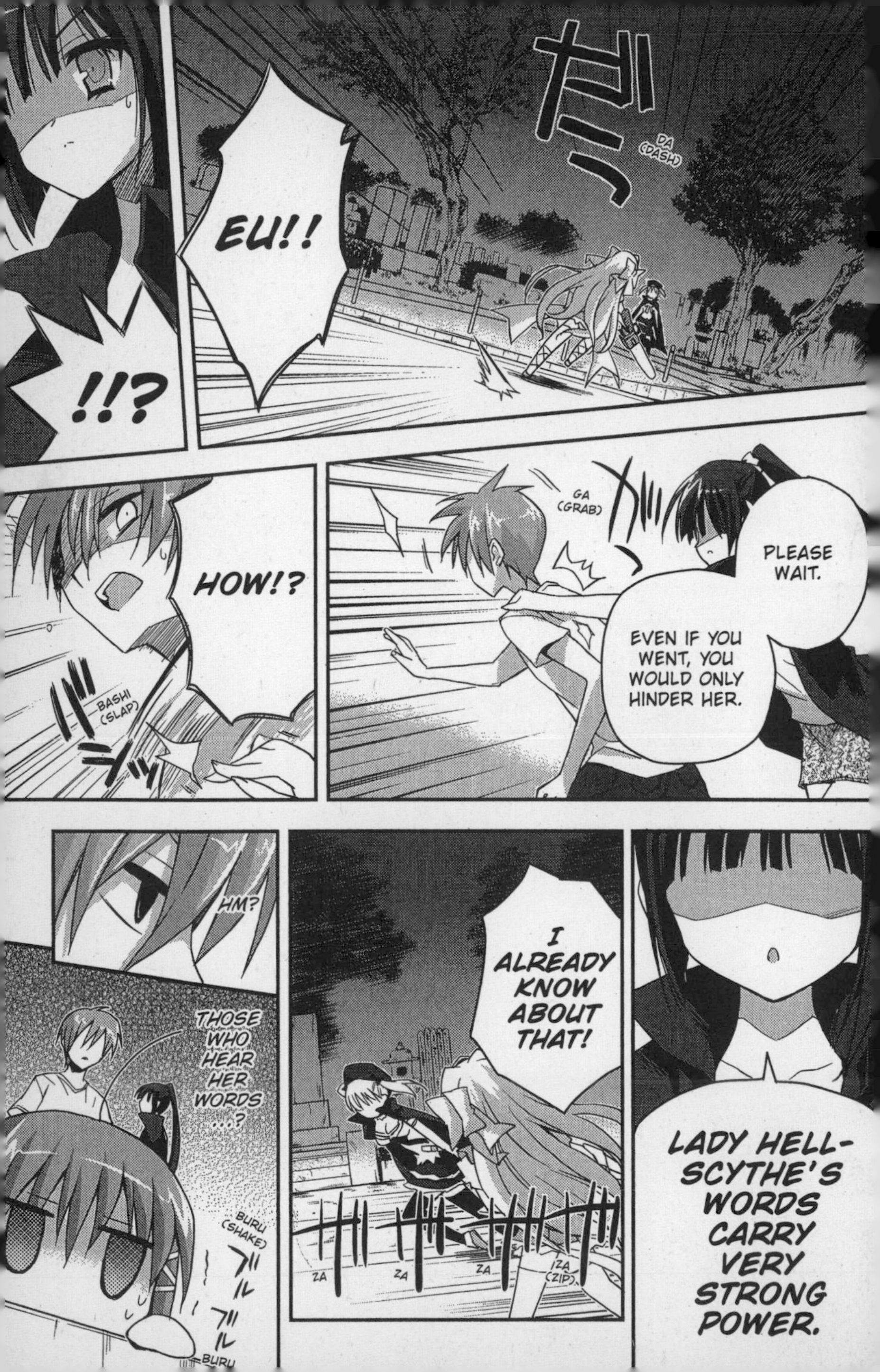

DA (DASH)
EU!!
!!?
GA (GRAB)
PLEASE WAIT.
EVEN IF YOU WENT, YOU WOULD ONLY HINDER HER.
HOW!?
BASHI (SLAP)
LADY HELL-SCYTHE'S WORDS CARRY VERY STRONG POWER.
I ALREADY KNOW ABOUT THAT!
ZA
ZA
ZA
ZA (ZIP)
HM?
THOSE WHO HEAR HER WORDS ...?
BURU (SHAKE)
BURU

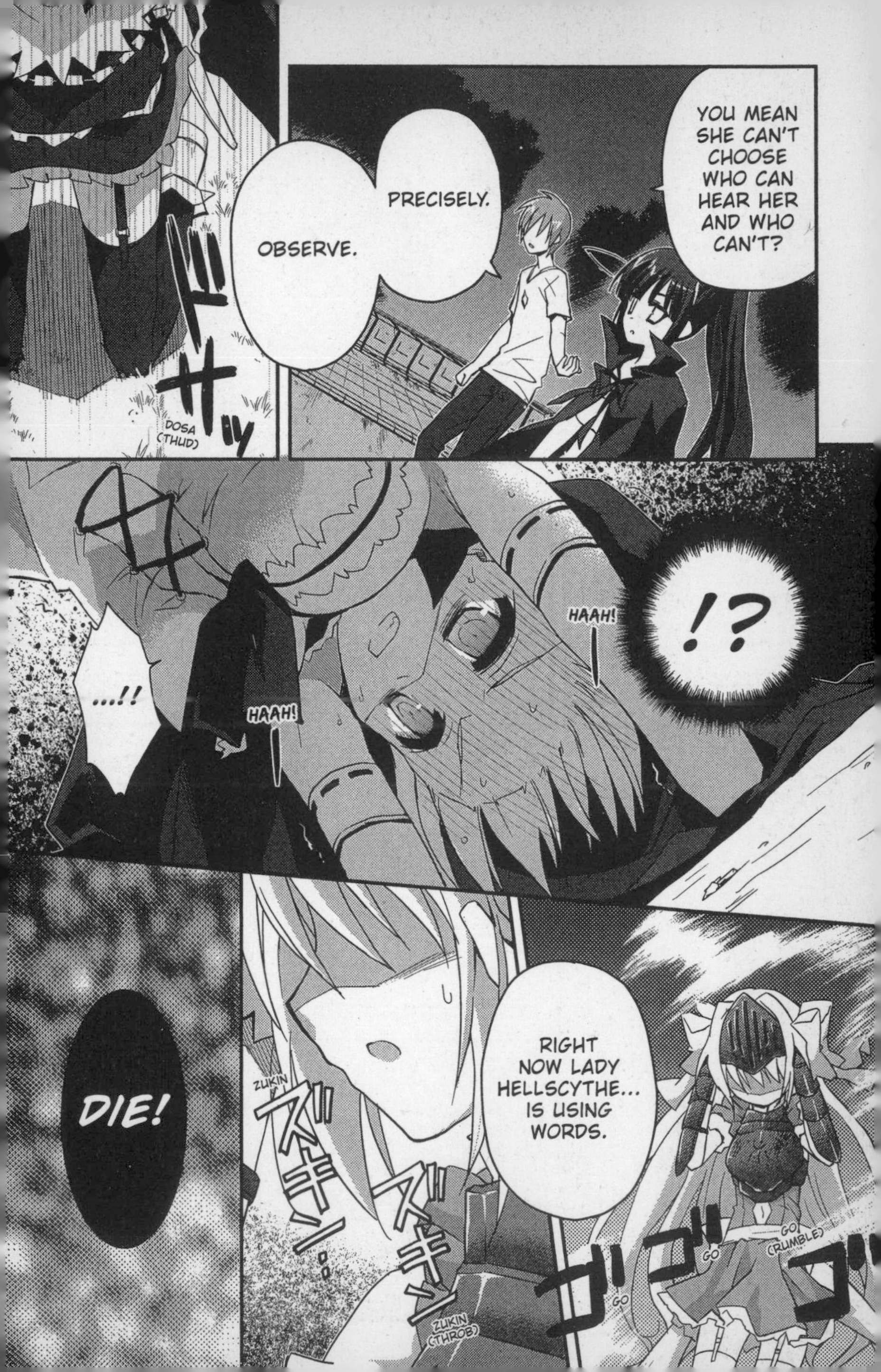

YOU MEAN SHE CAN'T CHOOSE WHO CAN HEAR HER AND WHO CAN'T?
PRECISELY.
OBSERVE.
DOSA (THUD)
!?
HAAH!
HAAH!
...!!
RIGHT NOW LADY HELLSCYTHE... IS USING WORDS.
GO GO (RUMBLE)
GO
ZUKIN
ZUKIN (THROB)
DIE!

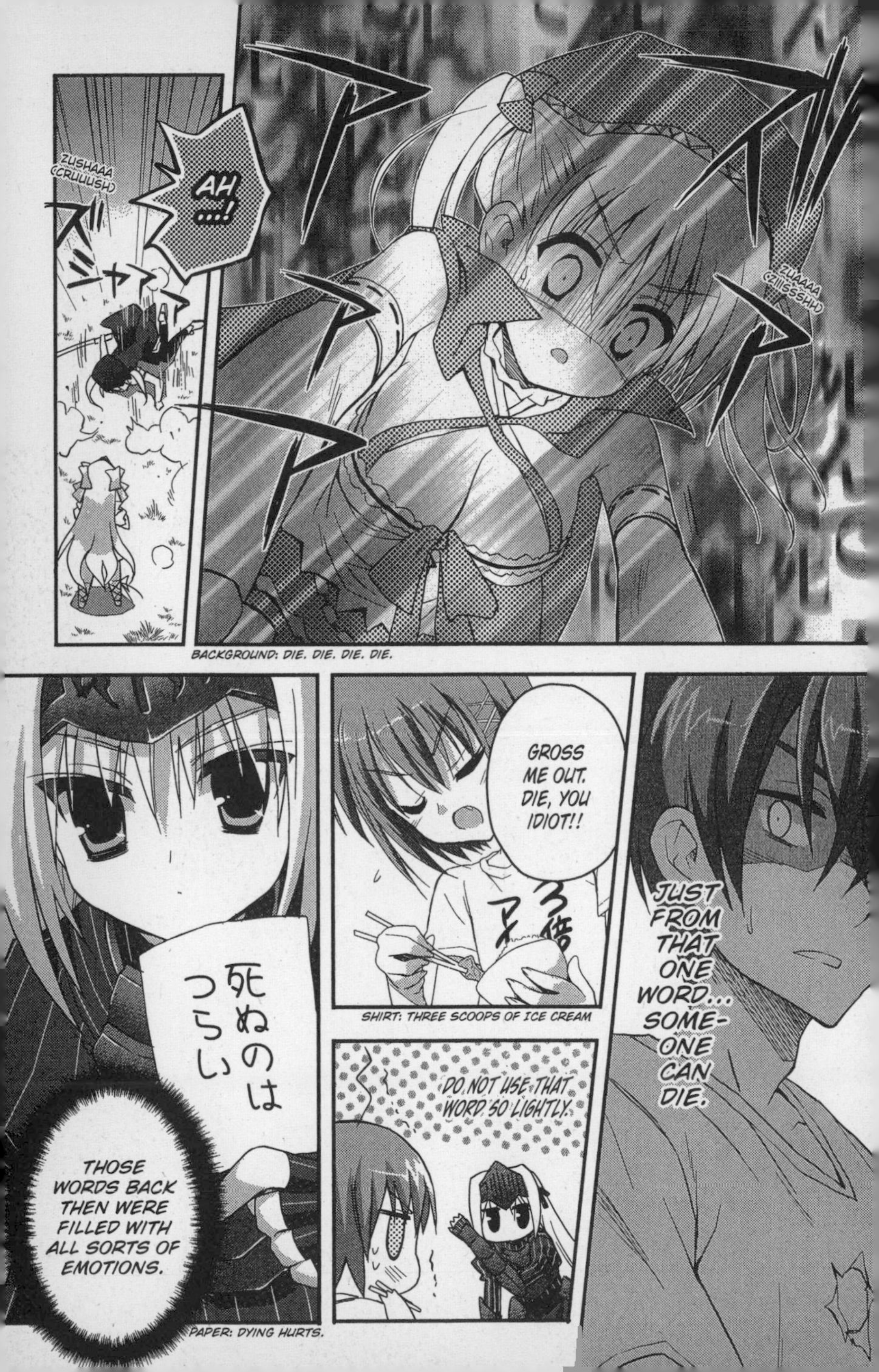
ZUAAAA (ZIIISSSHH)
ZUSHAAA (CRUUUSH)
AH ...!
BACKGROUND: DIE. DIE. DIE. DIE.
JUST FROM THAT ONE WORD... SOME-ONE CAN DIE.
GROSS ME OUT. DIE, YOU IDIOT!!
SHIRT: THREE SCOOPS OF ICE CREAM
死ぬのはつらい
THOSE WORDS BACK THEN WERE FILLED WITH ALL SORTS OF EMOTIONS.
PAPER: DYING HURTS.
DO NOT USE THAT WORD SO LIGHTLY.

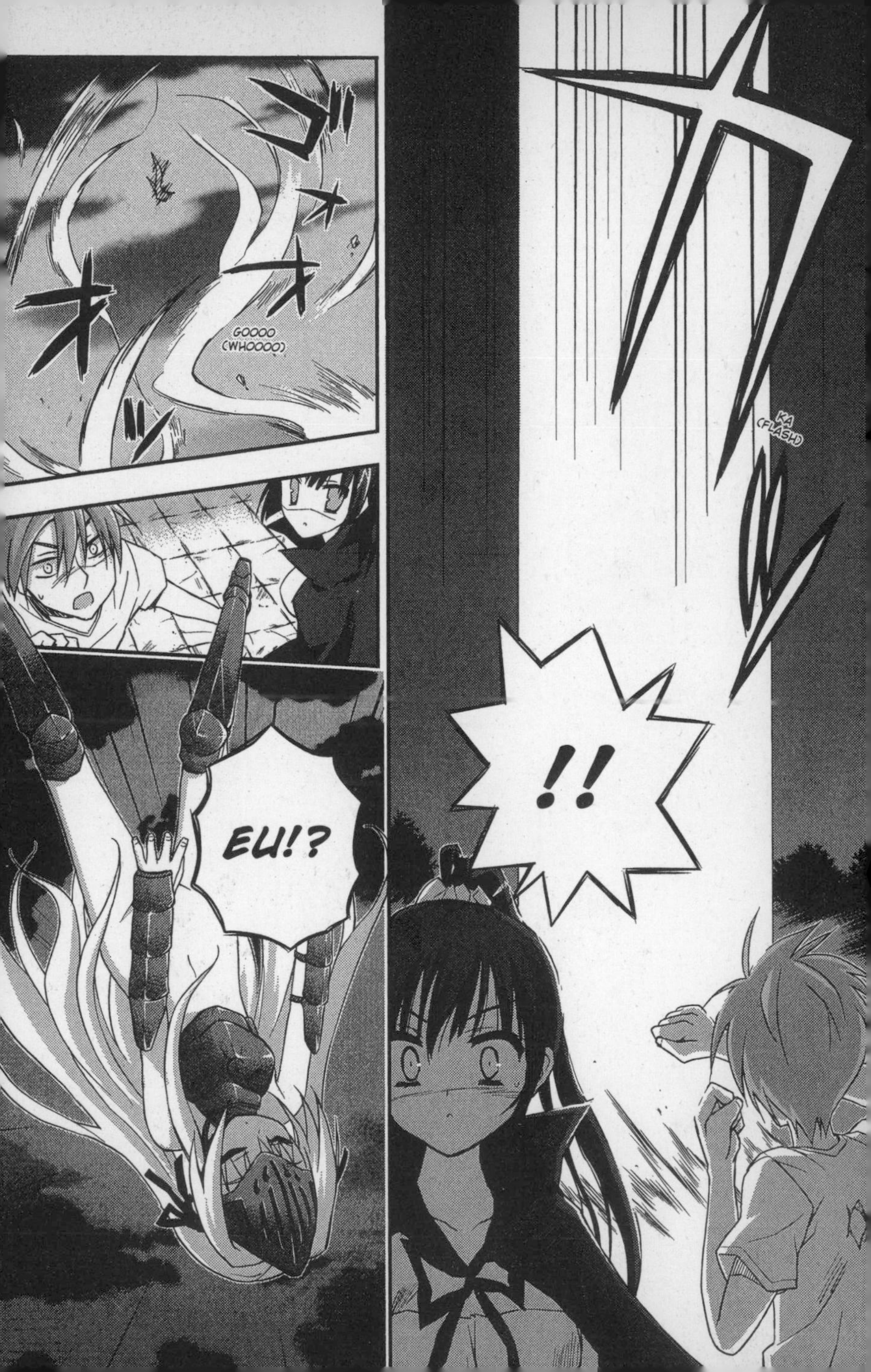
KA (FLASH)
!!
GOOOO (WHOOOO)
EU!?

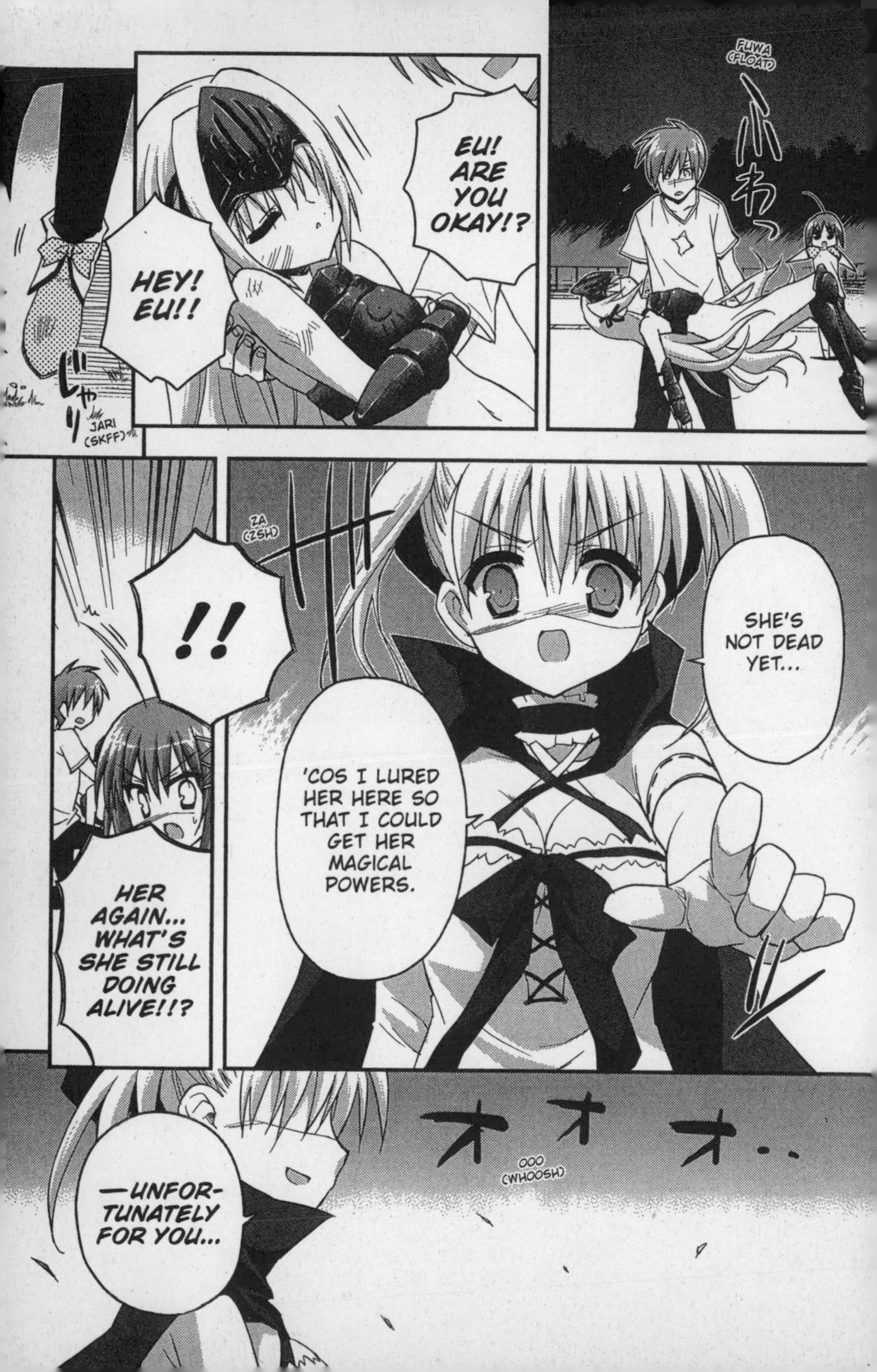
FUWA (FLOAT)
ふわっ
EU! ARE YOU OKAY!?
HEY! EU!!
JARI (SKFF)
じゃり
ZA (ZSH)
SHE'S NOT DEAD YET...
'COS I LURED HER HERE SO THAT I COULD GET HER MAGICAL POWERS.
!!
HER AGAIN... WHAT'S SHE STILL DOING ALIVE!!?
オオオ・・
OOO (WHOOSH)
—UNFORTUNATELY FOR YOU...

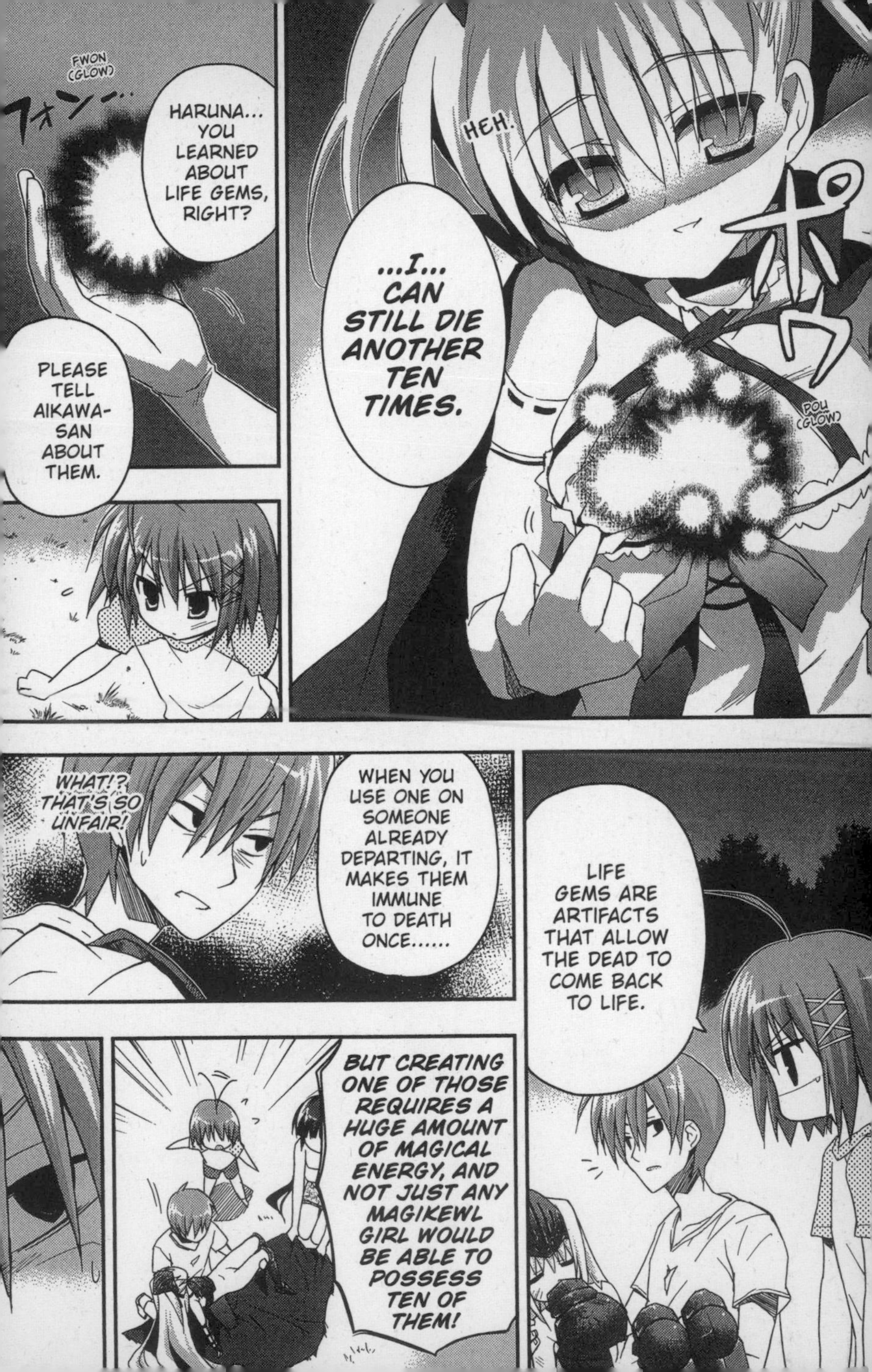
HEH.
...I... CAN STILL DIE ANOTHER TEN TIMES.
ポッ
POU (GLOW)
FWON (GLOW)
フォン一
HARUNA... YOU LEARNED ABOUT LIFE GEMS, RIGHT?
PLEASE TELL AIKAWA-SAN ABOUT THEM.
LIFE GEMS ARE ARTIFACTS THAT ALLOW THE DEAD TO COME BACK TO LIFE.
WHEN YOU USE ONE ON SOMEONE ALREADY DEPARTING, IT MAKES THEM IMMUNE TO DEATH ONCE......
WHAT!? THAT'S SO UNFAIR!
BUT CREATING ONE OF THOSE REQUIRES A HUGE AMOUNT OF MAGICAL ENERGY, AND NOT JUST ANY MAGIKEWL GIRL WOULD BE ABLE TO POSSESS TEN OF THEM!

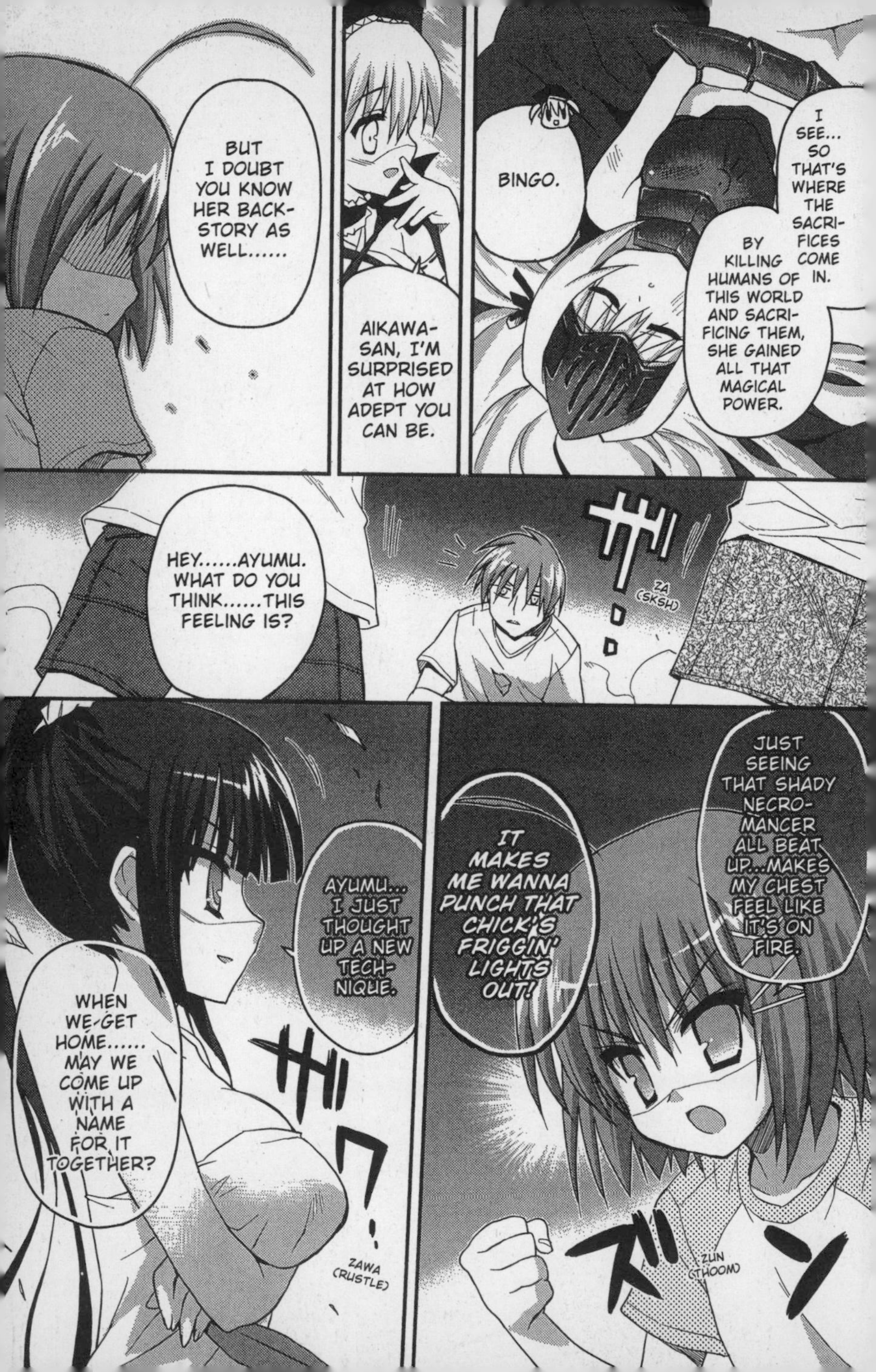

I SEE... SO THAT'S WHERE THE SACRIFICES COME IN.
BY KILLING HUMANS OF THIS WORLD AND SACRIFICING THEM, SHE GAINED ALL THAT MAGICAL POWER.
BINGO.
AIKAWA-SAN, I'M SURPRISED AT HOW ADEPT YOU CAN BE.
BUT I DOUBT YOU KNOW HER BACKSTORY AS WELL......
ZA (SKSH)
HEY......AYUMU. WHAT DO YOU THINK......THIS FEELING IS?
JUST SEEING THAT SHADY NECROMANCER ALL BEAT UP...MAKES MY CHEST FEEL LIKE IT'S ON FIRE.
IT MAKES ME WANNA PUNCH THAT CHICK'S FRIGGIN' LIGHTS OUT!
ZUN (THOOM)
AYUMU... I JUST THOUGHT UP A NEW TECHNIQUE.
WHEN WE GET HOME...... MAY WE COME UP WITH A NAME FOR IT TOGETHER?
ZAWA (RUSTLE)

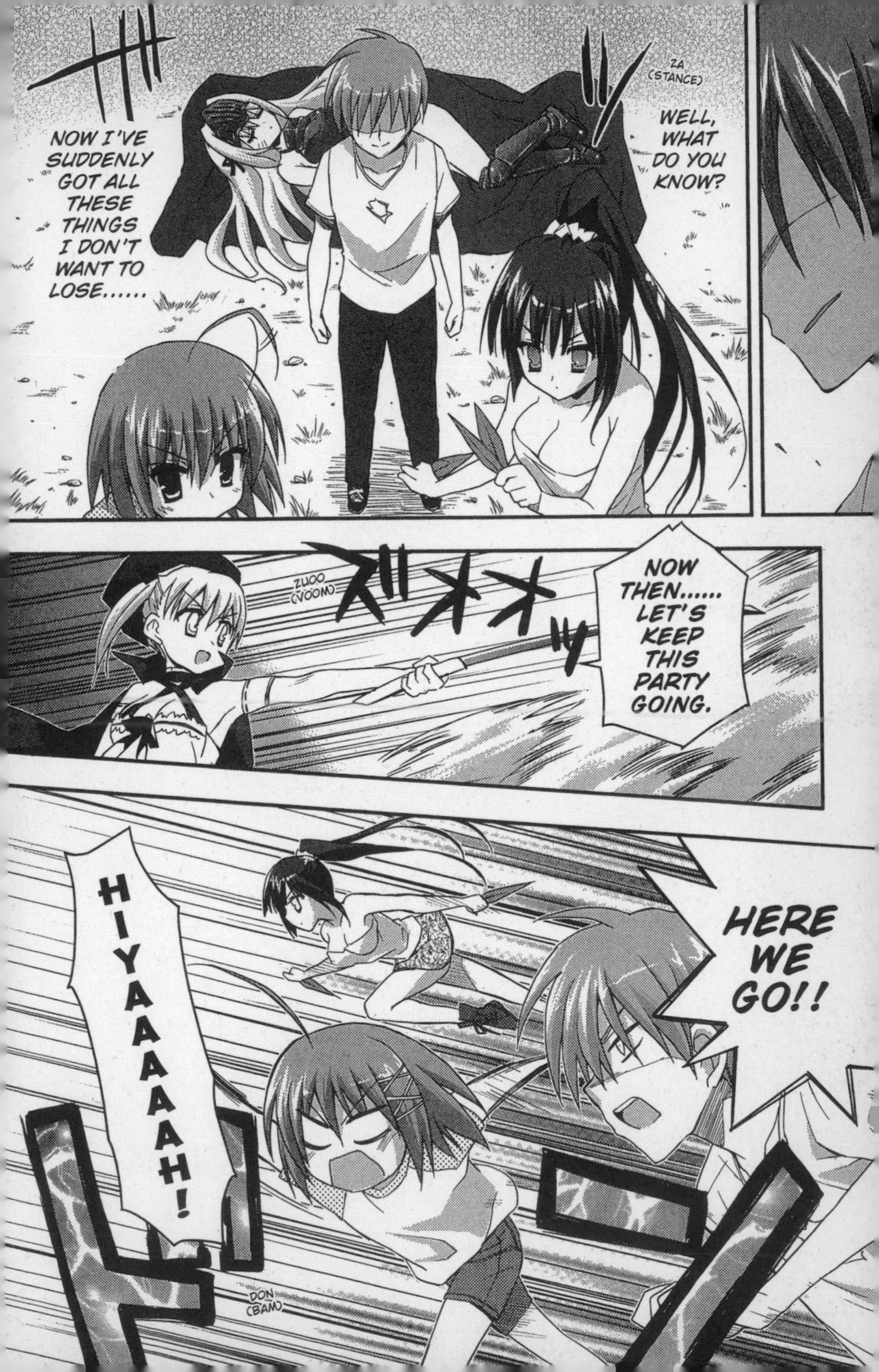
ZA (STANCE)
WELL, WHAT DO YOU KNOW?
NOW I'VE SUDDENLY GOT ALL THESE THINGS I DON'T WANT TO LOSE......
NOW THEN...... LET'S KEEP THIS PARTY GOING.
ZUOO (VOOM)
HERE WE GO!!
HIYAAAAAH!
DON (BAM)

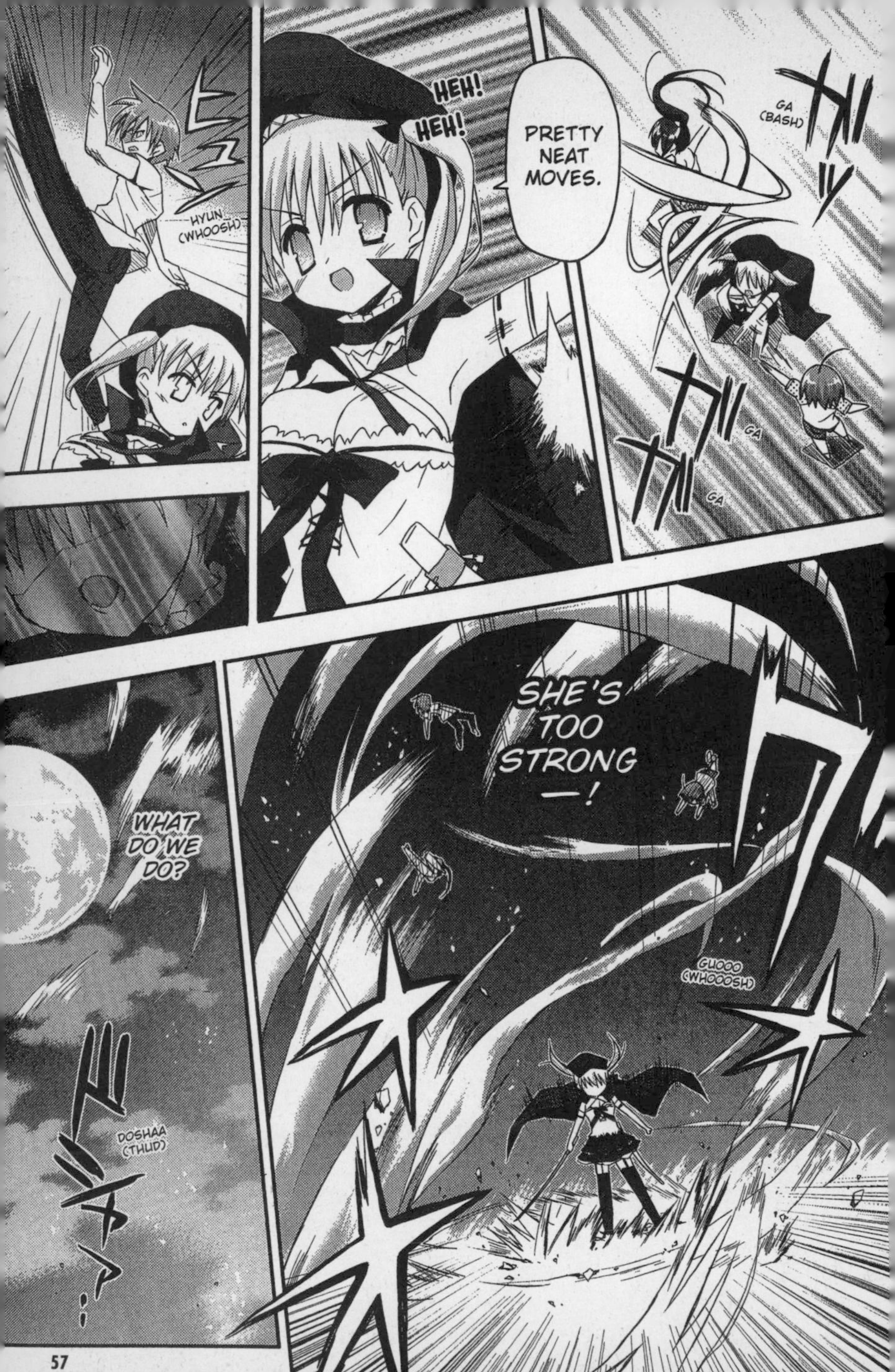
GA (BASH)
PRETTY NEAT MOVES.
HEH! HEH!
HYUN (WHOOSH)
GA
GA
SHE'S TOO STRONG—!
WHAT DO WE DO?
GUOOO (WHOOOSH)
DOSHAA (THUD)

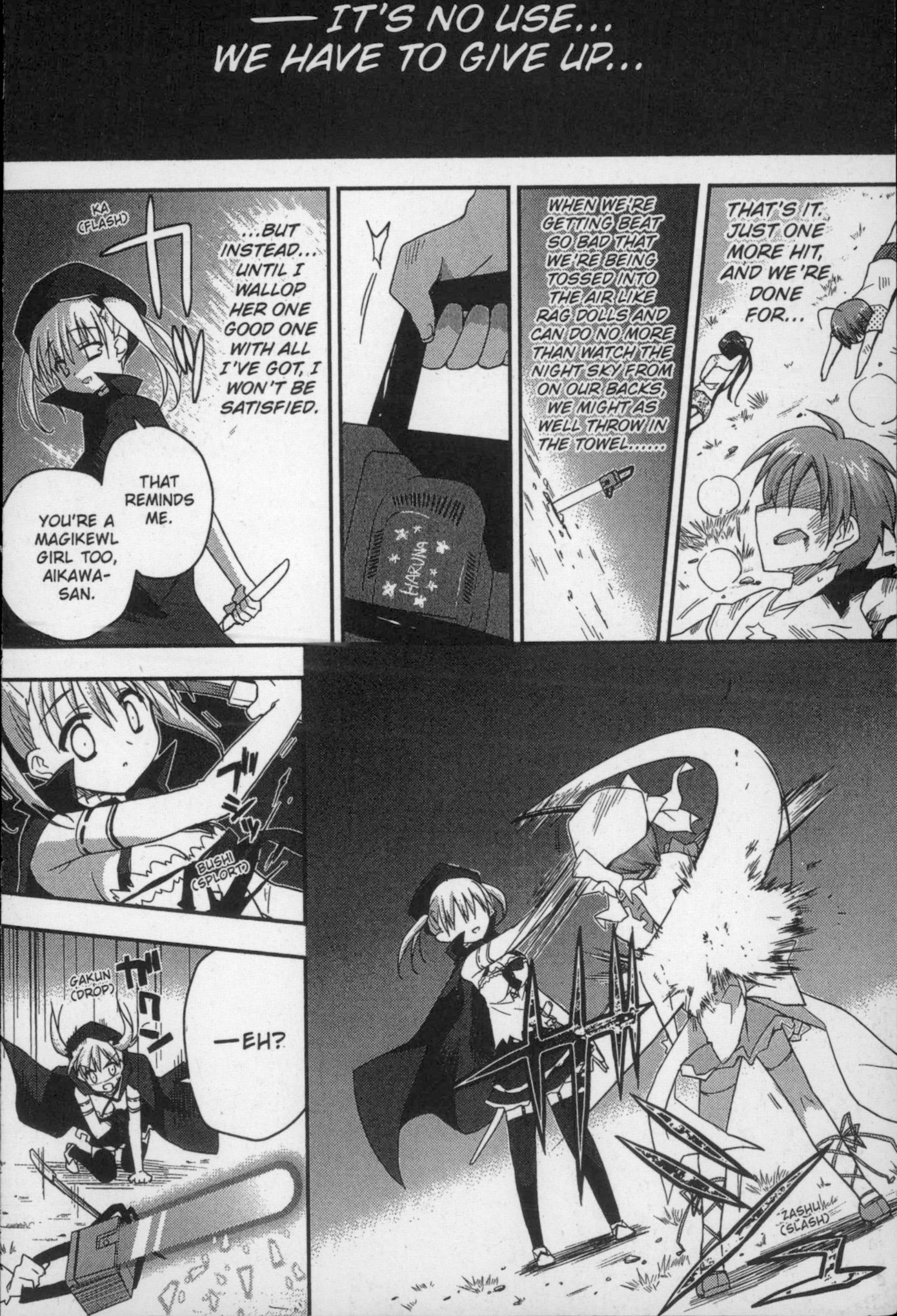
—IT'S NO USE...
WE HAVE TO GIVE UP...
THAT'S IT. JUST ONE MORE HIT, AND WE'RE DONE FOR...
WHEN WE'RE GETTING BEAT SO BAD THAT WE'RE BEING TOSSED INTO THE AIR LIKE RAG DOLLS AND CAN DO NO MORE THAN WATCH THE NIGHT SKY FROM ON OUR BACKS, WE MIGHT AS WELL THROW IN THE TOWEL......
HARUNA
KA (FLASH)
...BUT INSTEAD... UNTIL I WALLOP HER ONE GOOD ONE WITH ALL I'VE GOT, I WON'T BE SATISFIED.
THAT REMINDS ME.
YOU'RE A MAGIKEWL GIRL TOO, AIKAWA-SAN.
ZASHU (SLASH)
BUSHI (SPLORT)
GAKUN (DROP)
—EH?

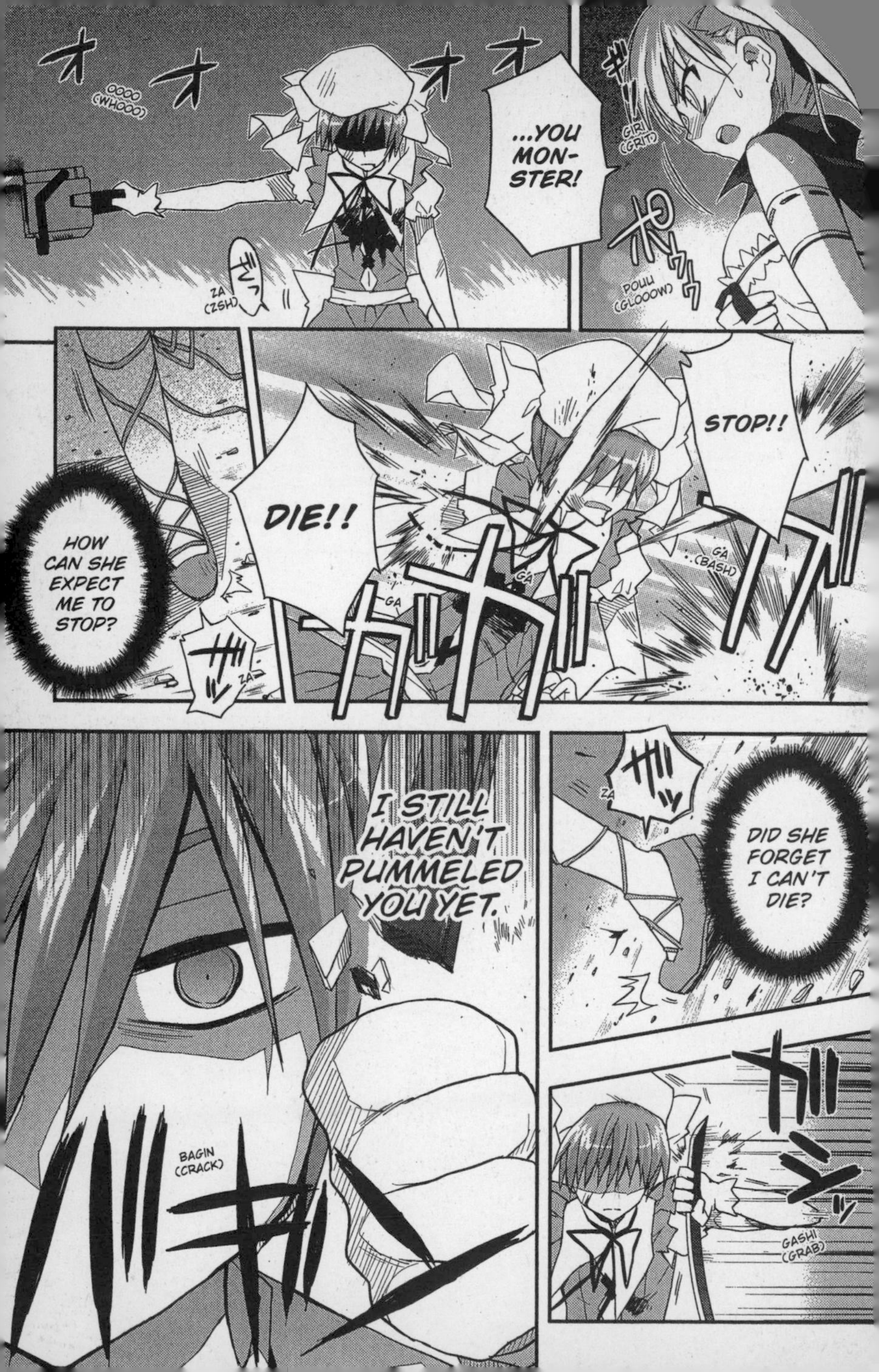

GIRI (GRIT)
POUU (GLOOOW)
...YOU MONSTER!
OOOO (WHOOO)
ZA (ZSH)
STOP!!
GA (BASH)
DIE!!
GA
GA
HOW CAN SHE EXPECT ME TO STOP?
ZA
ZA
DID SHE FORGET I CAN'T DIE?
GASHI (GRAB)
I STILL HAVEN'T PUMMELED YOU YET.
BAGIN (CRACK)

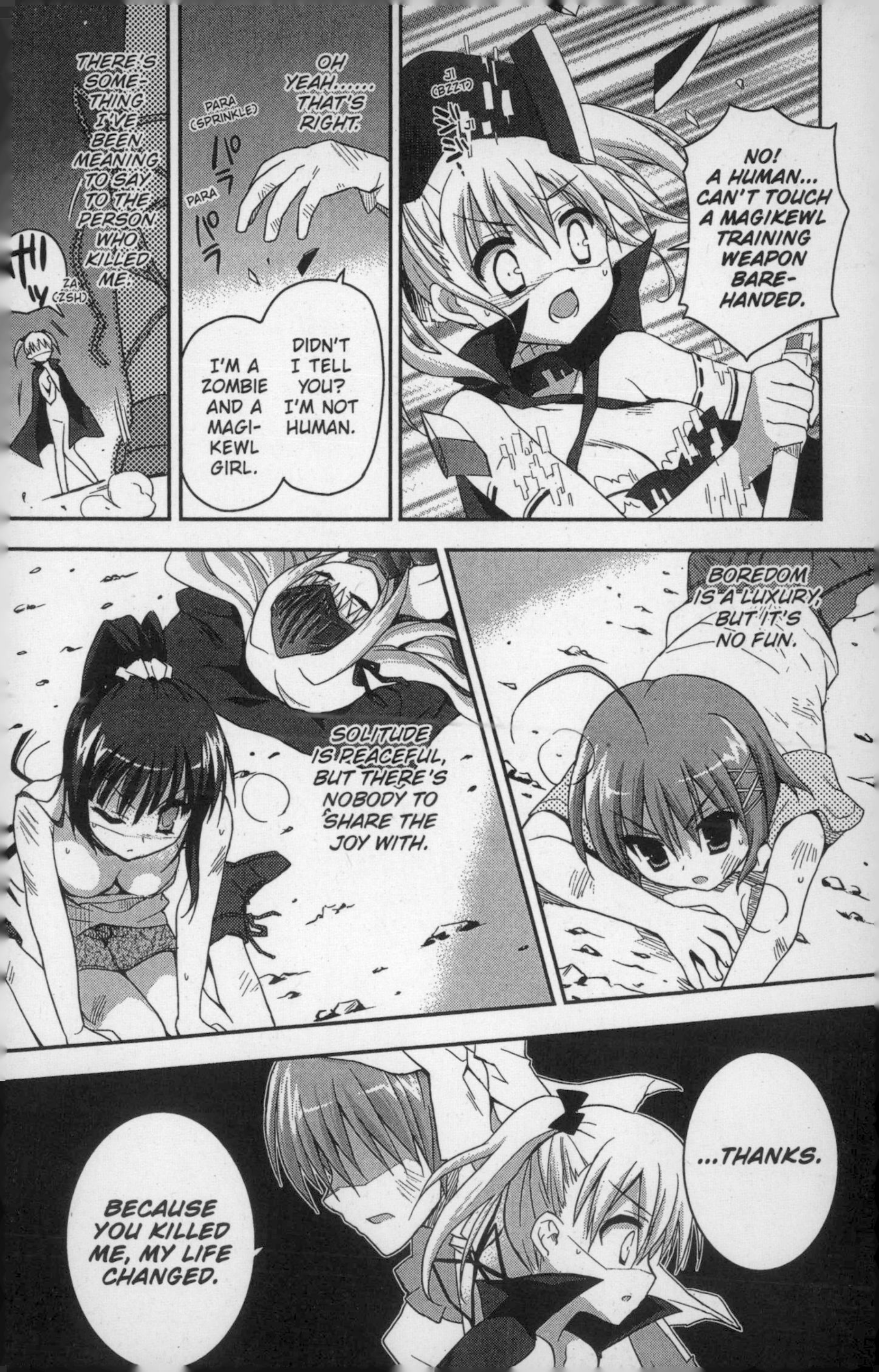
NO! A HUMAN... CAN'T TOUCH A MAGIKEWL TRAINING WEAPON BARE-HANDED.
JI (BZZT)
JI
OH YEAH...... THAT'S RIGHT.
PARA (SPRINKLE)
PARA
DIDN'T I TELL YOU? I'M NOT HUMAN.
I'M A ZOMBIE AND A MAGI-KEWL GIRL.
THERE'S SOME-THING I'VE BEEN MEANING TO SAY TO THE PERSON WHO KILLED ME.
ZA (ZSH)
BOREDOM IS A LUXURY, BUT IT'S NO FUN.
SOLITUDE IS PEACEFUL, BUT THERE'S NOBODY TO SHARE THE JOY WITH.
...THANKS.
BECAUSE YOU KILLED ME, MY LIFE CHANGED.

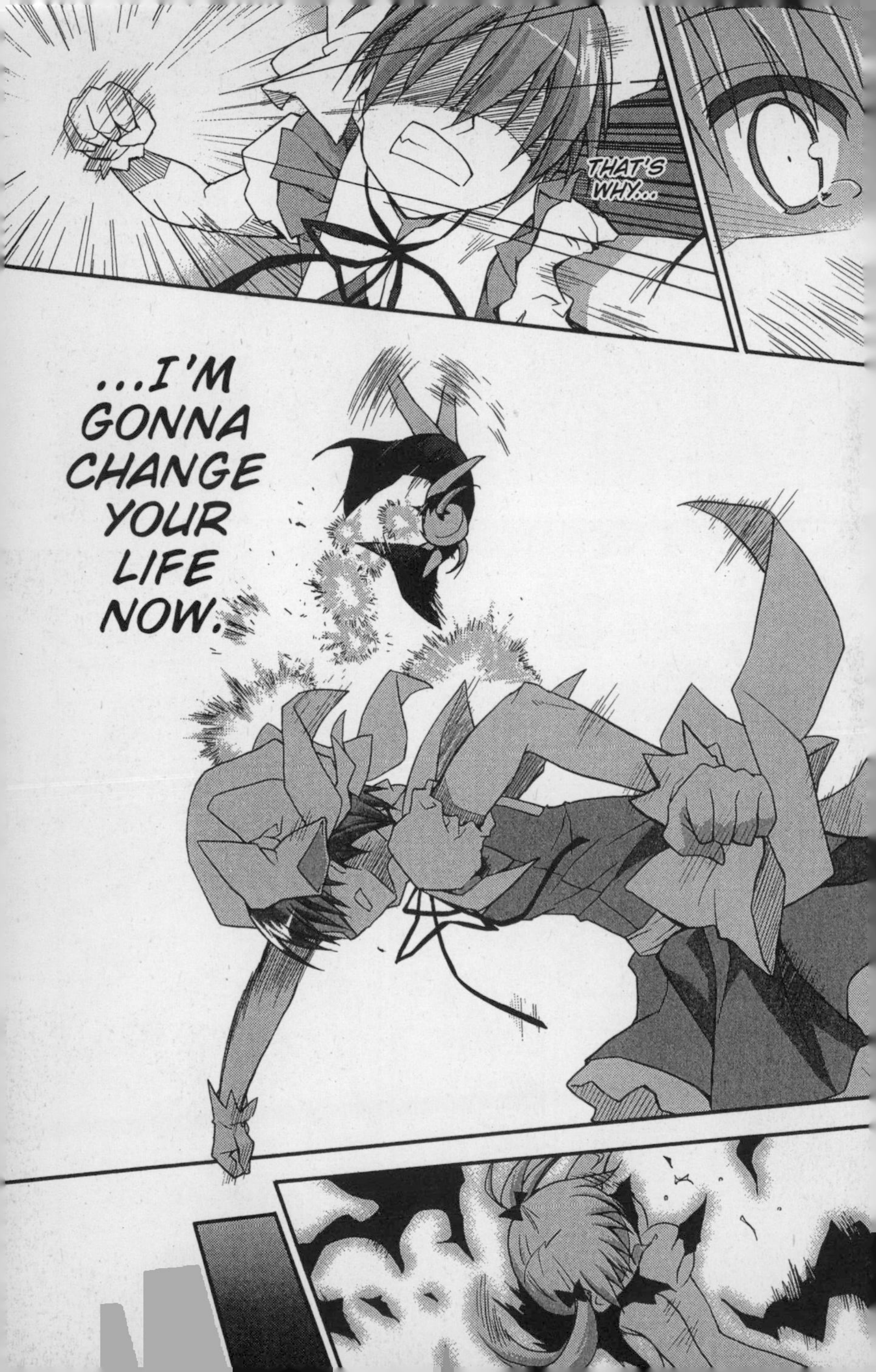
THAT'S WHY...
...I'M GONNA CHANGE YOUR LIFE NOW.

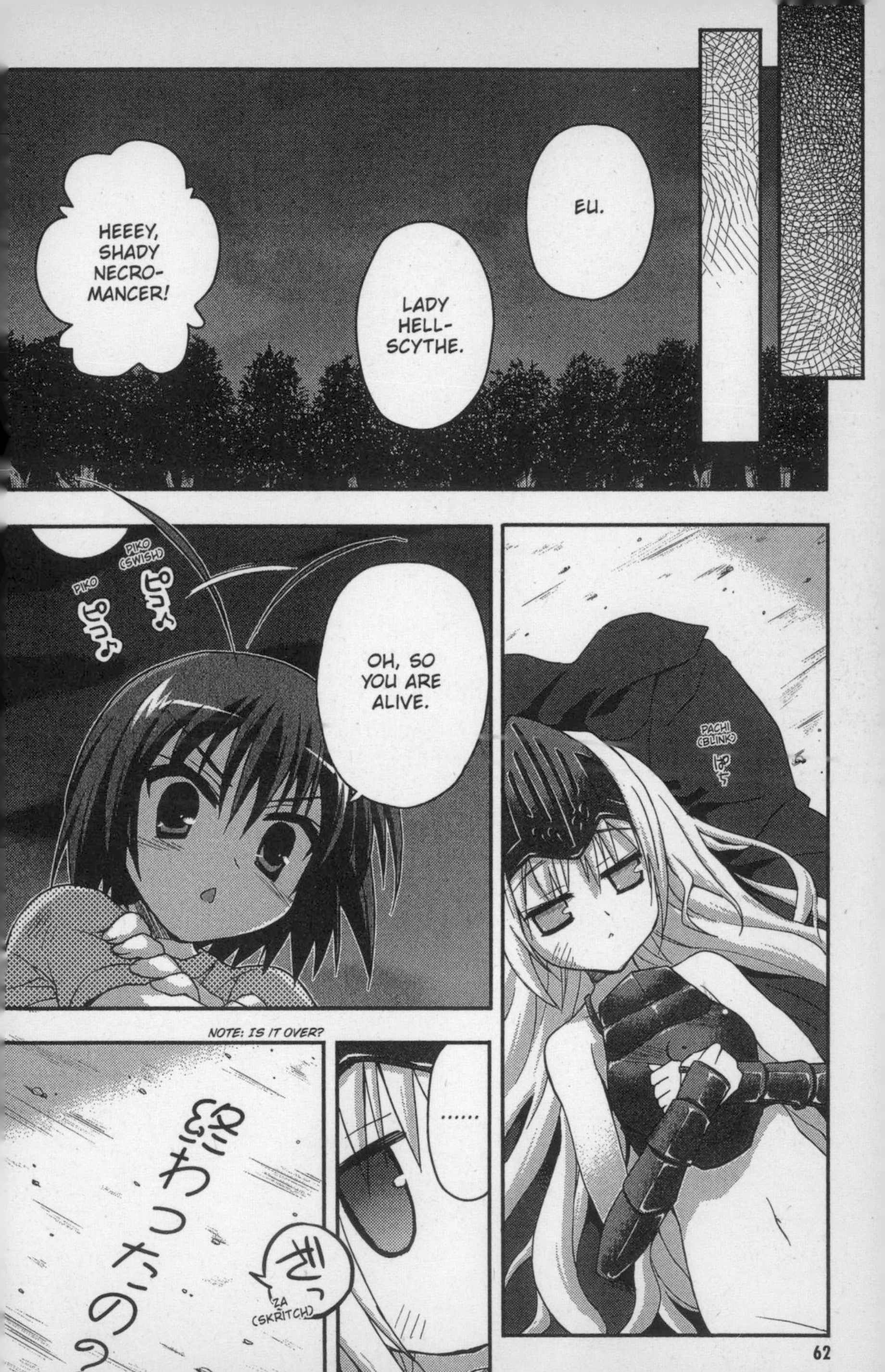
EU.
LADY HELL-SCYTHE.
HEEEY, SHADY NECRO-MANCER!
PIKO (SWISH)
ピコ
PIKO
ピコ
OH, SO YOU ARE ALIVE.
PACHI (BLINK)
ぱち
NOTE: IS IT OVER?
......
ざっ
ZA (SKRITCH)
終わったの？

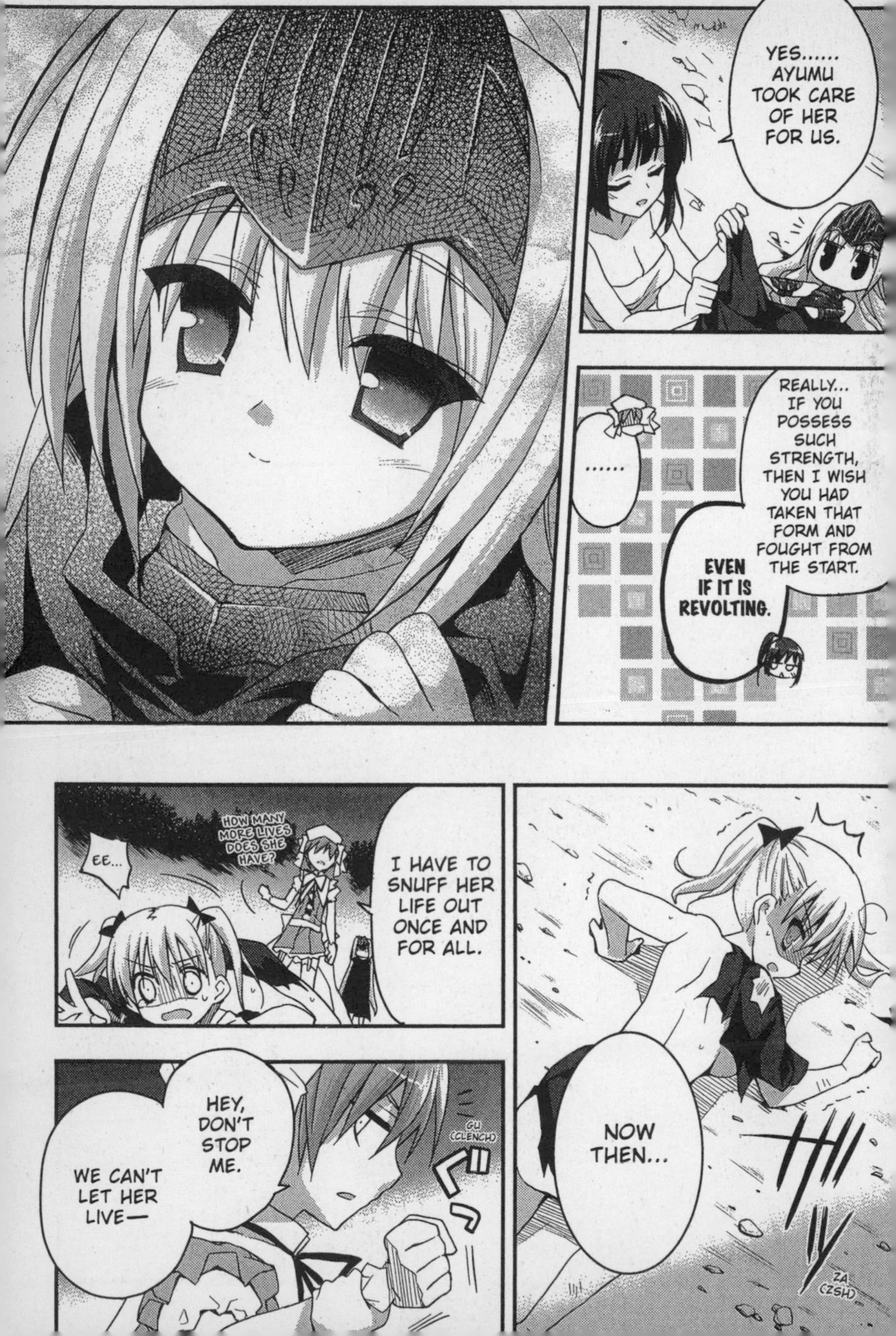

YES...... AYUMU TOOK CARE OF HER FOR US.
REALLY... IF YOU POSSESS SUCH STRENGTH, THEN I WISH YOU HAD TAKEN THAT FORM AND FOUGHT FROM THE START.
EVEN IF IT IS REVOLTING.
......
NOW THEN...
ZA (ZSH)
I HAVE TO SNUFF HER LIFE OUT ONCE AND FOR ALL.
HOW MANY MORE LIVES DOES SHE HAVE?
EE...
HEY, DON'T STOP ME.
GU (CLENCH)
WE CAN'T LET HER LIVE—

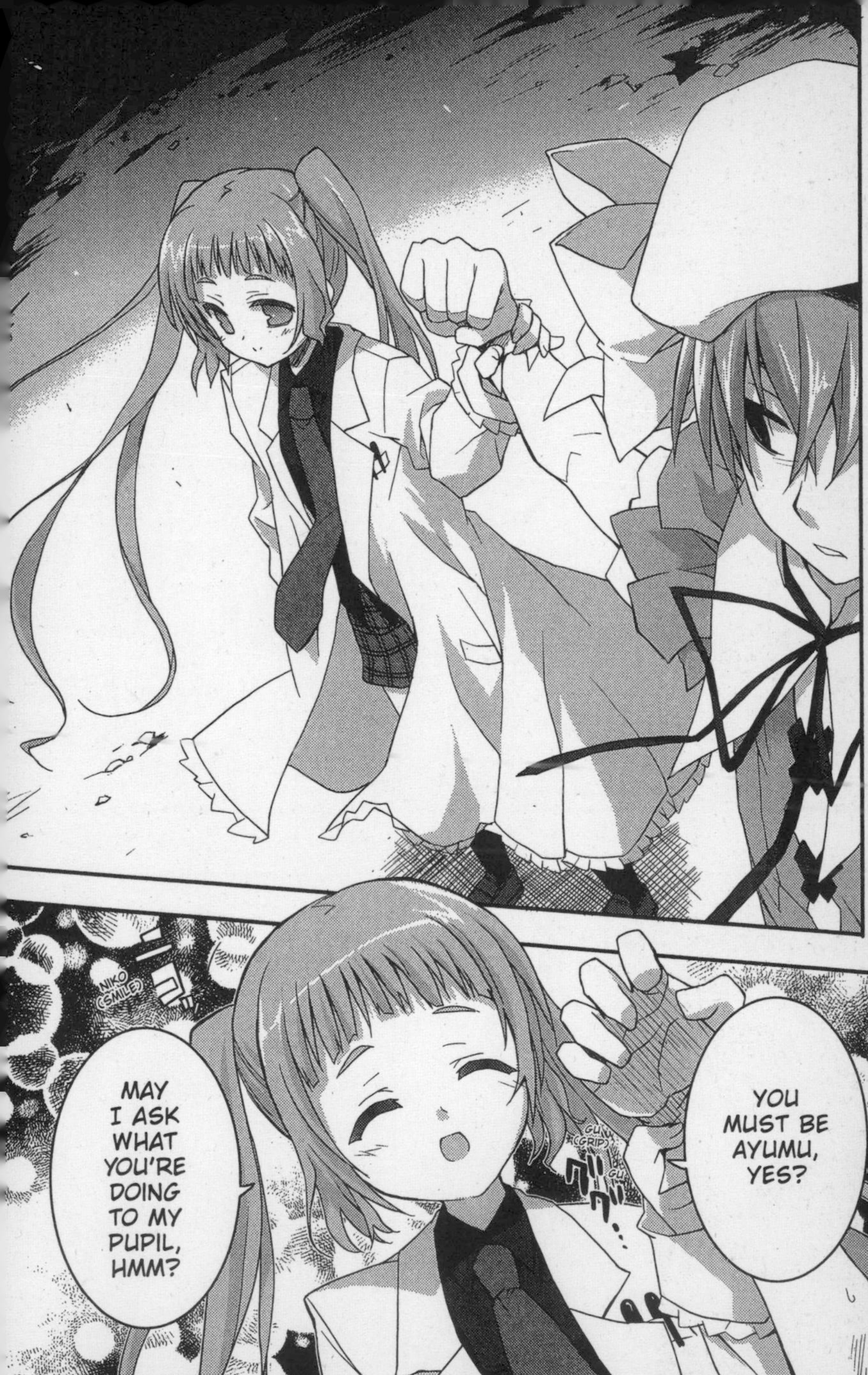
YOU MUST BE AYUMU, YES?
GYU (GRIP) GYU
NIKO (SMILE)
MAY I ASK WHAT YOU'RE DOING TO MY PUPIL, HMM?

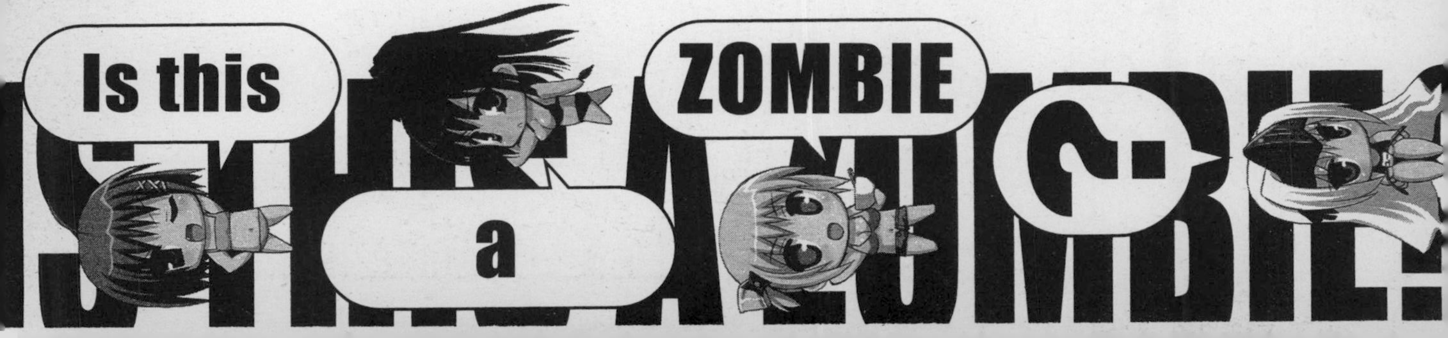
Is this
a
ZOMBIE
?

NECESSITIES OF LIFE

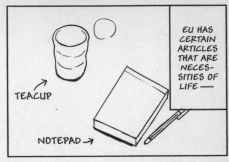

EU HAS CERTAIN ARTICLES THAT ARE NECES-SITIES OF LIFE —
TEACUP
NOTEPAD
VARIETY SHOWS.
WAH HA HA HA HA HA!
DIGITAL
HER HELL-SCYTHE.
AAAND HER PACIFIER!!
A MUST FOR KEEPING HERSELF FROM TALKING IN HER SLEEP!!
GOOO-GOO!
SHOKIIIIN (SHABANG)
ショキーーン!!

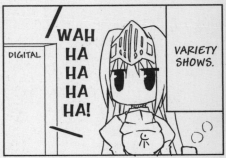

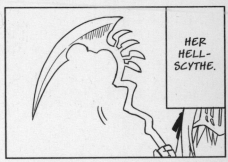

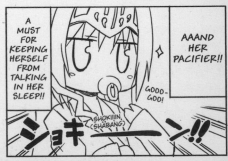

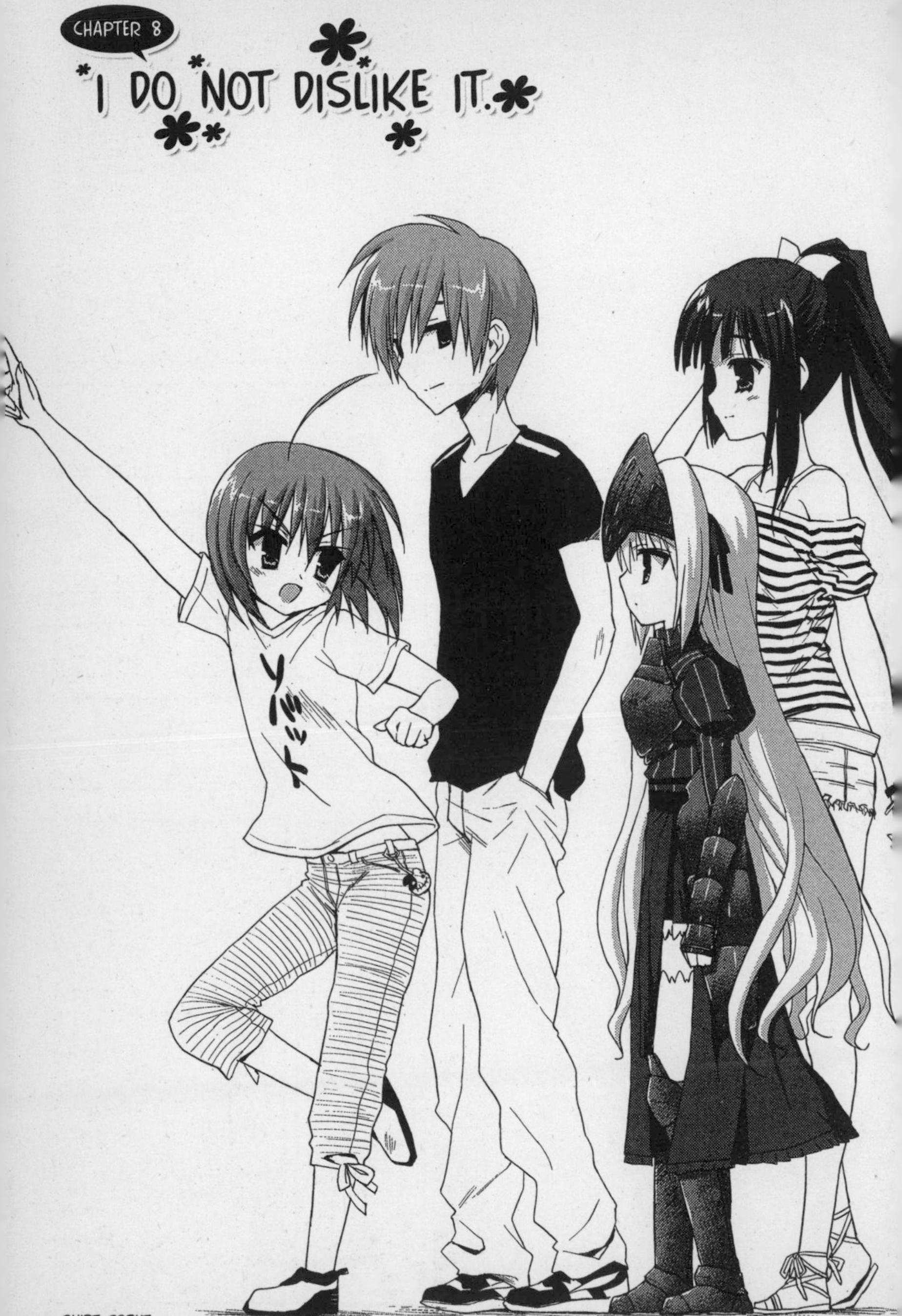
CHAPTER 8
I DO NOT DISLIKE IT.
ソバット
SHIRT: SOBUT

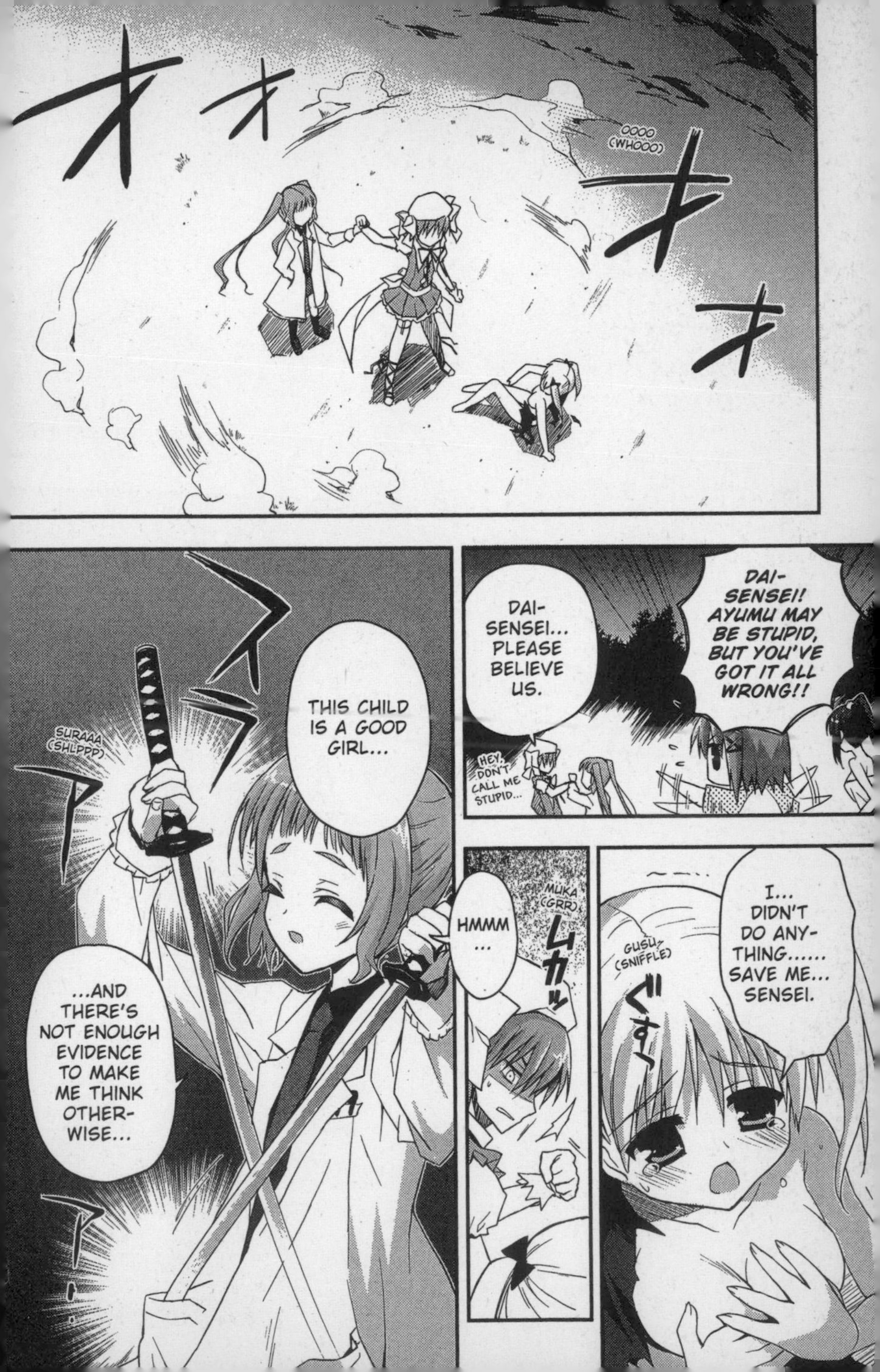
オオォ
OOOO (WHOOO)
DAI-SENSEI! AYUMU MAY BE STUPID, BUT YOU'VE GOT IT ALL WRONG!!
DAI-SENSEI... PLEASE BELIEVE US.
HEY, DON'T CALL ME STUPID...
THIS CHILD IS A GOOD GIRL...
SURAAA (SHLPPP)
I... DIDN'T DO ANYTHING...... SAVE ME... SENSEI.
GUSU (SNIFFLE)
MUKA (GRR)
HMMM...
...AND THERE'S NOT ENOUGH EVIDENCE TO MAKE ME THINK OTHERWISE...

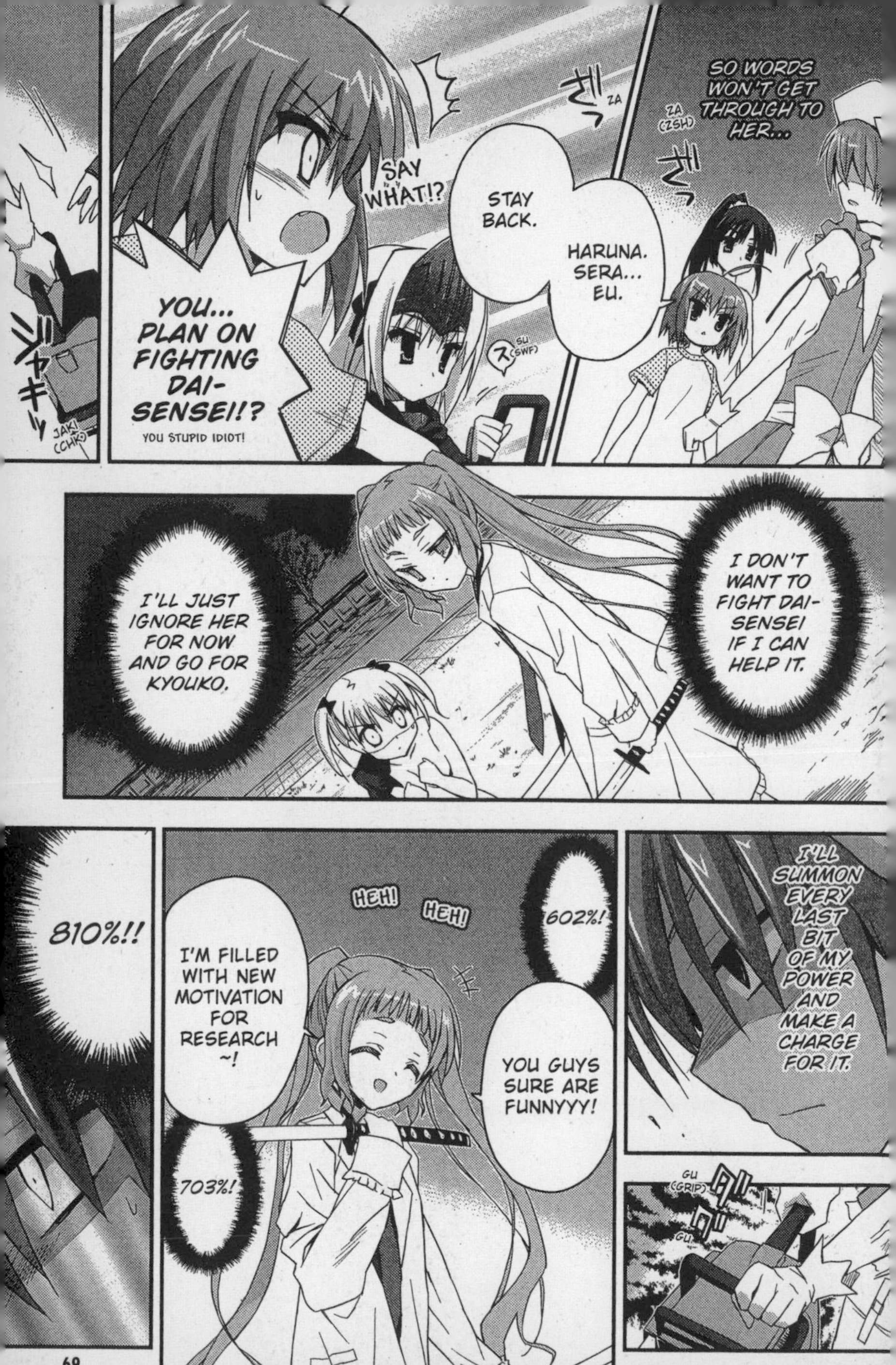
SO WORDS WON'T GET THROUGH TO HER...
ZA (ZSH)
ZA
HARUNA. SERA... EU.
STAY BACK.
SU (SWF)
SAY WHAT!?
YOU... PLAN ON FIGHTING DAI-SENSEI!?
YOU STUPID IDIOT!
JAKI (CHK)
I DON'T WANT TO FIGHT DAI-SENSEI IF I CAN HELP IT.
I'LL JUST IGNORE HER FOR NOW AND GO FOR KYOUKO.
I'LL SUMMON EVERY LAST BIT OF MY POWER AND MAKE A CHARGE FOR IT.
GU (GRIP)
GU
602%!
HEH!
HEH!
YOU GUYS SURE ARE FUNNYYY!
I'M FILLED WITH NEW MOTIVATION FOR RESEARCH ~!
703%!
810%!!

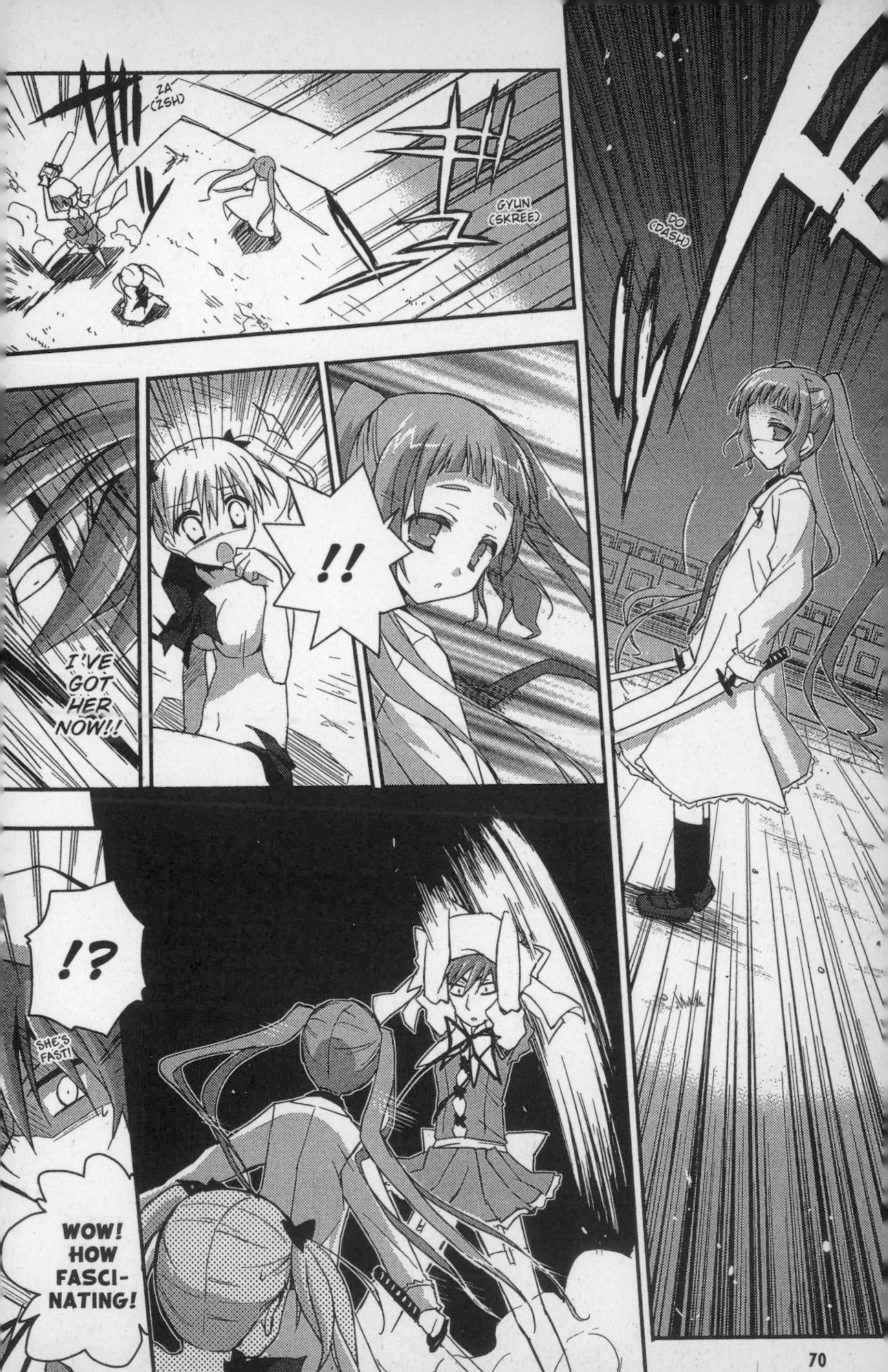
DO
(DASH)
GYUN
(SKREE)
ZA
(ZSH)
!!
I'VE GOT HER NOW!!
!?
SHE'S FAST!
WOW! HOW FASCI-NATING!

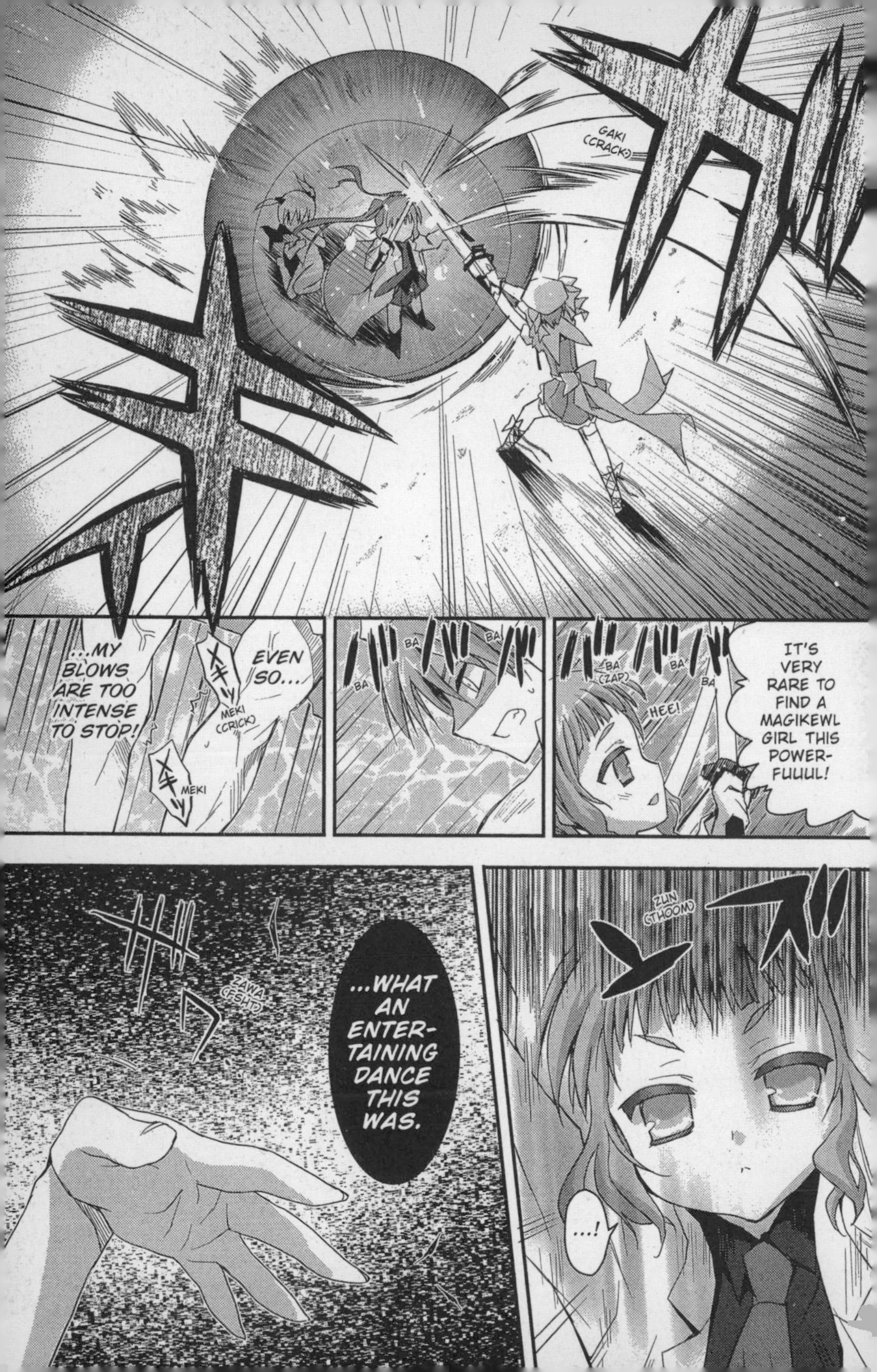
GAKI (CRACK)
IT'S VERY RARE TO FIND A MAGIKEWL GIRL THIS POWER-FUUUL!
BA (ZAP)
BA
BA
HEE!
BA
BA
BA
EVEN SO...
MEKI (CRICK)
...MY BLOWS ARE TOO INTENSE TO STOP!
MEKI
ZUN (THOOM)
...!
...WHAT AN ENTER-TAINING DANCE THIS WAS.
ZAWA (FSHT)

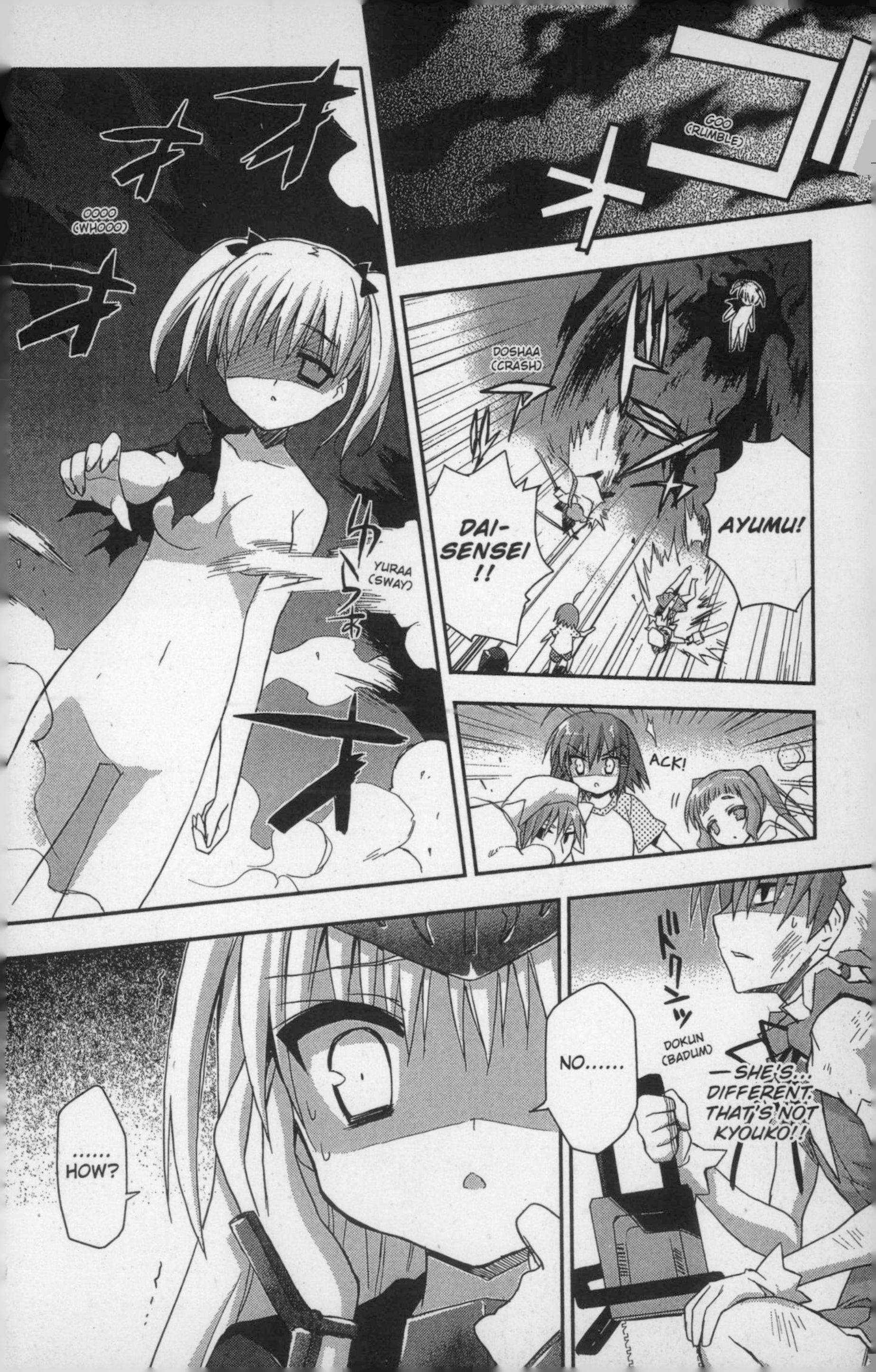
GOO
(RUMBLE)
OOOO
(WHOOO)
DOSHAA
(CRASH)
AYUMU!
DAI-
SENSEI
!!
YURAA
(SWAY)
ACK!
DOKUN
(BADUM)
—SHE'S...
DIFFERENT.
THAT'S NOT
KYOUKO!!
NO......
......
HOW?

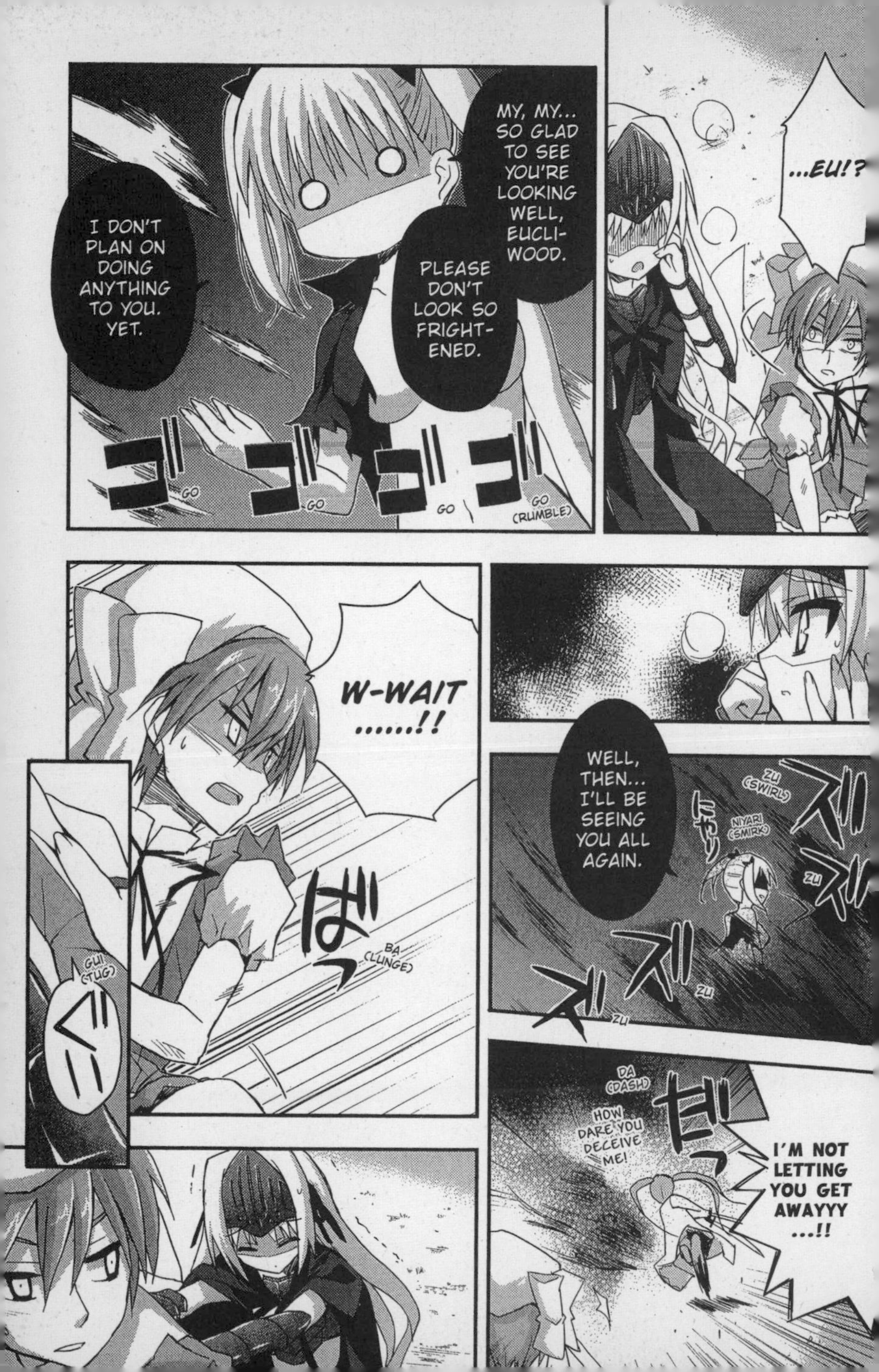
...EU!?
MY, MY... SO GLAD TO SEE YOU'RE LOOKING WELL, EUCLI-WOOD.
PLEASE DON'T LOOK SO FRIGHT-ENED.
I DON'T PLAN ON DOING ANYTHING TO YOU. YET.
GO GO GO GO (RUMBLE)
WELL, THEN... I'LL BE SEEING YOU ALL AGAIN.
ZU (SWIRL)
NIYARI (SMIRK)
ZU
ZU
ZU
W-WAIT ......!!
BA (LUNGE)
GUI (TUG)
DA (DASH)
HOW DARE YOU DECEIVE ME!
I'M NOT LETTING YOU GET AWAYYY ...!!

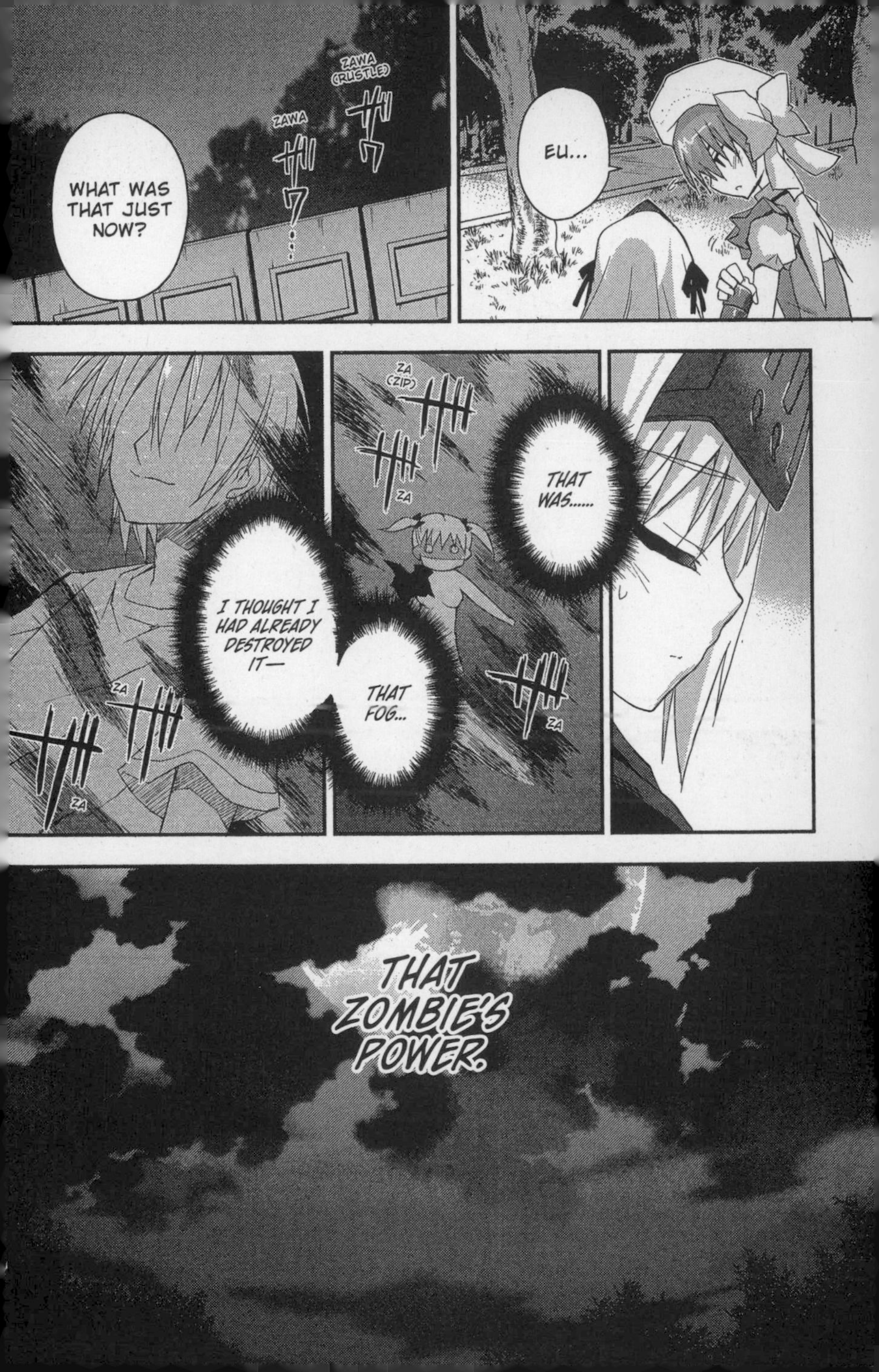
EU...
WHAT WAS THAT JUST NOW?
ZAWA (RUSTLE)
ZAWA
THAT WAS......
ZA (ZIP)
ZA
ZA
I THOUGHT I HAD ALREADY DESTROYED IT—
THAT FOG...
ZA
ZA
THAT ZOMBIE'S POWER.

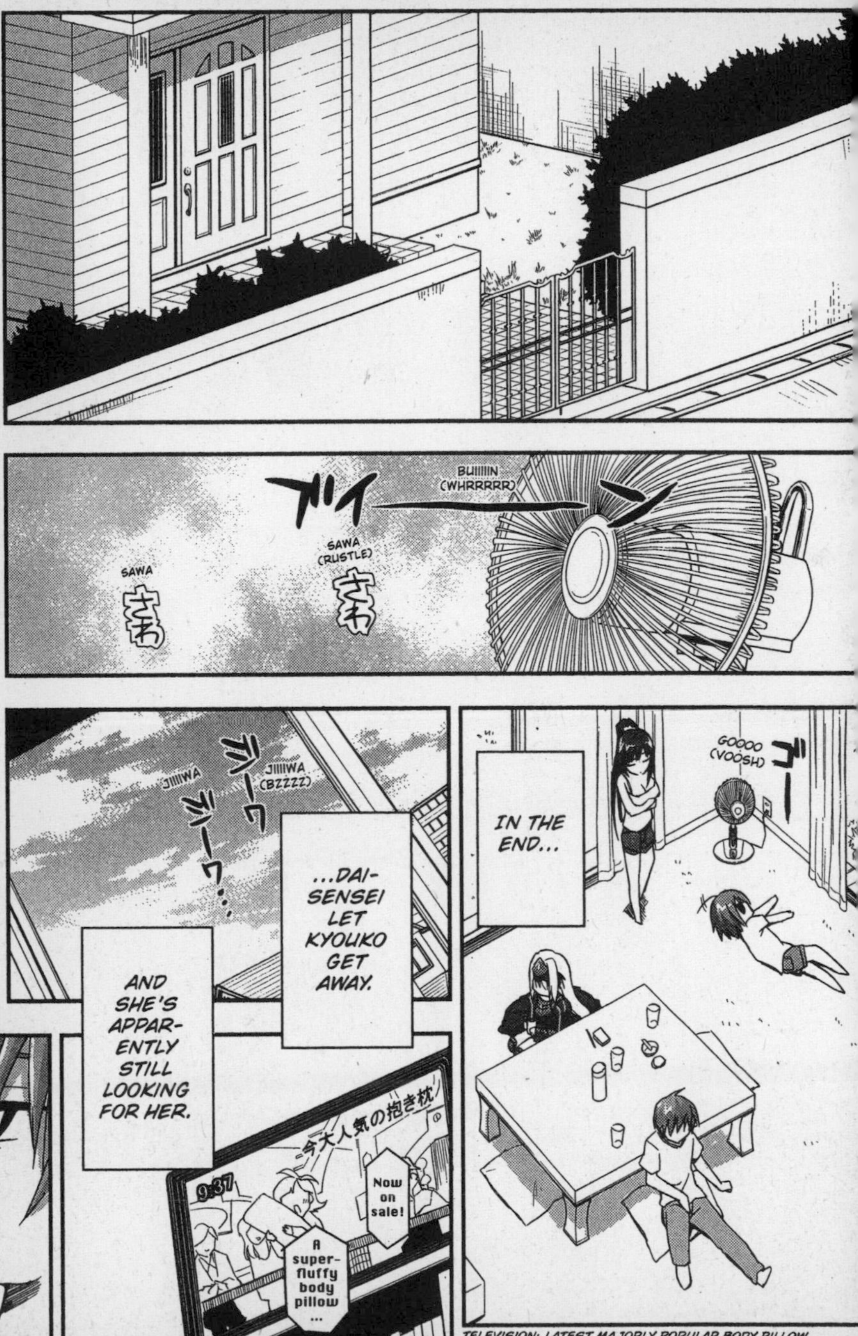
BUIIIIN (WHRRRRR)
ブイーン
SAWA (RUSTLE)
さわ
SAWA
さわ
GOOOO (VOOSH)
ゴー
IN THE END...
JIIIIWA (BZZZZ)
ジーワ
JIIIIWA
ジーワ...
...DAI-SENSEI LET KYOUKO GET AWAY.
AND SHE'S APPARENTLY STILL LOOKING FOR HER.
今大人気の抱き枕
9:37
Now on sale!
A super-fluffy body pillow...

TELEVISION: LATEST MAJORLY POPULAR BODY PILLOW

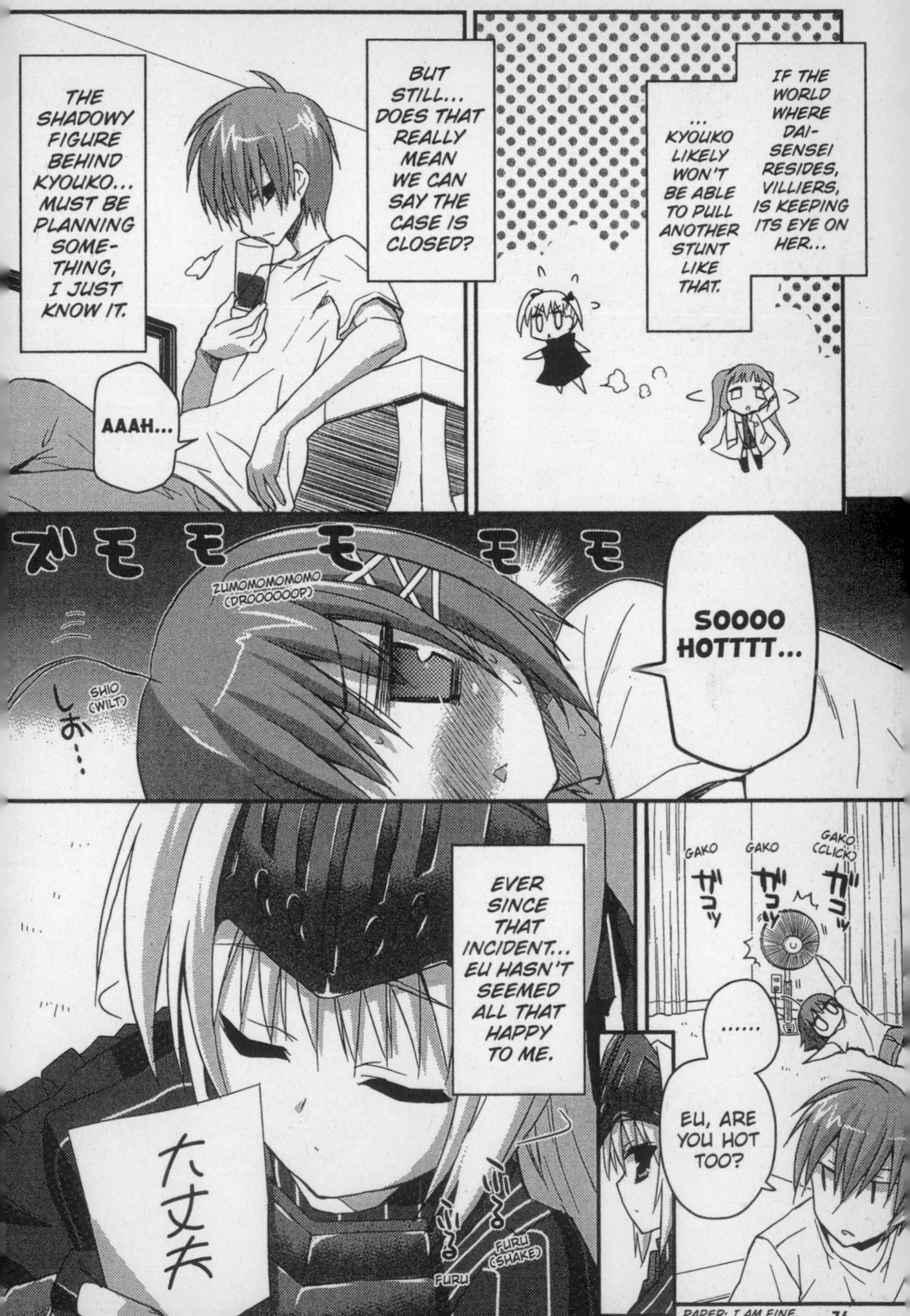
IF THE WORLD WHERE DAI-SENSEI RESIDES, VILLIERS, IS KEEPING ITS EYE ON HER...
...KYOUKO LIKELY WON'T BE ABLE TO PULL ANOTHER STUNT LIKE THAT.
BUT STILL... DOES THAT REALLY MEAN WE CAN SAY THE CASE IS CLOSED?
THE SHADOWY FIGURE BEHIND KYOUKO... MUST BE PLANNING SOME-THING, I JUST KNOW IT.
AAAH...
ズモモモモモ
ZUMOMOMOMOMO (DROOOOOOP)
SOOOO HOTTTT...
しお…
SHIO (WILT)
ガコッ
GAKO (CLICK)
ガコッ
GAKO
ガコッ
GAKO
......
EU, ARE YOU HOT TOO?
EVER SINCE THAT INCIDENT... EU HASN'T SEEMED ALL THAT HAPPY TO ME.
ふる
FURU (SHAKE)
ふる
FURU
大丈夫
PAPER: I AM FINE.

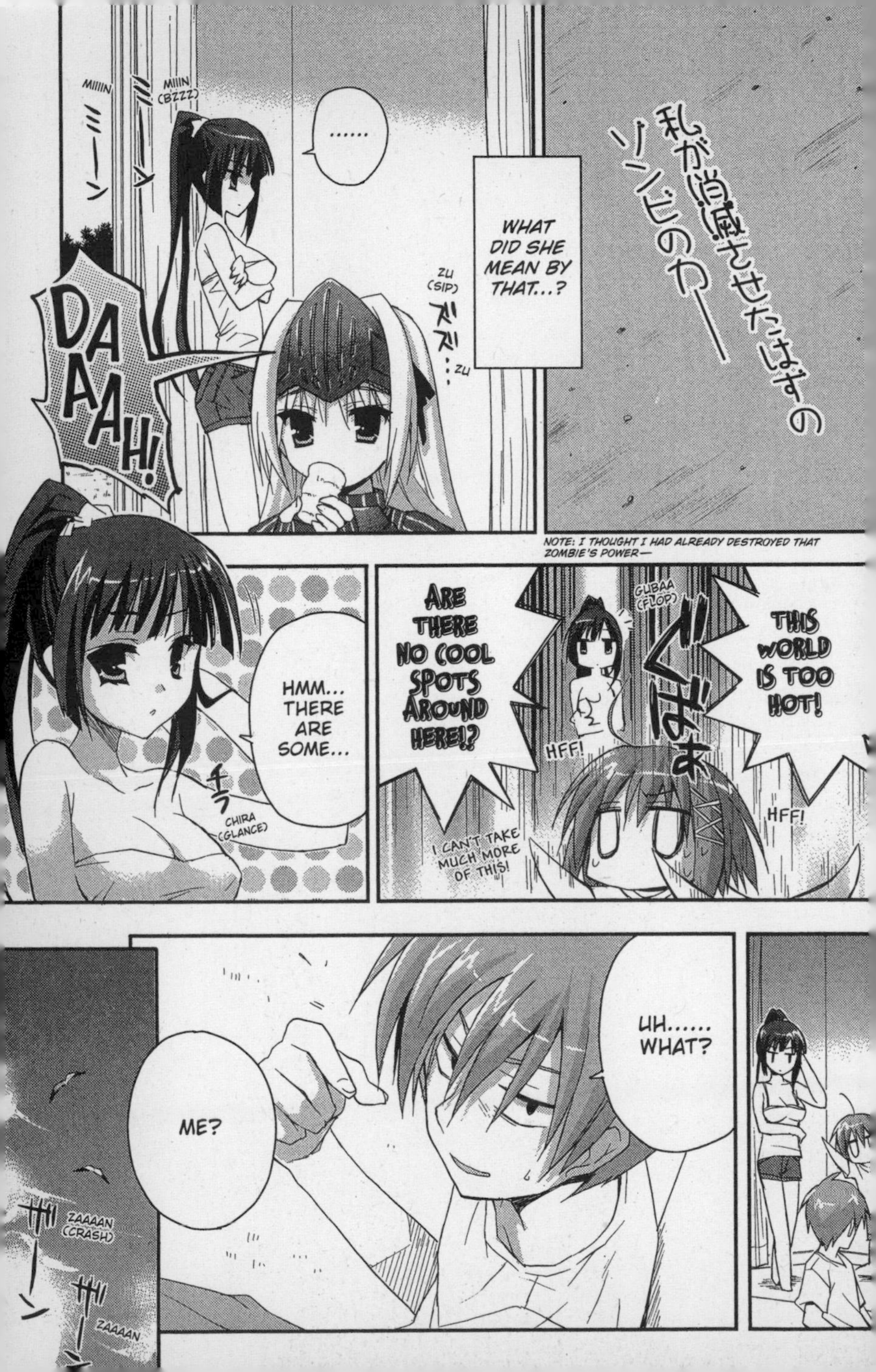
私が消滅させたはずのゾンビの力ーー
WHAT DID SHE MEAN BY THAT...?
......
MIIIN (BZZZ)
MIIIN
ZU (SIP)
ZU
DAAAH!
NOTE: I THOUGHT I HAD ALREADY DESTROYED THAT ZOMBIE'S POWER—
THIS WORLD IS TOO HOT!
GUBAA (FLOP)
ARE THERE NO COOL SPOTS AROUND HERE!?
HFF!
HFF!
I CAN'T TAKE MUCH MORE OF THIS!
HMM... THERE ARE SOME...
CHIRA (GLANCE)
UH...... WHAT?
ME?
ZAAAAN (CRASH)
ZAAAAN

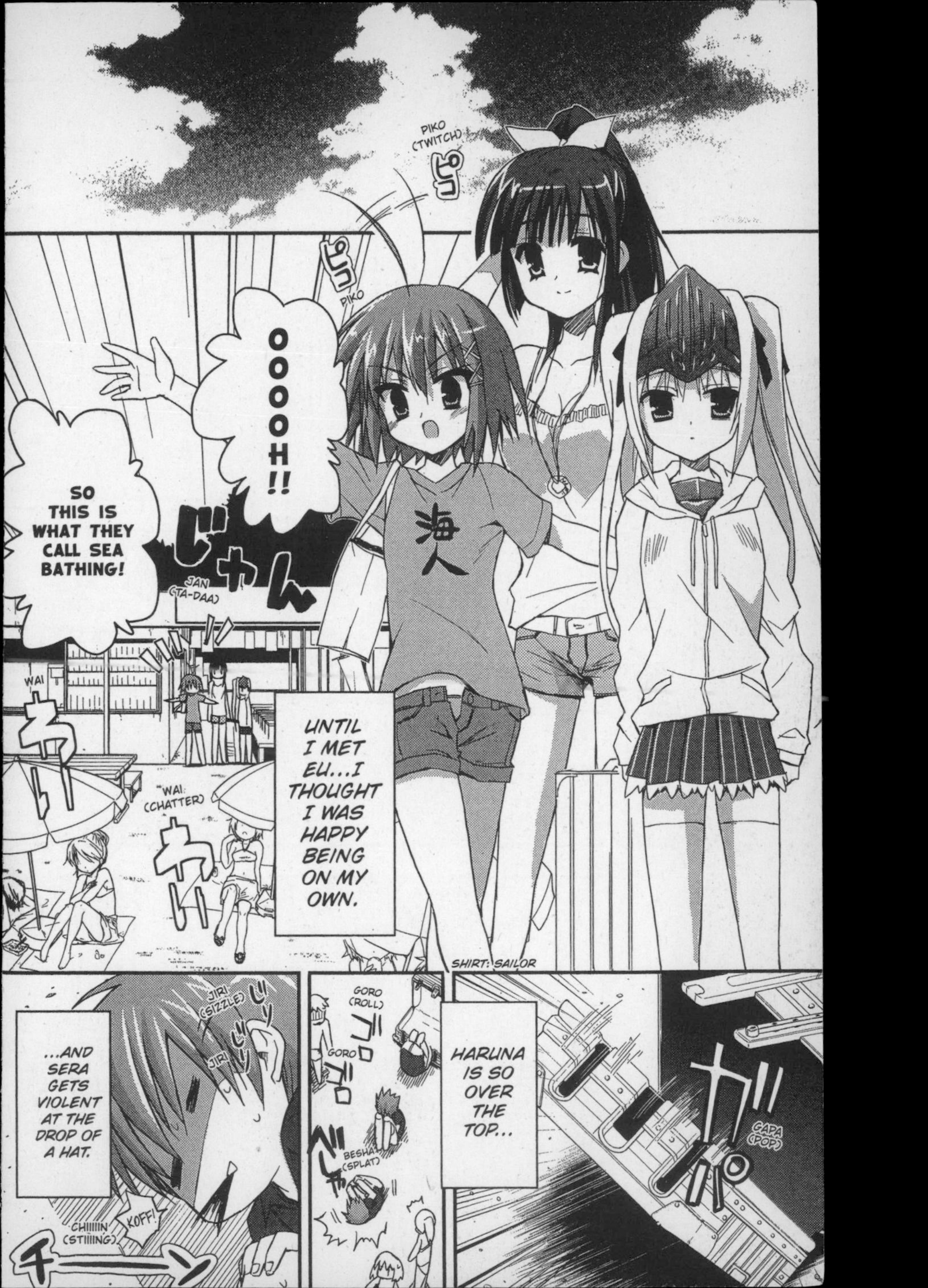

PIKO (TWITCH)
ピコ
ピコ
PIKO
OOOOOH!!
SO THIS IS WHAT THEY CALL SEA BATHING!
じゃん
JAN (TA-DAA)
UNTIL I MET EU...I THOUGHT I WAS HAPPY BEING ON MY OWN.
WAI
わい
WAI (CHATTER)
わい
海人
SHIRT: SAILOR
HARUNA IS SO OVER THE TOP...
GAPA (POP)
ガパ
GORO (ROLL)
ゴロ
GORO
ゴロ
BESHA (SPLAT)
べしゃ
...AND SERA GETS VIOLENT AT THE DROP OF A HAT.
JIRI (SIZZLE)
じり
JIRI
じり
KOFF!
CHIIIIIN (STIIIING)
チーン

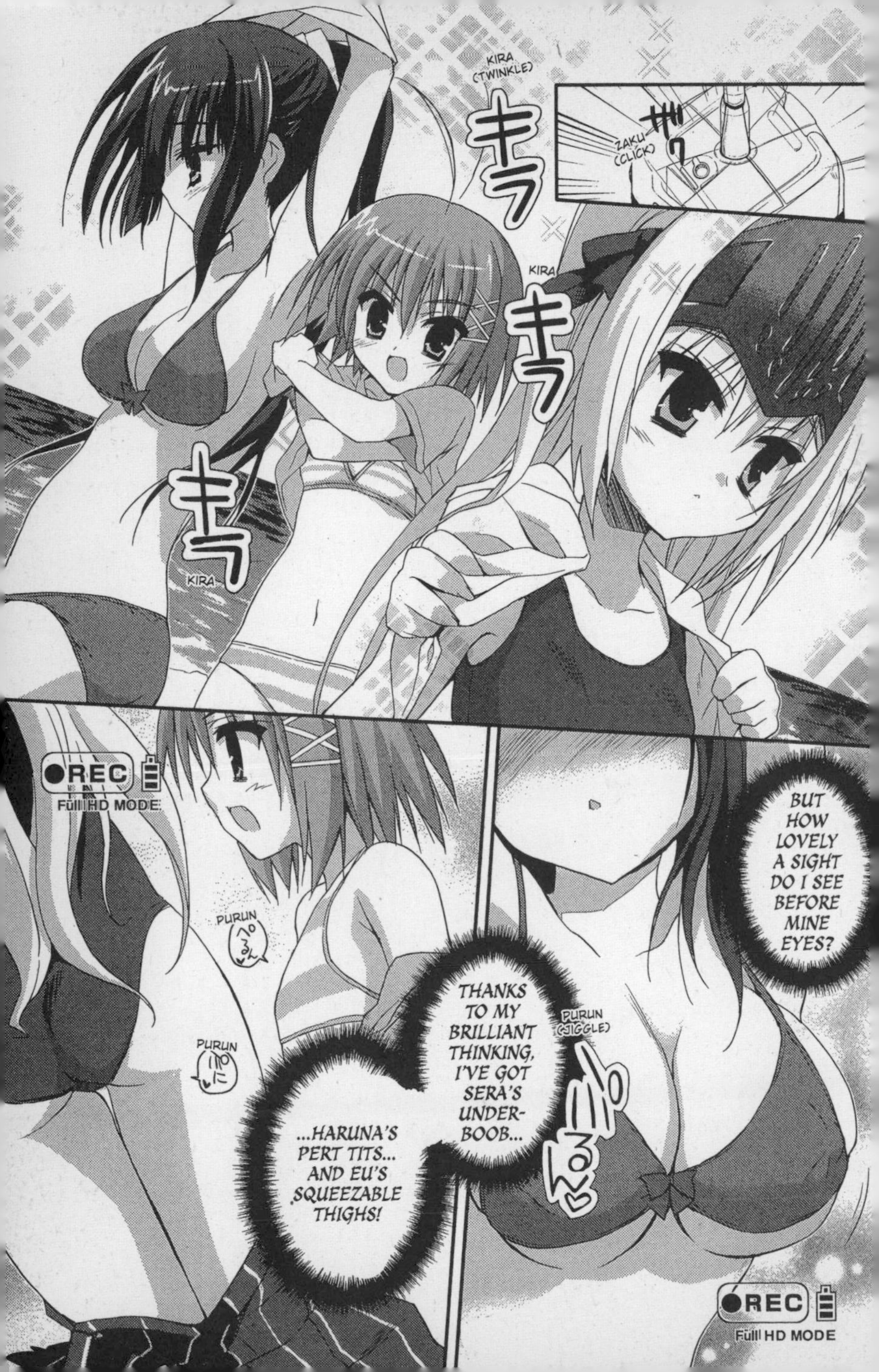
ZAKU (CLICK)
ザク
KIRA (TWINKLE)
キラ
KIRA
キラ
KIRA
キラ
REC
Full HD MODE
BUT HOW LOVELY A SIGHT DO I SEE BEFORE MINE EYES?
THANKS TO MY BRILLIANT THINKING, I'VE GOT SERA'S UNDER-BOOB...
PURUN (JIGGLE)
PURUN
...HARUNA'S PERT TITS... AND EU'S SQUEEZABLE THIGHS!
PURUN
REC
Full HD MODE

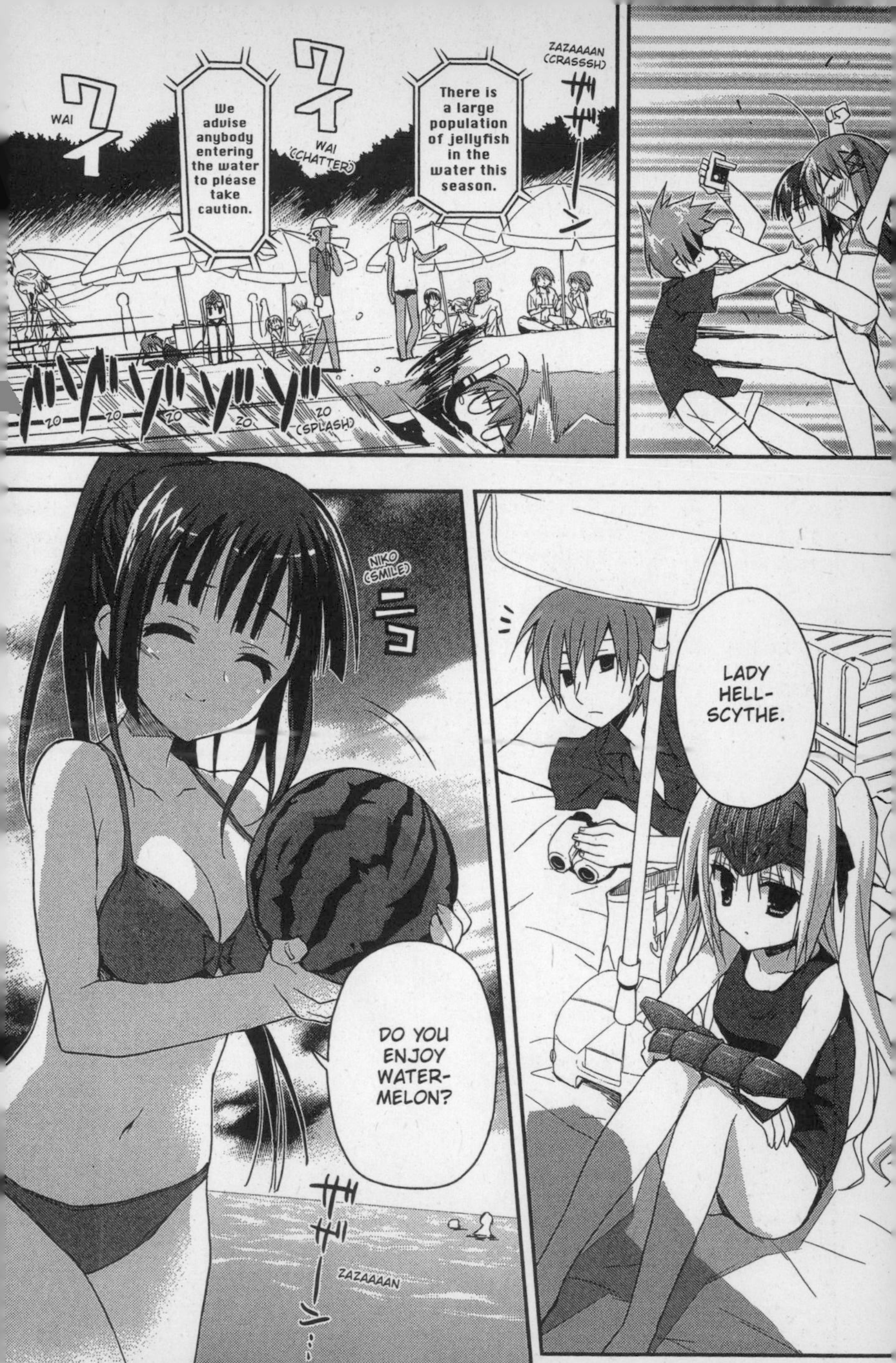
ZAZAAAAN (CRASSSH)
There is a large population of jellyfish in the water this season.
WAI (CHATTER)
We advise anybody entering the water to please take caution.
WAI
ZO ZO ZO ZO ZO (SPLASH)
LADY HELL-SCYTHE.
NIKO (SMILE)
DO YOU ENJOY WATER-MELON?
ZAZAAAAN

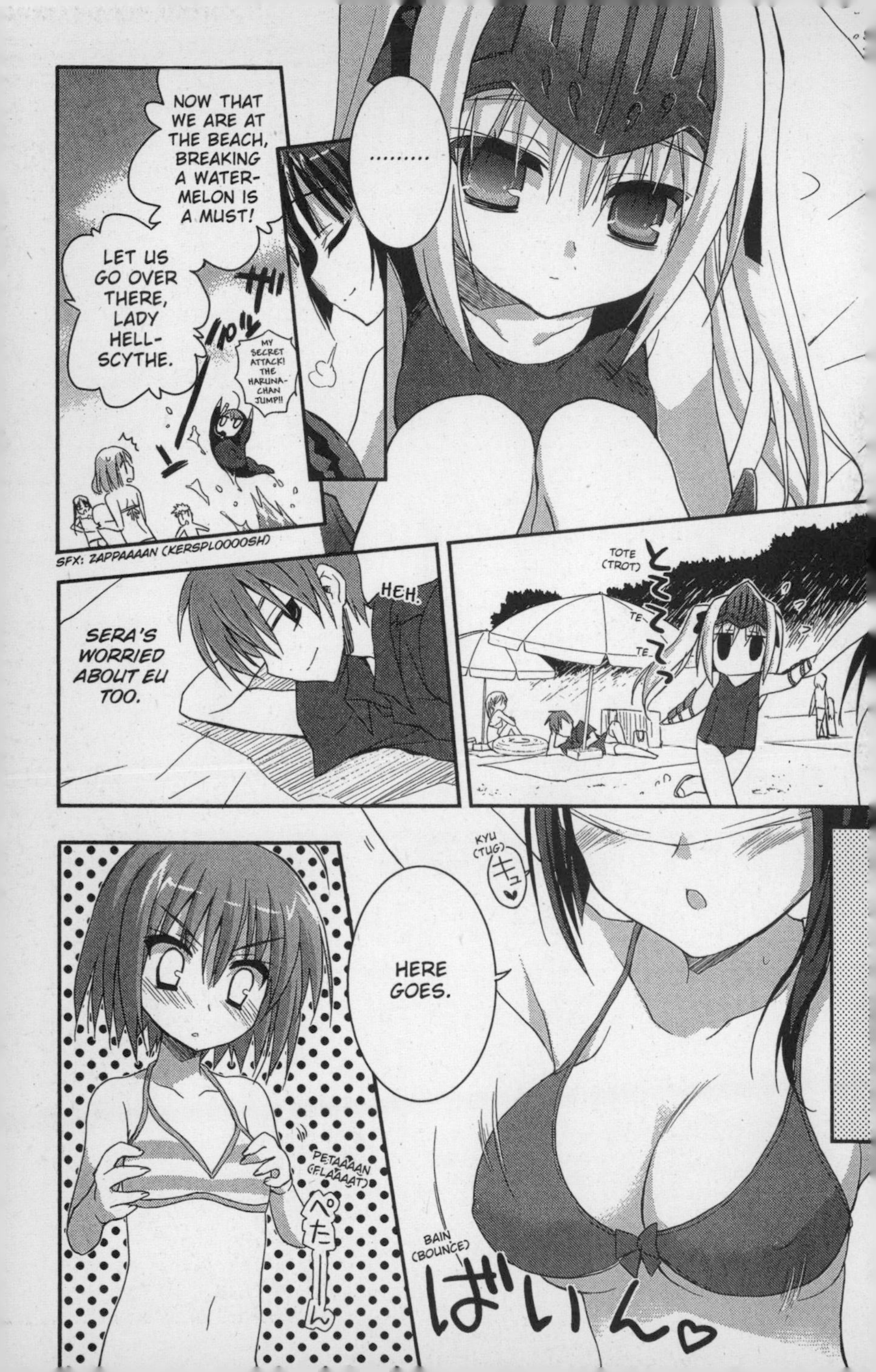
....
NOW THAT WE ARE AT THE BEACH, BREAKING A WATER-MELON IS A MUST!
LET US GO OVER THERE, LADY HELL-SCYTHE.
MY SECRET ATTACK! THE HARUNA-CHAN JUMP!!
SFX: ZAPPAAAAN (KERSPLOOOOSH)
TOTE (TROT)
TE
TE
HEH.
SERA'S WORRIED ABOUT EU TOO.
KYU (TUG)
HERE GOES.
BAIN (BOUNCE)
PETAAAAN (FLAAAAT)

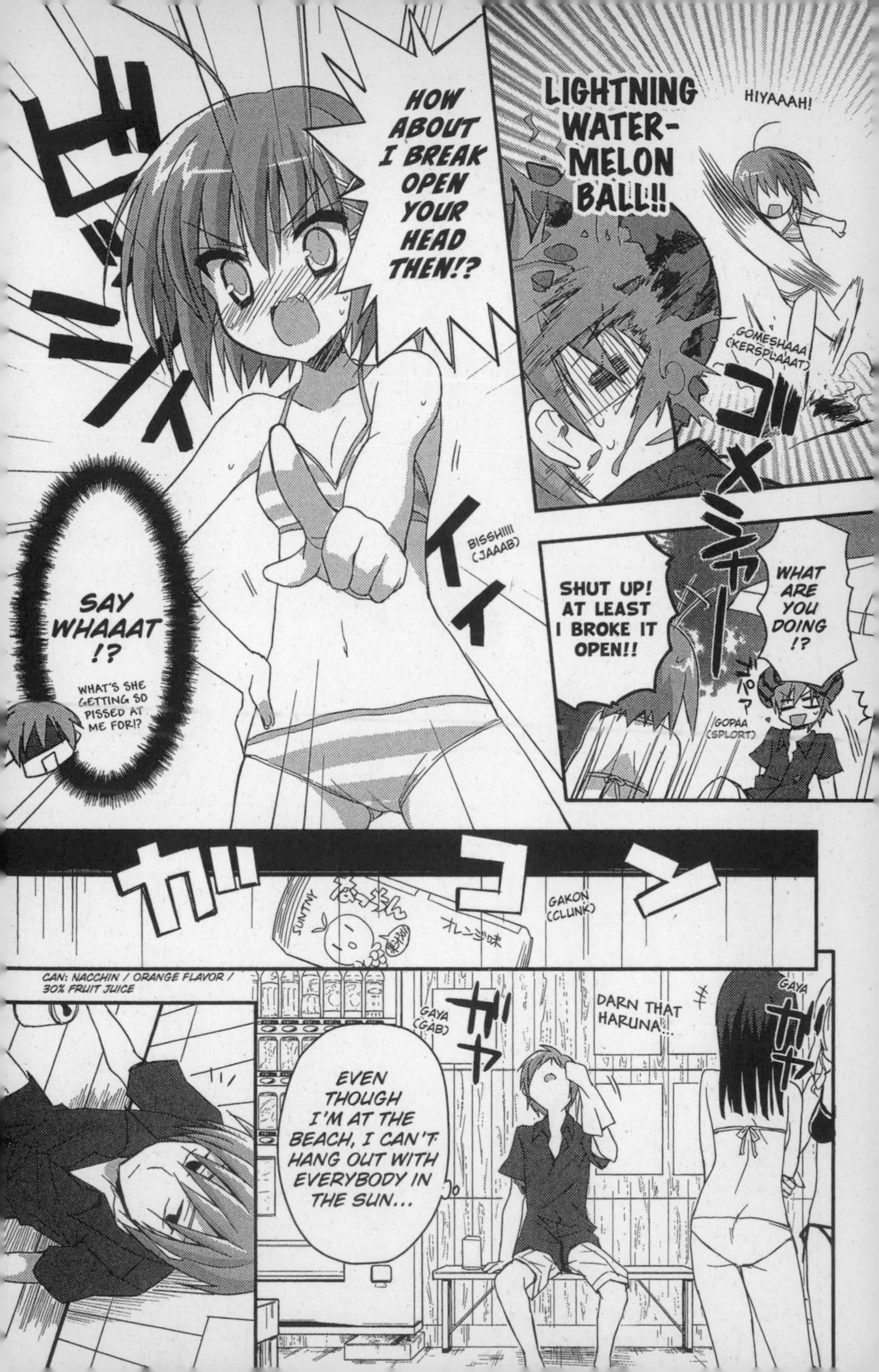

HIYAAAH!
LIGHTNING WATER-MELON BALL!!
HOW ABOUT I BREAK OPEN YOUR HEAD THEN!?
GOMESHAAA (KERSPLAAAT)
BISSHIIII (JAAAB)
WHAT ARE YOU DOING!?
SHUT UP! AT LEAST I BROKE IT OPEN!!
GOPAA (SPLORT)
SAY WHAAAT!?
WHAT'S SHE GETTING SO PISSED AT ME FOR!?
GAKON (CLUNK)
SUNTNY
オレンジ味
CAN: NACCHIN / ORANGE FLAVOR / 30% FRUIT JUICE
GAYA
DARN THAT HARUNA...
GAYA (GAB)
EVEN THOUGH I'M AT THE BEACH, I CAN'T HANG OUT WITH EVERYBODY IN THE SUN...

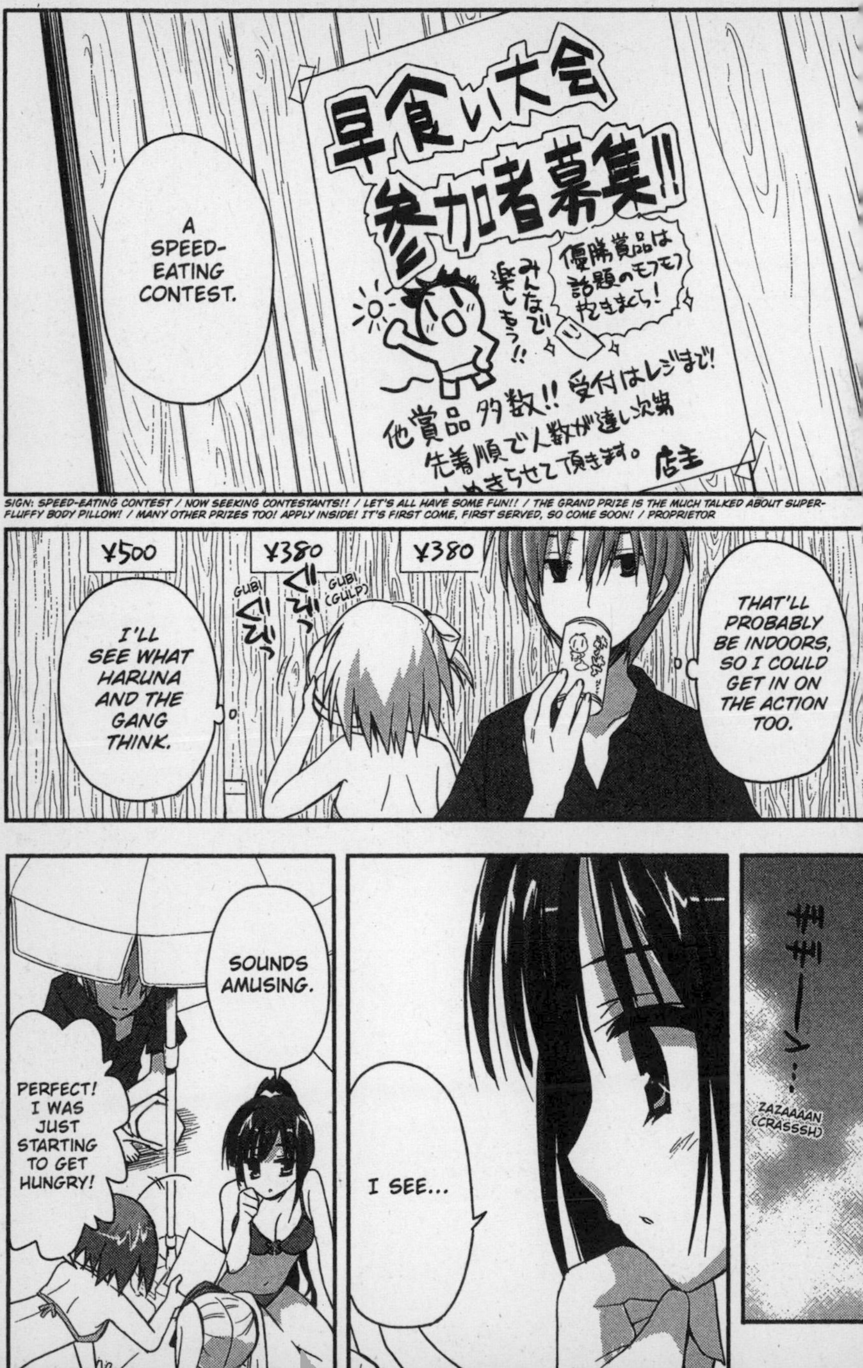
早食い大会
参加者募集!!
優勝賞品は話題のモフモフ抱きまくら!
みんなで楽しもう!!
他賞品多数!! 受付はレジまで!
先着順で人数が達し次第
店主
A SPEED-EATING CONTEST.
SIGN: SPEED-EATING CONTEST / NOW SEEKING CONTESTANTS!! / LET'S ALL HAVE SOME FUN!! / THE GRAND PRIZE IS THE MUCH TALKED ABOUT SUPER-FLUFFY BODY PILLOW! / MANY OTHER PRIZES TOO! APPLY INSIDE! IT'S FIRST COME, FIRST SERVED, SO COME SOON! / PROPRIETOR
¥380
¥380
¥500
THAT'LL PROBABLY BE INDOORS, SO I COULD GET IN ON THE ACTION TOO.
GUBI (GULP)
GUBI
I'LL SEE WHAT HARUNA AND THE GANG THINK.
ZAZAAAAN (CRASSSH)
I SEE...
SOUNDS AMUSING.
PERFECT! I WAS JUST STARTING TO GET HUNGRY!

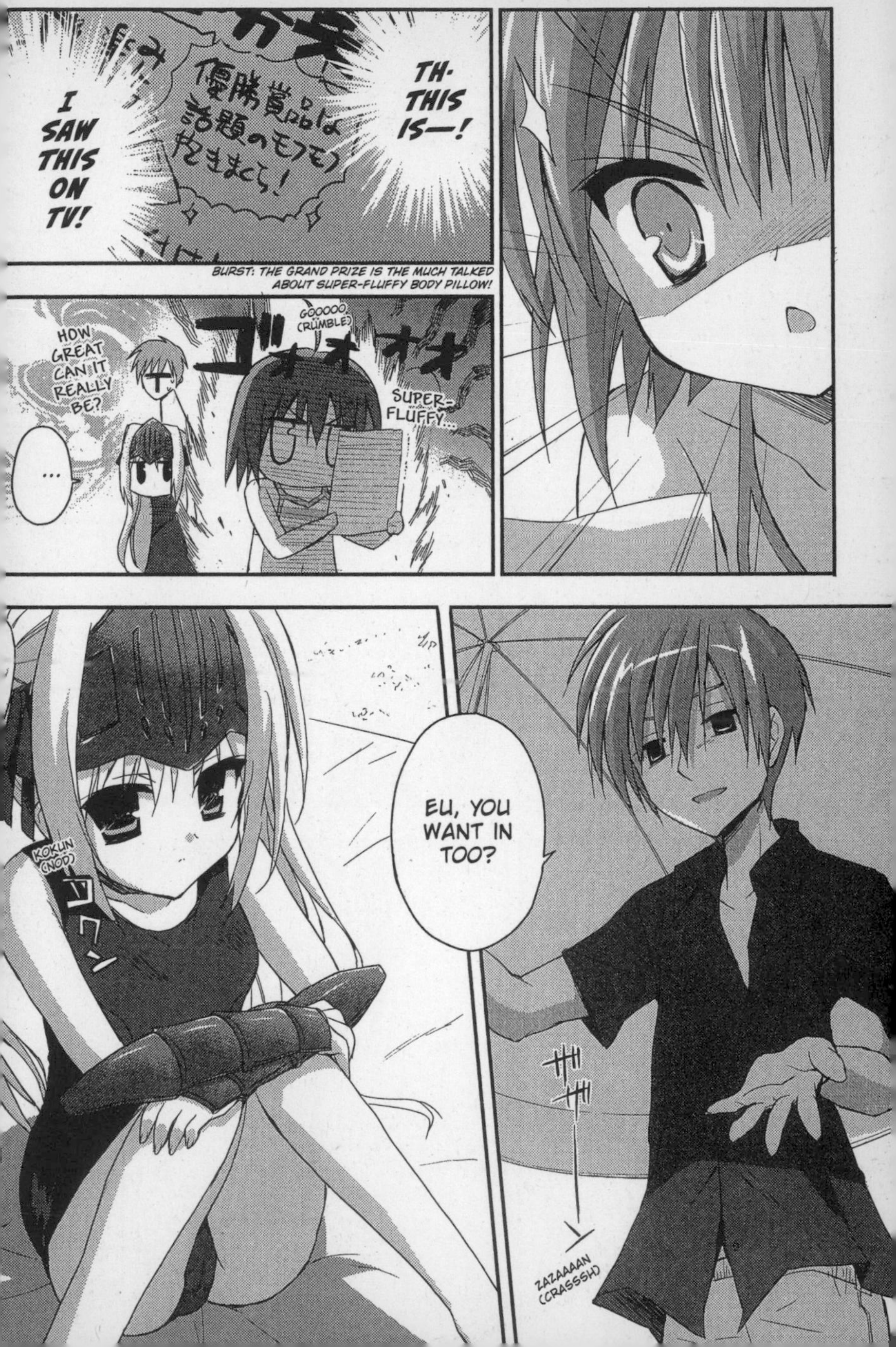
TH-THIS IS—!
I SAW THIS ON TV!
優勝賞品は話題のモフモフ抱きまくら！
BURST: THE GRAND PRIZE IS THE MUCH TALKED ABOUT SUPER-FLUFFY BODY PILLOW!
GOOOOO (RUMBLE)
SUPER-FLUFFY...
HOW GREAT CAN IT REALLY BE?
...
EU, YOU WANT IN TOO?
KOKUN (NOD)
ZAZAAAAN (CRASSSH)

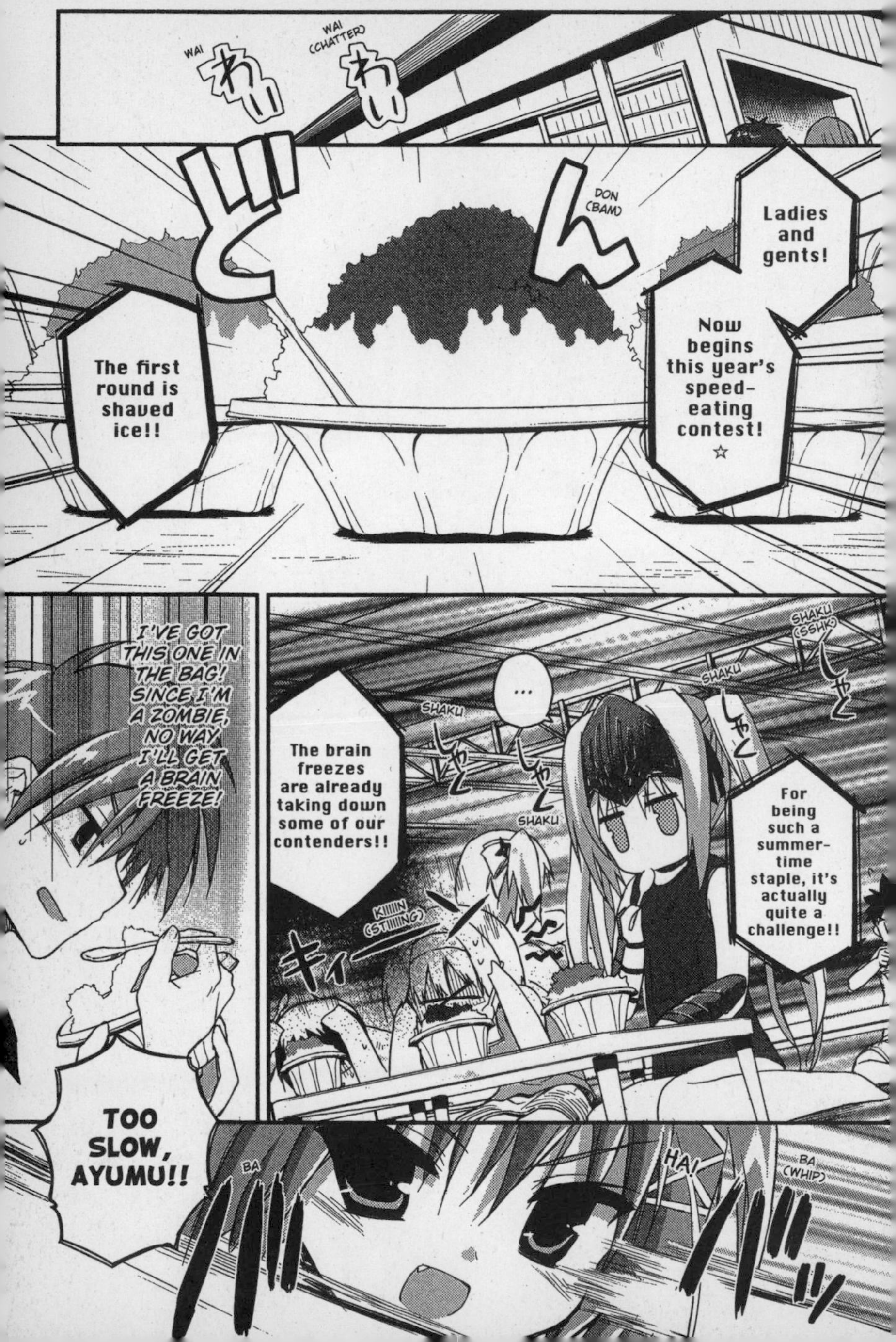

WAI (CHATTER)
WAI
わい
わい
DON (BAM)
どん
Ladies and gents!
Now begins this year's speed-eating contest! ☆
The first round is shaved ice!!
SHAKU (SSHK)
SHAKU
SHAKU
SHAKU
...
For being such a summer-time staple, it's actually quite a challenge!!
The brain freezes are already taking down some of our contenders!!
KIIIIN (STIIIING)
I'VE GOT THIS ONE IN THE BAG! SINCE I'M A ZOMBIE, NO WAY I'LL GET A BRAIN FREEZE!
BA (WHIP)
HA!
BA
TOO SLOW, AYUMU!!

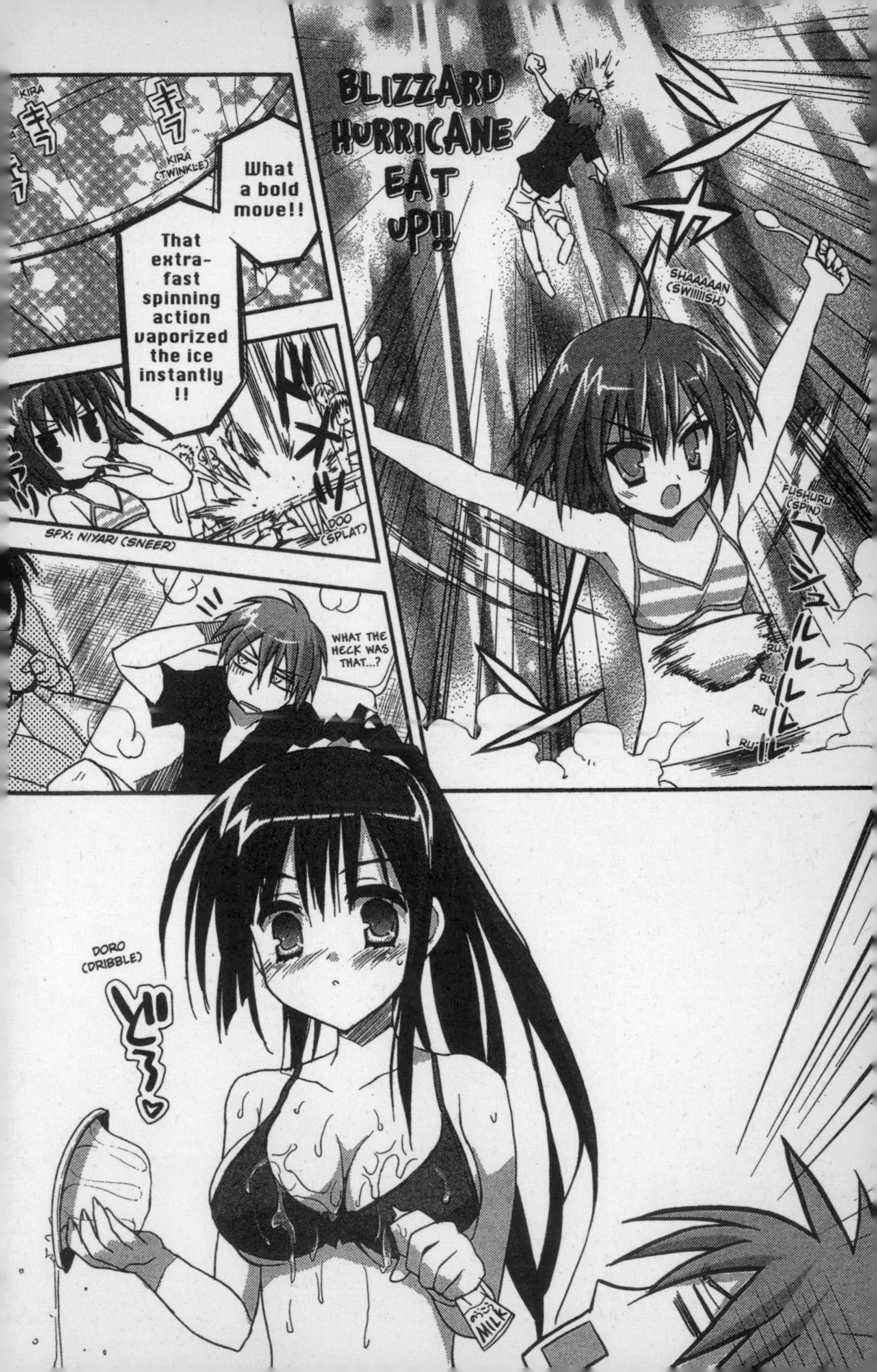
BLIZZARD HURRICANE EAT UP!!
SHAAAAAN (SWIIIIISH)
FUSHURU (SPIN)
RU
RU
RU
RU
KIRA
KIRA (TWINKLE)
What a bold move!!
That extra-fast spinning action vaporized the ice instantly!!
DOO (SPLAT)
SFX: NIYARI (SNEER)
WHAT THE HECK WAS THAT...?
DORO (DRIBBLE)
MILK

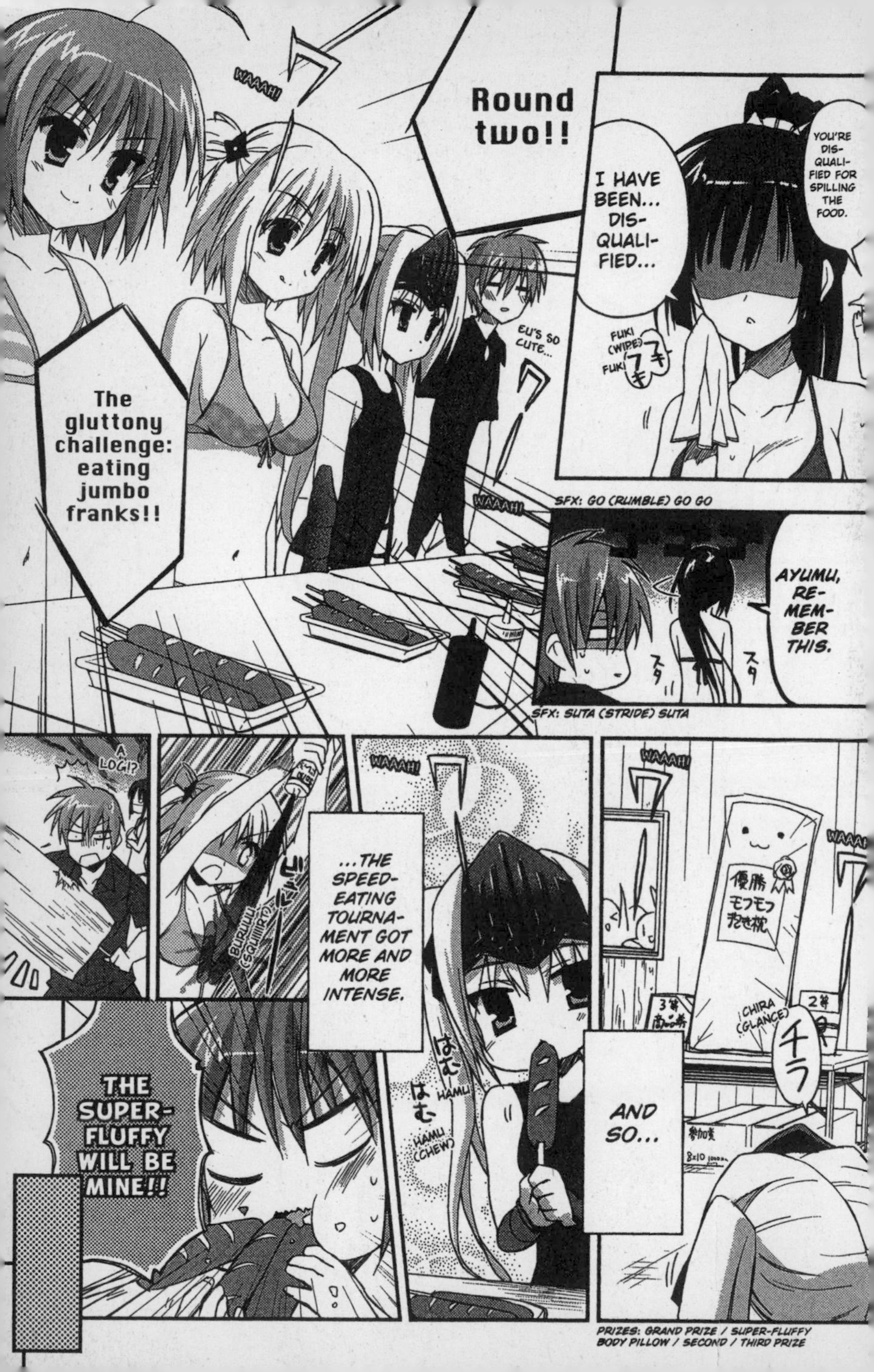

YOU'RE DIS-QUALI-FIED FOR SPILLING THE FOOD.
I HAVE BEEN... DIS-QUALI-FIED...
FUKI (WIPE) FUKI
SFX: GO (RUMBLE) GO GO
Round two!!
WAAAH!
The gluttony challenge: eating jumbo franks!!
EU'S SO CUTE...
WAAAH!
AYUMU, RE-MEM-BER THIS.
SFX: SUTA (STRIDE) SUTA
WAAAH!
WAAAH!
優勝 モフモフ抱き枕
CHIRA (GLANCE)
AND SO...
WAAAH!
...THE SPEED-EATING TOURNA-MENT GOT MORE AND MORE INTENSE.
HAMU HAMU (CHEW)
BURUUU (SQUIIIIRT)
A LOG!?
THE SUPER-FLUFFY WILL BE MINE!!
PRIZES: GRAND PRIZE / SUPER-FLUFFY BODY PILLOW / SECOND / THIRD PRIZE

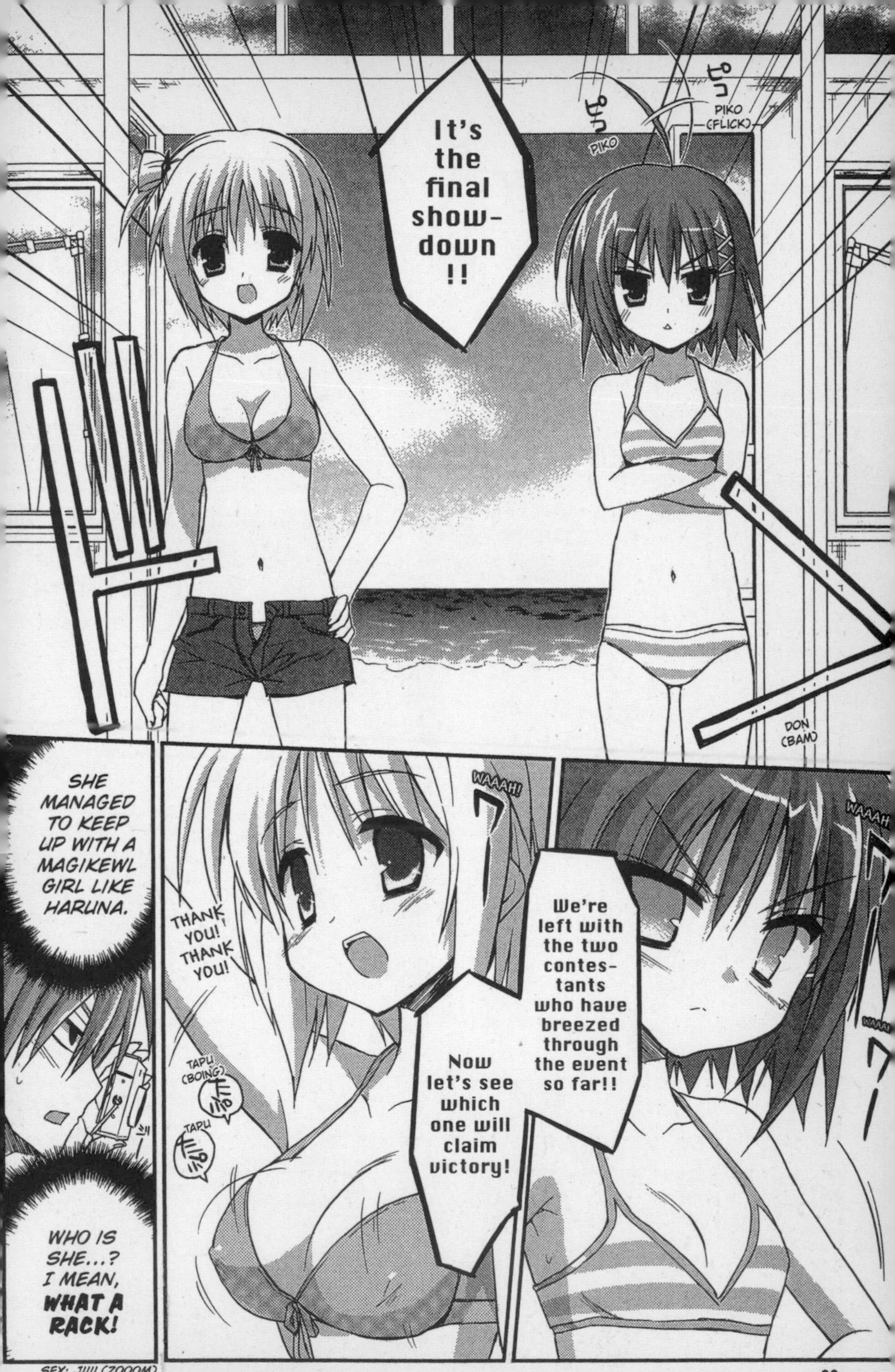

PIKO (FLICK)
PIKO
It's the final show-down!!
DON (BAM)
WAAAH!
We're left with the two contestants who have breezed through the event so far!!
Now let's see which one will claim victory!
WAAAH!
THANK YOU! THANK YOU!
TAPU (BOING)
TAPU
SHE MANAGED TO KEEP UP WITH A MAGIKEWL GIRL LIKE HARUNA.
WHO IS SHE...? I MEAN, **WHAT A RACK!**

SFX: JIIII (ZOOOM)

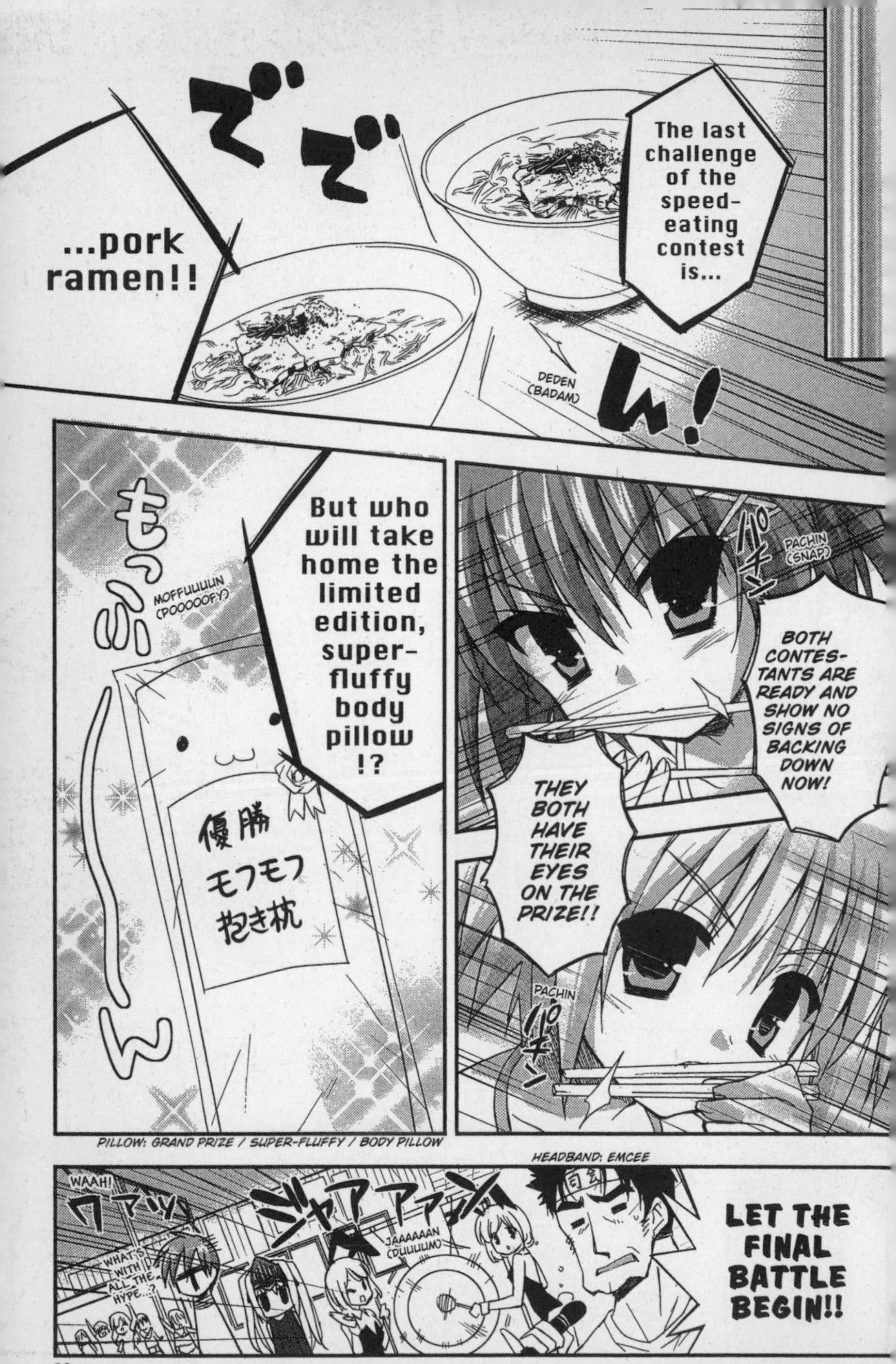
The last challenge of the speed-eating contest is...
...pork ramen!!
DEDEN (BADAM)
PACHIN (SNAP)
BOTH CONTESTANTS ARE READY AND SHOW NO SIGNS OF BACKING DOWN NOW!
THEY BOTH HAVE THEIR EYES ON THE PRIZE!!
PACHIN
But who will take home the limited edition, super-fluffy body pillow!?
MOFFUUUUN (POOOOOFY)
優勝
モフモフ
抱き枕
PILLOW: GRAND PRIZE / SUPER-FLUFFY / BODY PILLOW
HEADBAND: EMCEE
LET THE FINAL BATTLE BEGIN!!
JAAAAAAN (DUUUUUN)
WAAH!
WHAT'S WITH ALL THE HYPE...?

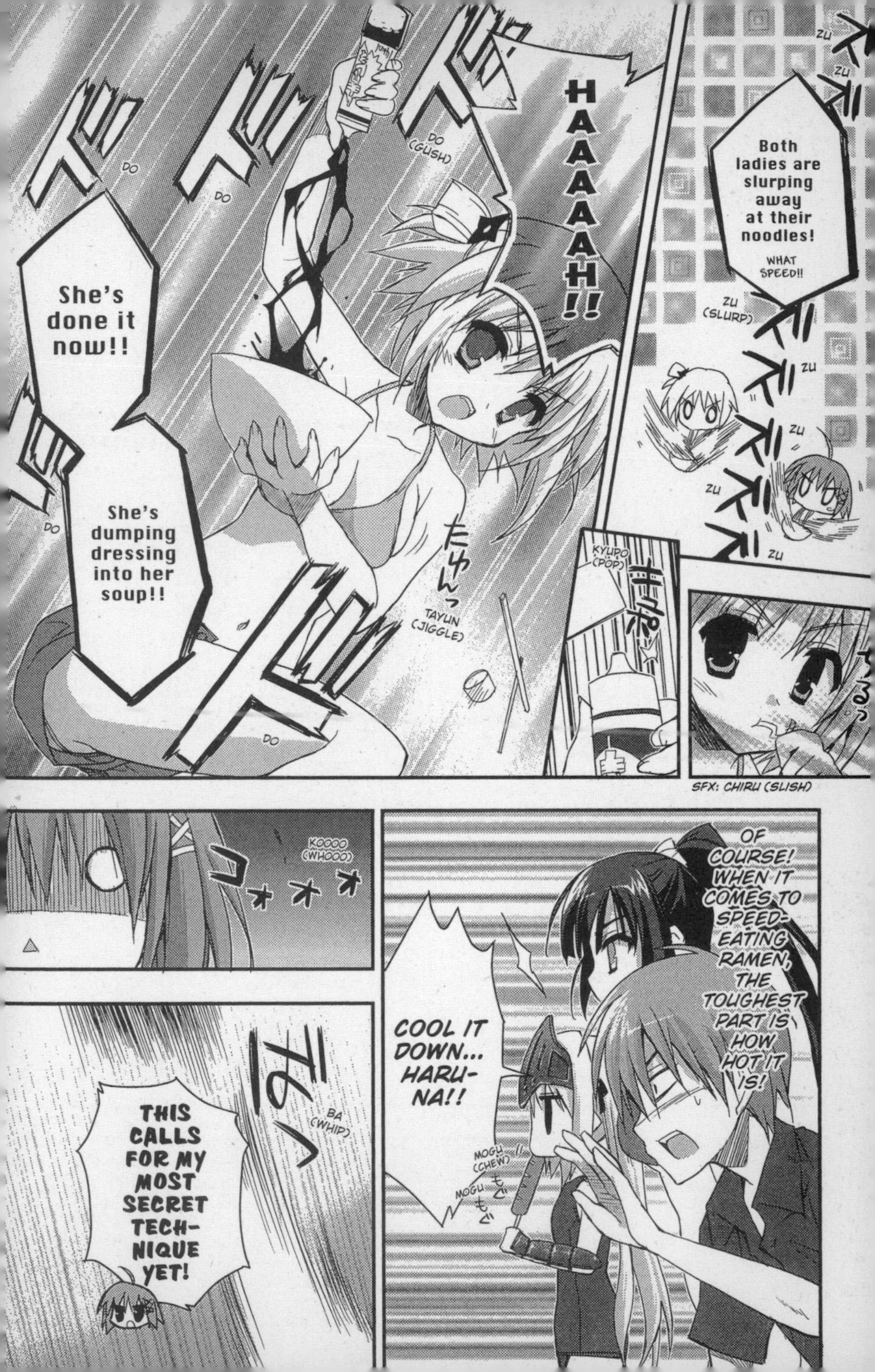
ZU
ZU
Both ladies are slurping away at their noodles!
WHAT SPEED!!
ZU (SLURP)
ZU
ZU
ZU
ZU
HAAAAAAH!!
DO (GUSH)
DO
DO
She's done it now!!
She's dumping dressing into her soup!!
DO
TAYUN (JIGGLE)
DO
KYUPO (POP)
SFX: CHIRU (SLISH)
OF COURSE! WHEN IT COMES TO SPEED-EATING RAMEN, THE TOUGHEST PART IS HOW HOT IT IS!
COOL IT DOWN... HARUNA!!
MOGU (CHEW)
MOGU
KOOOO (WHOOO)
BA (WHIP)
THIS CALLS FOR MY MOST SECRET TECHNIQUE YET!

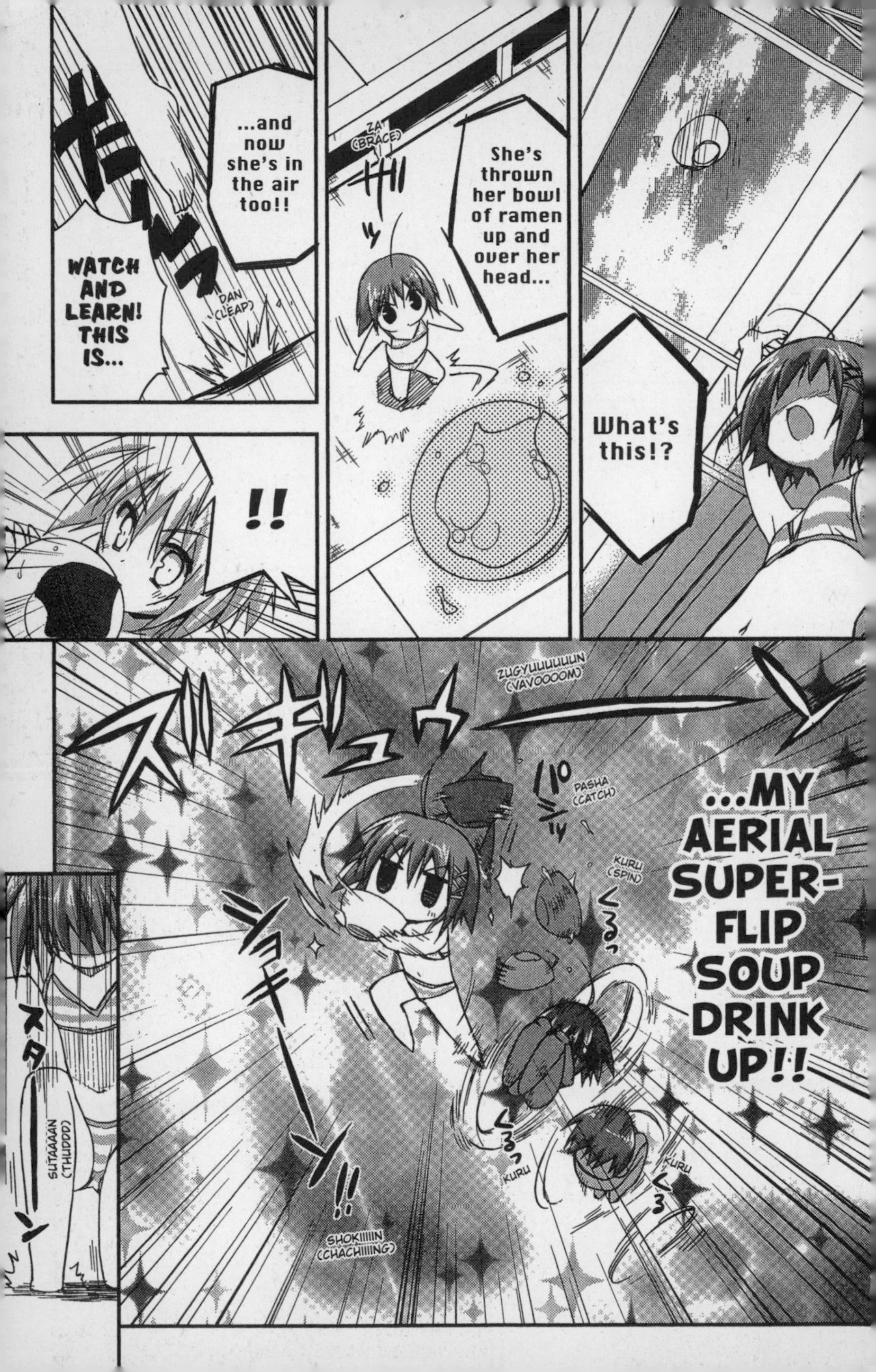
What's this!?
She's thrown her bowl of ramen up and over her head...
ZA (BRACE)
...and now she's in the air too!!
DAN (LEAP)
WATCH AND LEARN! THIS IS...
!!
ZUGYUUUUUUN (VAVOOOOM)
PASHA (CATCH)
KURU (SPIN)
...MY AERIAL SUPER-FLIP SOUP DRINK UP!!
KURU
KURU
SHOKIIIIIN (CHACHIIIING)
SUTAAAAN (THUDDD)

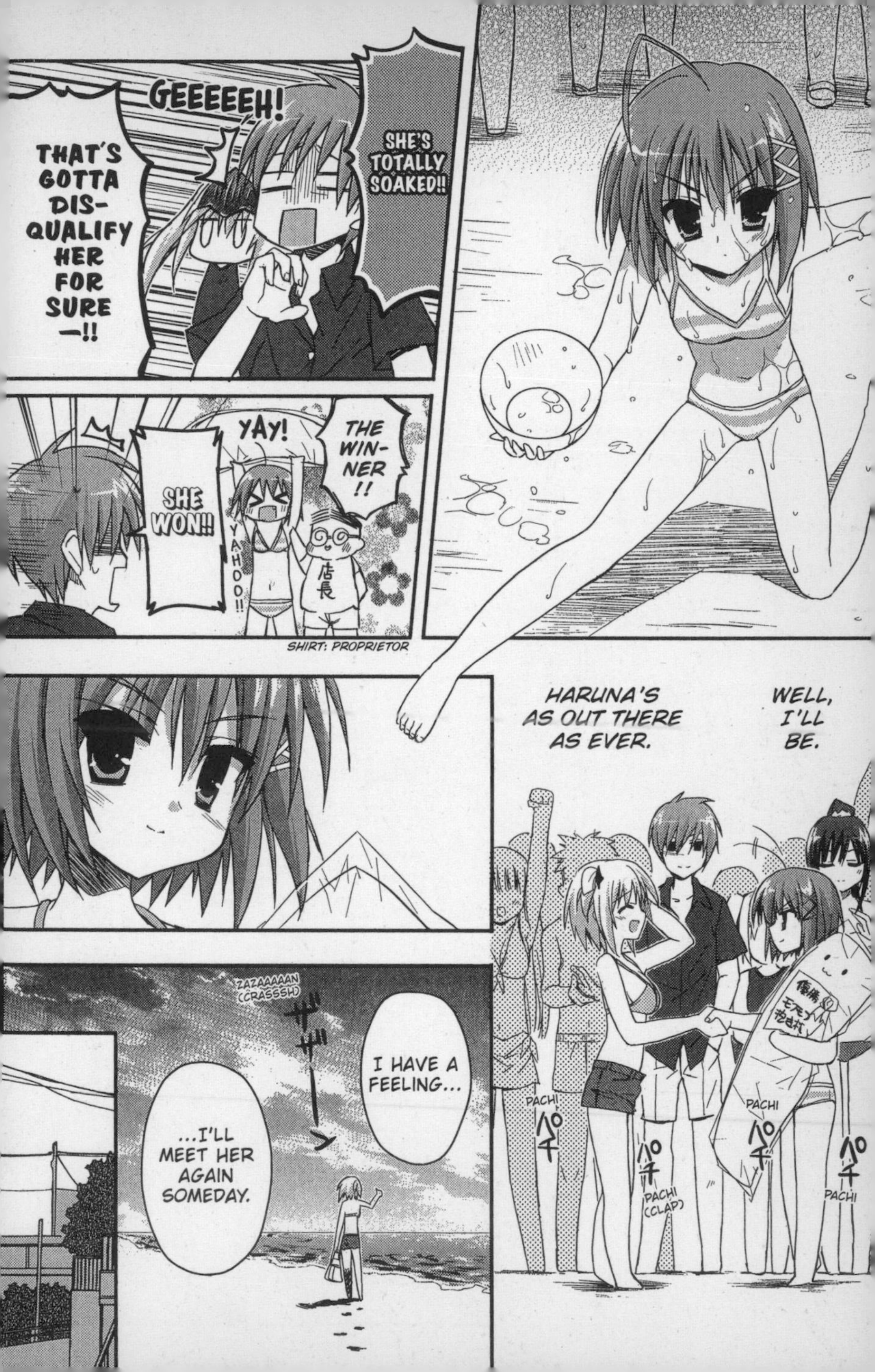

SHE'S TOTALLY SOAKED!!
GEEEEEH!
THAT'S GOTTA DIS-QUALIFY HER FOR SURE—!!
THE WINNER!!
YAY!
YAHOOO!!
店長
SHE WON!!
SHIRT: PROPRIETOR
WELL, I'LL BE.
HARUNA'S AS OUT THERE AS EVER.
PACHI
PACHI
PACHI (CLAP)
PACHI
ZAZAAAAAN (CRASSSH)
I HAVE A FEELING...
...I'LL MEET HER AGAIN SOMEDAY.

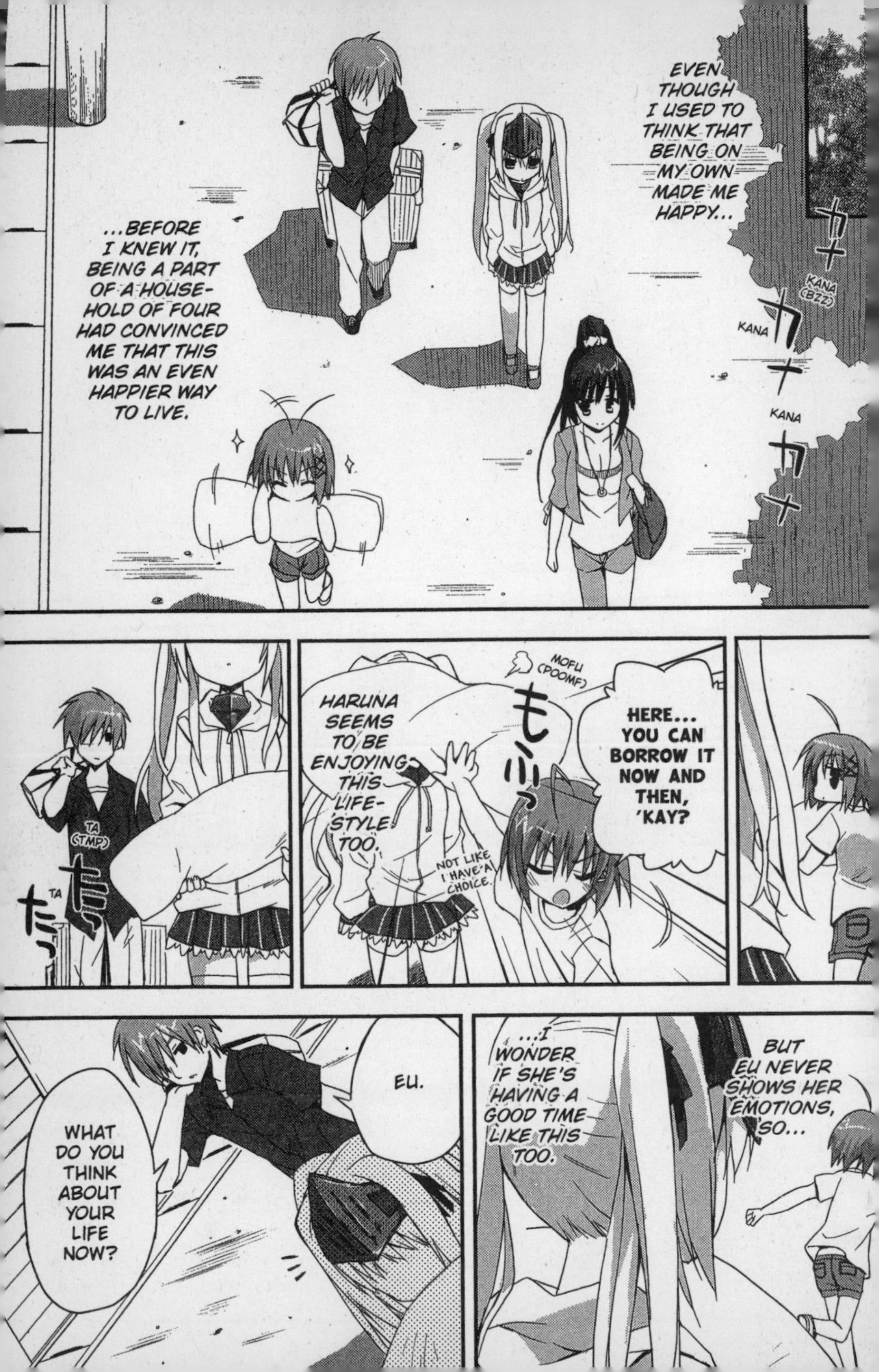
EVEN THOUGH I USED TO THINK THAT BEING ON MY OWN MADE ME HAPPY...
カナ
KANA (BZZ)
カナ
KANA
カナ
KANA
カナ
...BEFORE I KNEW IT, BEING A PART OF A HOUSE-HOLD OF FOUR HAD CONVINCED ME THAT THIS WAS AN EVEN HAPPIER WAY TO LIVE.
HERE... YOU CAN BORROW IT NOW AND THEN, 'KAY?
MOFU (POOMF)
もふっ
HARUNA SEEMS TO BE ENJOYING THIS LIFE-STYLE TOO.
NOT LIKE I HAVE A CHOICE.
TA (TMP)
たっ
TA
たっ
BUT EU NEVER SHOWS HER EMOTIONS, SO...
...I WONDER IF SHE'S HAVING A GOOD TIME LIKE THIS TOO.
EU.
WHAT DO YOU THINK ABOUT YOUR LIFE NOW?

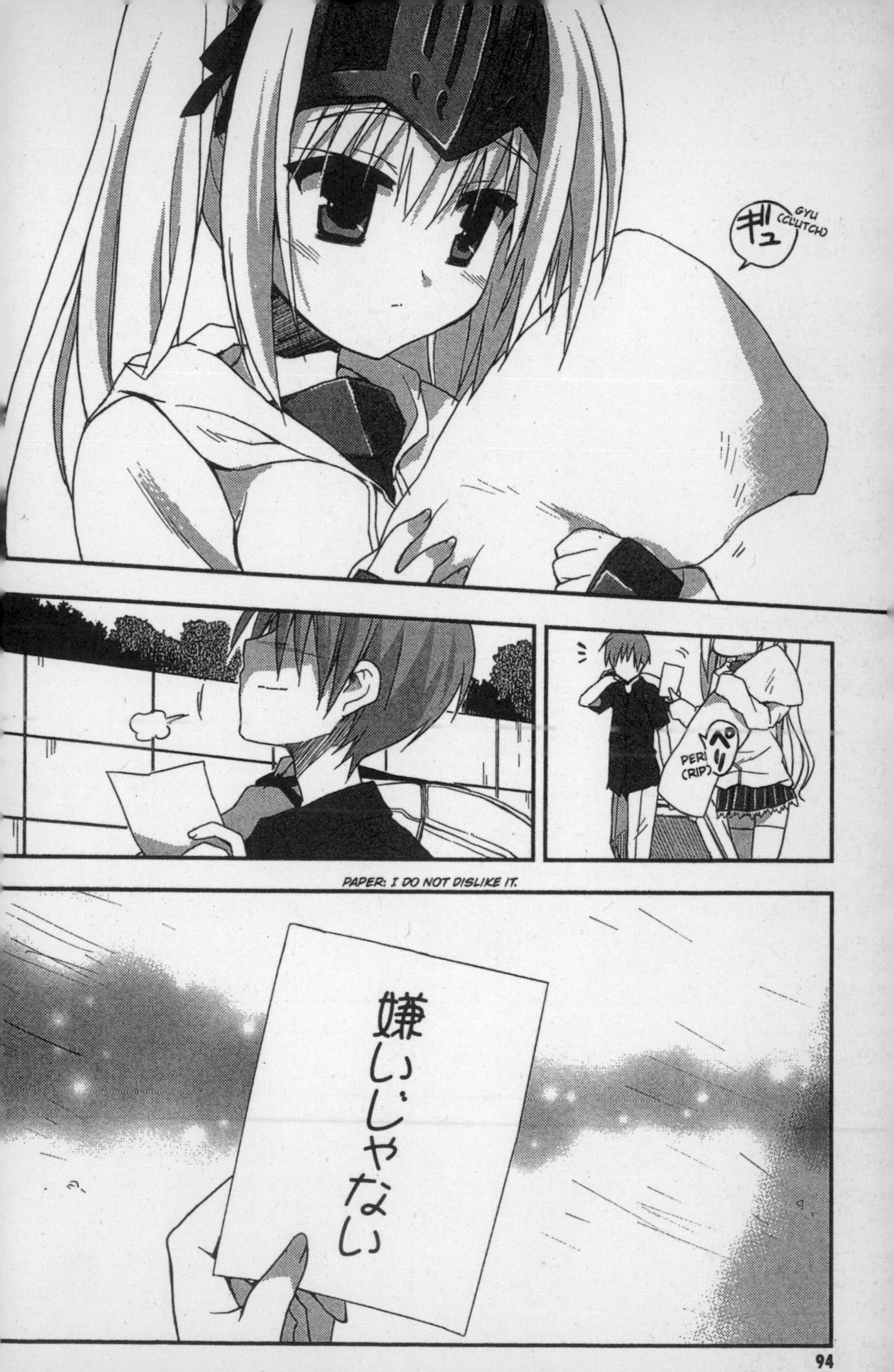
ギュ
GYU (CLUTCH)
ペリ
PERI (RIP)
嫌いじゃない

PAPER: I DO NOT DISLIKE IT.

IS THIS A ZOMBIE?

MATERNITY

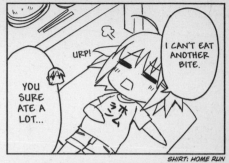

I CAN'T EAT ANOTHER BITE.
URP!
YOU SURE ATE A LOT...
SHIRT: HOME RUN
ACK!
...
I FELT IT KICK!!
SASU (RUB)
SASU
......
GAFU (SPLORT)
A- AYUMU, YOU PERV!!
GA (STOMP)
IF YOU'RE GONNA GET ALL EMBAR-RASSED ABOUT IT, DON'T SAY CRAP LIKE THAT!
GA

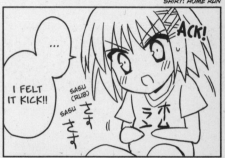

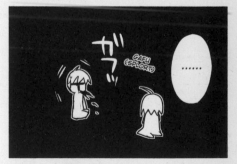

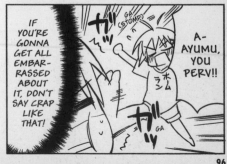

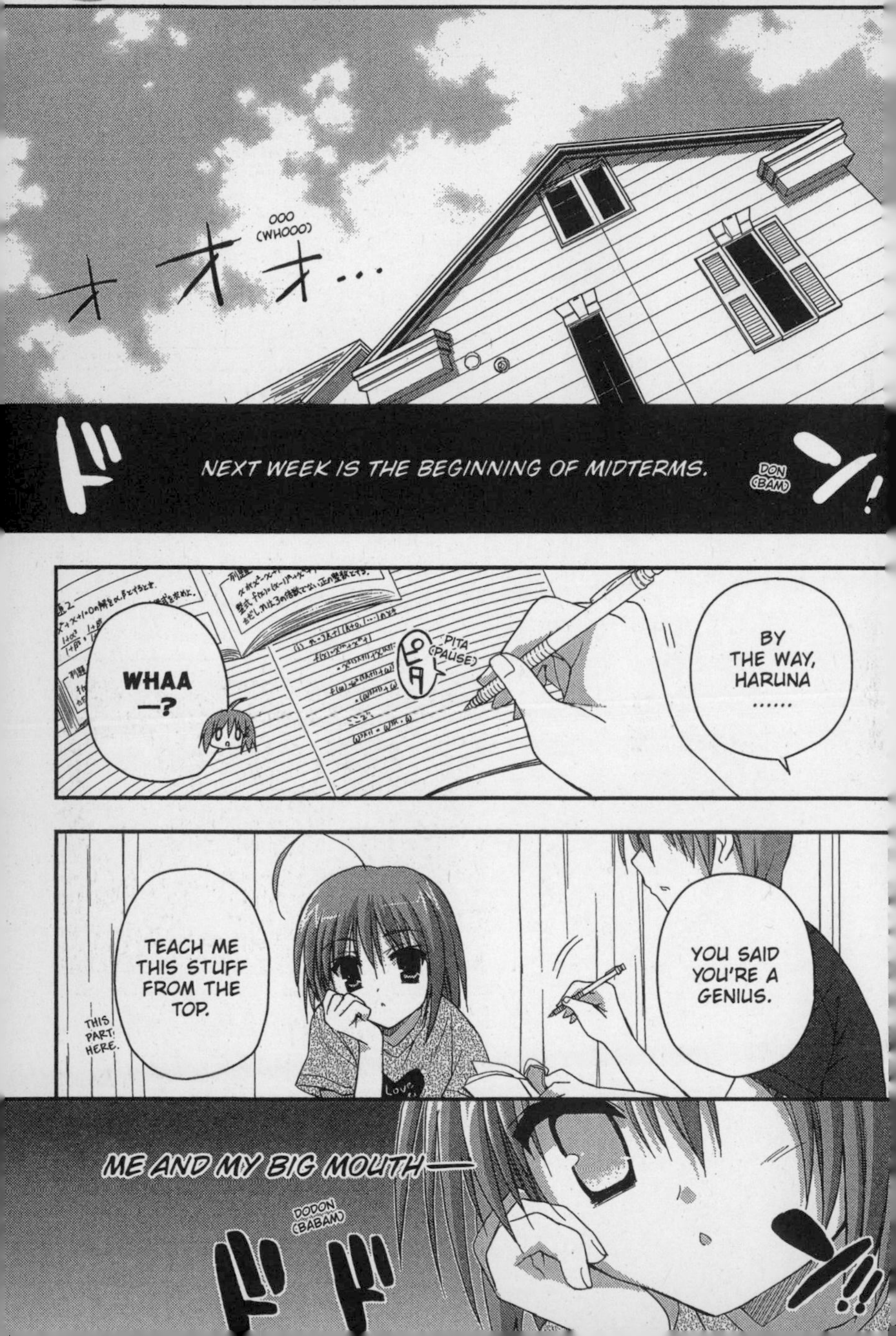
OOO (WHOOO)
NEXT WEEK IS THE BEGINNING OF MIDTERMS.
DON (BAM)
BY THE WAY, HARUNA ......
PITA (PAUSE)
WHAA —?
YOU SAID YOU'RE A GENIUS.
TEACH ME THIS STUFF FROM THE TOP.
THIS PART HERE.
ME AND MY BIG MOUTH—
DODON (BABAM)

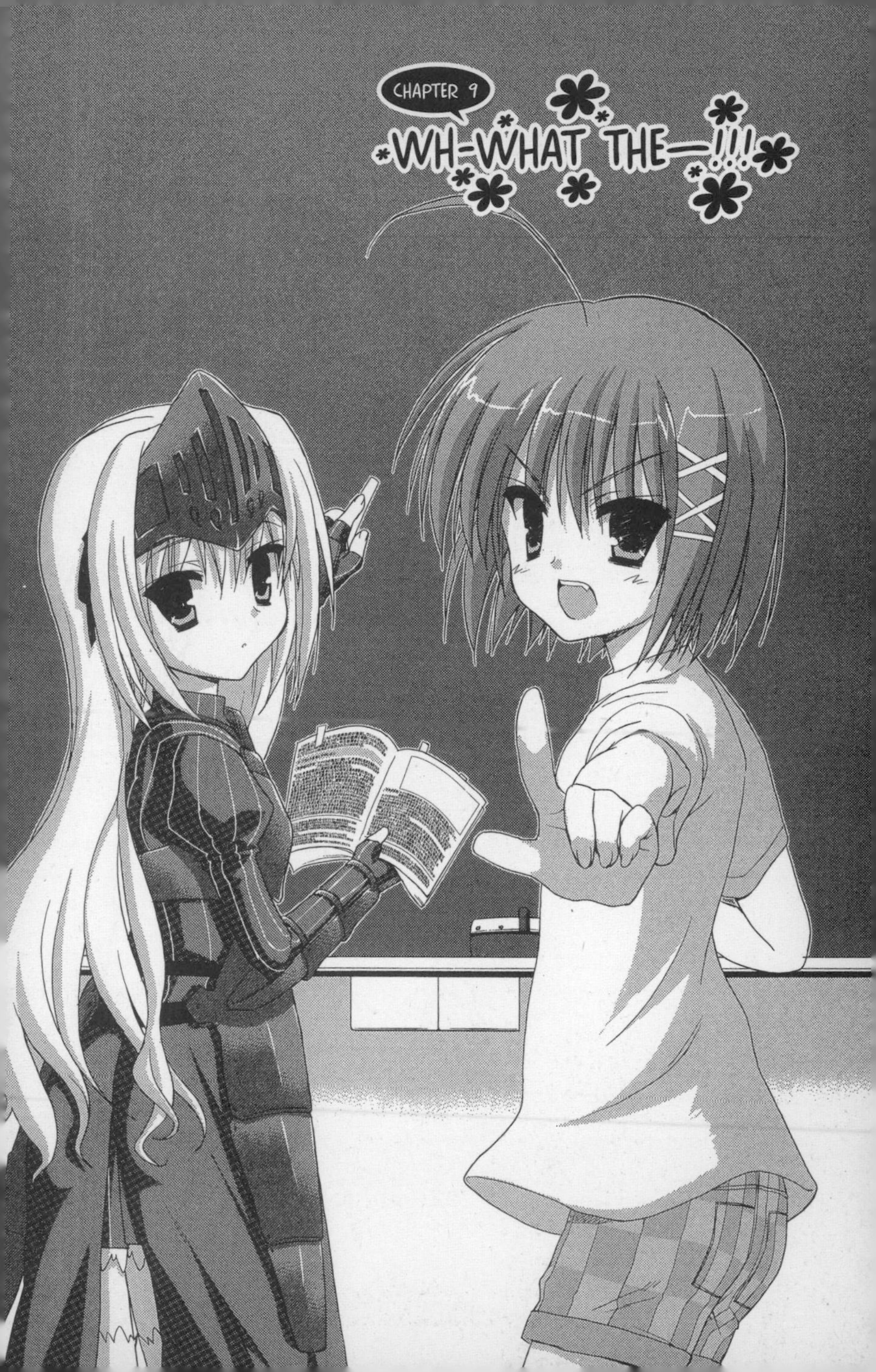
CHAPTER 9
WH-WHAT THE—!!!

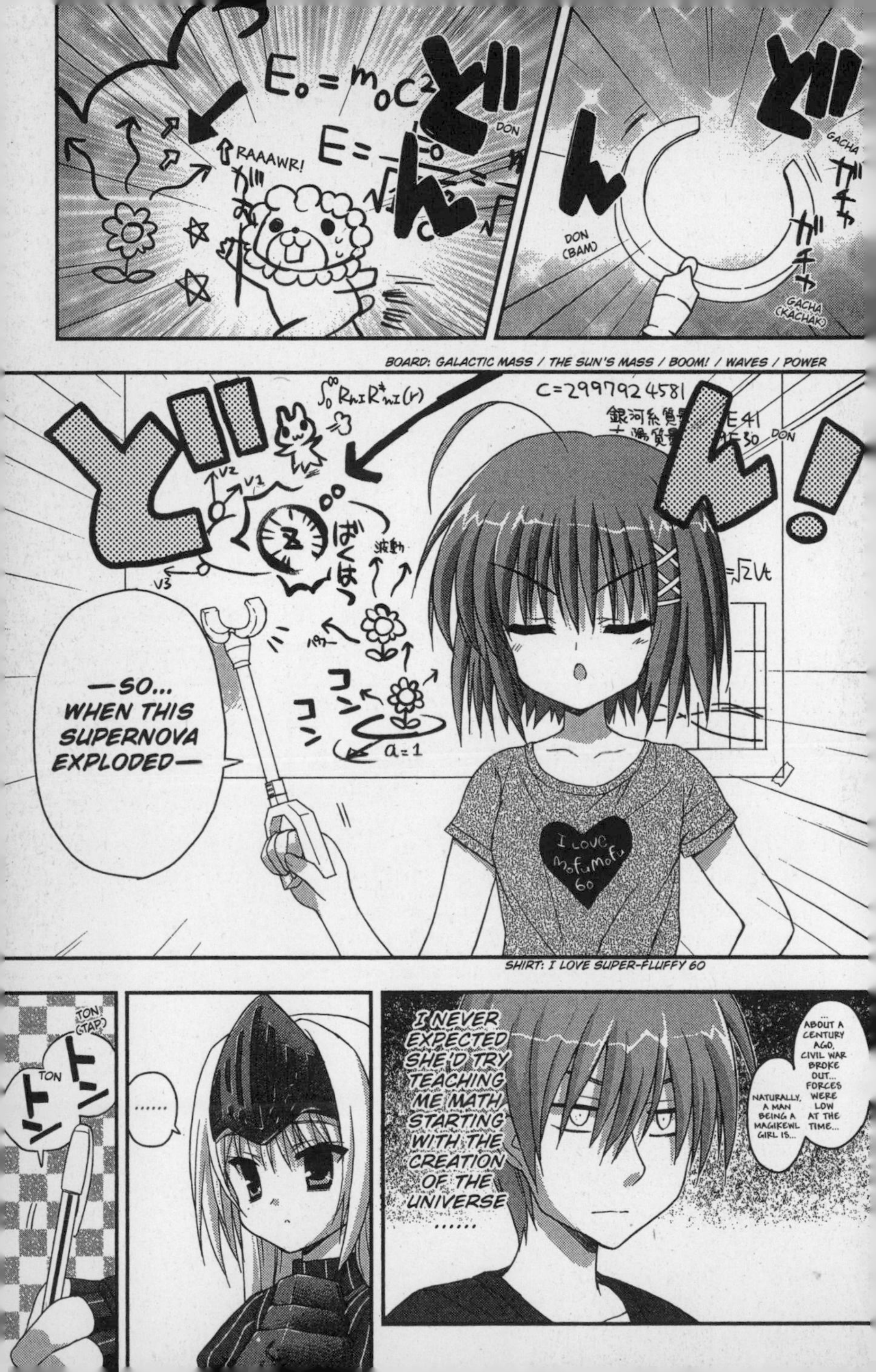
GACHA
DON
GACHA (KACHAK)
DON (BAM)
DON
RAAAWR!
$E_0 = m_0c^2$
BOARD: GALACTIC MASS / THE SUN'S MASS / BOOM! / WAVES / POWER
C=2997924581
DON
—SO... WHEN THIS SUPERNOVA EXPLODED—
SHIRT: I LOVE SUPER-FLUFFY 60
I LOVE mofumofu 60
...ABOUT A CENTURY AGO, CIVIL WAR BROKE OUT... FORCES WERE LOW AT THE TIME...
NATURALLY, A MAN BEING A MAGIKEWL GIRL IS...
I NEVER EXPECTED SHE'D TRY TEACHING ME MATH STARTING WITH THE CREATION OF THE UNIVERSE......
......
TON (TAP)
TON

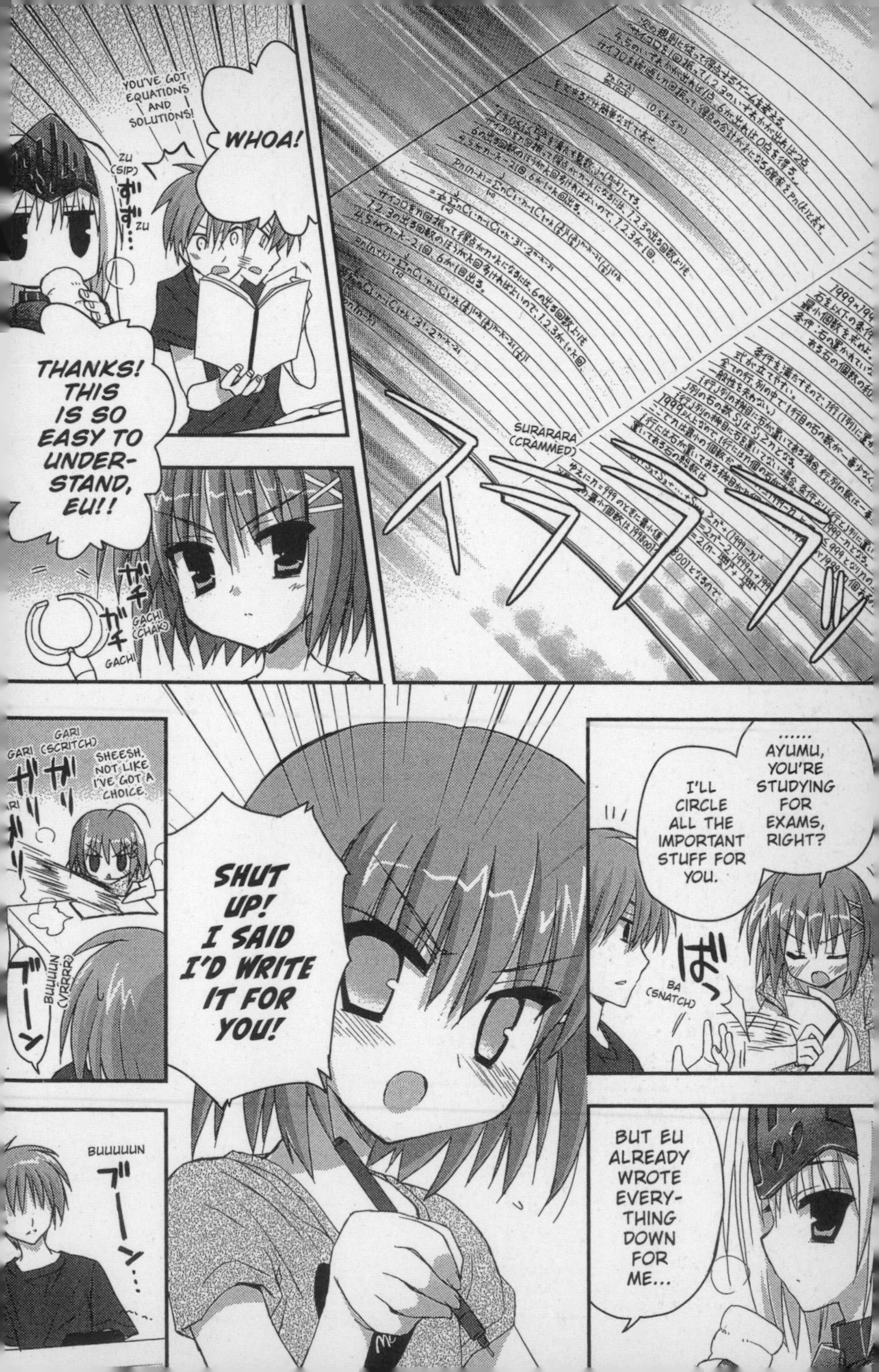

SURARARA (CRAMMED)
スラララッ
WHOA!
YOU'VE GOT EQUATIONS AND SOLUTIONS!
ZU (SIP)
ずずっ
ZU...
THANKS! THIS IS SO EASY TO UNDER-STAND, EU!!
ガチ ガチ
GACHI (CHAK)
GACHI
......
AYUMU, YOU'RE STUDYING FOR EXAMS, RIGHT?
I'LL CIRCLE ALL THE IMPORTANT STUFF FOR YOU.
ばっ
BA (SNATCH)
SHUT UP! I SAID I'D WRITE IT FOR YOU!
GARI (SCRITCH)
GARI
SHEESH, NOT LIKE I'VE GOT A CHOICE
ガリ ガリ
BUUUUN (VRRRR)
ブーン
BUT EU ALREADY WROTE EVERY-THING DOWN FOR ME...
BUUUUUN
ブーン...

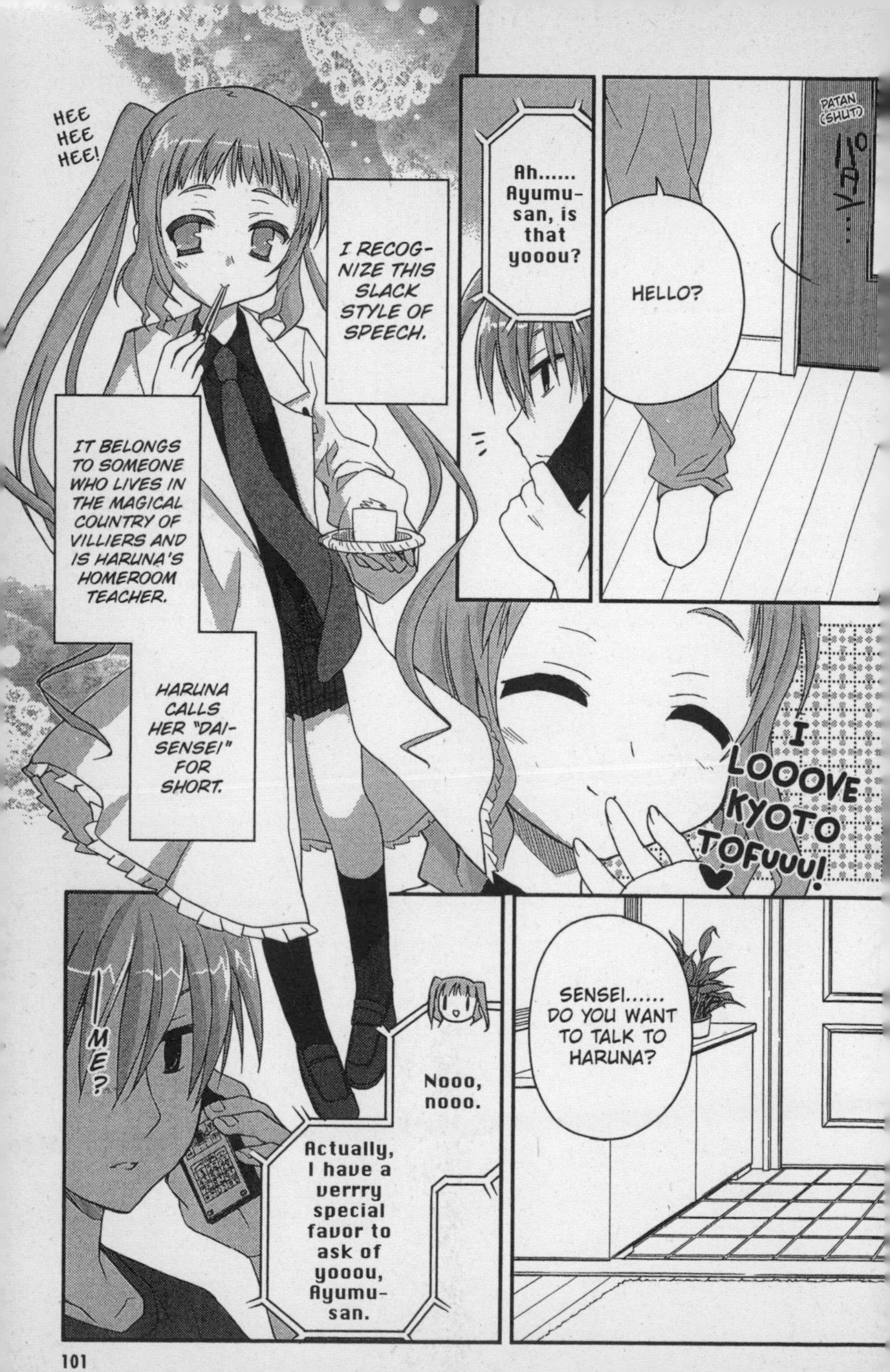
PATAN (SHUT)
HELLO?
Ah...... Ayumu-san, is that yooou?
HEE HEE HEE!
I RECOGNIZE THIS SLACK STYLE OF SPEECH.
IT BELONGS TO SOMEONE WHO LIVES IN THE MAGICAL COUNTRY OF VILLIERS AND IS HARUNA'S HOMEROOM TEACHER.
HARUNA CALLS HER "DAI-SENSEI" FOR SHORT.
I LOOOVE KYOTO TOFUUU!
SENSEI...... DO YOU WANT TO TALK TO HARUNA?
Nooo, nooo.
Actually, I have a verrry special favor to ask of yooou, Ayumu-san.
ME?

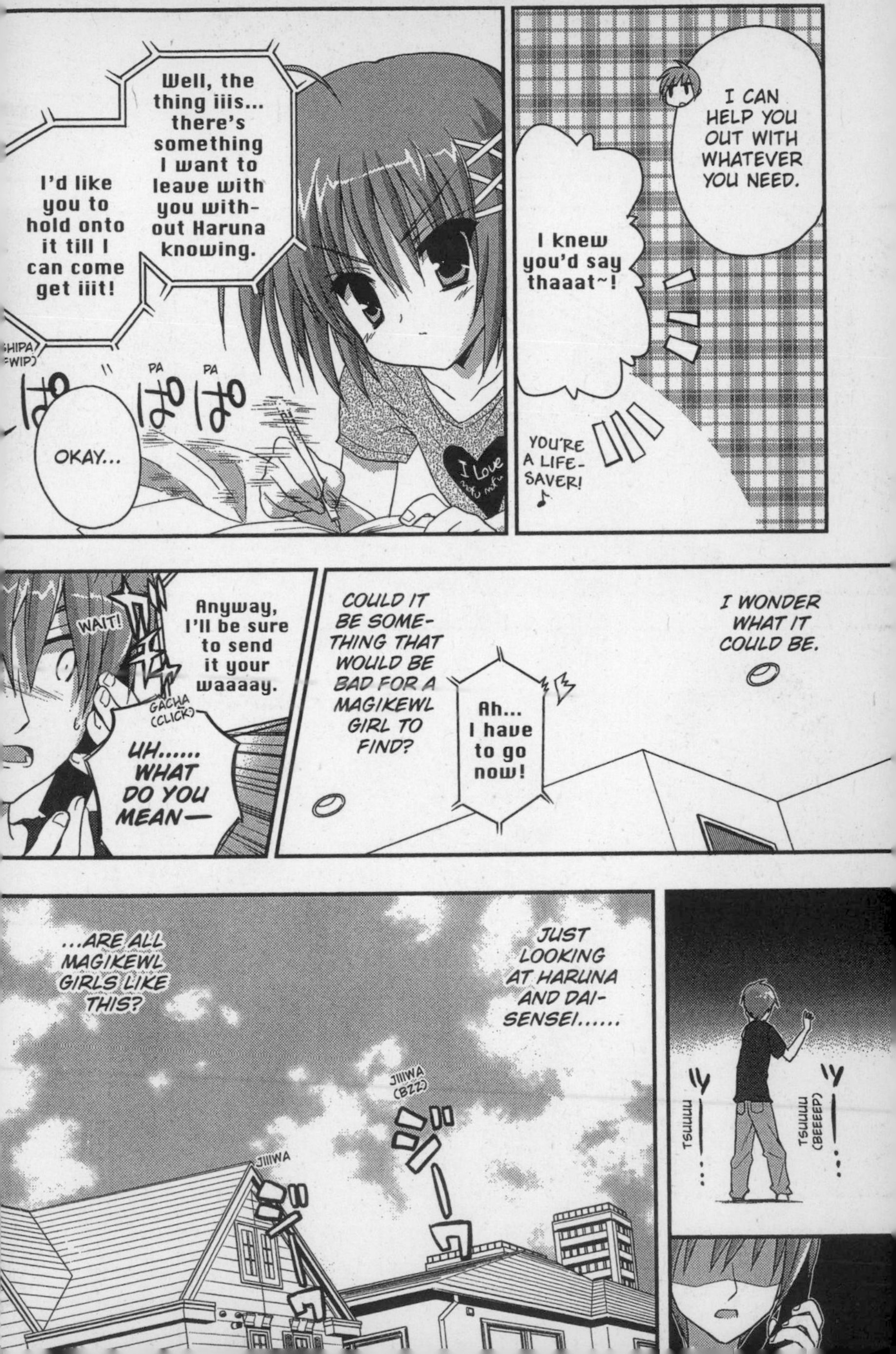
I CAN HELP YOU OUT WITH WHATEVER YOU NEED.
I knew you'd say thaaat~!
YOU'RE A LIFE-SAVER! ♪
Well, the thing iiis... there's something I want to leave with you with-out Haruna knowing.
I'd like you to hold onto it till I can come get iiit!
SHIPA (FWIP)
PA
PA
OKAY...
I WONDER WHAT IT COULD BE.
COULD IT BE SOME-THING THAT WOULD BE BAD FOR A MAGIKEWL GIRL TO FIND?
Ah... I have to go now!
Anyway, I'll be sure to send it your waaaay.
WAIT!
GACHA (CLICK)
UH...... WHAT DO YOU MEAN—
TSUUUUN (BEEEEP)...
TSUUUUN...
JUST LOOKING AT HARUNA AND DAI-SENSEI......
...ARE ALL MAGIKEWL GIRLS LIKE THIS?
JIIIWA (BZZ)
JIIIWA

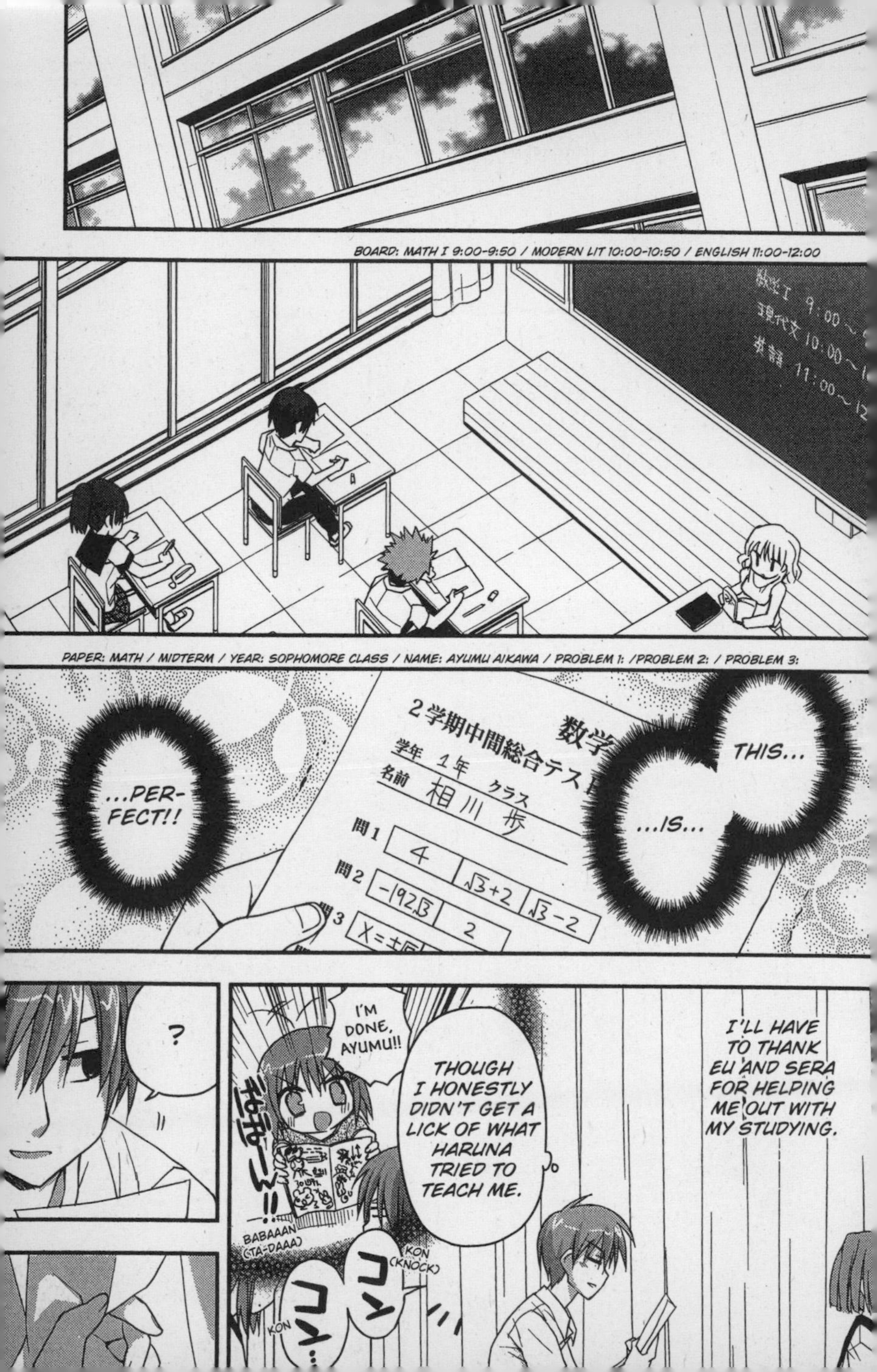
BOARD: MATH I 9:00-9:50 / MODERN LIT 10:00-10:50 / ENGLISH 11:00-12:00
PAPER: MATH / MIDTERM / YEAR: SOPHOMORE CLASS / NAME: AYUMU AIKAWA / PROBLEM 1: /PROBLEM 2: / PROBLEM 3:
THIS...
...IS...
...PER-FECT!!
I'LL HAVE TO THANK EU AND SERA FOR HELPING ME OUT WITH MY STUDYING.
THOUGH I HONESTLY DIDN'T GET A LICK OF WHAT HARUNA TRIED TO TEACH ME.
I'M DONE, AYUMU!!
BABAAAN (TA-DAAA)
KON (KNOCK)
KON
?

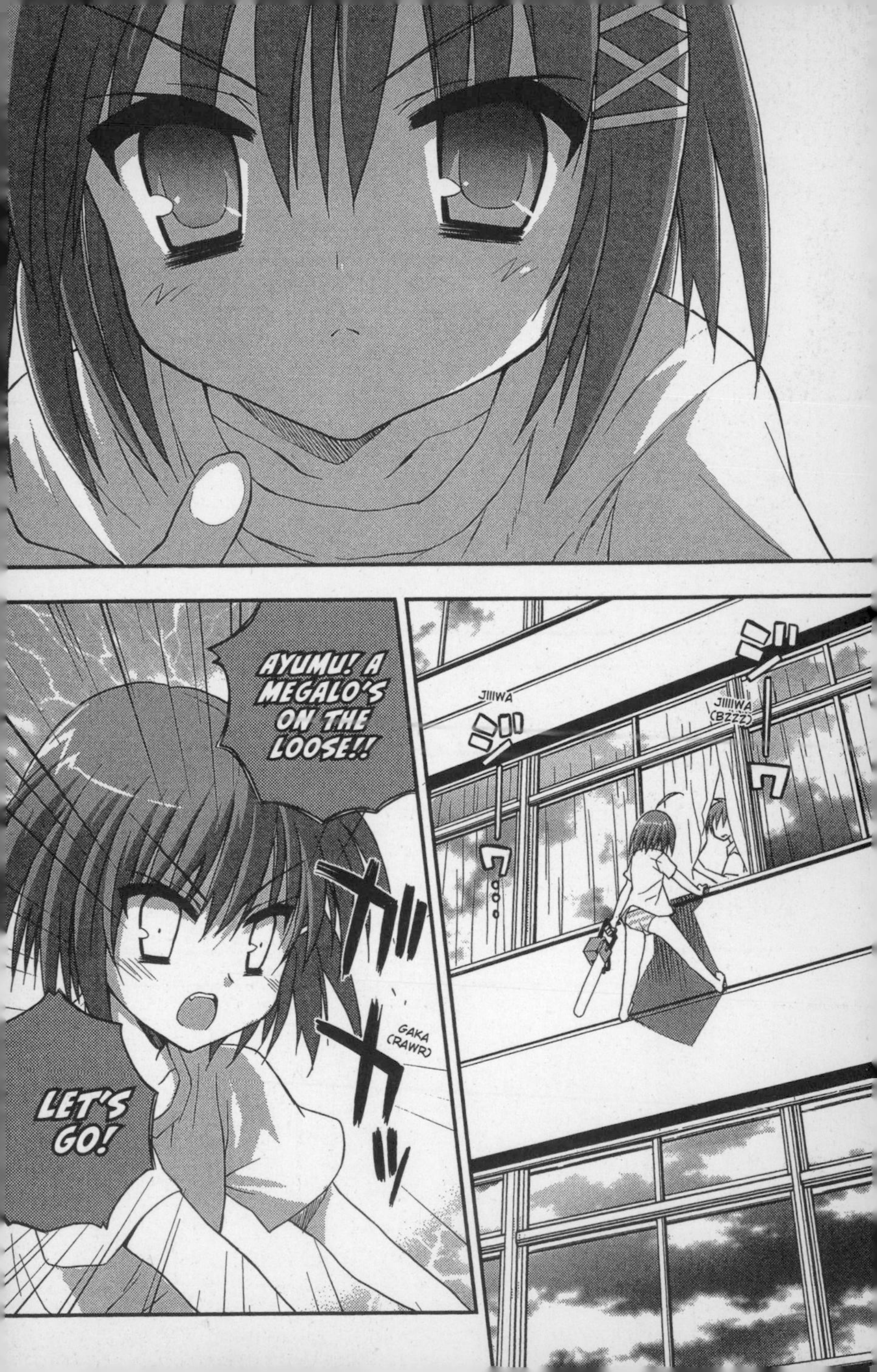

JIIIWA
JIIIWA (BZZZ)
AYUMU! A MEGALO'S ON THE LOOSE!!
GAKA (RAWR)
LET'S GO!

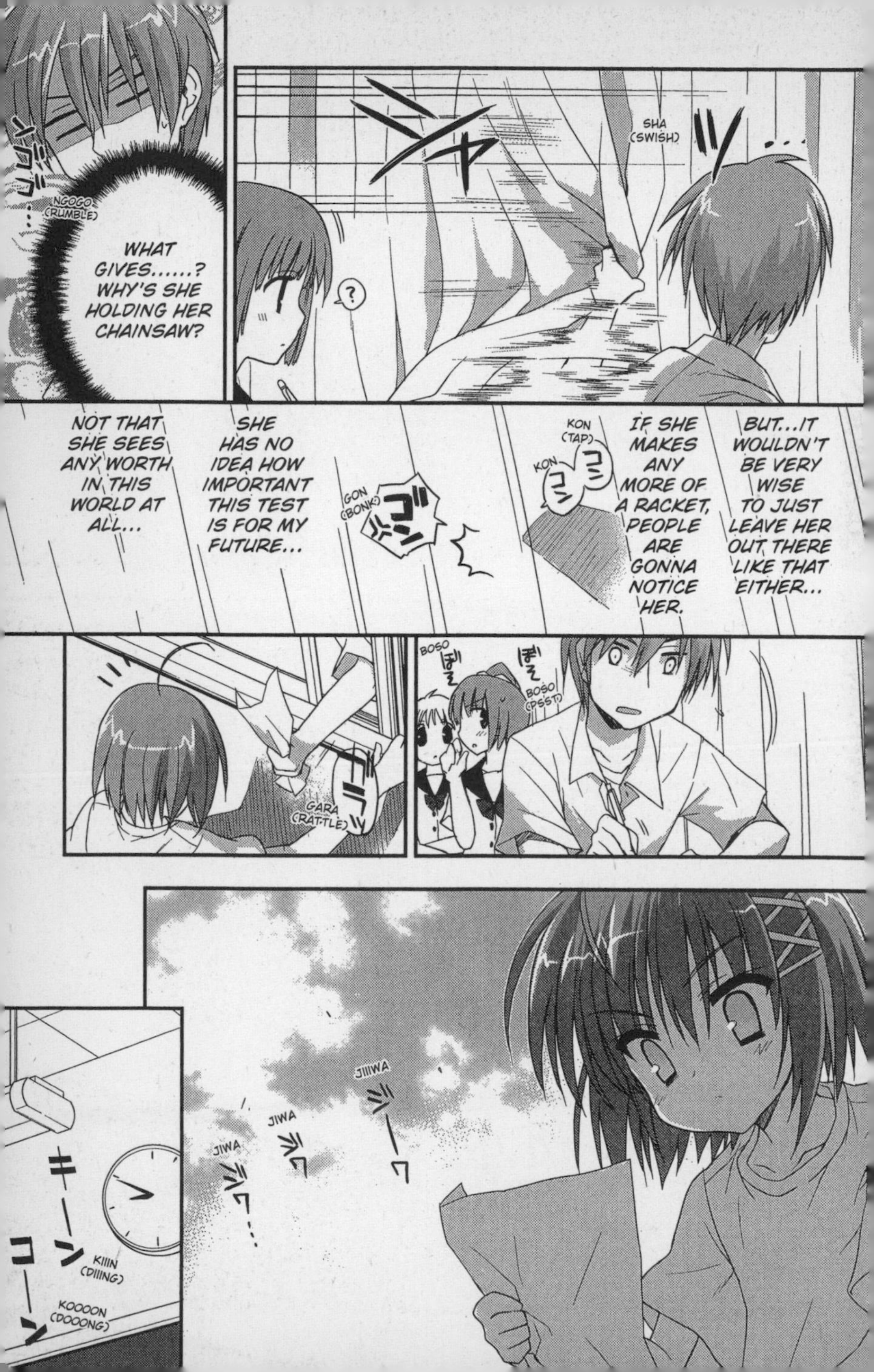
SHA (SWISH)
NGOGO (RUMBLE)
WHAT GIVES......? WHY'S SHE HOLDING HER CHAINSAW?
BUT...IT WOULDN'T BE VERY WISE TO JUST LEAVE HER OUT THERE LIKE THAT EITHER...
IF SHE MAKES ANY MORE OF A RACKET, PEOPLE ARE GONNA NOTICE HER.
KON (TAP)
KON
GON (BONK!)
SHE HAS NO IDEA HOW IMPORTANT THIS TEST IS FOR MY FUTURE...
NOT THAT SHE SEES ANY WORTH IN THIS WORLD AT ALL...
BOSO
BOSO (PSST)
GARA (RATTLE)
JIIIWA
JIWA
JIWA
KIIIN (DIIING)
KOOOON (DOOONG)

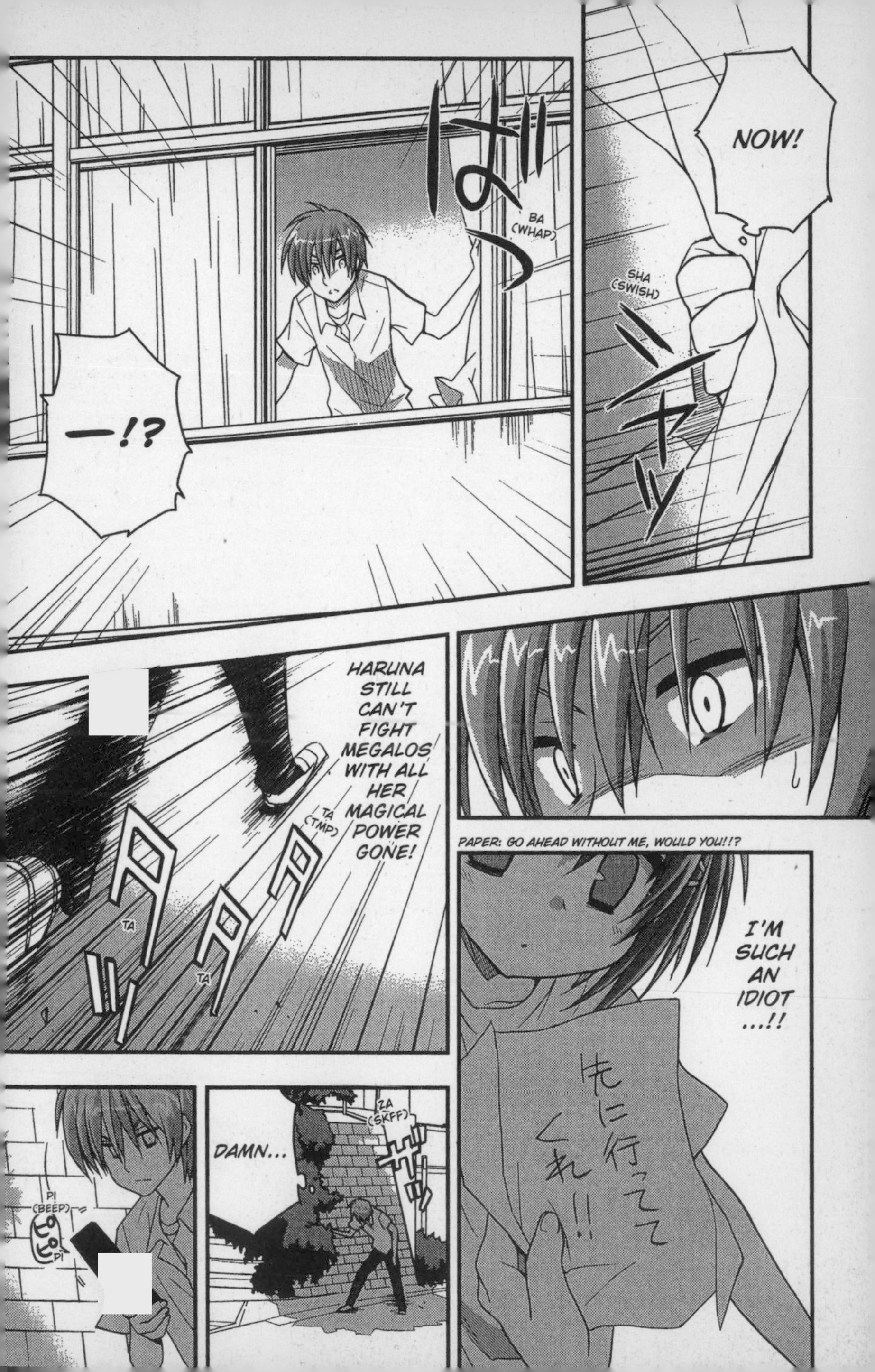
NOW!
SHA (SWISH)
BA (WHAP)
—!?
HARUNA STILL CAN'T FIGHT MEGALOS WITH ALL HER MAGICAL POWER GONE!
TA (TMP)
TA
TA
PAPER: GO AHEAD WITHOUT ME, WOULD YOU!!?
I'M SUCH AN IDIOT ...!!
先に行っててくれ!!
ZA (SKFF)
DAMN...
PI (BEEP)
PI

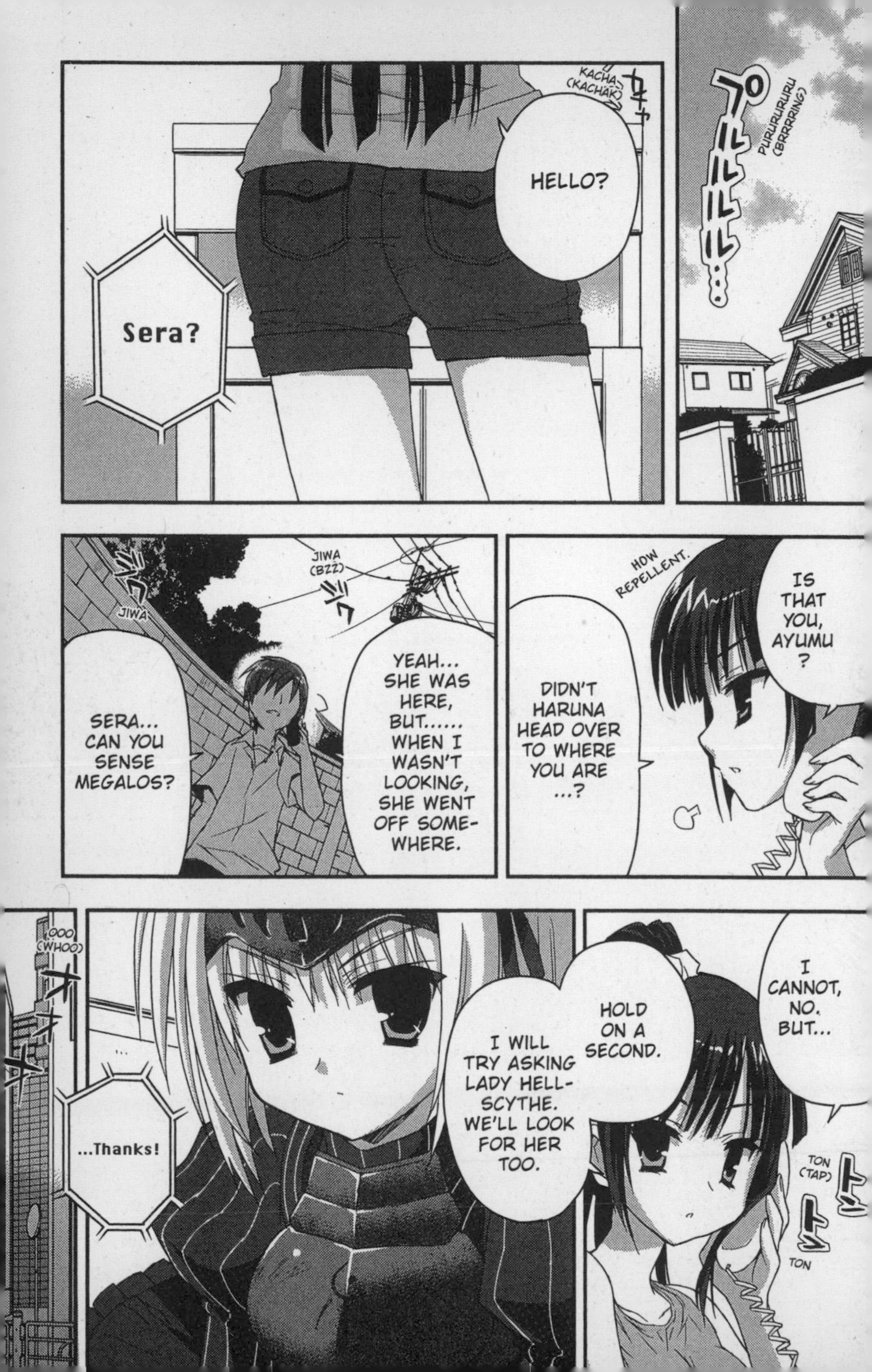
PURURURURU (BRRRRING)
KACHA (KACHAK)
HELLO?
Sera?
IS THAT YOU, AYUMU?
HOW REPELLENT.
DIDN'T HARUNA HEAD OVER TO WHERE YOU ARE ...?
JIWA (BZZ)
JIWA
YEAH... SHE WAS HERE, BUT...... WHEN I WASN'T LOOKING, SHE WENT OFF SOME-WHERE.
SERA... CAN YOU SENSE MEGALOS?
I CANNOT, NO. BUT...
TON (TAP)
TON
HOLD ON A SECOND.
I WILL TRY ASKING LADY HELL-SCYTHE. WE'LL LOOK FOR HER TOO.
...
...Thanks!
OOO (WHOO)

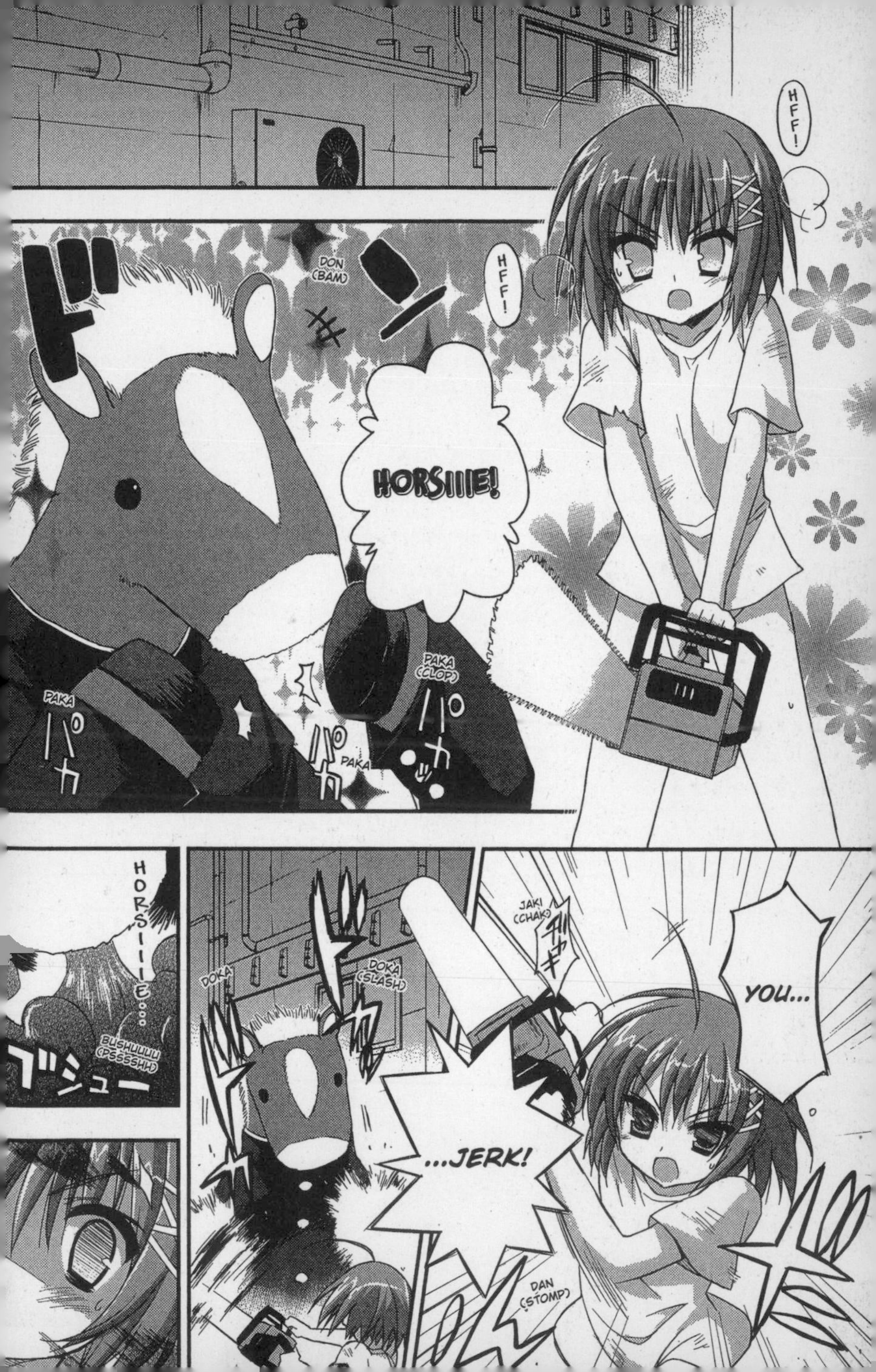
HFF!
HFF!
ド
DON (BAM)
HORSIIIE!
PAKA (CLOP)
パカ
PAKA
パカ
PAKA
パカ
YOU...
JAKI (CHAK)
DOKA (SLASH)
DOKA
HORSIIIE...
BUSHUUUU (PSSSSHH)
ブシュー
...JERK!
DAN (STOMP)

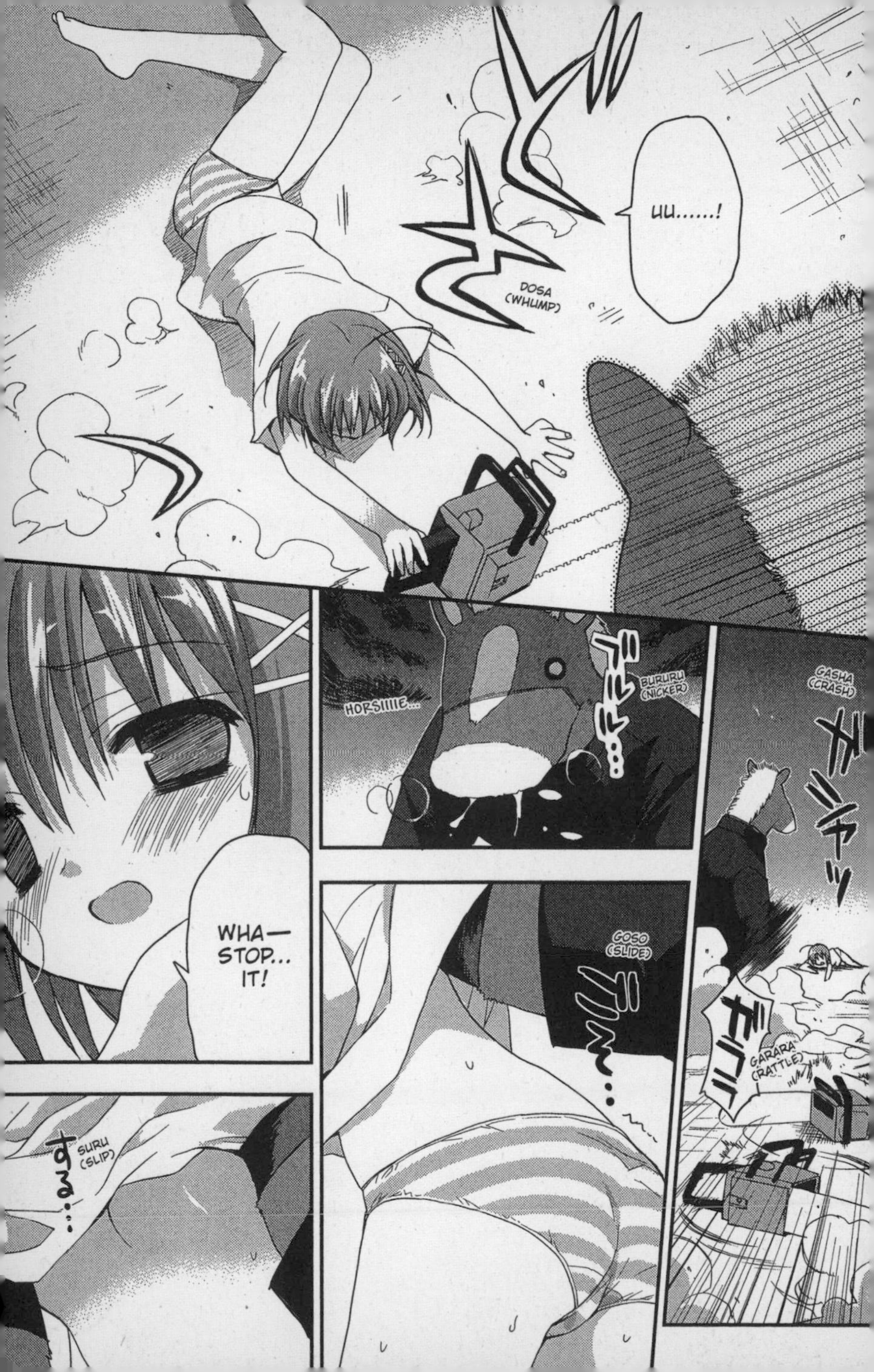

UU......!
DOSA (WHUMP)
BURURU (NICKER)
HORSIIIIE...
GASHA (CRASH)
WHA—STOP... IT!
GOSO (SLIDE)
GARARA (RATTLE)
SURU (SLIP)

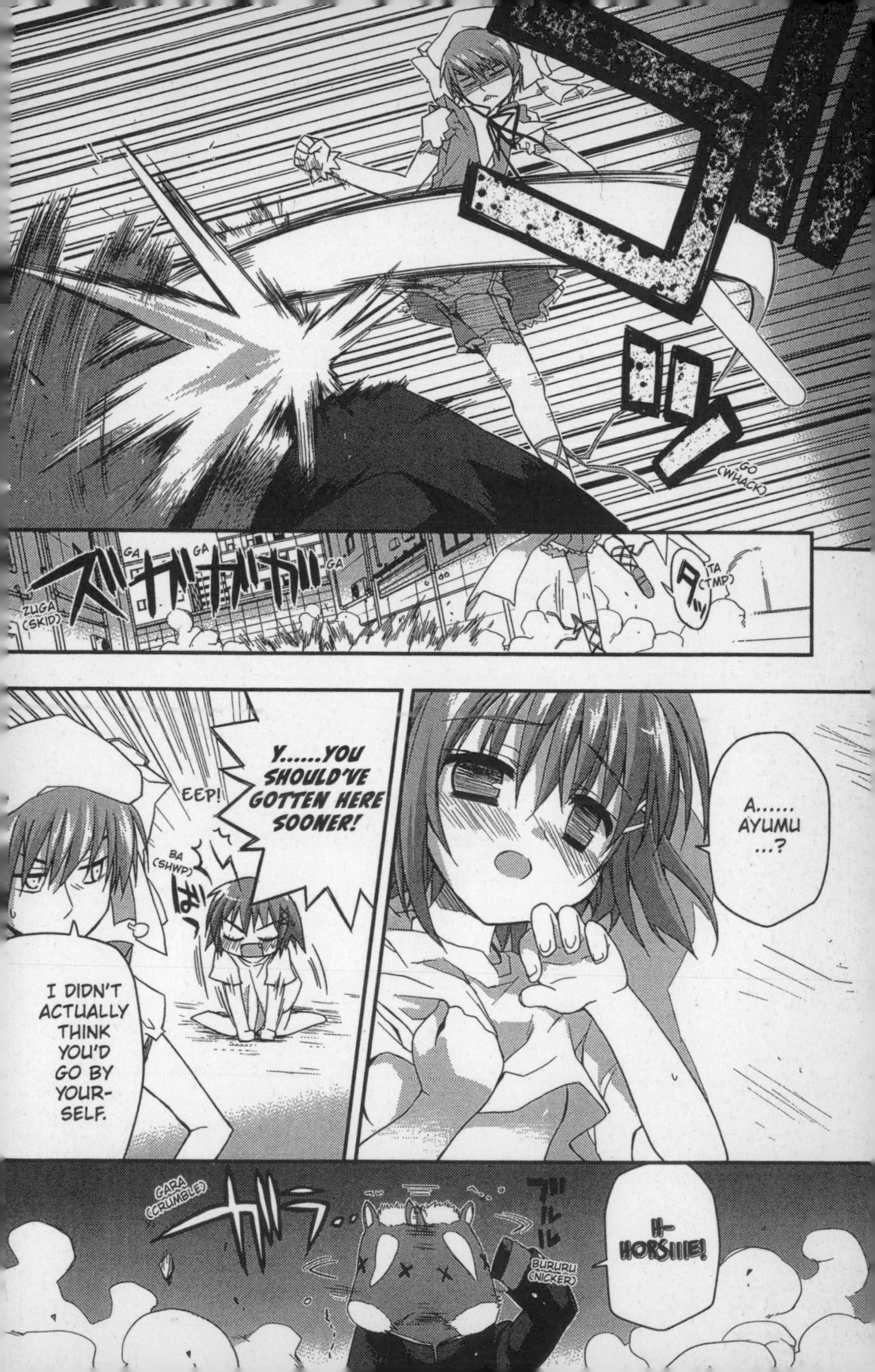

GO (WHACK)
TA (TMP)
GA
GA
GA
ZUGA (SKID)
A...... AYUMU ...?
Y......YOU SHOULD'VE GOTTEN HERE SOONER!
EEP!
BA (SHWP)
I DIDN'T ACTUALLY THINK YOU'D GO BY YOURSELF.
H-HORSIIIE!
BURURU (NICKER)
GARA (CRUMBLE)

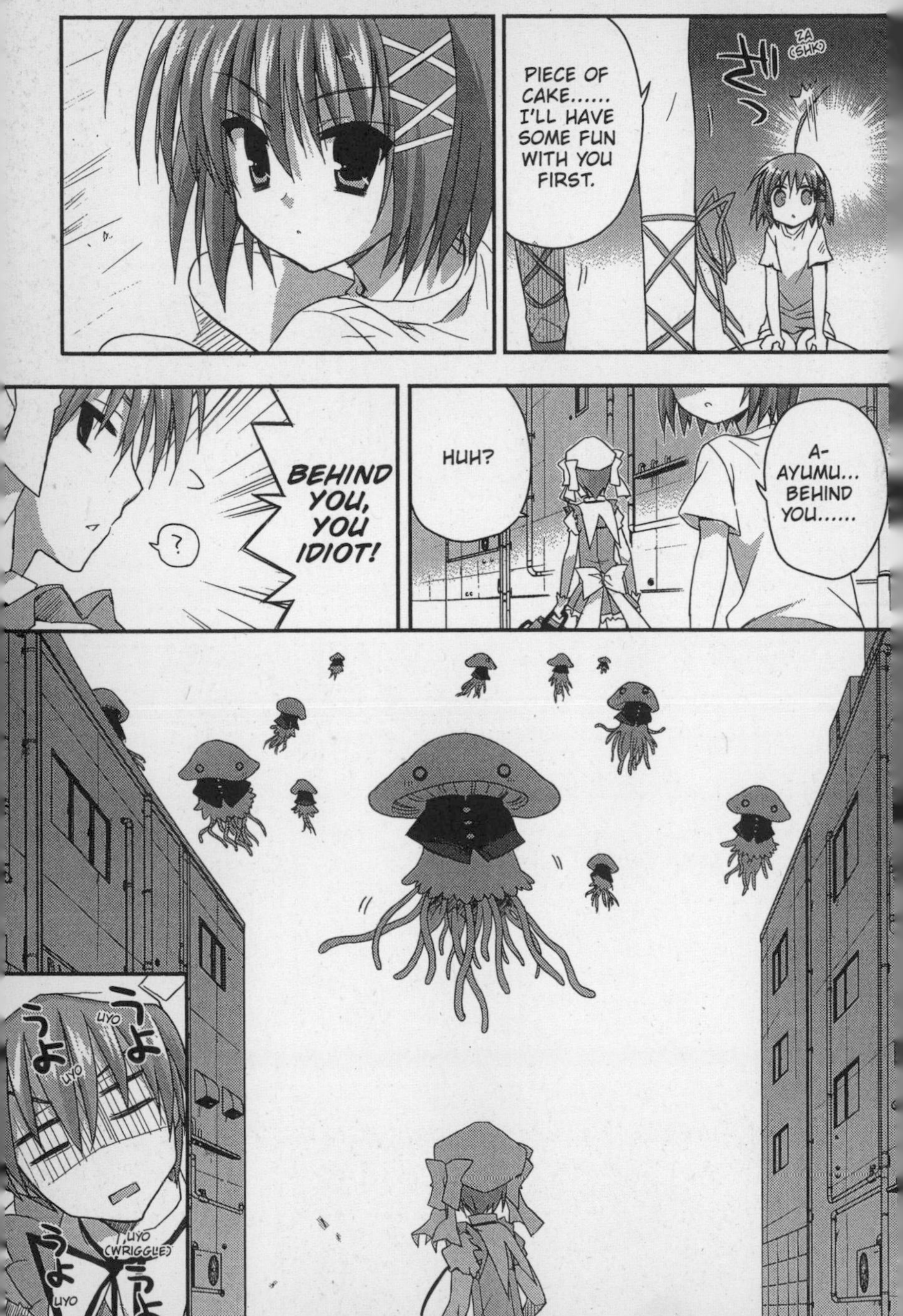

ZA (SHK)
PIECE OF CAKE...... I'LL HAVE SOME FUN WITH YOU FIRST.
A- AYUMU... BEHIND YOU......
HUH?
BEHIND YOU, YOU IDIOT!
?
UYO
UYO
UYO (WRIGGLE)
UYO

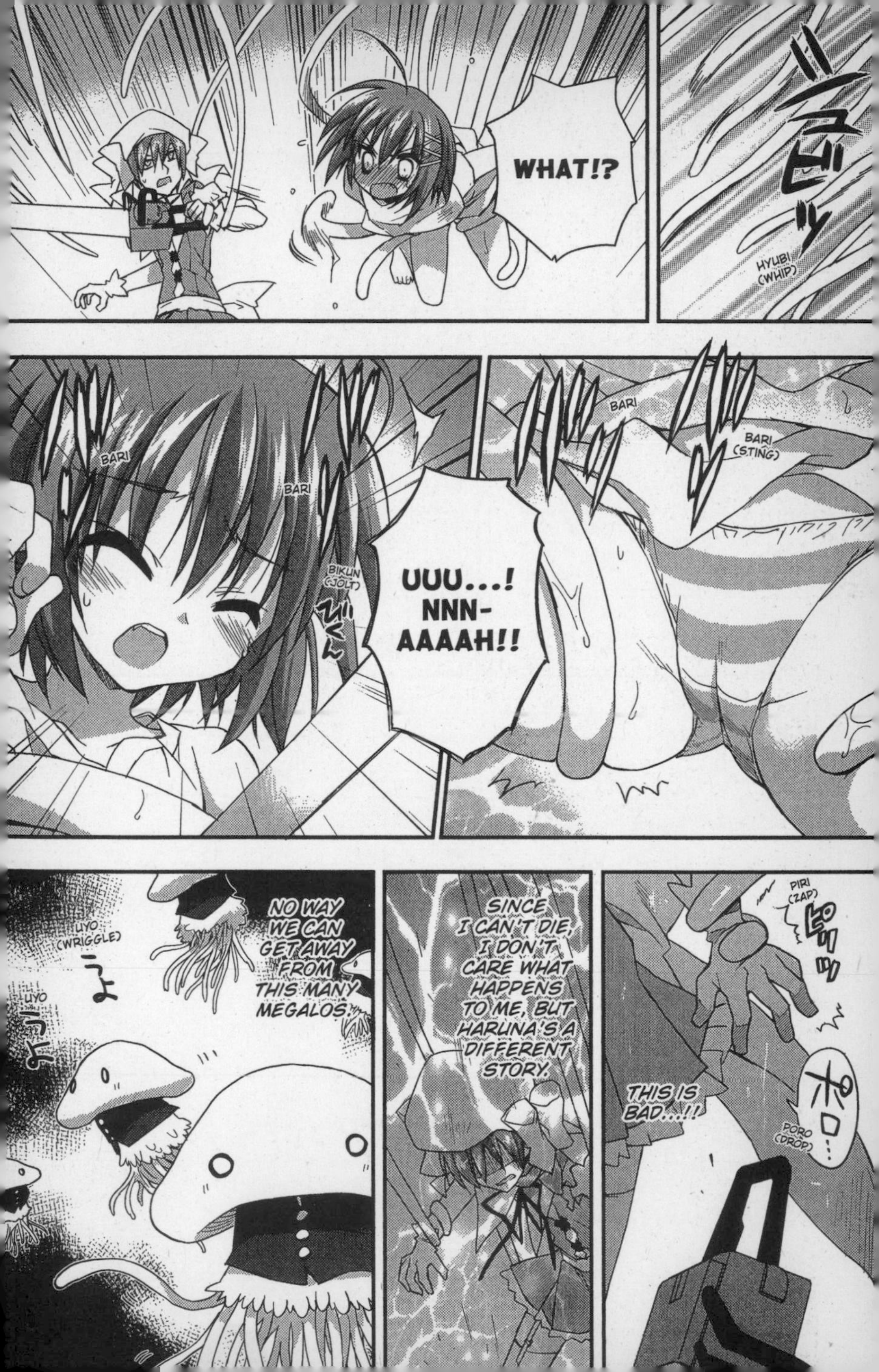

HYUBI (WHIP)
WHAT!?
BARI
BARI (STING)
UUU...! NNN-AAAAH!!
BIKUN (JOLT)
BARI
BARI
PIRI (ZAP)
PORO (DROP)
THIS IS BAD...!!
SINCE I CAN'T DIE, I DON'T CARE WHAT HAPPENS TO ME, BUT HARUNA'S A DIFFERENT STORY.
NO WAY WE CAN GET AWAY FROM THIS MANY MEGALOS.
UYO (WRIGGLE)
UYO

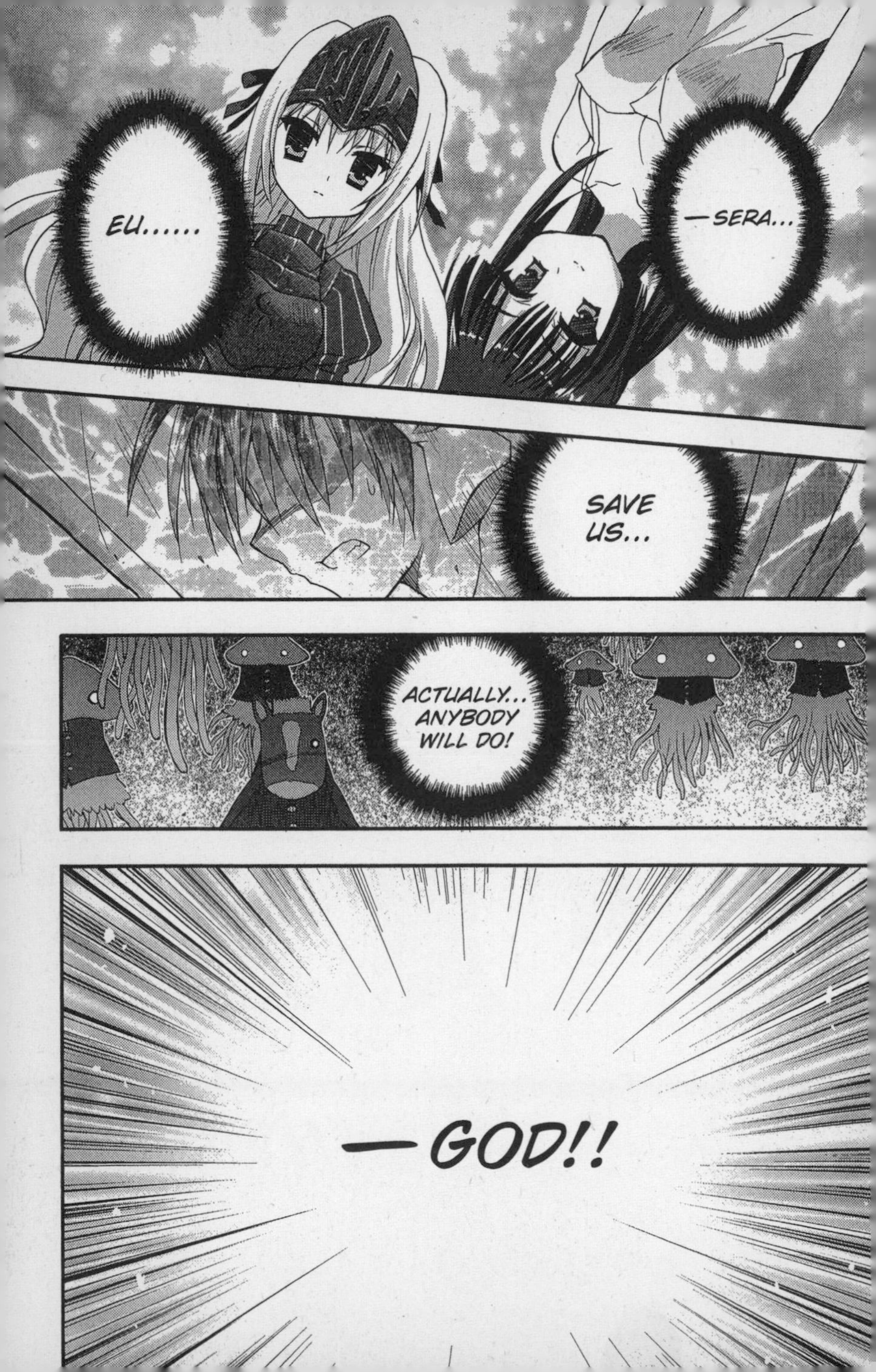
—SERA...
EU......
SAVE US...
ACTUALLY... ANYBODY WILL DO!
—GOD!!

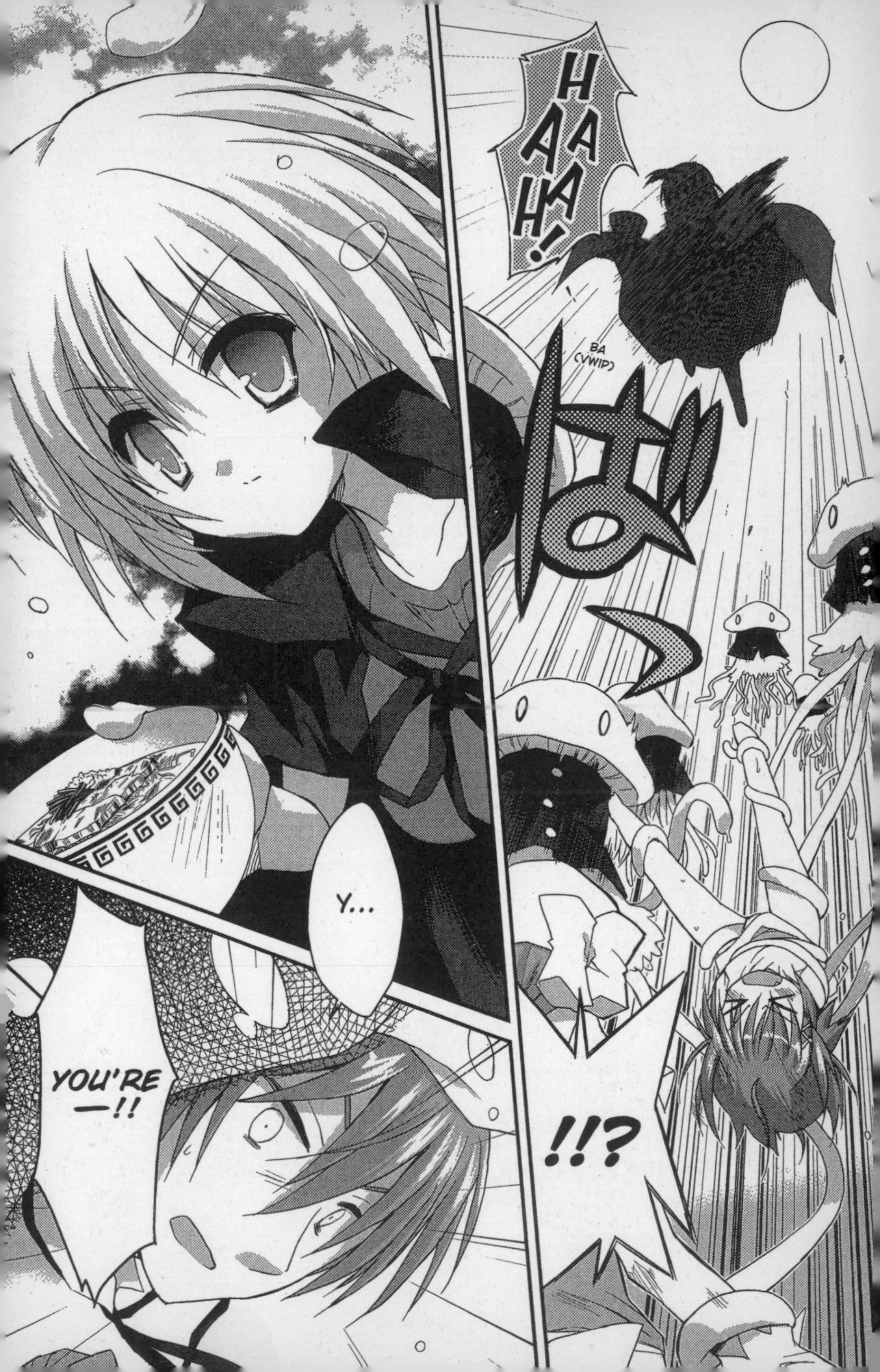
HAAAAH!
BA (VWIP)
ば
!!?
Y...
YOU'RE —!!

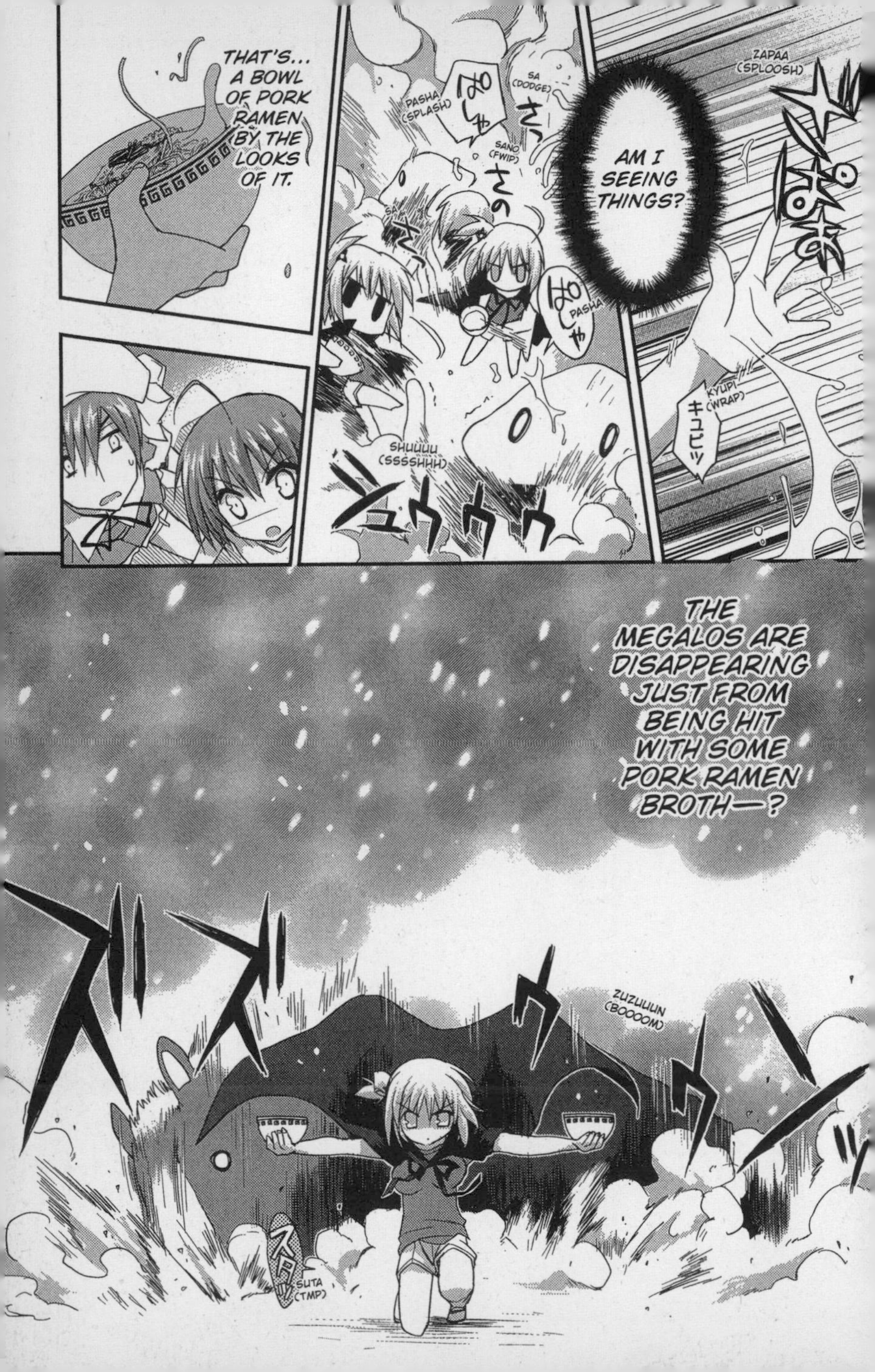

ZAPAA (SPLOOSH)
AM I SEEING THINGS?
KYUPI (WRAP)
キュピッ
SA (DODGE)
PASHA (SPLASH)
SANO (FWIP)
さの
SA
PASHA
SHUUUU (SSSSHHH)
シュウウウウ
THAT'S... A BOWL OF PORK RAMEN BY THE LOOKS OF IT.
THE MEGALOS ARE DISAPPEARING JUST FROM BEING HIT WITH SOME PORK RAMEN BROTH—?
ZUZUUUN (BOOOOM)
SUTA (TMP)

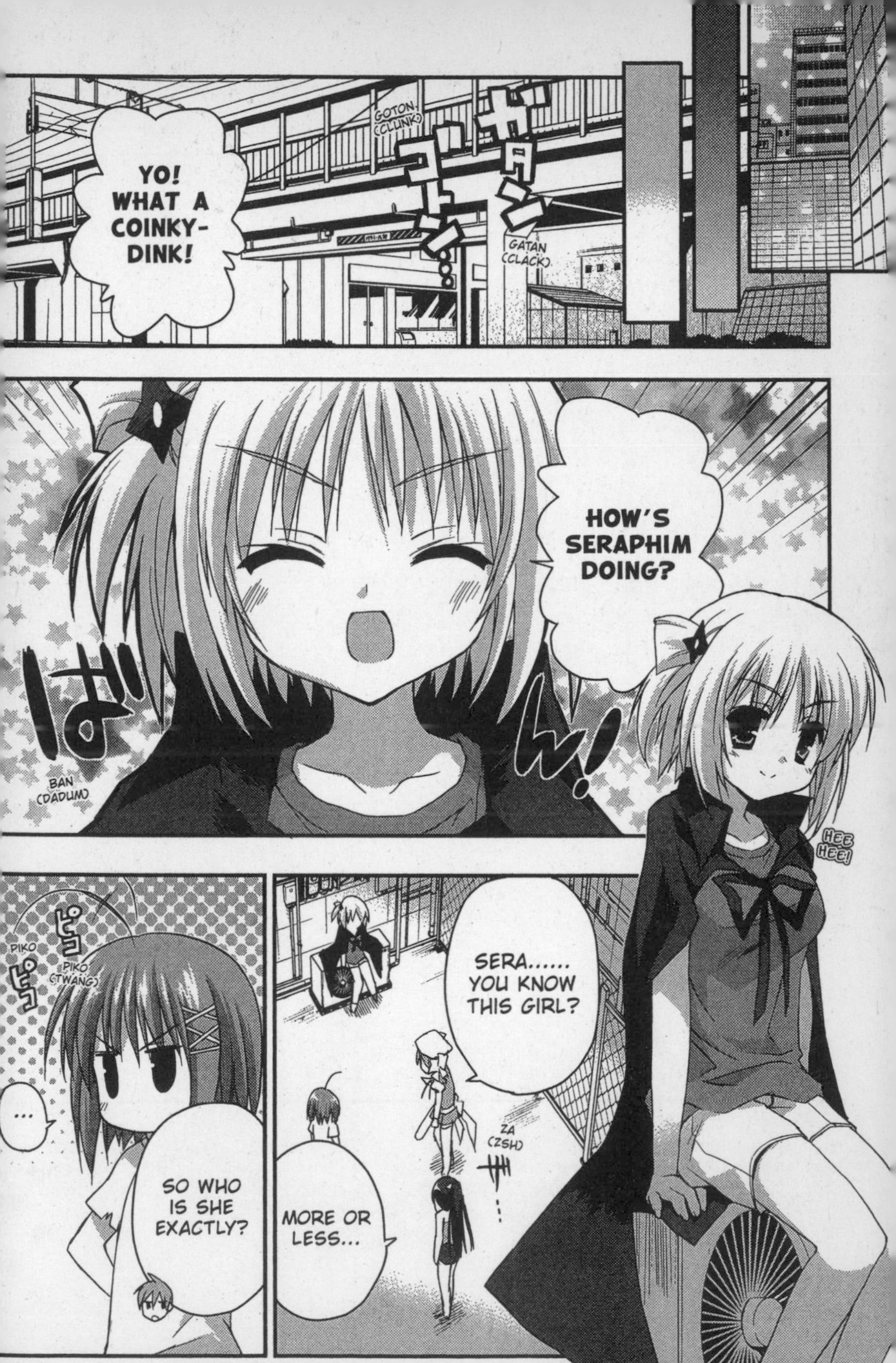
GOTON (CLUNK)
GATAN (CLACK)
YO! WHAT A COINKY-DINK!
HOW'S SERAPHIM DOING?
BAN (DADUM)
HEE HEE!
SERA...... YOU KNOW THIS GIRL?
ZA (ZSH)
MORE OR LESS...
PIKO PIKO (TWANG)
...
SO WHO IS SHE EXACTLY?

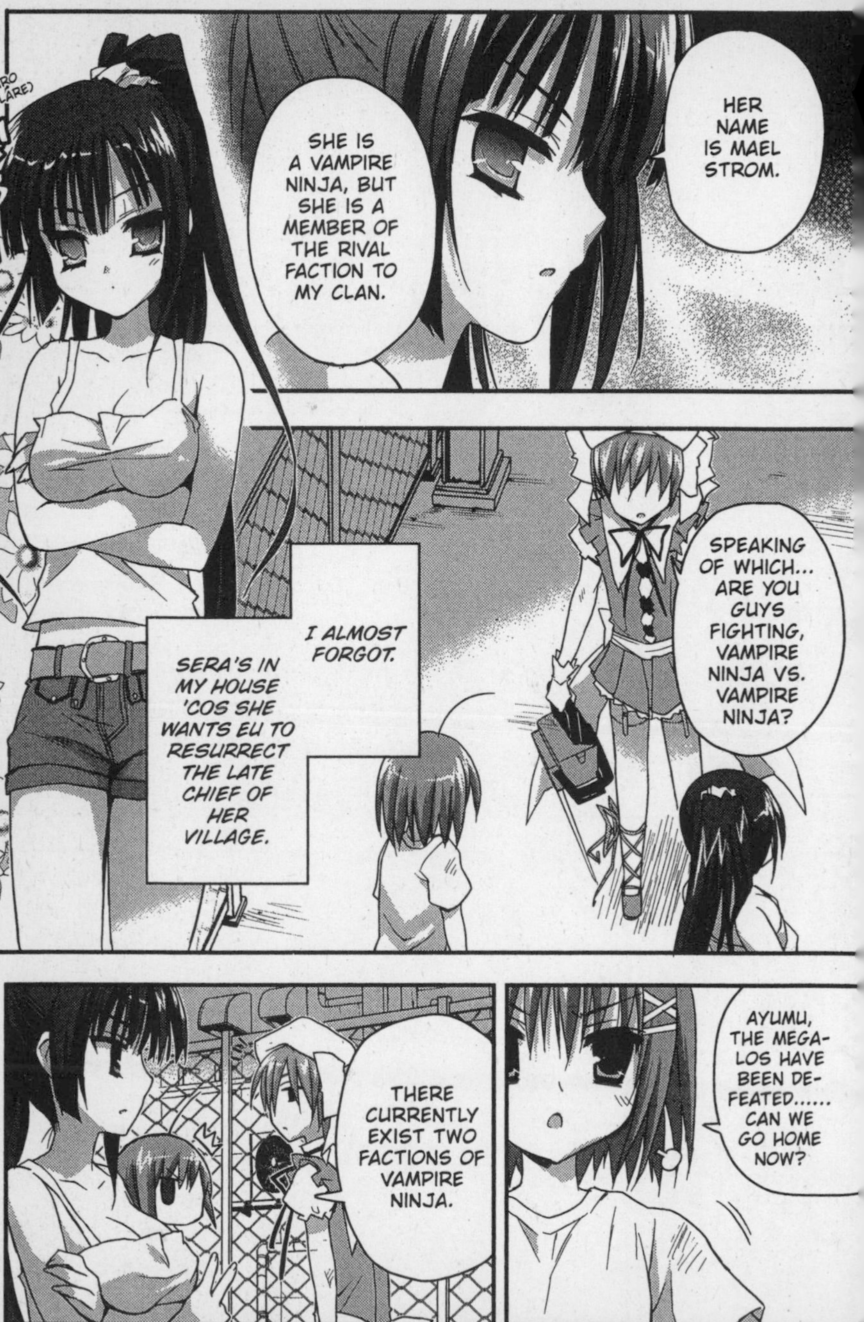
HER NAME IS MAEL STROM.
SHE IS A VAMPIRE NINJA, BUT SHE IS A MEMBER OF THE RIVAL FACTION TO MY CLAN.
JIRO (GLARE)
SPEAKING OF WHICH... ARE YOU GUYS FIGHTING, VAMPIRE NINJA VS. VAMPIRE NINJA?
I ALMOST FORGOT.
SERA'S IN MY HOUSE 'COS SHE WANTS EU TO RESURRECT THE LATE CHIEF OF HER VILLAGE.
AYUMU, THE MEGA-LOS HAVE BEEN DE-FEATED...... CAN WE GO HOME NOW?
THERE CURRENTLY EXIST TWO FACTIONS OF VAMPIRE NINJA.

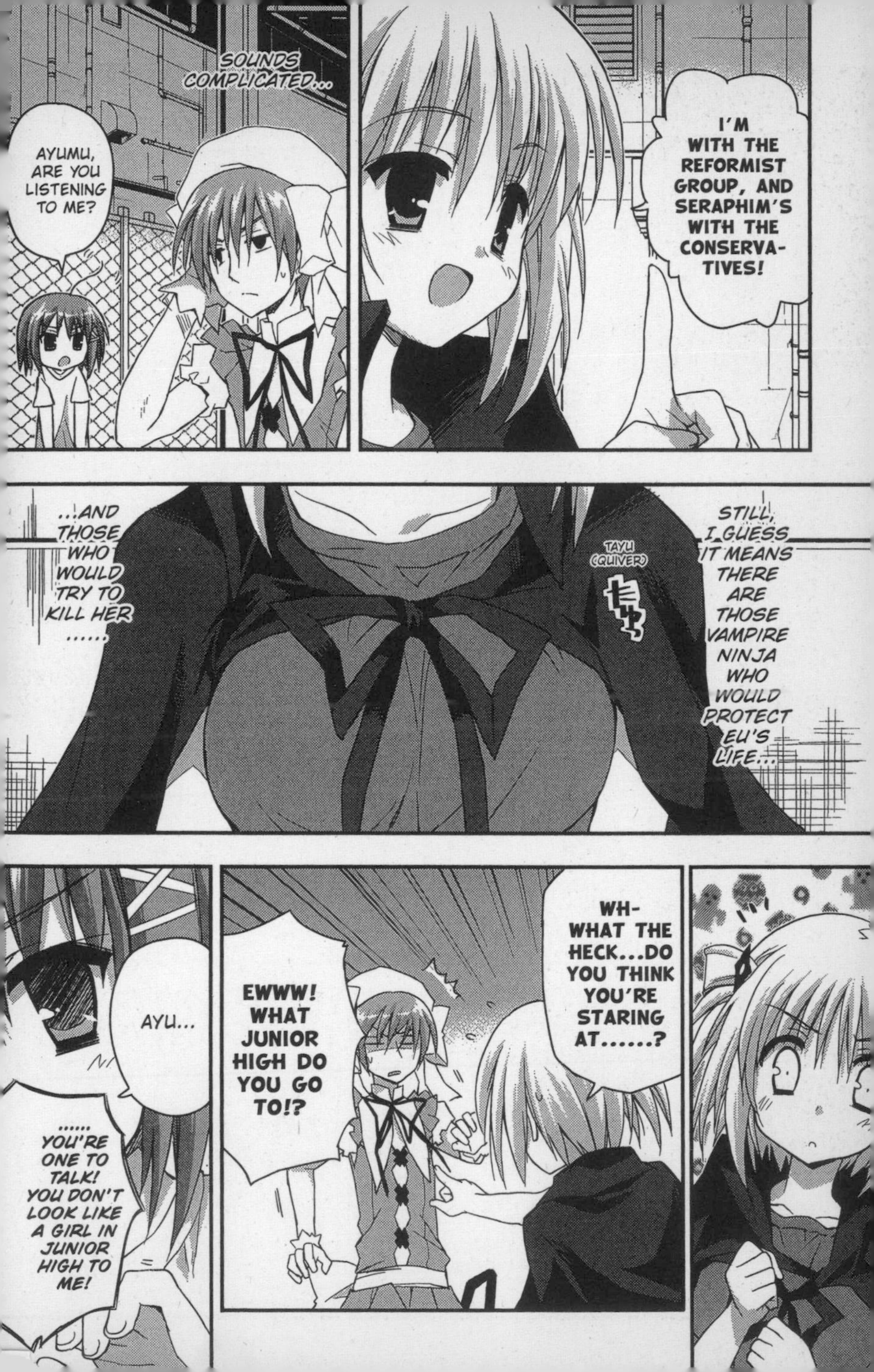
I'M WITH THE REFORMIST GROUP, AND SERAPHIM'S WITH THE CONSERVATIVES!
SOUNDS COMPLICATED...
AYUMU, ARE YOU LISTENING TO ME?
STILL, I GUESS IT MEANS THERE ARE THOSE VAMPIRE NINJA WHO WOULD PROTECT EU'S LIFE...
TAYU (QUIVER)
...AND THOSE WHO WOULD TRY TO KILL HER ......
WH-WHAT THE HECK...DO YOU THINK YOU'RE STARING AT......?
EWWW! WHAT JUNIOR HIGH DO YOU GO TO!?
AYU...
......YOU'RE ONE TO TALK! YOU DON'T LOOK LIKE A GIRL IN JUNIOR HIGH TO ME!

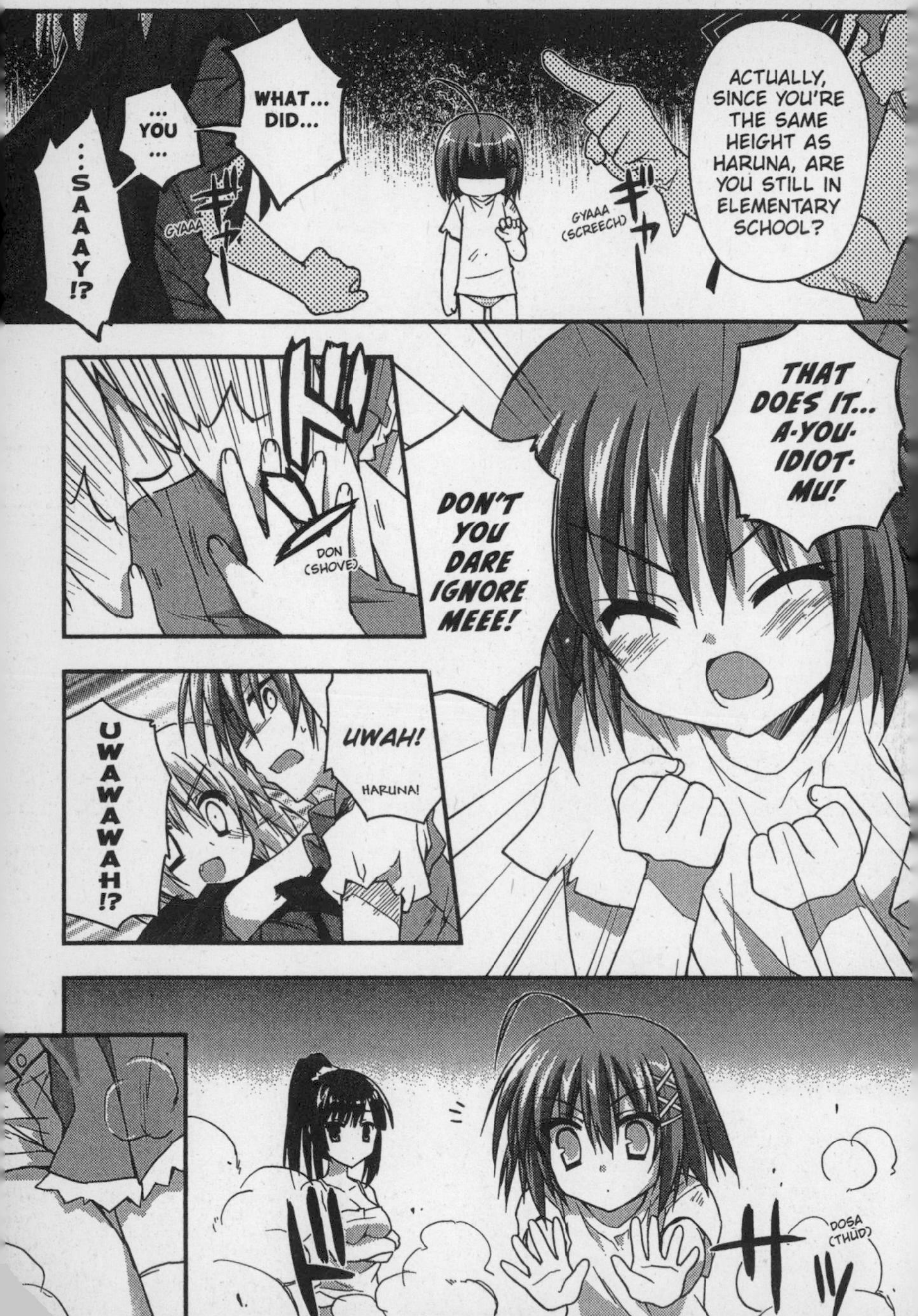
ACTUALLY, SINCE YOU'RE THE SAME HEIGHT AS HARUNA, ARE YOU STILL IN ELEMENTARY SCHOOL?
GYAAA (SCREECH)
WHAT... DID...
... YOU ...
...SAAAAY!?
GYAAA
THAT DOES IT... A-YOU-IDIOT-MU!
DON'T YOU DARE IGNORE MEEE!
DON (SHOVE)
UWAH!
HARUNA!
UWAWAWAH!?
DOSA (THUD)

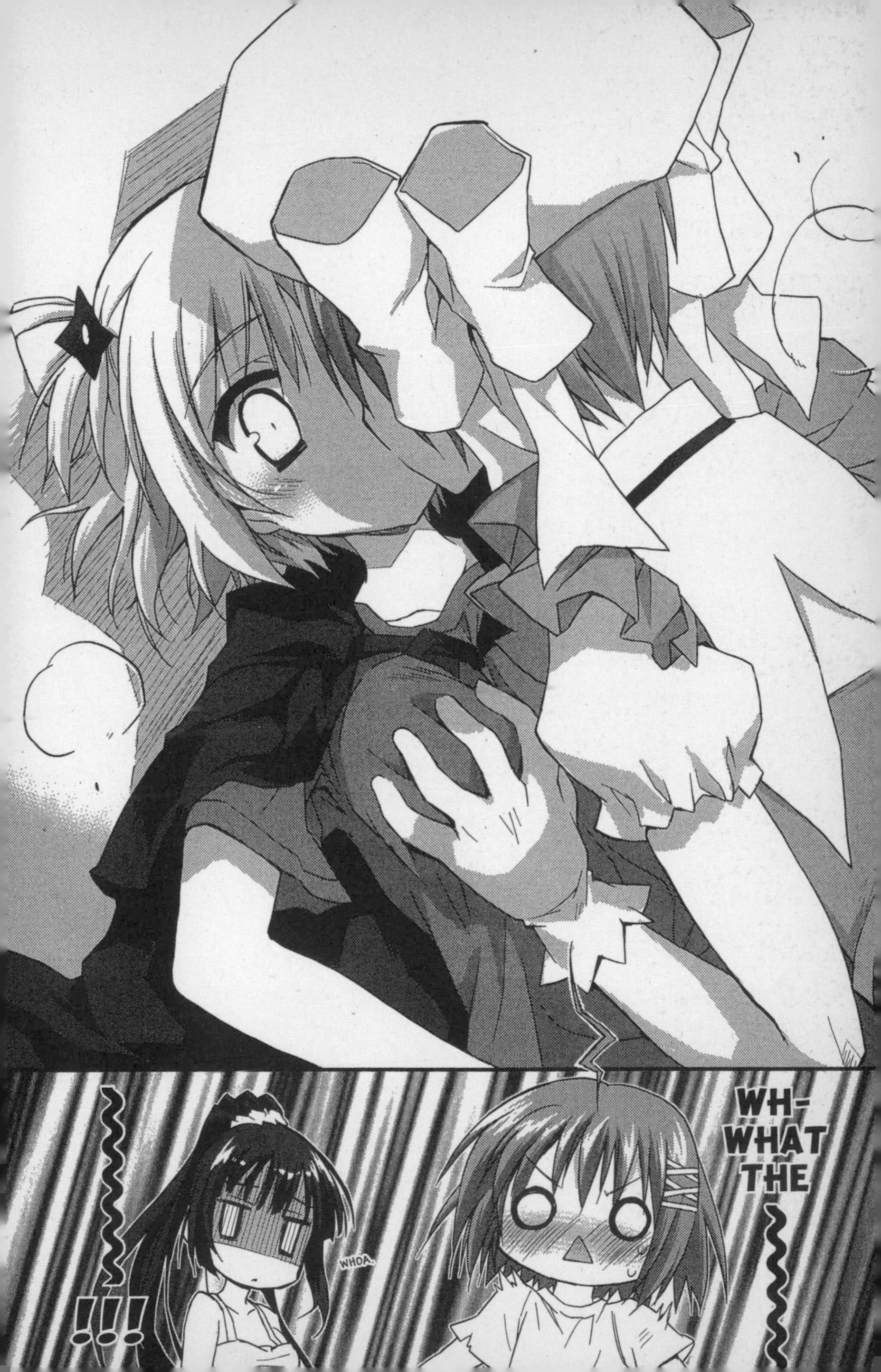
WH-WHAT THE ~~~!!!
WHOA.

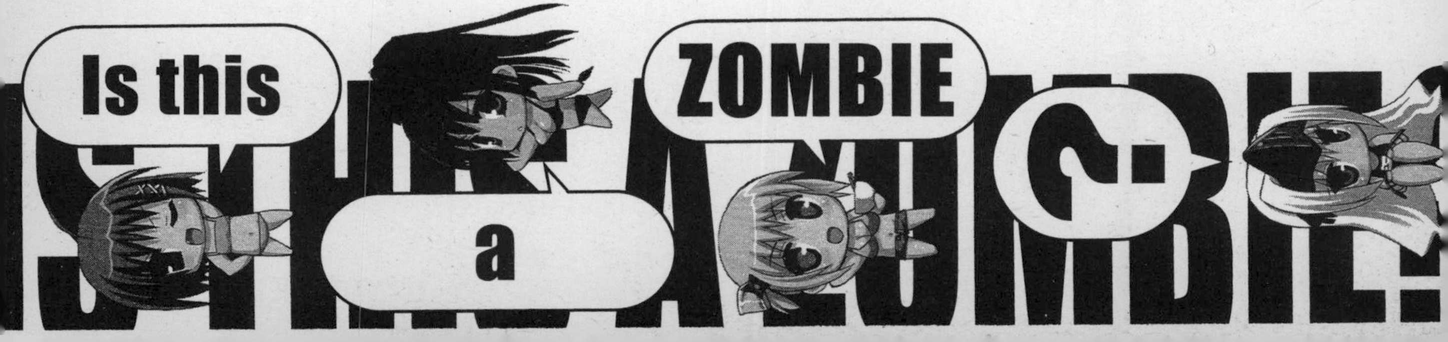
Is this
a
ZOMBIE
?

A YOUNG BRIDE'S HEART

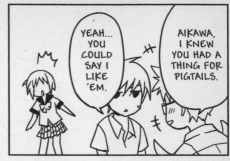

AIKAWA, I KNEW YOU HAD A THING FOR PIGTAILS.
YEAH... YOU COULD SAY I LIKE 'EM.
I SEE... PIG-TAILS, HUH?
A FEW DAYS LATER
ZA (STAND)
HEY, AIKAWA!
OH...HEY, TOMONO—
AIKAWA, YOU GET OFF...ON THIS SORT OF THING, RIGHT?
I CAN ACCEPT THAT.
WHAT THE HECK IS SHE TALKING ABOUT?
FWASA
FWASA (WAG)

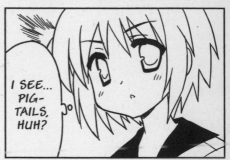

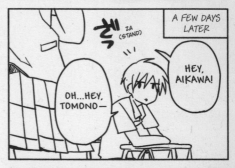

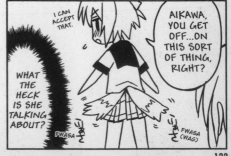

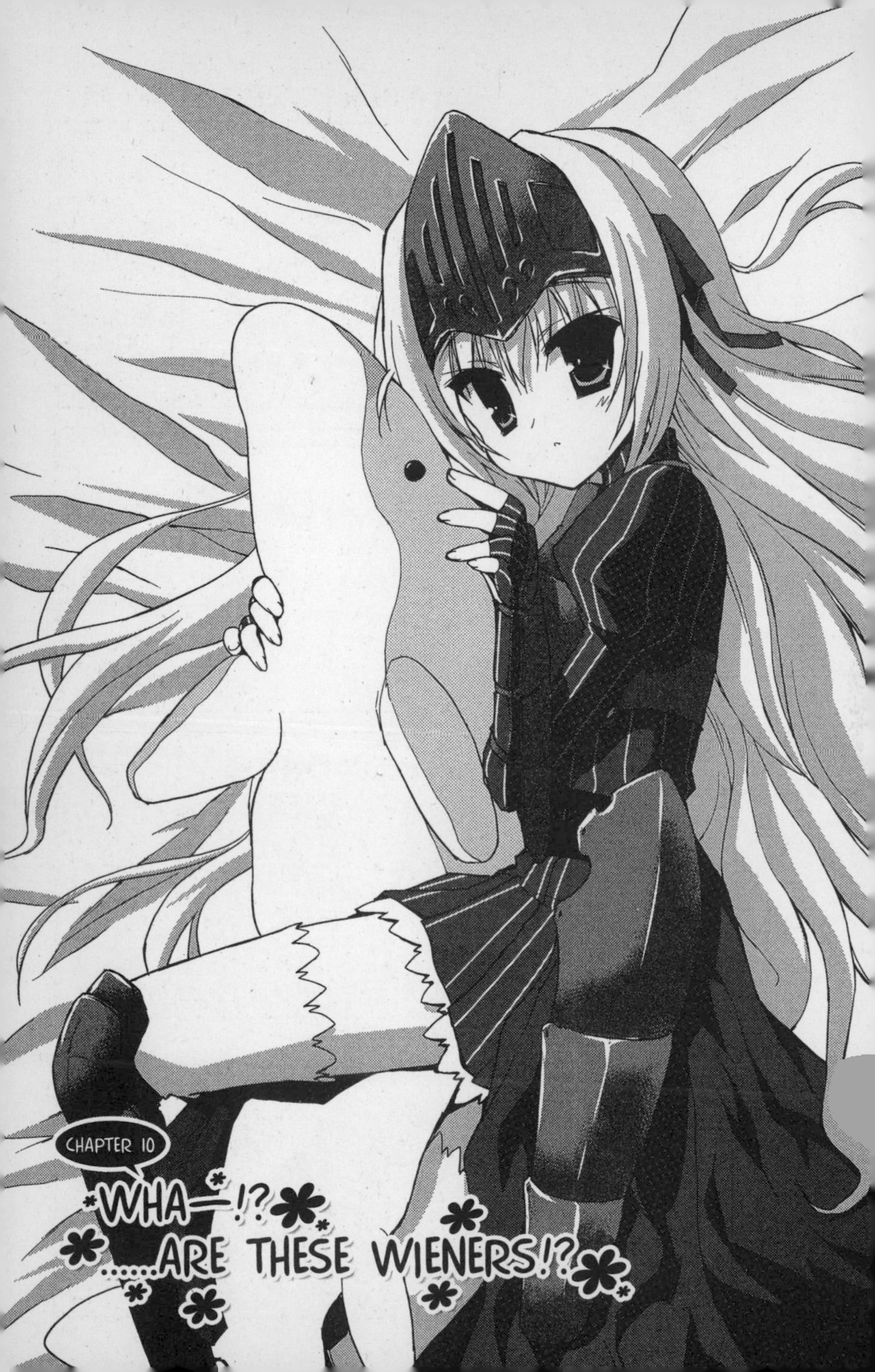
CHAPTER 10
WHA—!?
......ARE THESE WIENERS!?

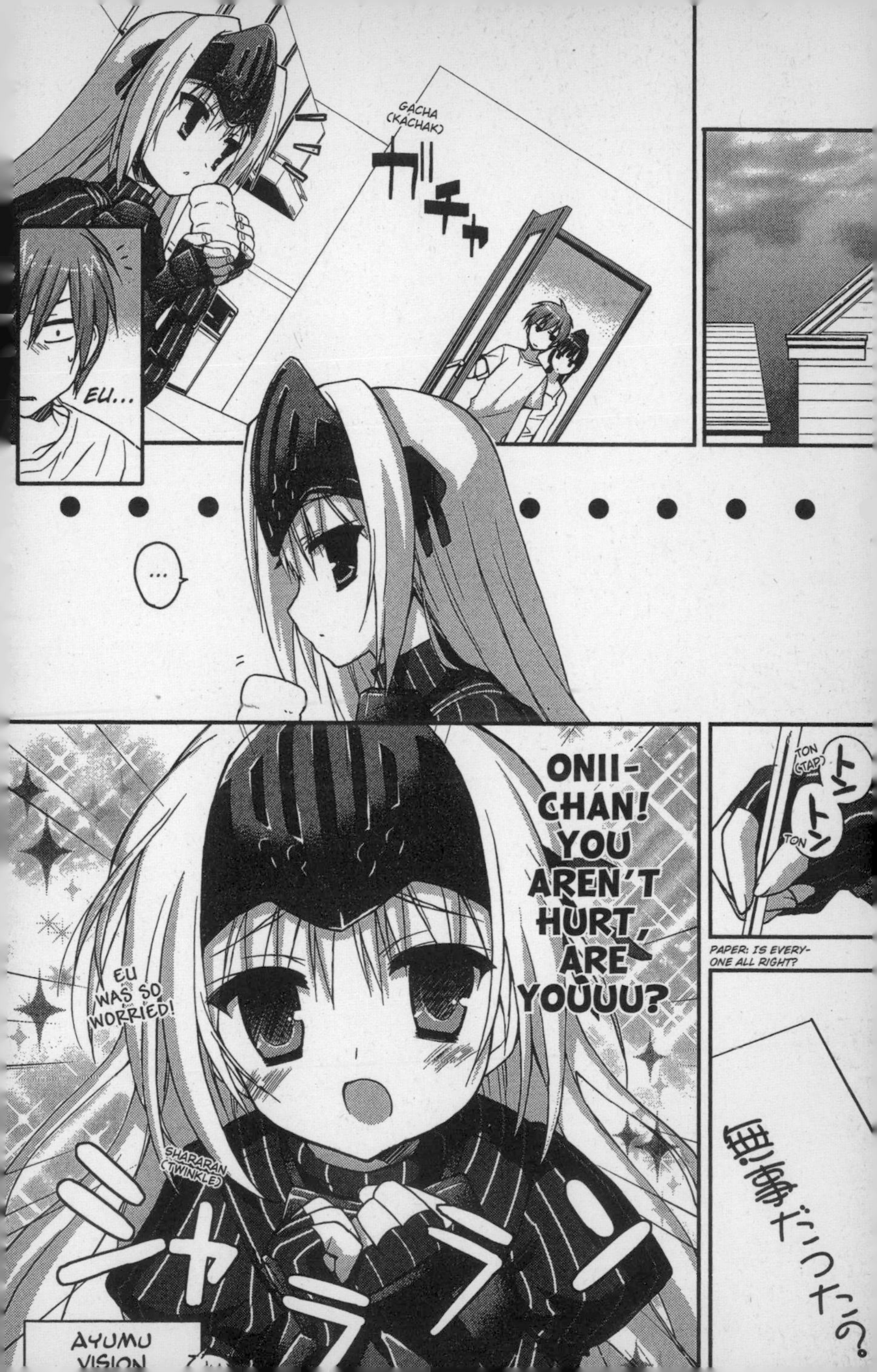

GACHA (KACHAK)
ガチャ
EU...
...
TON (STAP)
トン
TON
トン
PAPER: IS EVERY-ONE ALL RIGHT?
無事だったの？
ONII-CHAN! YOU AREN'T HURT, ARE YOUUU?
EU WAS SO WORRIED!
SHARARAN (TWINKLE)
AYUMU VISION

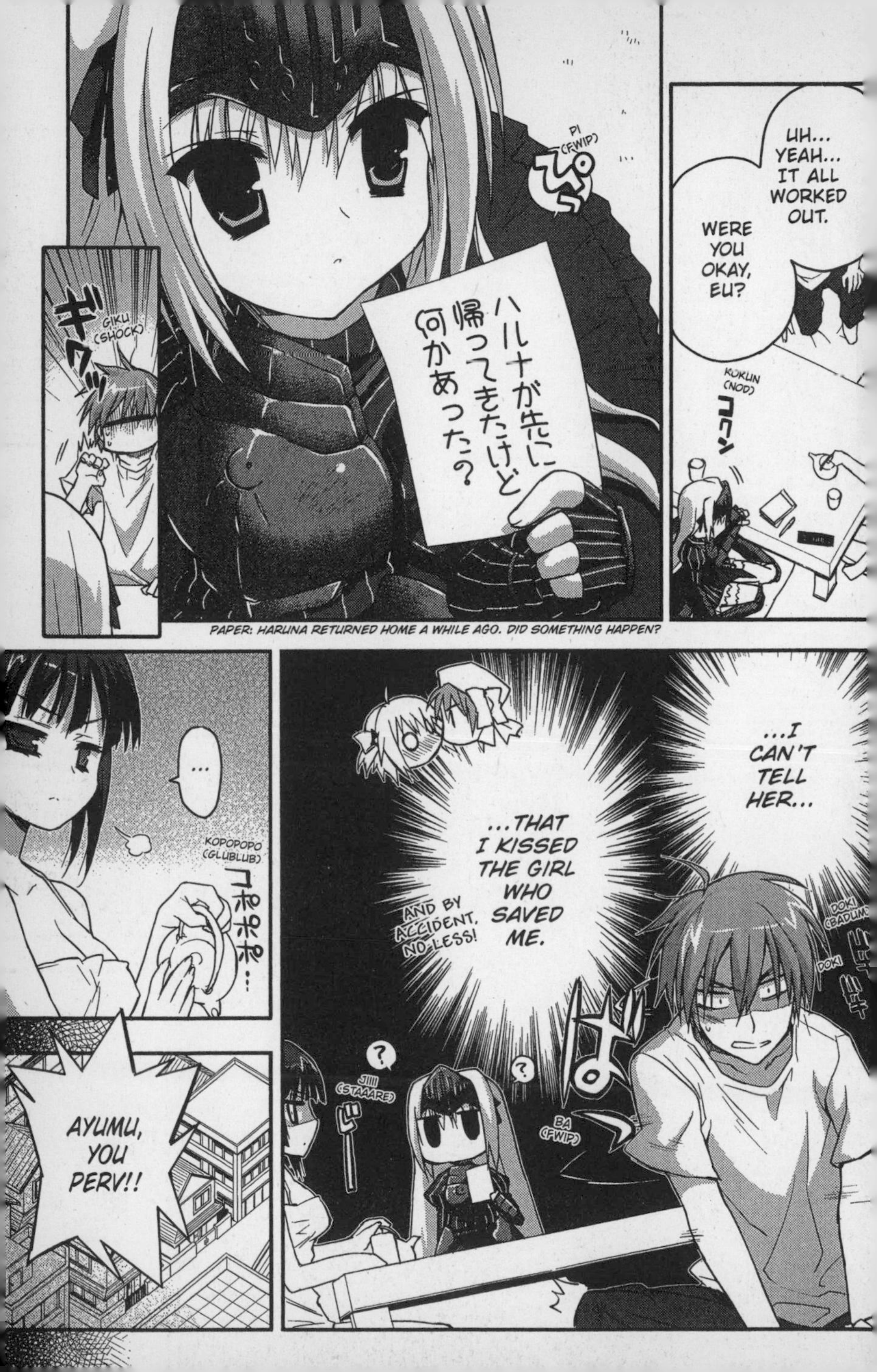
WERE YOU OKAY, EU?
KOKUN (NOD)
コクン
PI (FWIP)
ぴっ
ハルナが先に帰ってきたけど何かあったの？
PAPER: HARUNA RETURNED HOME A WHILE AGO. DID SOMETHING HAPPEN?
GIKU (SHOCK)
ギクッ
UH... YEAH... IT ALL WORKED OUT.
...I CAN'T TELL HER...
...THAT I KISSED THE GIRL WHO SAVED ME.
AND BY ACCIDENT, NO LESS!
DOKI (BADUM)
DOKI
BA (FWIP)
ば
JIII (STAAARE)
じ
...
KOPOPOPO (GLUBLUB)
コポポポ...
AYUMU, YOU PERV!!

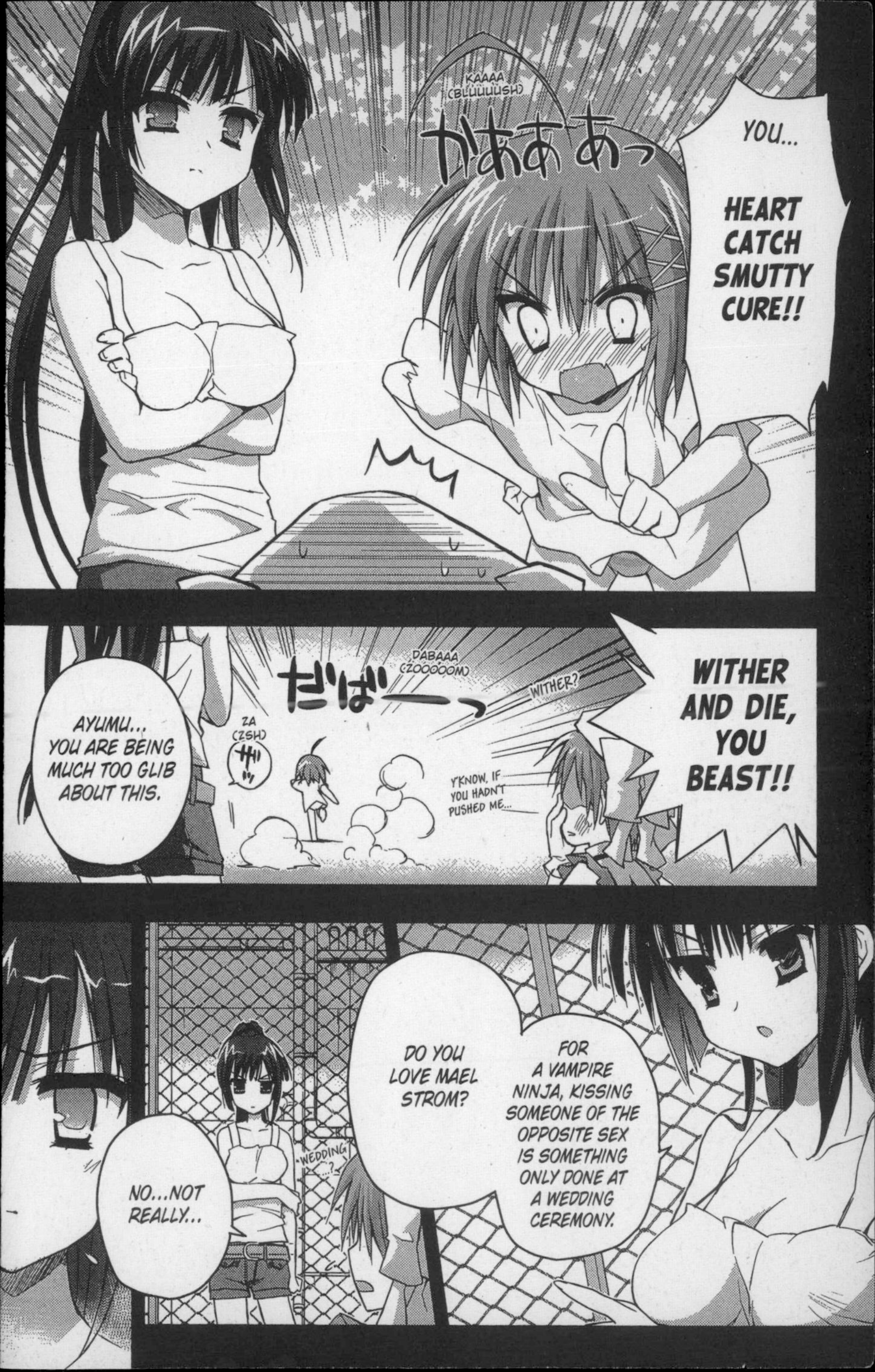
YOU...
HEART CATCH SMUTTY CURE!!
KAAAA (BLUUUUUSH)
かあああっ
WITHER AND DIE, YOU BEAST!!
DABAAA (ZOOOOOOM)
だばーっ
WITHER?
Y'KNOW, IF YOU HADN'T PUSHED ME...
ZA (ZSH)
AYUMU... YOU ARE BEING MUCH TOO GLIB ABOUT THIS.
FOR A VAMPIRE NINJA, KISSING SOMEONE OF THE OPPOSITE SEX IS SOMETHING ONLY DONE AT A WEDDING CEREMONY.
DO YOU LOVE MAEL STROM?
WEDDING...?
NO...NOT REALLY...

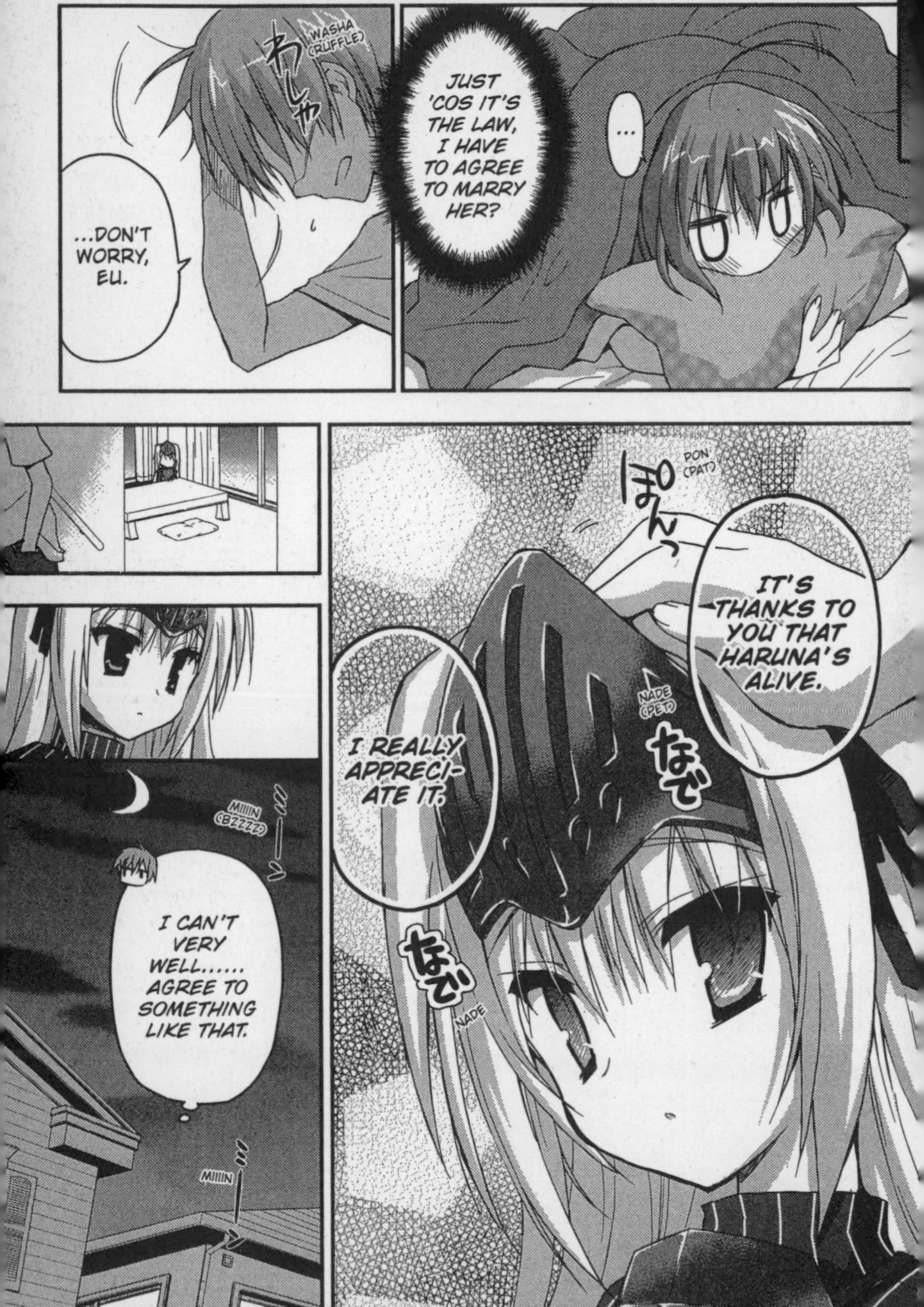
...
JUST 'COS IT'S THE LAW, I HAVE TO AGREE TO MARRY HER?
WASHA (RUFFLE)
わしゃ
...DON'T WORRY, EU.
PON (PAT)
ぽんっ
IT'S THANKS TO YOU THAT HARUNA'S ALIVE.
NADE (PET)
なで
I REALLY APPRECI-ATE IT.
なで
NADE
MIIIIN (BZZZZ)
I CAN'T VERY WELL...... AGREE TO SOMETHING LIKE THAT.
MIIIN

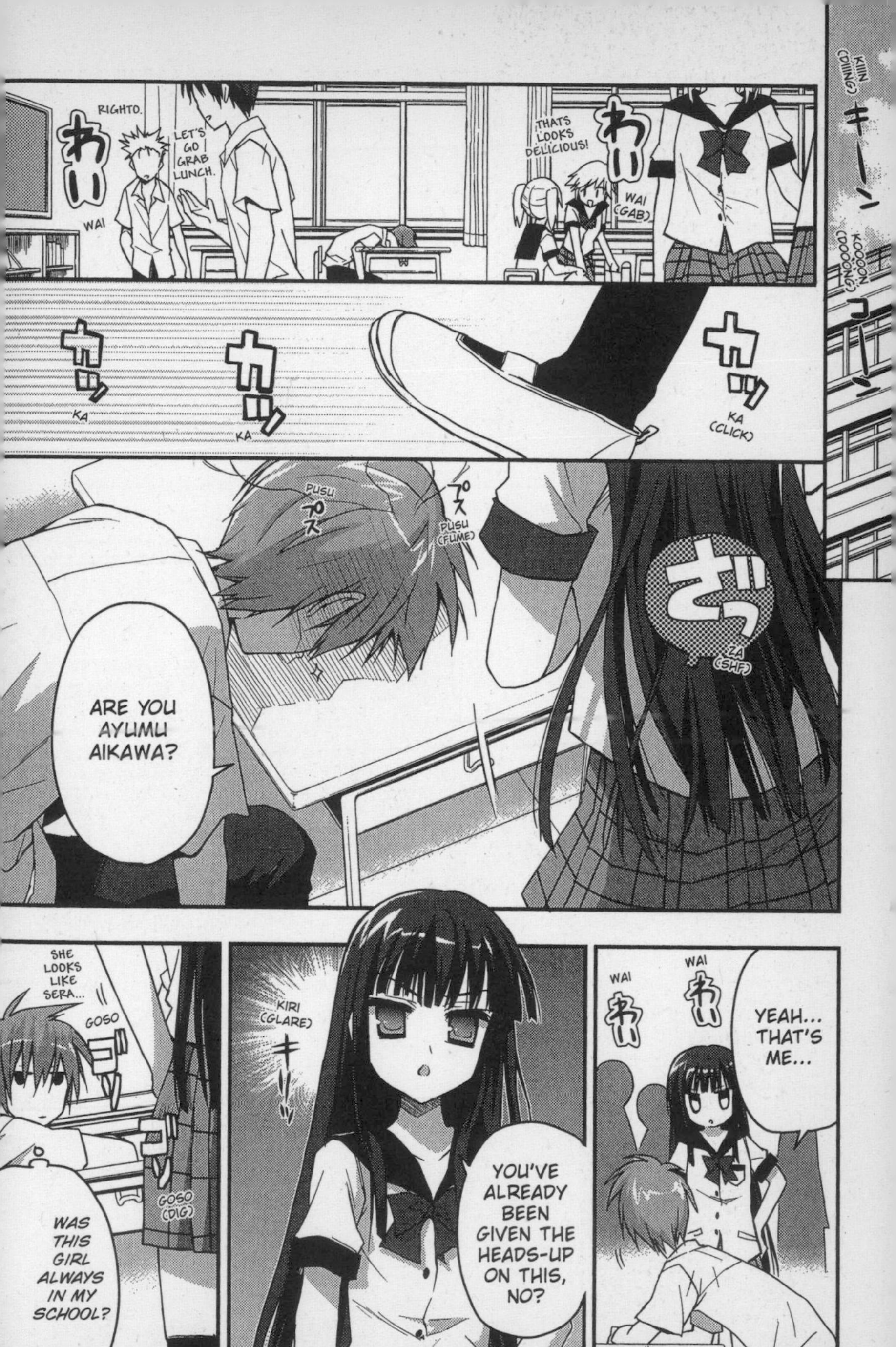
キーン
KIIN (DIIING)
コーン
KOOON (DOOONG)
わい
WAI (GAB)
THATS LOOKS DELICIOUS!
わい
WAI
RIGHTO.
LET'S GO GRAB LUNCH.
カッ
KA (CLICK)
カッ
KA
カッ
KA
ざっ
ZA (SHF)
プス
PUSU (FUME)
プス
PUSU
ARE YOU AYUMU AIKAWA?
YEAH... THAT'S ME...
わい
WAI
わい
WAI
KIRI (GLARE)
キッ
YOU'VE ALREADY BEEN GIVEN THE HEADS-UP ON THIS, NO?
SHE LOOKS LIKE SERA...
GOSO
GOSO (DIG)
WAS THIS GIRL ALWAYS IN MY SCHOOL?

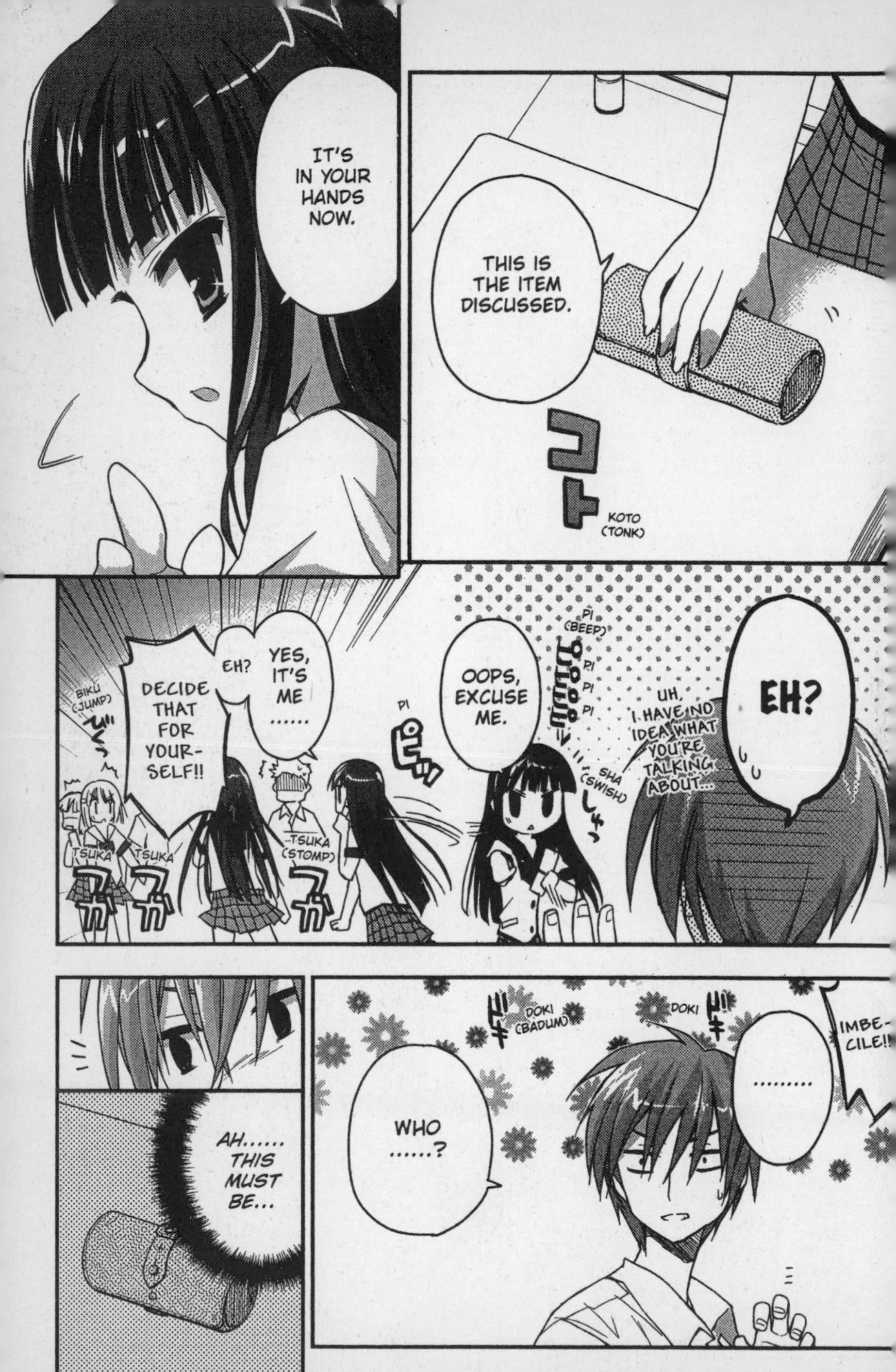
THIS IS THE ITEM DISCUSSED.
KOTO (TONK)
IT'S IN YOUR HANDS NOW.
EH?
UH, I HAVE NO IDEA WHAT YOU'RE TALKING ABOUT...
PI (BEEP) PI PI PI
SHA (SWISH)
OOPS, EXCUSE ME.
PI
YES, IT'S ME ......
EH?
DECIDE THAT FOR YOUR-SELF!!
BIKU (JUMP)
TSUKA (STOMP)
TSUKA
TSUKA
IMBE-CILE!!
....
DOKI
DOKI (BADUM)
WHO ......?
AH...... THIS MUST BE...

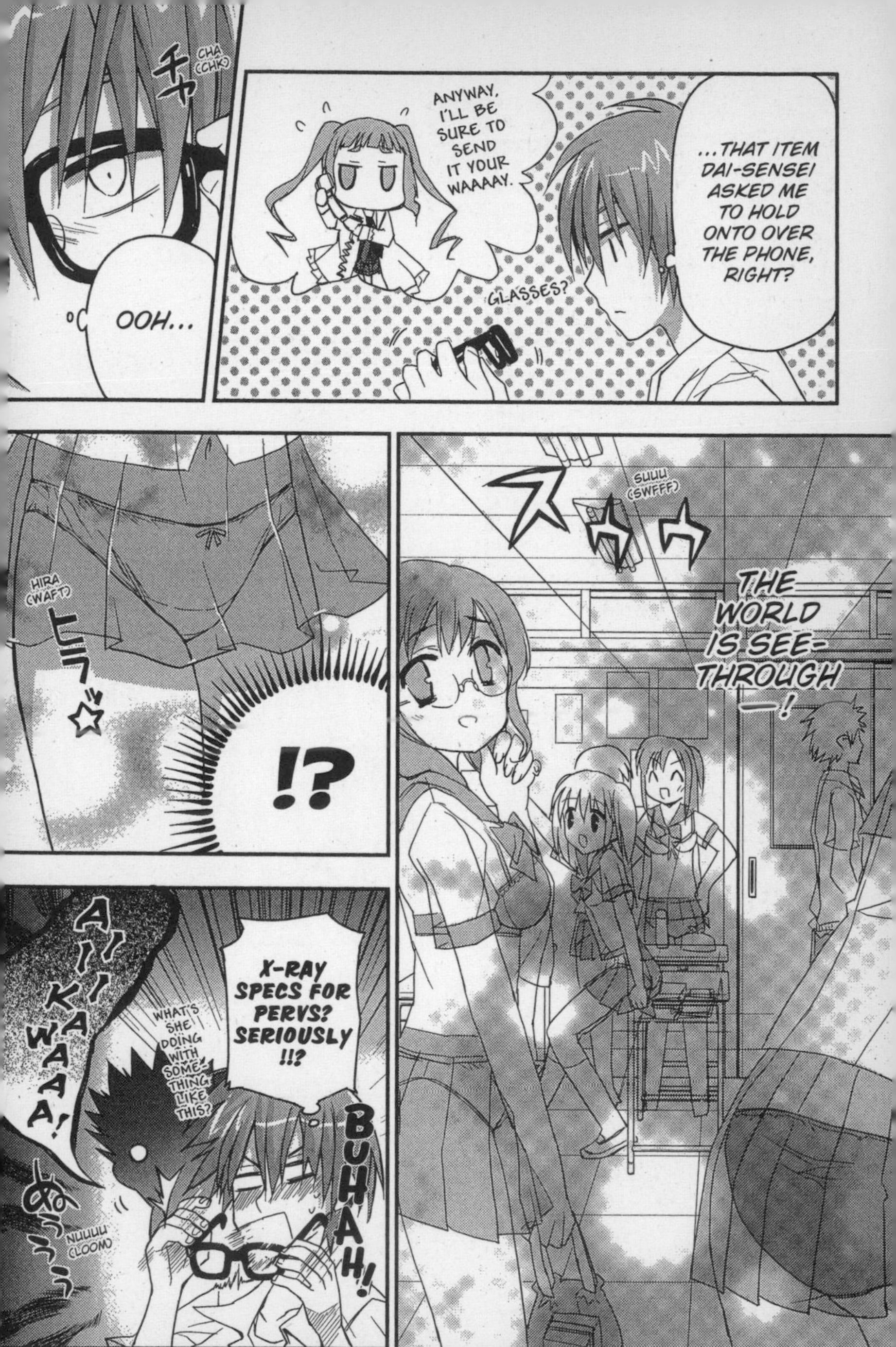

...THAT ITEM DAI-SENSEI ASKED ME TO HOLD ONTO OVER THE PHONE, RIGHT?
ANYWAY, I'LL BE SURE TO SEND IT YOUR WAAAAY.
GLASSES?
チャ
CHA (CHK)
OOH...
スゥゥ
SUUU (SWFFF)
THE WORLD IS SEE-THROUGH—!
ヒラ☆
HIRA (WAFT)
!?
X-RAY SPECS FOR PERVS? SERIOUSLY!!?
WHAT'S SHE DOING WITH SOMETHING LIKE THIS?
BUHAH!
AIIIKAWAAA!
ぬうう
NUUUU (LOOM)

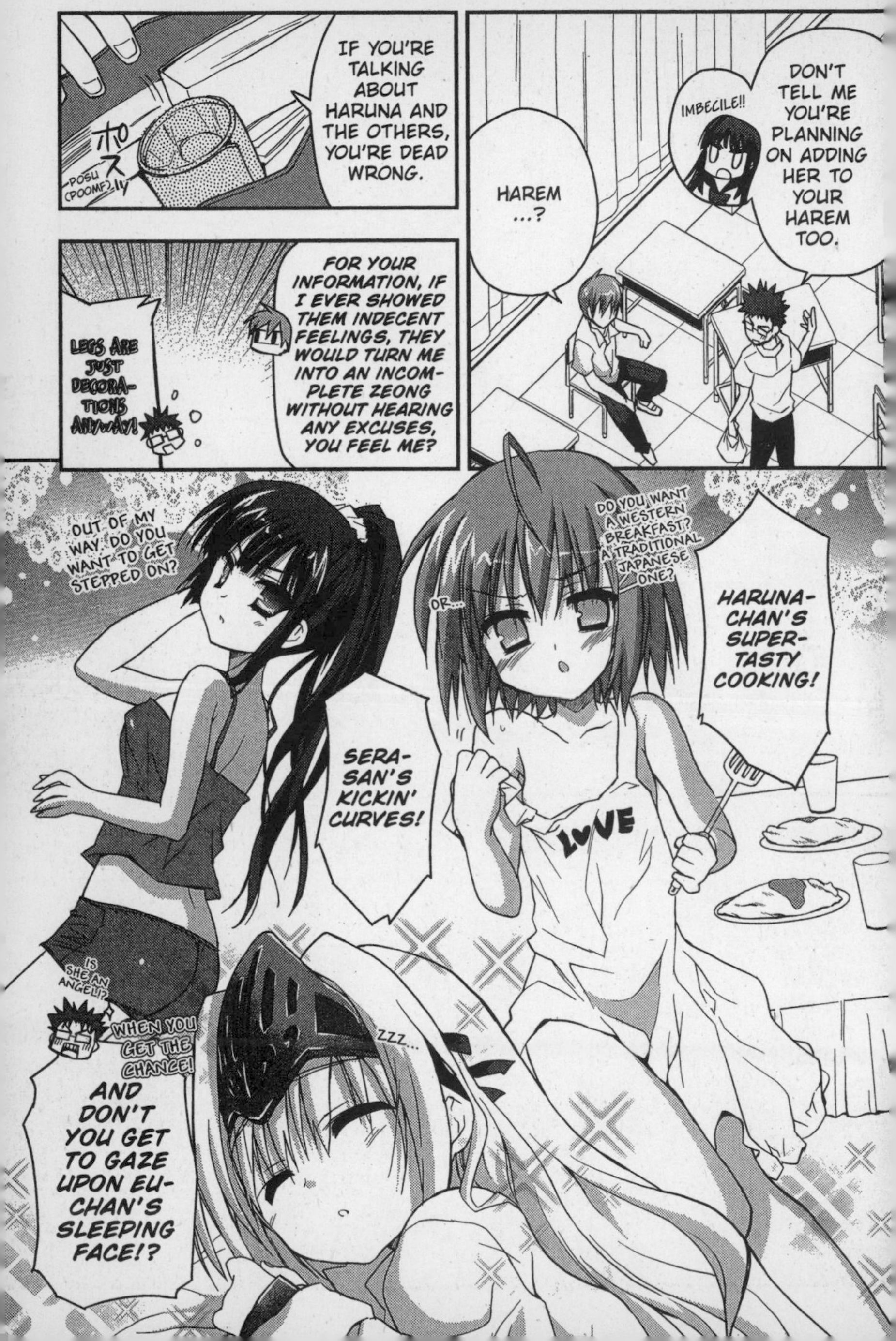
DON'T TELL ME YOU'RE PLANNING ON ADDING HER TO YOUR HAREM TOO.
IMBECILE!!
HAREM ...?
IF YOU'RE TALKING ABOUT HARUNA AND THE OTHERS, YOU'RE DEAD WRONG.
POSU (POOMF)
FOR YOUR INFORMATION, IF I EVER SHOWED THEM INDECENT FEELINGS, THEY WOULD TURN ME INTO AN INCOMPLETE ZEONG WITHOUT HEARING ANY EXCUSES, YOU FEEL ME?
LEGS ARE JUST DECORATIONS ANYWAY!
HARUNA-CHAN'S SUPER-TASTY COOKING!
DO YOU WANT A WESTERN BREAKFAST? A TRADITIONAL JAPANESE ONE?
OR...
SERA-SAN'S KICKIN' CURVES!
OUT OF MY WAY. DO YOU WANT TO GET STEPPED ON?
LOVE
ZZZ...
AND DON'T YOU GET TO GAZE UPON EU-CHAN'S SLEEPING FACE!?
WHEN YOU GET THE CHANCE!
IS SHE AN ANGEL!?

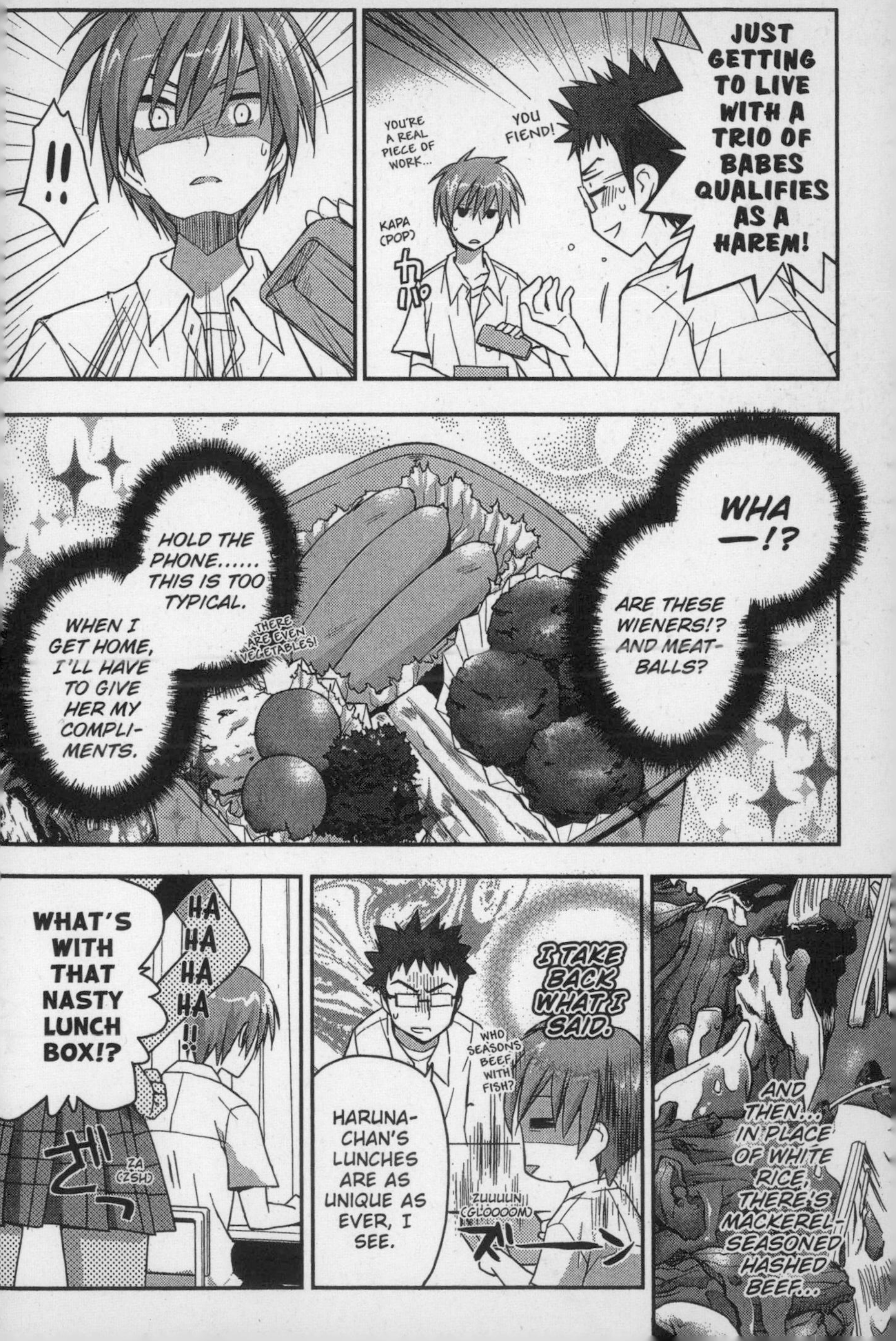

JUST GETTING TO LIVE WITH A TRIO OF BABES QUALIFIES AS A HAREM!
YOU FIEND!
YOU'RE A REAL PIECE OF WORK...
KAPA (POP)
!!
WHA—!?
ARE THESE WIENERS!? AND MEAT-BALLS?
HOLD THE PHONE...... THIS IS TOO TYPICAL.
THERE ARE EVEN VEGETABLES!
WHEN I GET HOME, I'LL HAVE TO GIVE HER MY COMPLI-MENTS.
AND THEN... IN PLACE OF WHITE RICE, THERE'S MACKEREL-SEASONED HASHED BEEF...
I TAKE BACK WHAT I SAID.
WHO SEASONS BEEF WITH FISH?
HARUNA-CHAN'S LUNCHES ARE AS UNIQUE AS EVER, I SEE.
ZUUUUN (GLOOOOM)
WHAT'S WITH THAT NASTY LUNCH BOX!?
HA HA HA HA!!
ZA (ZSH)

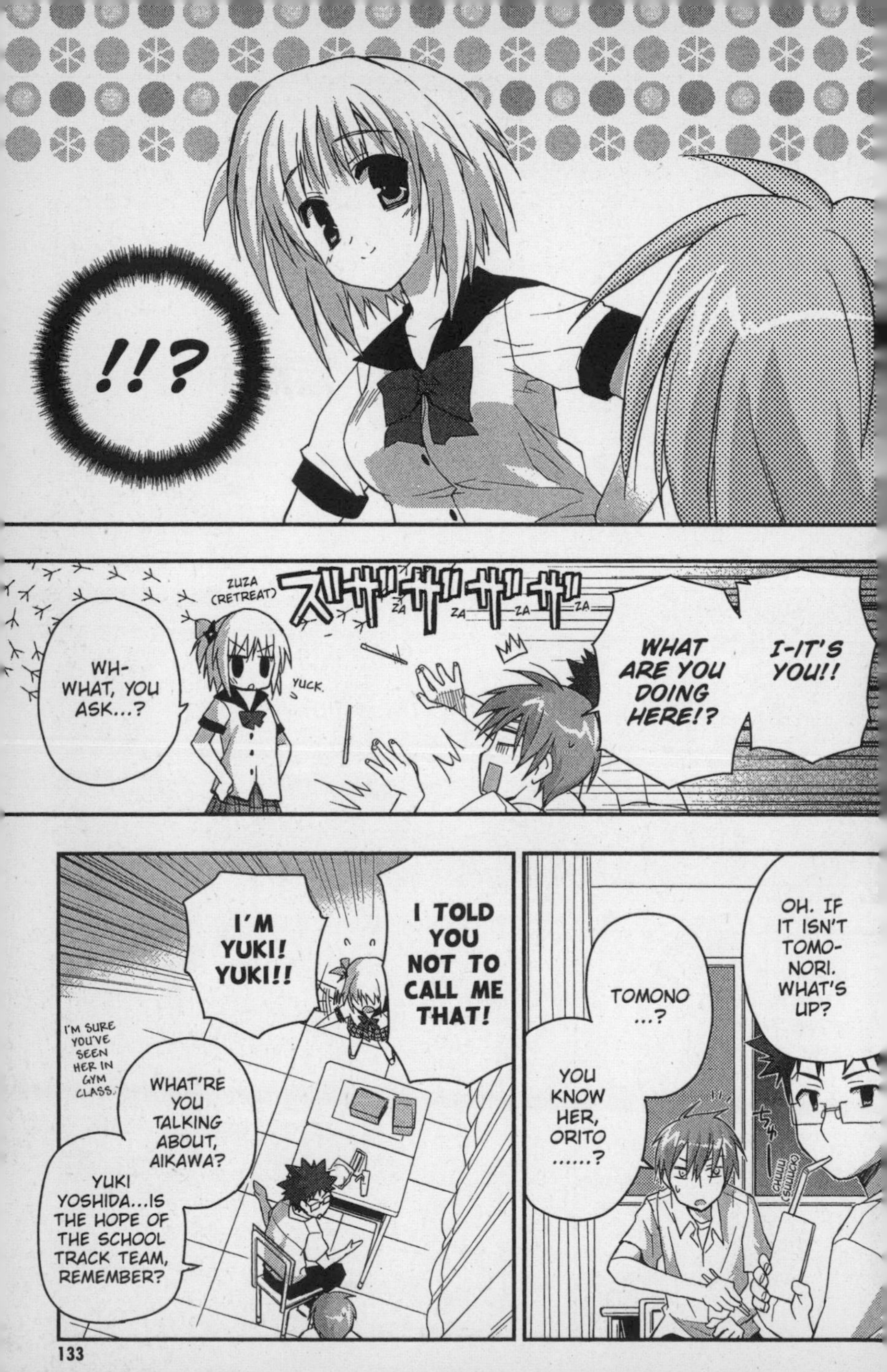
!!?
I-IT'S YOU!!
WHAT ARE YOU DOING HERE!?
ZA
ZA
ZA
ZA
ZUZA (RETREAT)
YUCK.
WH- WHAT, YOU ASK...?
OH. IF IT ISN'T TOMO- NORI. WHAT'S UP?
TOMONO ...?
YOU KNOW HER, ORITO ......?
I TOLD YOU NOT TO CALL ME THAT!
I'M YUKI! YUKI!!
WHAT'RE YOU TALKING ABOUT, AIKAWA?
YUKI YOSHIDA...IS THE HOPE OF THE SCHOOL TRACK TEAM, REMEMBER?
I'M SURE YOU'VE SEEN HER IN GYM CLASS.

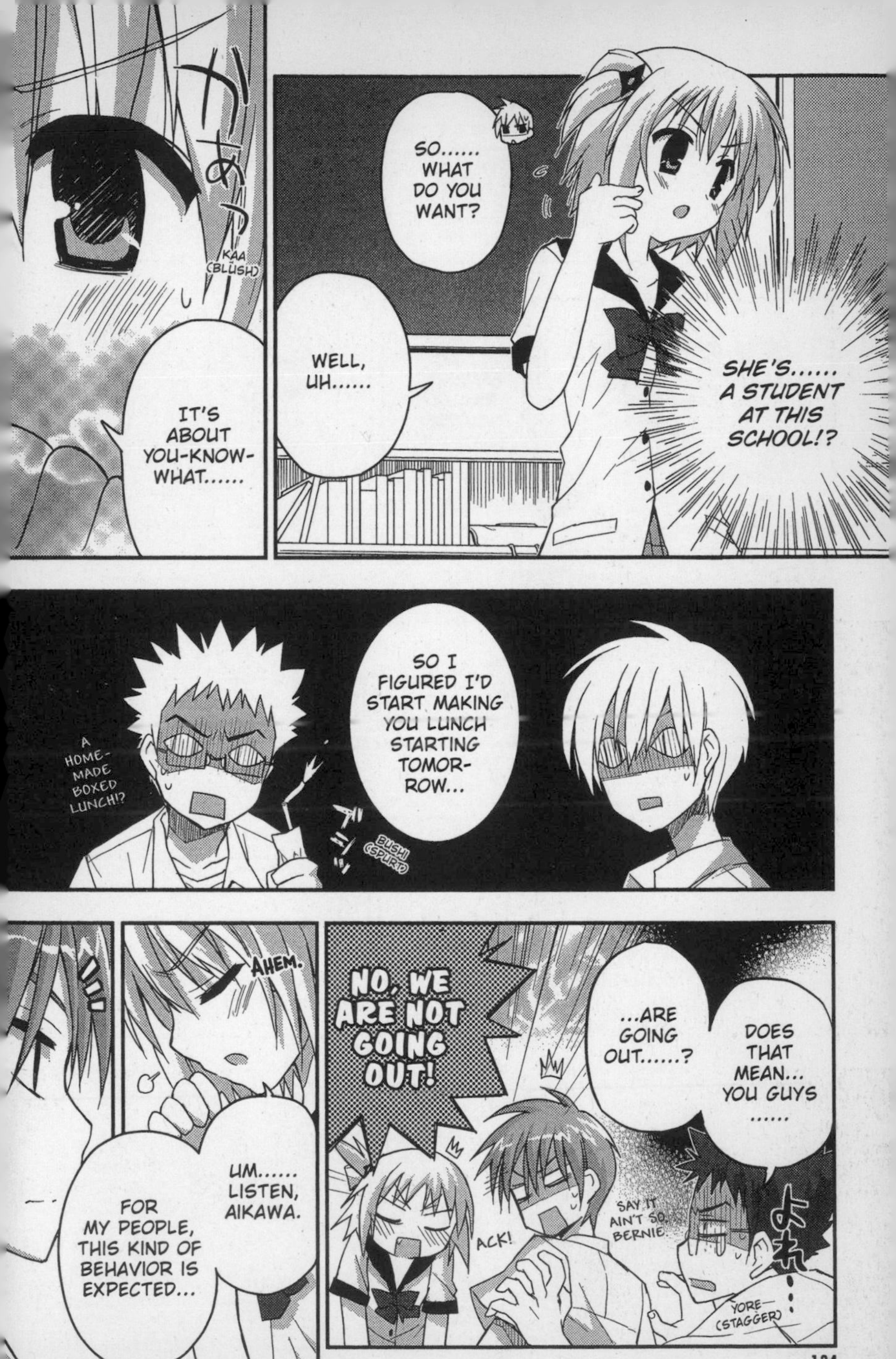
SO...... WHAT DO YOU WANT?
KAA (BLUSH)
SHE'S...... A STUDENT AT THIS SCHOOL!?
WELL, UH......
IT'S ABOUT YOU-KNOW-WHAT......
SO I FIGURED I'D START MAKING YOU LUNCH STARTING TOMORROW...
BUSHI (SPURT)
A HOME-MADE BOXED LUNCH!?
DOES THAT MEAN... YOU GUYS ......
...ARE GOING OUT......?
NO, WE ARE NOT GOING OUT!
AHEM.
ACK!
SAY IT AIN'T SO, BERNIE.
YORE (STAGGER)
UM...... LISTEN, AIKAWA.
FOR MY PEOPLE, THIS KIND OF BEHAVIOR IS EXPECTED...

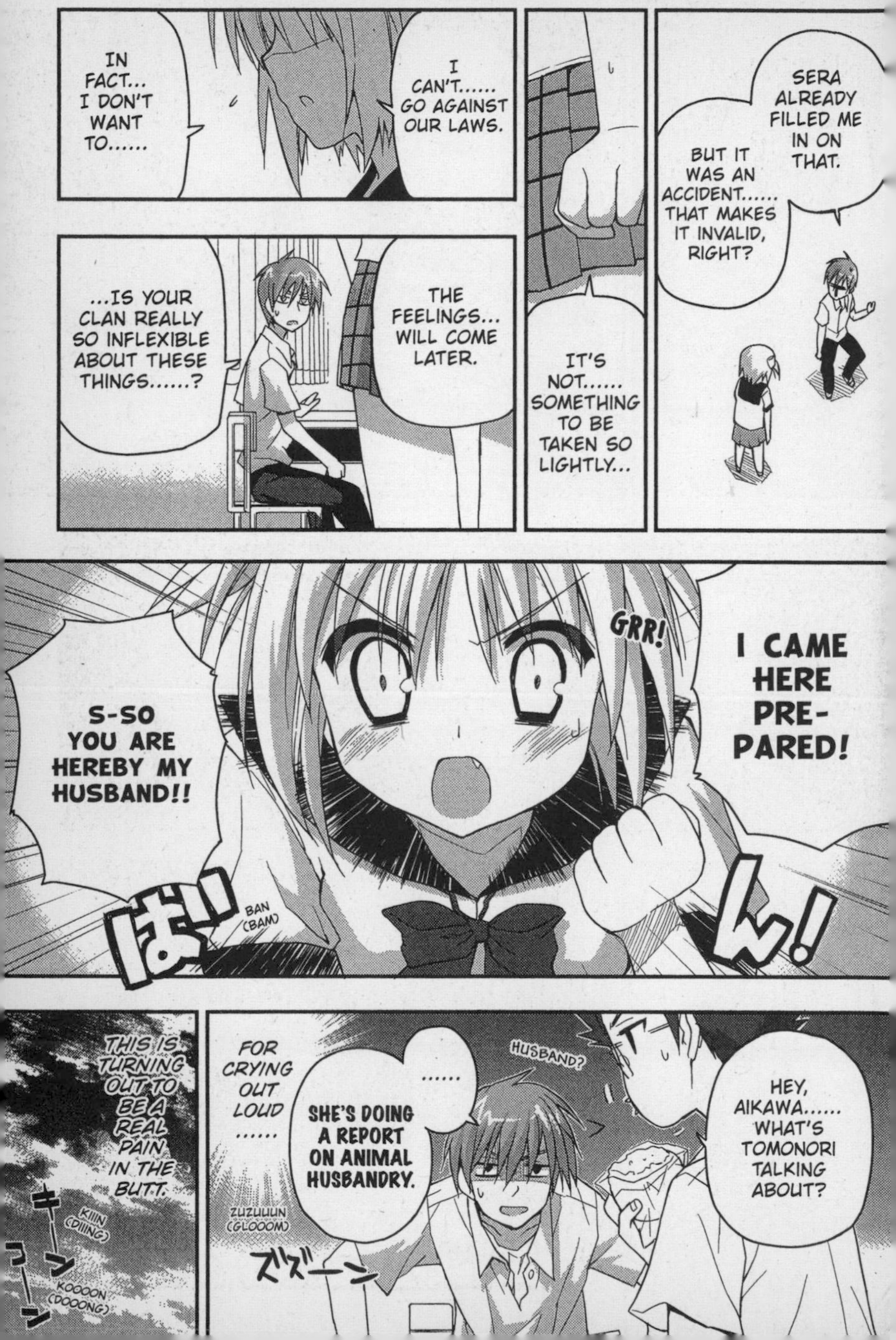
SERA ALREADY FILLED ME IN ON THAT.
BUT IT WAS AN ACCIDENT...... THAT MAKES IT INVALID, RIGHT?
IT'S NOT...... SOMETHING TO BE TAKEN SO LIGHTLY...
I CAN'T...... GO AGAINST OUR LAWS.
IN FACT... I DON'T WANT TO......
THE FEELINGS... WILL COME LATER.
...IS YOUR CLAN REALLY SO INFLEXIBLE ABOUT THESE THINGS......?
I CAME HERE PRE-PARED!
GRR!
S-SO YOU ARE HEREBY MY HUSBAND!!
ばーん!
BAN (BAM)
HEY, AIKAWA...... WHAT'S TOMONORI TALKING ABOUT?
HUSBAND?
......
SHE'S DOING A REPORT ON ANIMAL HUSBANDRY.
FOR CRYING OUT LOUD ......
ズズーン
ZUZUUUN (GLOOOM)
THIS IS TURNING OUT TO BE A REAL PAIN IN THE BUTT.
キーン
コーン
KIIIN (DIIING)
KOOOON (DOOONG)

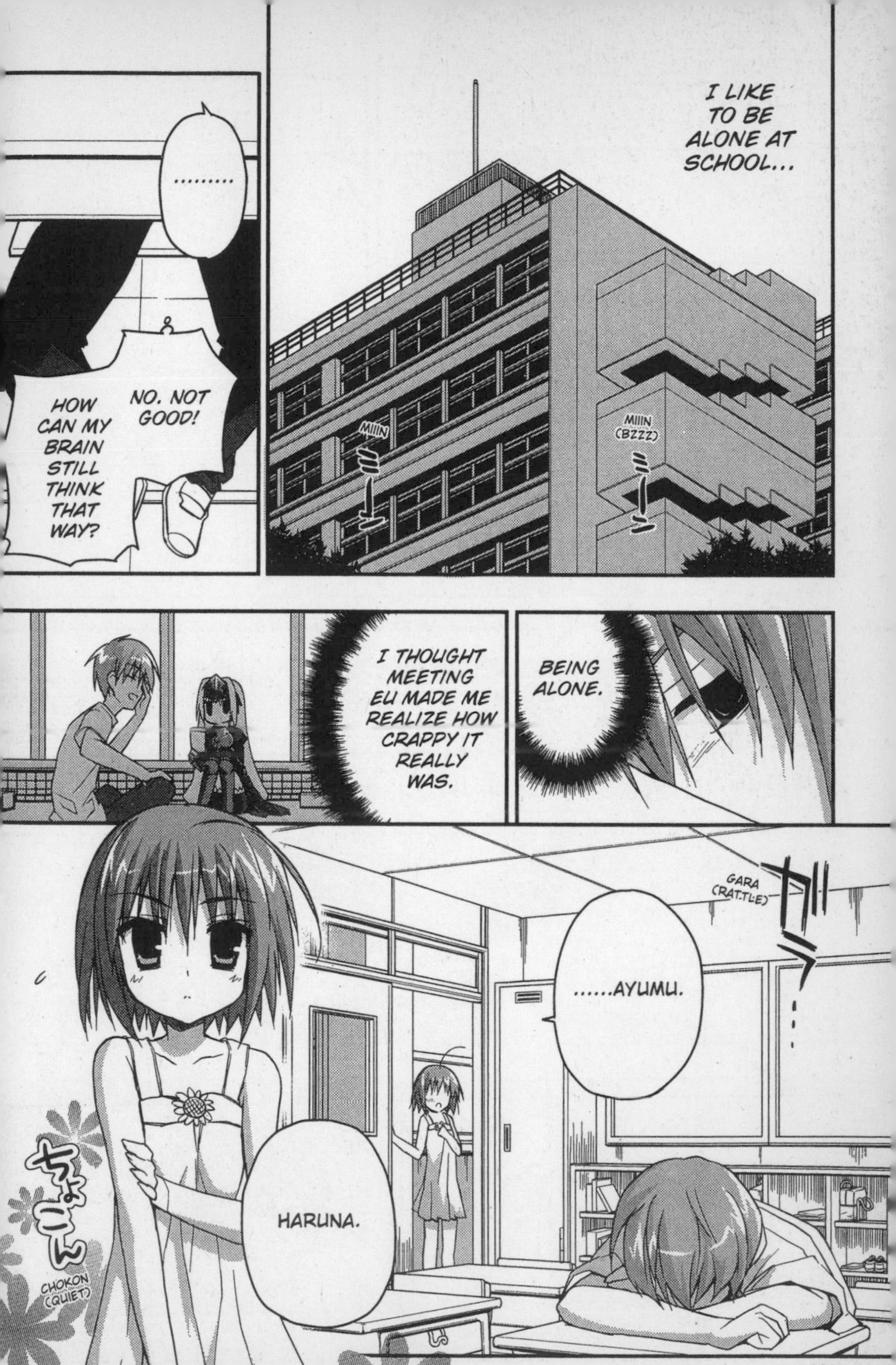
I LIKE TO BE ALONE AT SCHOOL...
MIIN
MIIN (BZZZ)
....
NO. NOT GOOD!
HOW CAN MY BRAIN STILL THINK THAT WAY?
BEING ALONE.
I THOUGHT MEETING EU MADE ME REALIZE HOW CRAPPY IT REALLY WAS.
GARA (RATTLE)
......AYUMU.
HARUNA.
ちょこん
CHOKON (QUIET)

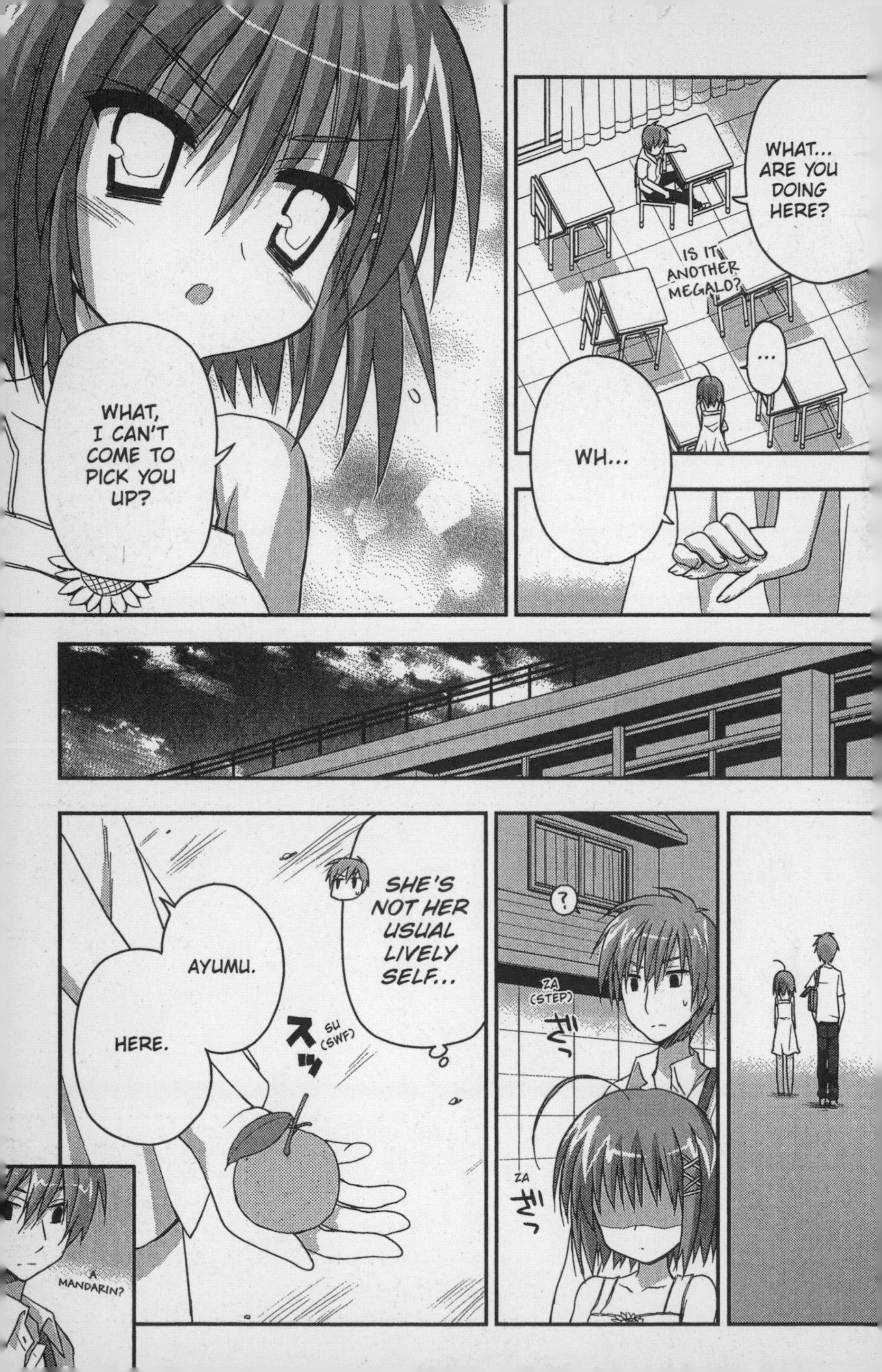
WHAT... ARE YOU DOING HERE?
IS IT ANOTHER MEGALO?
...
WH...
WHAT, I CAN'T COME TO PICK YOU UP?
?
ZA (STEP)
ZA
SHE'S NOT HER USUAL LIVELY SELF...
AYUMU.
HERE.
SU (SWF)
A MANDARIN?

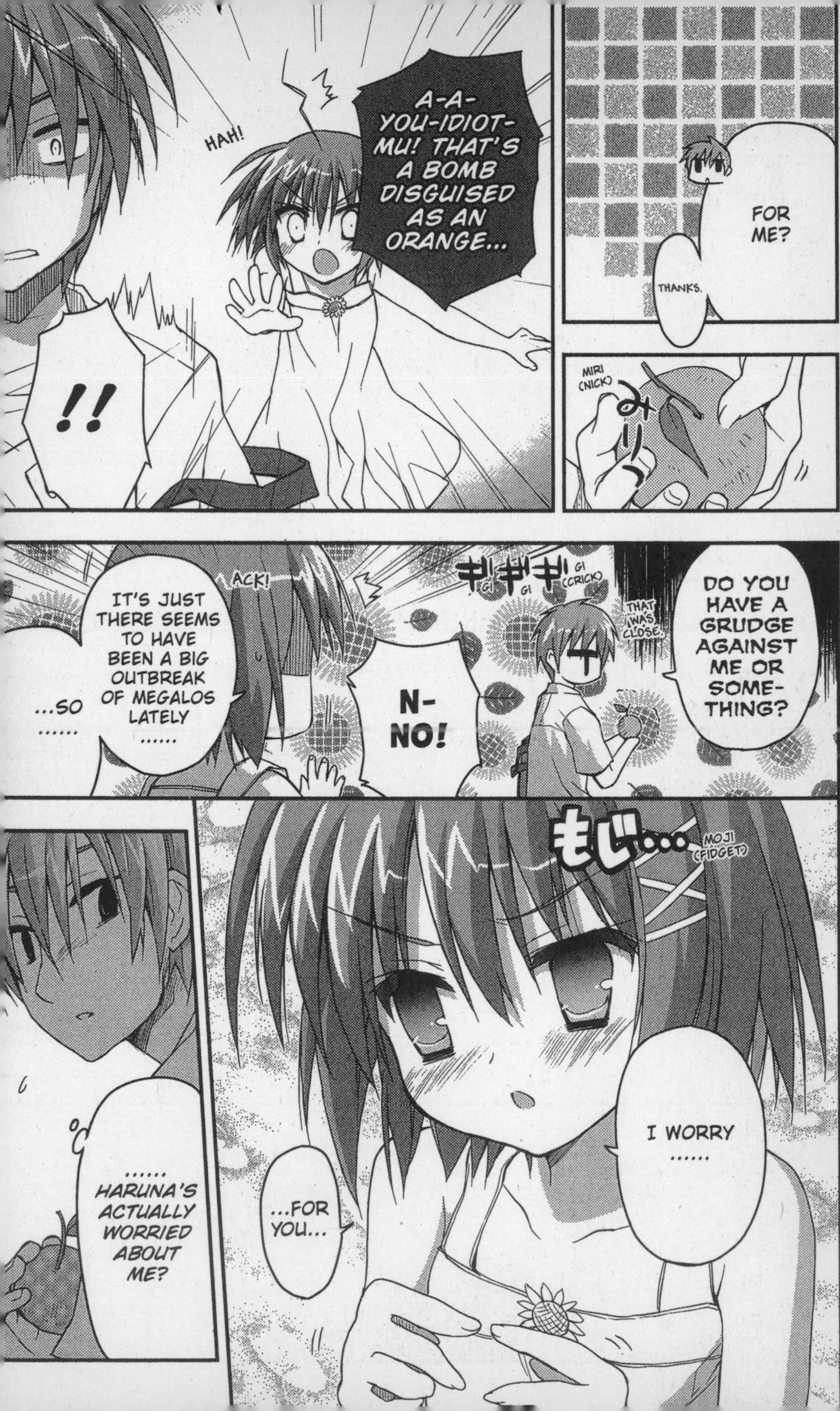
FOR ME?
THANKS.
みーっ
MIRI (NICK)
A-A-YOU-IDIOT-MU! THAT'S A BOMB DISGUISED AS AN ORANGE...
HAH!
!!
DO YOU HAVE A GRUDGE AGAINST ME OR SOME-THING?
THAT WAS CLOSE.
ギギギ
GI GI GI (CRICK)
ACK!
N-NO!
IT'S JUST THERE SEEMS TO HAVE BEEN A BIG OUTBREAK OF MEGALOS LATELY ......
...SO ......
もじ...
MOJI (FIDGET)
I WORRY ......
...FOR YOU...
...... HARUNA'S ACTUALLY WORRIED ABOUT ME?

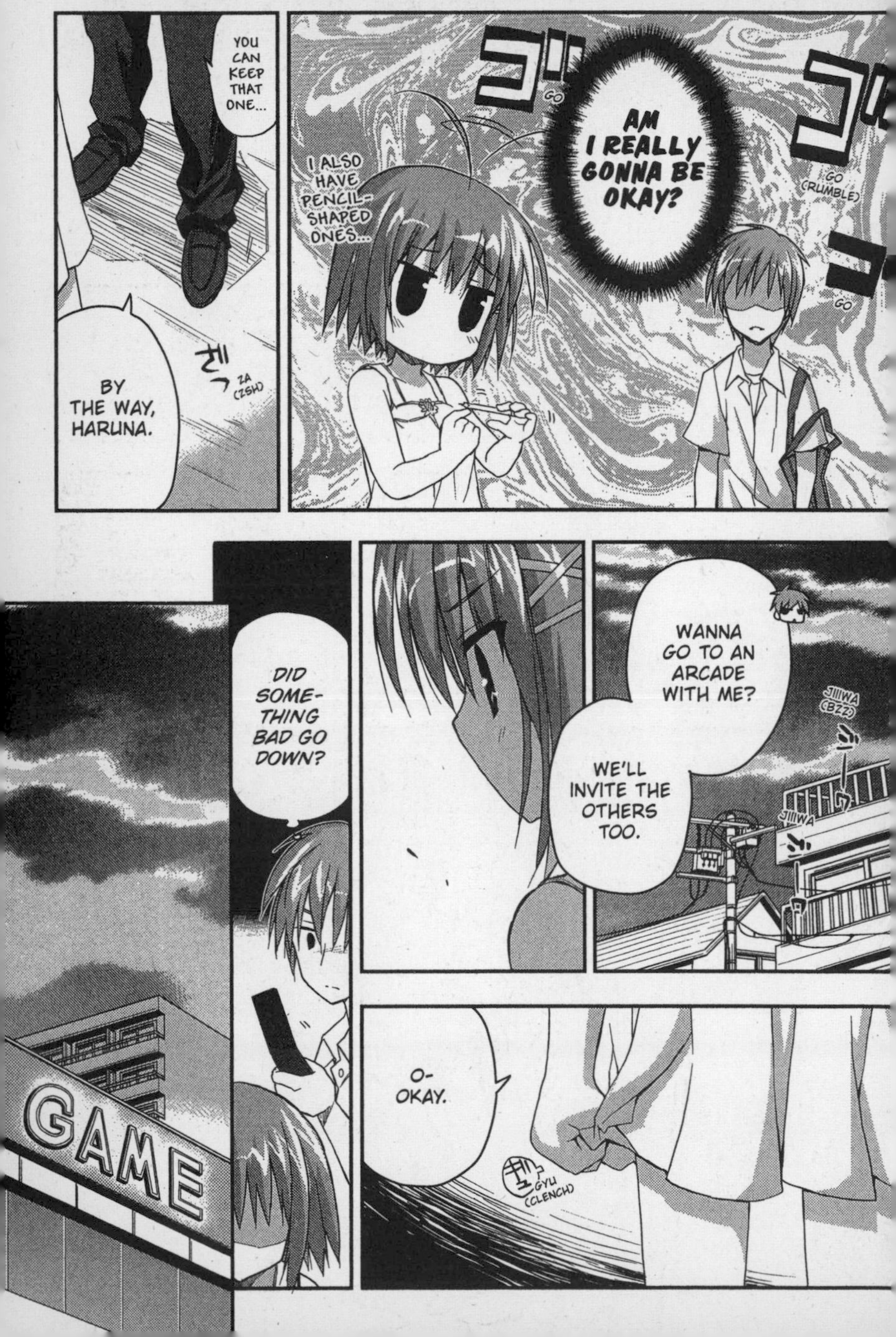
AM I REALLY GONNA BE OKAY?
GO
GO (RUMBLE)
GO
I ALSO HAVE PENCIL-SHAPED ONES...
YOU CAN KEEP THAT ONE...
ZA (ZSH)
BY THE WAY, HARUNA.
WANNA GO TO AN ARCADE WITH ME?
WE'LL INVITE THE OTHERS TOO.
JIIIWA (BZZ)
JIIIWA
O-OKAY.
GYU (CLENCH)
DID SOME-THING BAD GO DOWN?
GAME

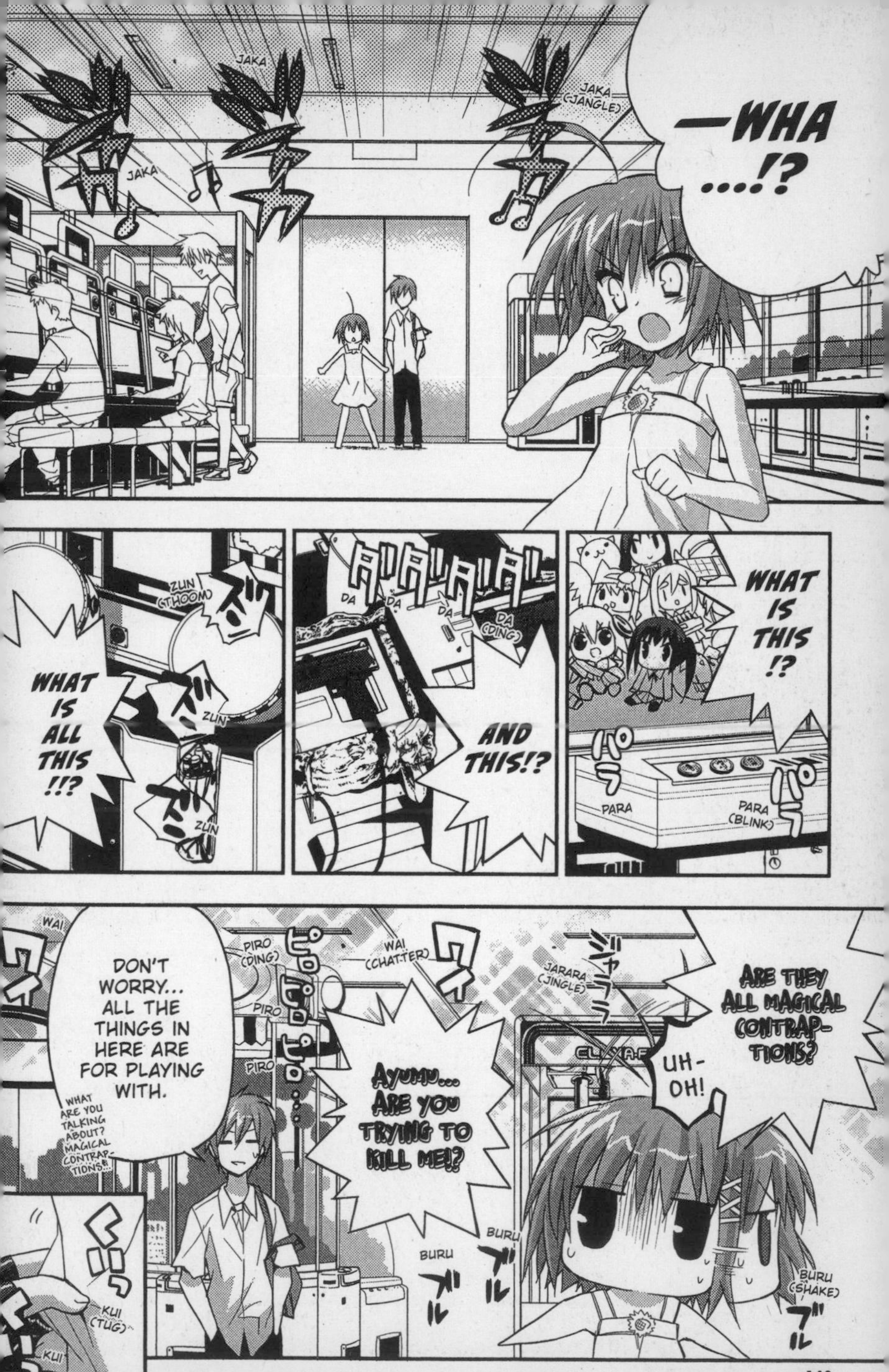
JAKA (JANGLE)
JAKA
JAKA
—WHA ...!?
WHAT IS THIS !?
PARA
PARA (BLINK)
DA
DA
DA
DA (DING)
AND THIS!?
ZUN (THOOM)
ZUN
ZUN
WHAT IS ALL THIS !!?
ARE THEY ALL MAGICAL CONTRAP-TIONS?
UH-OH!
JARARA (JINGLE)
AYUMU... ARE YOU TRYING TO KILL ME!?
WAI (CHATTER)
PIRO (DING)
PIRO
PIRO
WAI
DON'T WORRY... ALL THE THINGS IN HERE ARE FOR PLAYING WITH.
WHAT ARE YOU TALKING ABOUT? MAGICAL CONTRAP-TIONS...
BURU
BURU
BURU (SHAKE)
KUI (TUG)
KUI

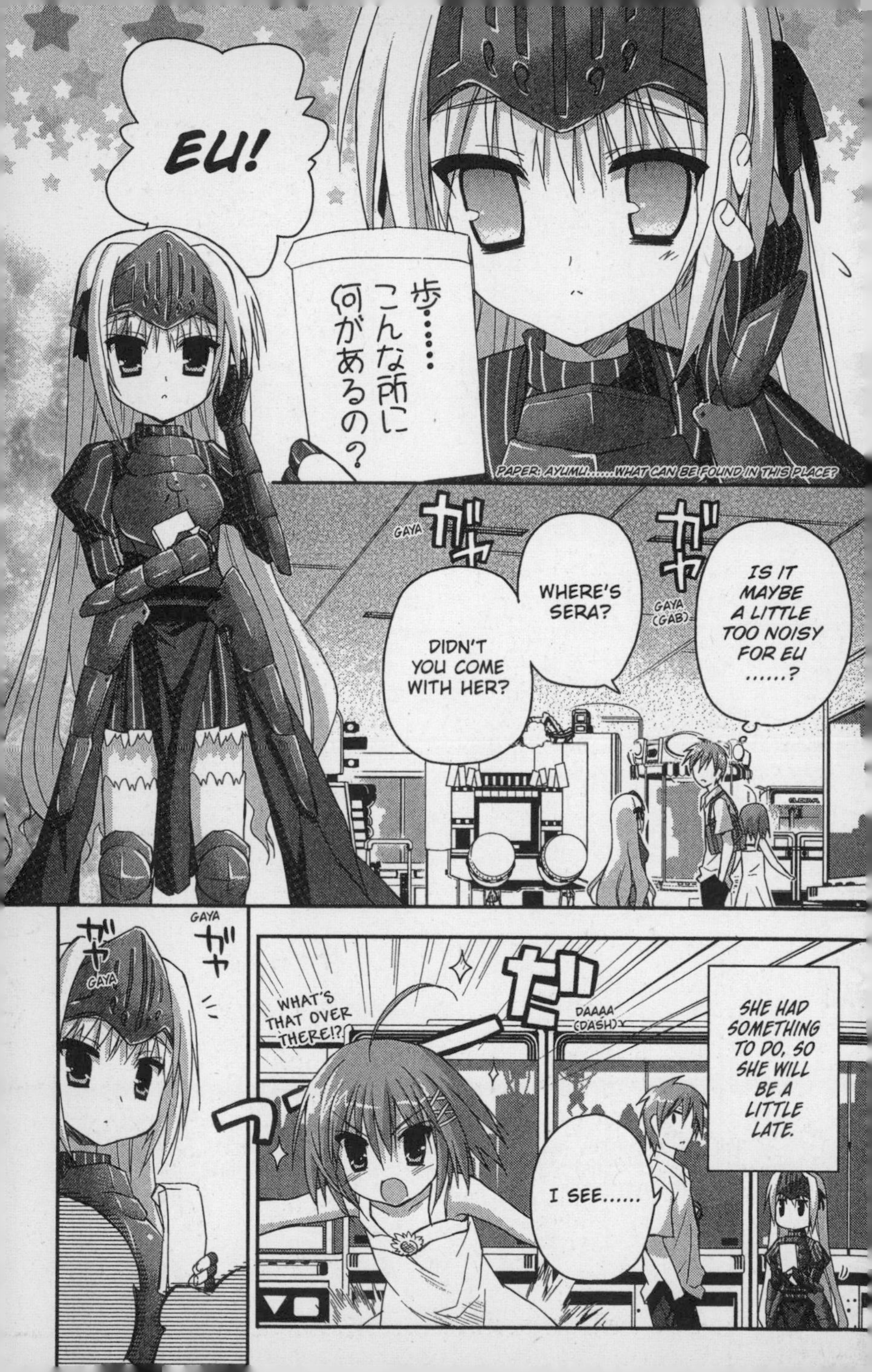
歩……こんな所に何があるの？
PAPER: AYUMU......WHAT CAN BE FOUND IN THIS PLACE?
EU!
ガヤ
GAYA (GAB)
IS IT MAYBE A LITTLE TOO NOISY FOR EU ......?
ガヤ
GAYA
WHERE'S SERA?
DIDN'T YOU COME WITH HER?
SHE HAD SOMETHING TO DO, SO SHE WILL BE A LITTLE LATE.
I SEE......
だっ
DAAAA (DASH)
WHAT'S THAT OVER THERE!?
ガヤ
GAYA
GAYA

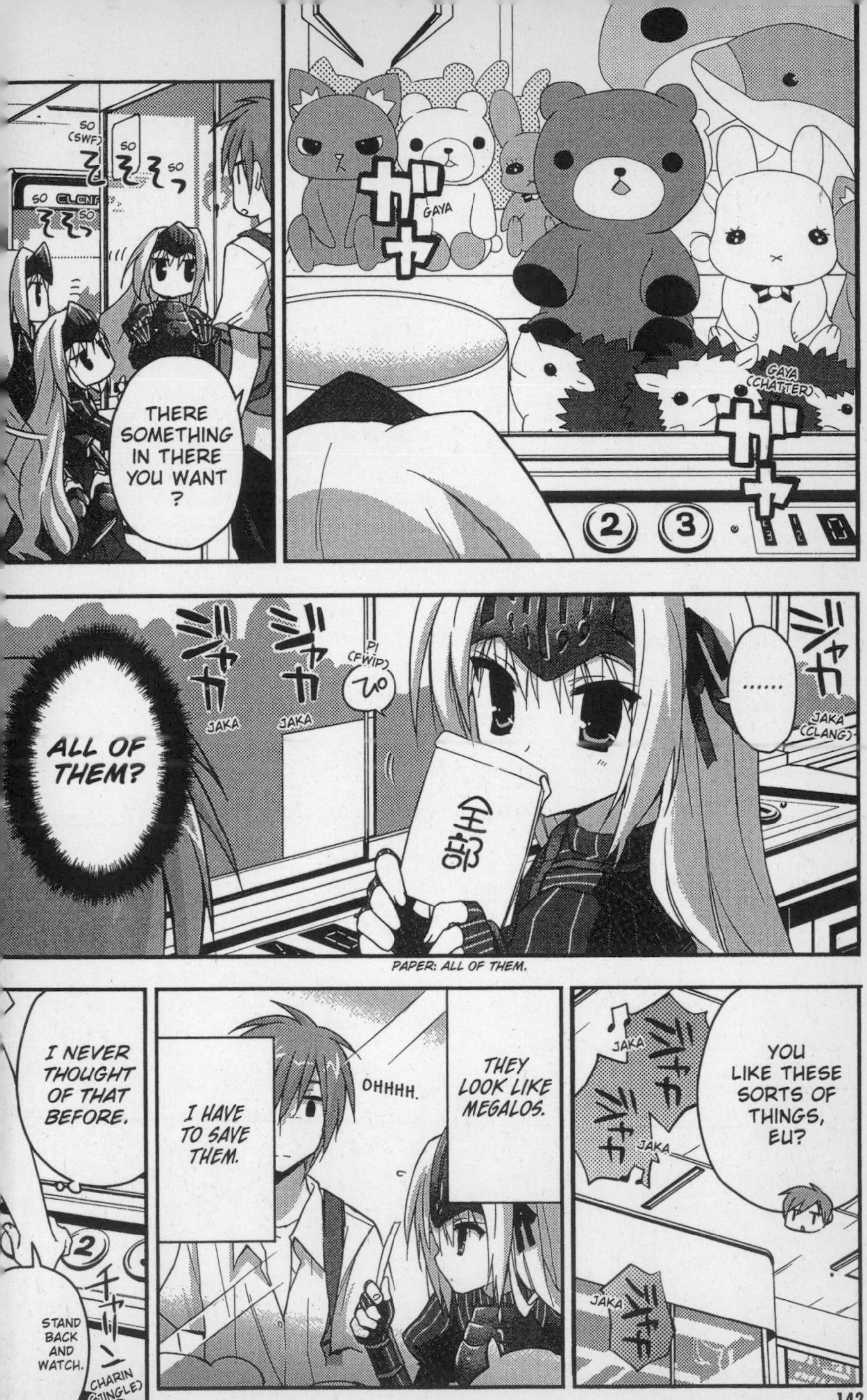
GAYA
GAYA (CHATTER)
SO (SWF)
SO
SO
SO
SO
THERE SOMETHING IN THERE YOU WANT?
JAKA (CLANG)
......
PI (FWIP)
JAKA
JAKA
ALL OF THEM?
PAPER: ALL OF THEM.
YOU LIKE THESE SORTS OF THINGS, EU?
JAKA
JAKA
JAKA
THEY LOOK LIKE MEGALOS.
OHHHH.
I HAVE TO SAVE THEM.
I NEVER THOUGHT OF THAT BEFORE.
STAND BACK AND WATCH.
CHARIN (JINGLE)

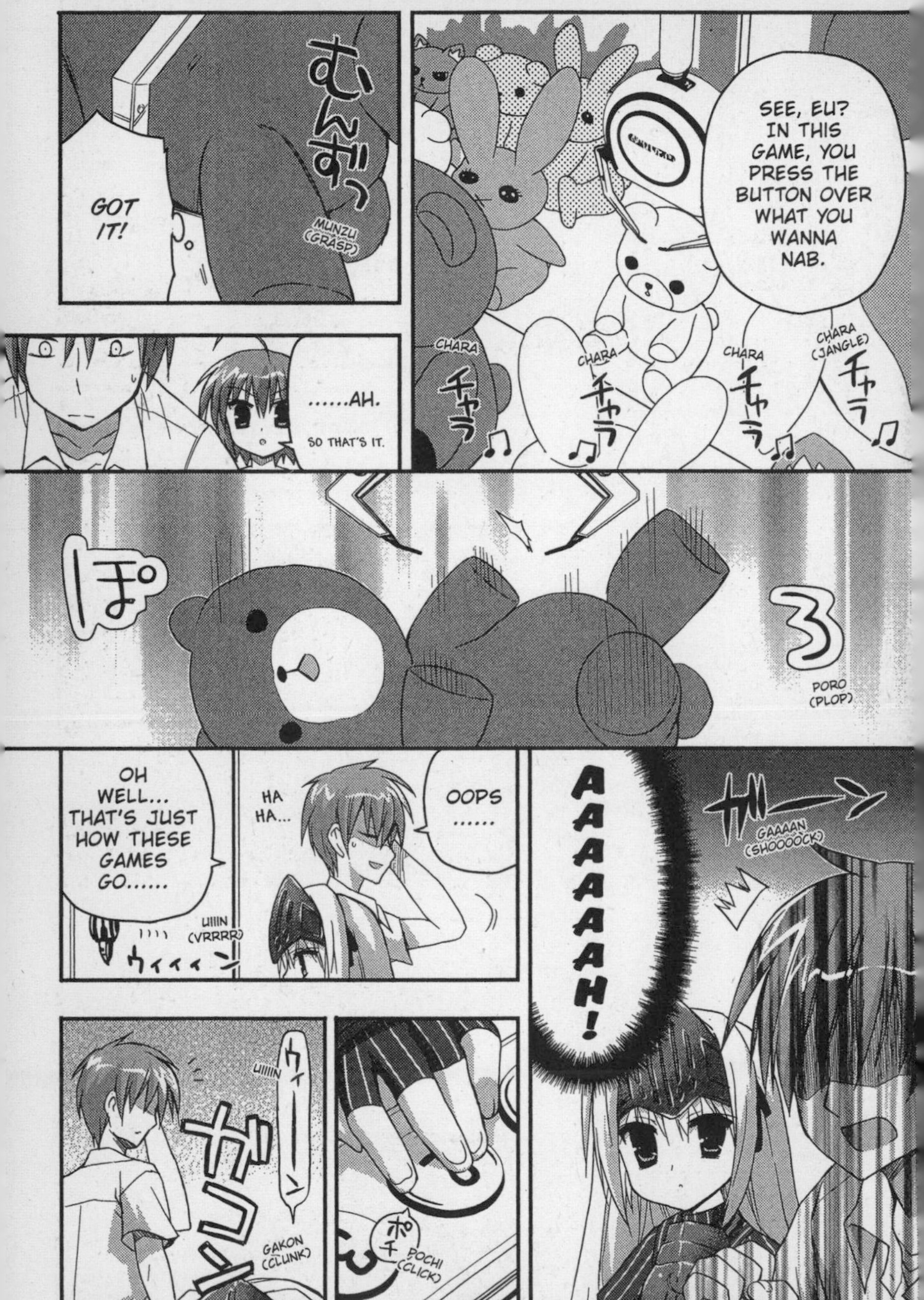

SEE, EU? IN THIS GAME, YOU PRESS THE BUTTON OVER WHAT YOU WANNA NAB.
チャラ CHARA (JANGLE)
チャラ CHARA
チャラ CHARA
チャラ CHARA
むんずっ MUNZU (GRASP)
GOT IT!
......AH.
SO THAT'S IT.
ぽろ PORO (PLOP)
AAAAAAAH!
ガーン GAAAAN (SHOOOOCK)
OOPS ......
HA HA...
OH WELL... THAT'S JUST HOW THESE GAMES GO......
ウィィィン UIIIN (VRRRR)
ポチ POCHI (CLICK)
ウィーン UIIIIN
がこん GAKON (CLUNK)

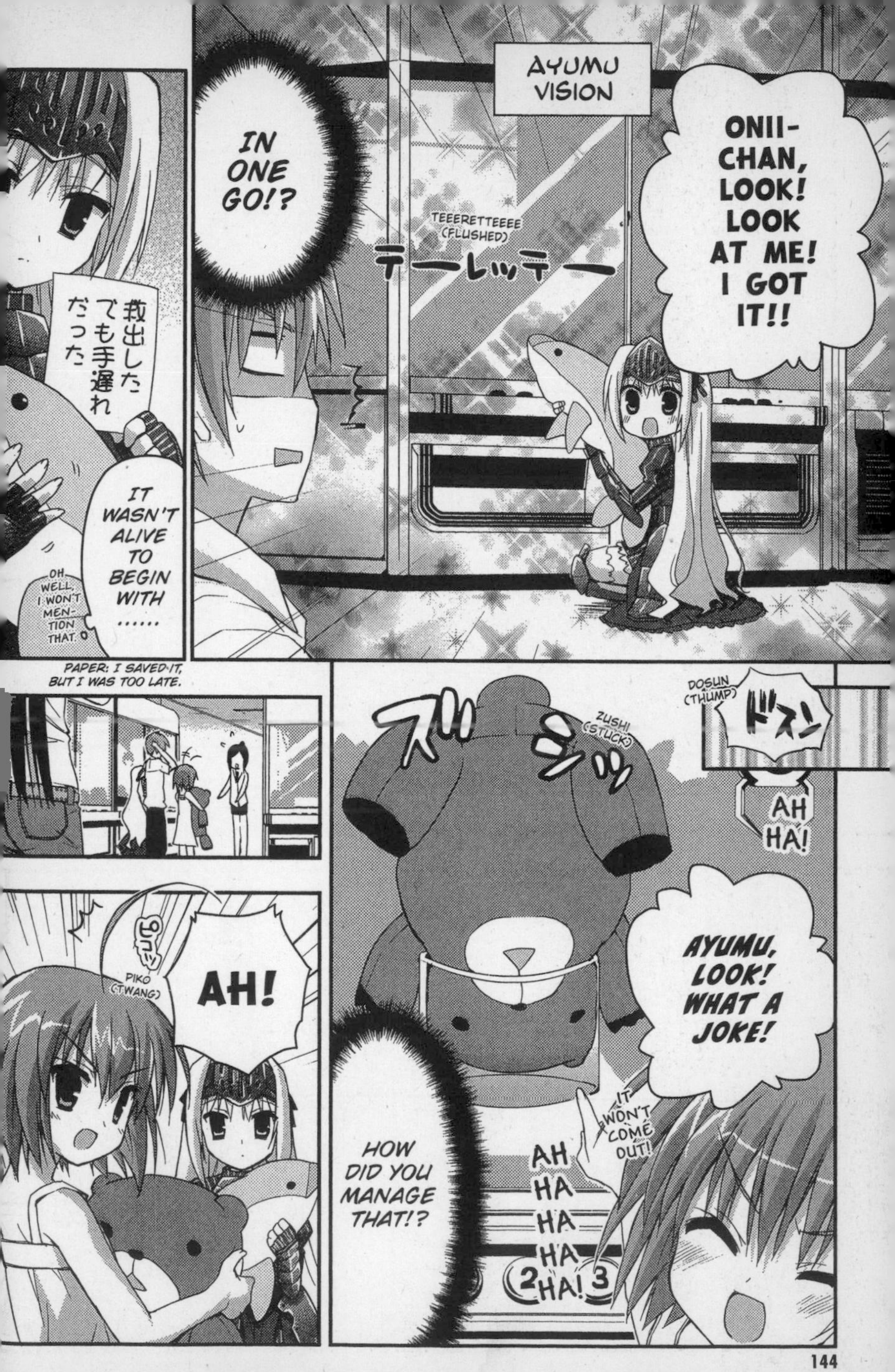
AYUMU VISION
ONII-CHAN, LOOK! LOOK AT ME! I GOT IT!!
TEEERETTEEEE (FLUSHED)
テーレッテー
IN ONE GO!?
救出したでも手遅れだった
IT WASN'T ALIVE TO BEGIN WITH ......
OH WELL, I WON'T MENTION THAT.
PAPER: I SAVED IT, BUT I WAS TOO LATE.
DOSUN (THUMP)
ドスン
AH HA!
ZUSHI (STUCK)
ズシッ
AYUMU, LOOK! WHAT A JOKE!
IT WON'T COME OUT!
AH HA HA HA HA!
2
3
HOW DID YOU MANAGE THAT!?
PIKO (TWANG)
ピコッ
AH!

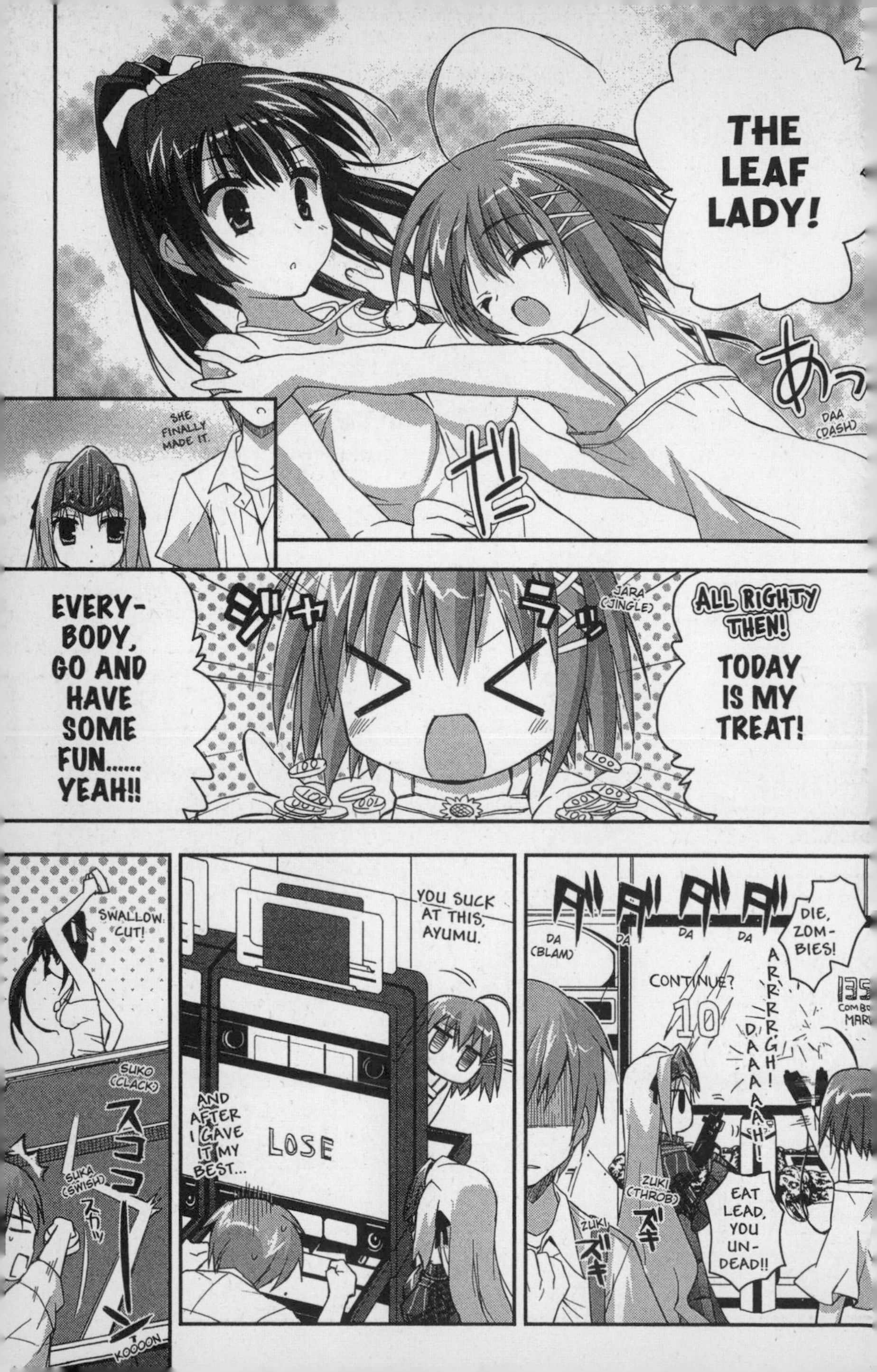
THE LEAF LADY!
あっ
DAA (DASH)
SHE FINALLY MADE IT.
ALL RIGHTY THEN!
TODAY IS MY TREAT!
JARA (JINGLE)
EVERY-BODY, GO AND HAVE SOME FUN...... YEAH!!
DIE, ZOM-BIES!
DA (BLAM)
DA
DA
DA
CONTINUE?
10
ARRRRGH!
DAAAAAH!
EAT LEAD, YOU UN-DEAD!!
ZUKI (THROB)
ZUKI
ズキ
ズキ
YOU SUCK AT THIS, AYUMU.
AND AFTER I GAVE IT MY BEST...
LOSE
SWALLOW CUT!
SUKO (CLACK)
スコーン
SUKA (SWISH)
スカッ
KOOOON

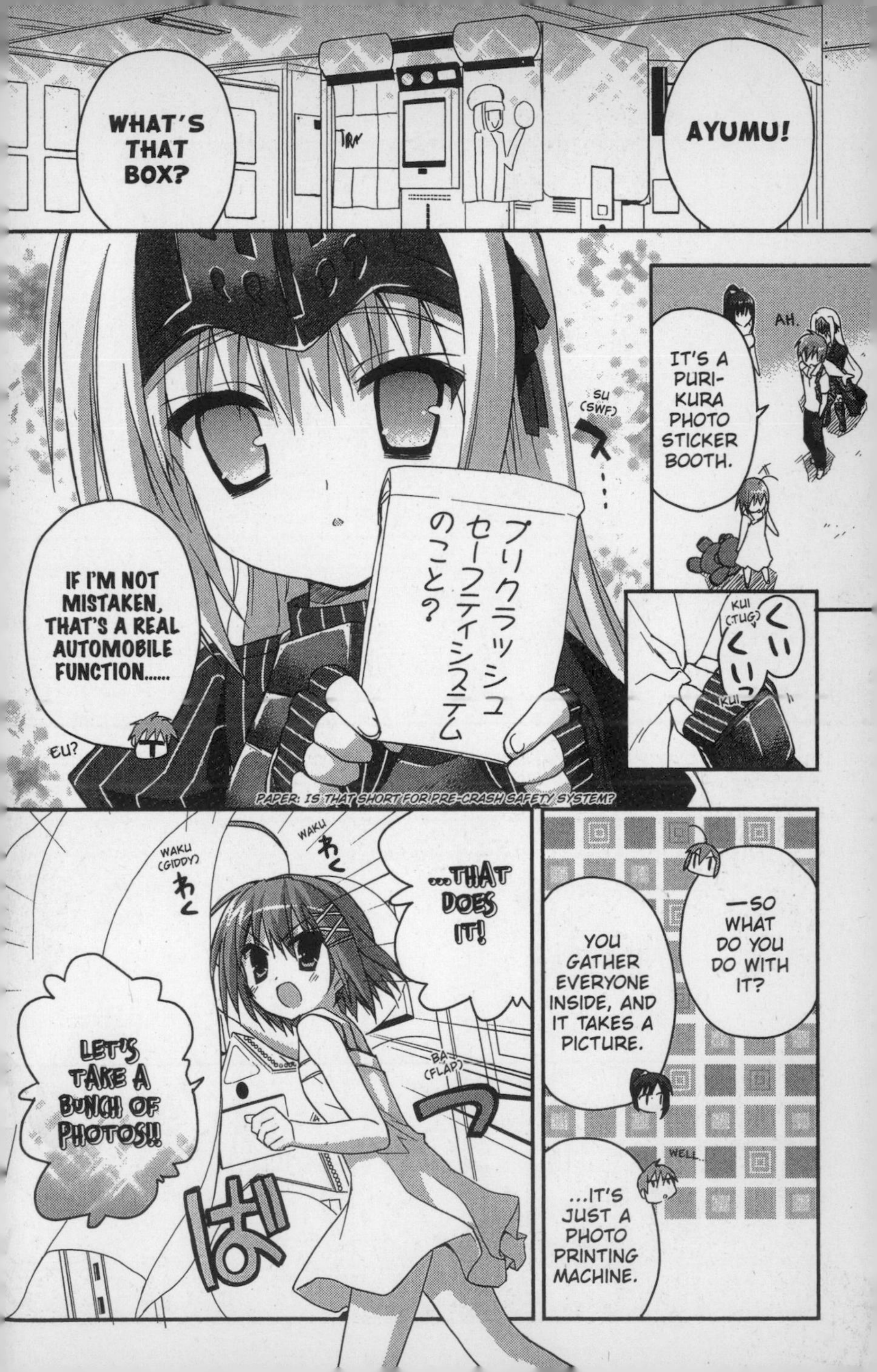
AYUMU!
WHAT'S THAT BOX?
AH.
IT'S A PURI-KURA PHOTO STICKER BOOTH.
SU (SWF)
IF I'M NOT MISTAKEN, THAT'S A REAL AUTOMOBILE FUNCTION......
EU?
プリクラッシュセーフティシステムのこと？
PAPER: IS THAT SHORT FOR PRE-CRASH SAFETY SYSTEM?
KUI (TUG)
くいくいっ
KUI
—SO WHAT DO YOU DO WITH IT?
YOU GATHER EVERYONE INSIDE, AND IT TAKES A PICTURE.
WELL...
...IT'S JUST A PHOTO PRINTING MACHINE.
WAKU
わく
WAKU (GIDDY)
わく
...THAT DOES IT!
LET'S TAKE A BUNCH OF PHOTOS!!
BA (FLAP)
ばっ

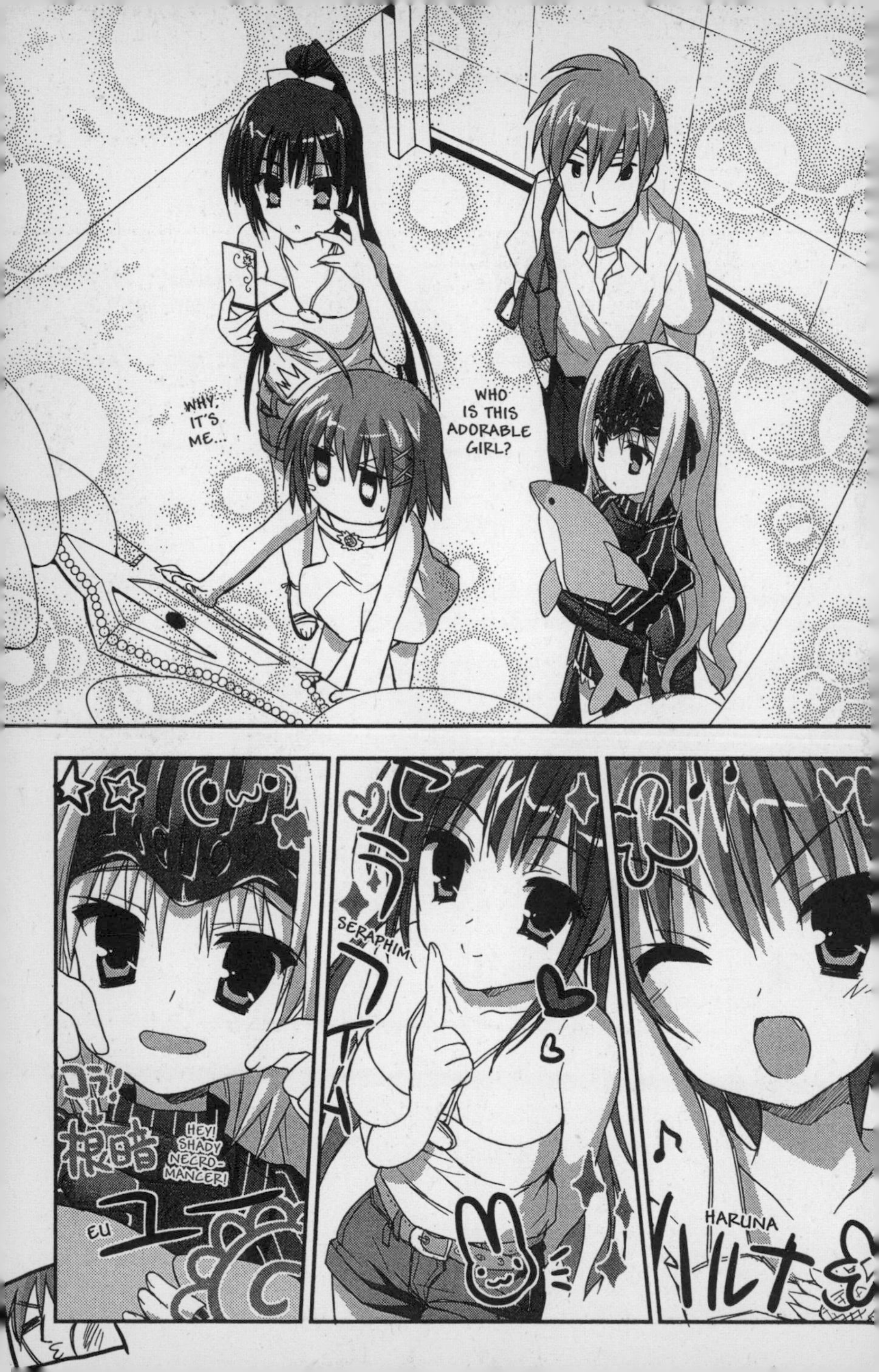
WHO IS THIS ADORABLE GIRL?
WHY, IT'S ME...
HARUNA
SERAPHIM
HEY! SHADY NECRO-MANCER!
EU
根暗
ユー
ハルナ

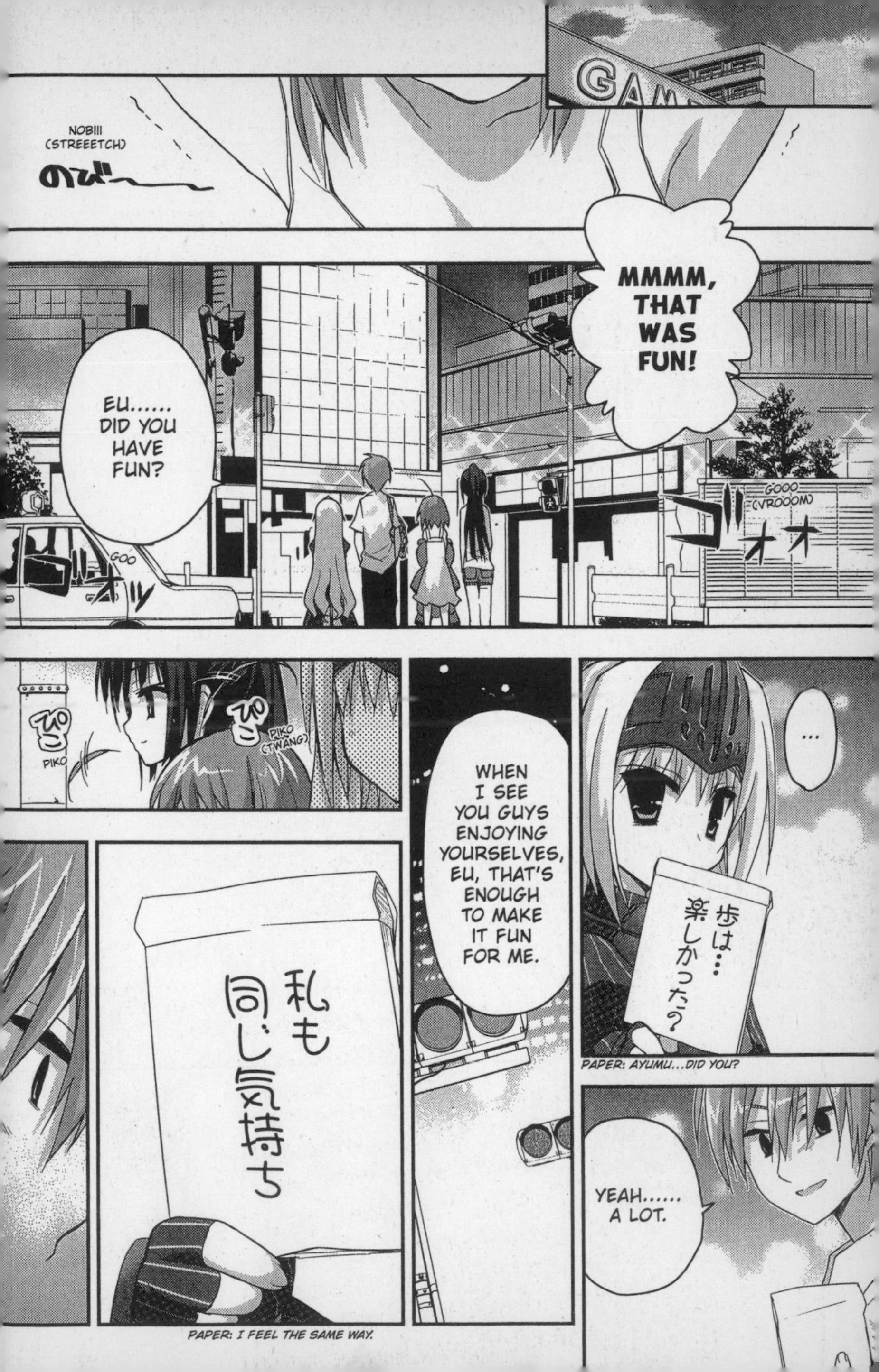

GAM
MMMM, THAT WAS FUN!
NOBIII (STREEETCH)
のびー
GOOO (VROOOM)
ゴオオ
EU...... DID YOU HAVE FUN?
GOO
ゴオッ
...
歩は…楽しかった？
PAPER: AYUMU...DID YOU?
WHEN I SEE YOU GUYS ENJOYING YOURSELVES, EU, THAT'S ENOUGH TO MAKE IT FUN FOR ME.
ぴこ
PIKO (TWANG)
ぴこ
PIKO
YEAH...... A LOT.
私も同じ気持ち
PAPER: I FEEL THE SAME WAY.

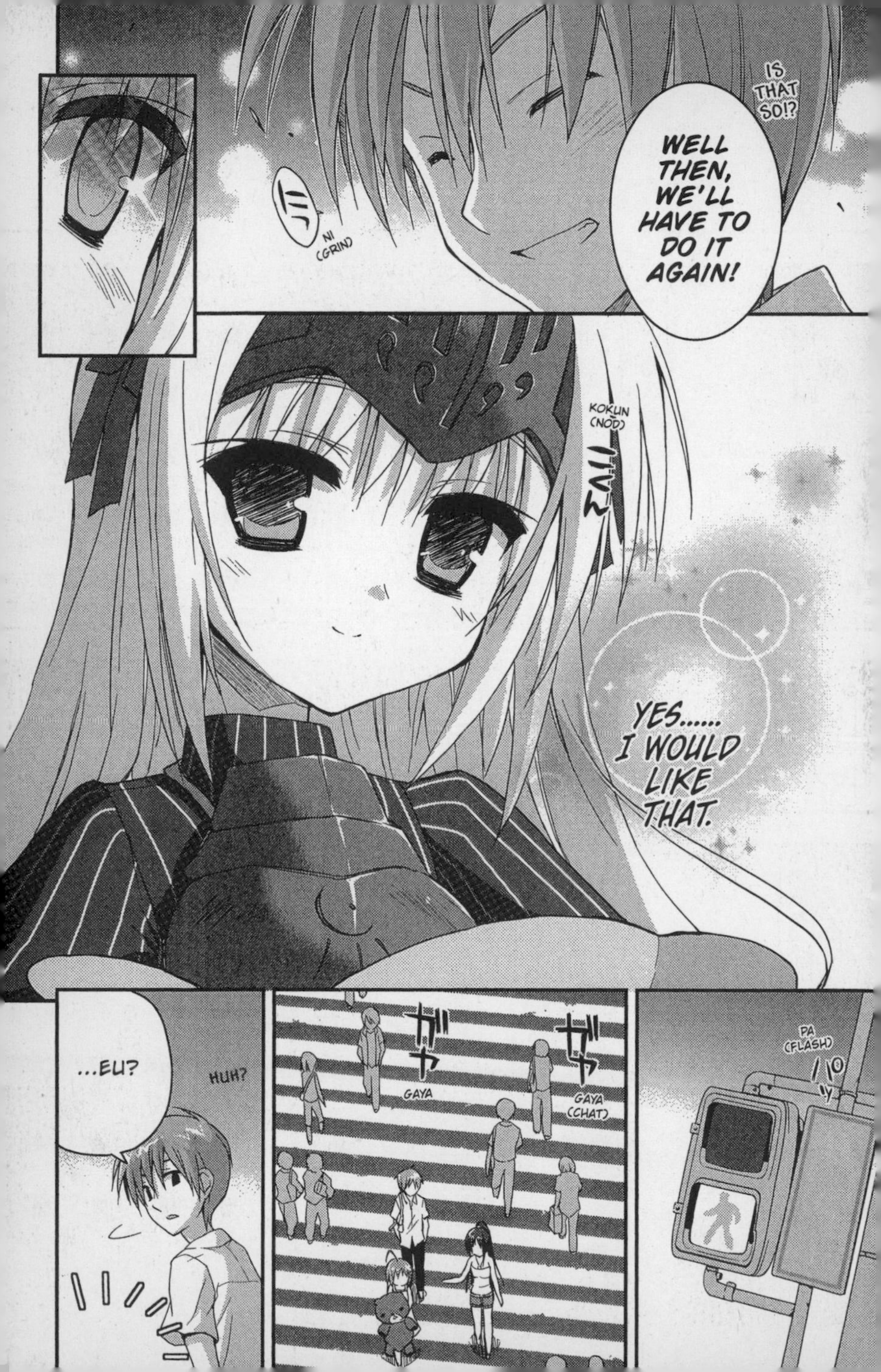

IS THAT SO!?
WELL THEN, WE'LL HAVE TO DO IT AGAIN!
NI (GRIN)
KOKUN (NOD)
YES...... I WOULD LIKE THAT.
PA (FLASH)
GAYA (CHAT)
GAYA
...EU?
HUH?

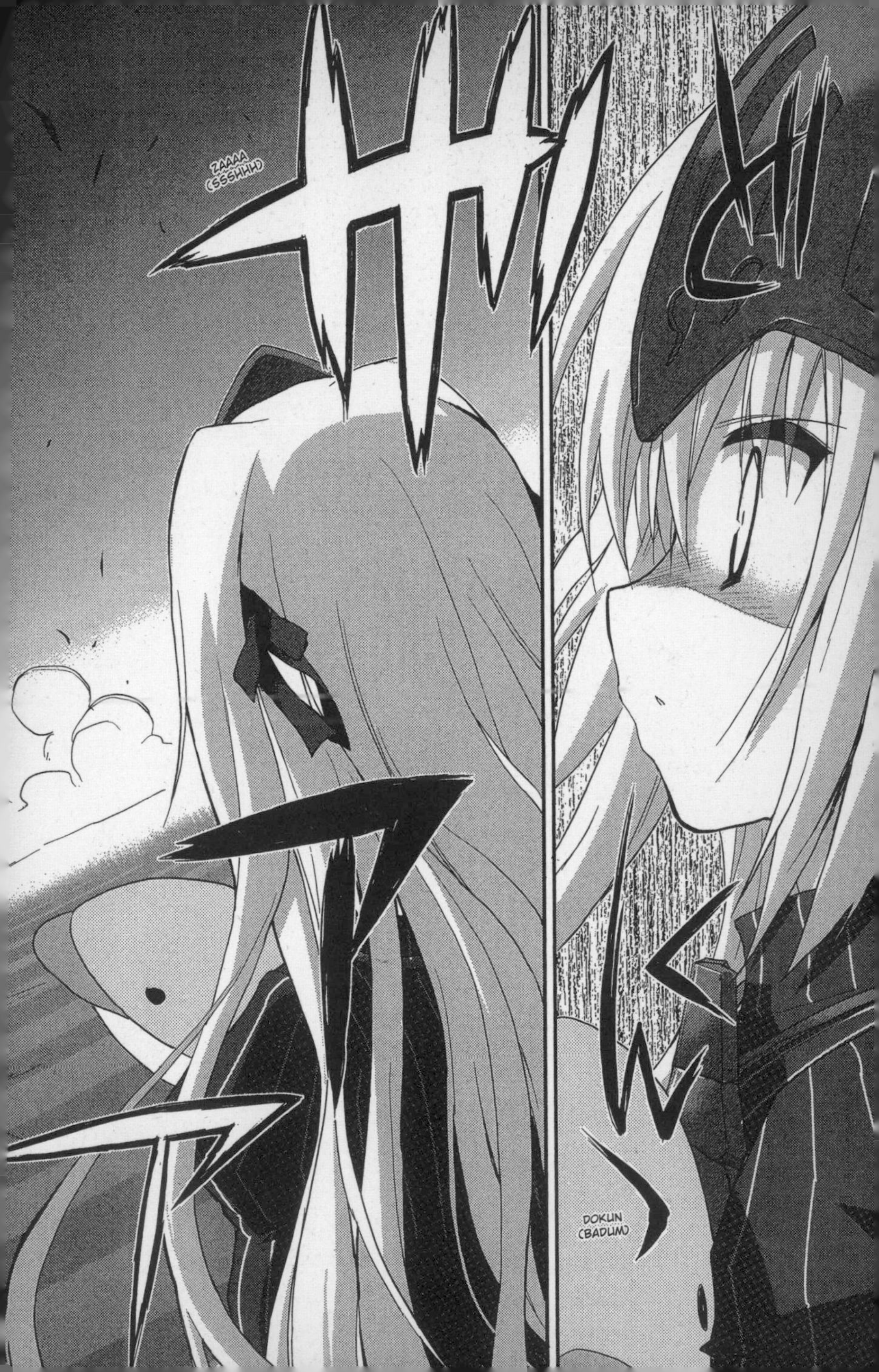
ZAAAA (SSSHHH)
DOKUN (BADUM)

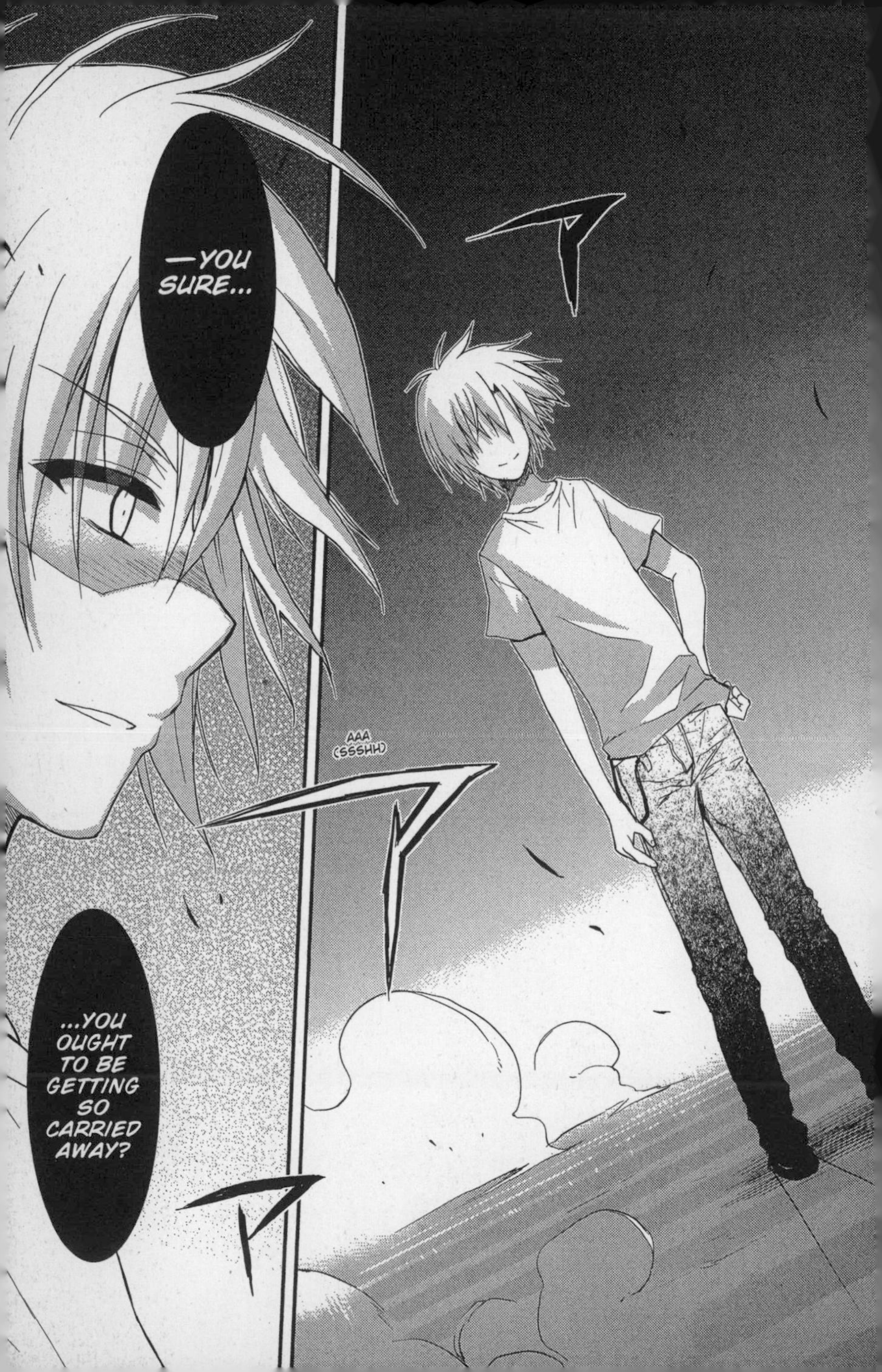
—YOU SURE...
AAA (SSSHH)
...YOU OUGHT TO BE GETTING SO CARRIED AWAY?

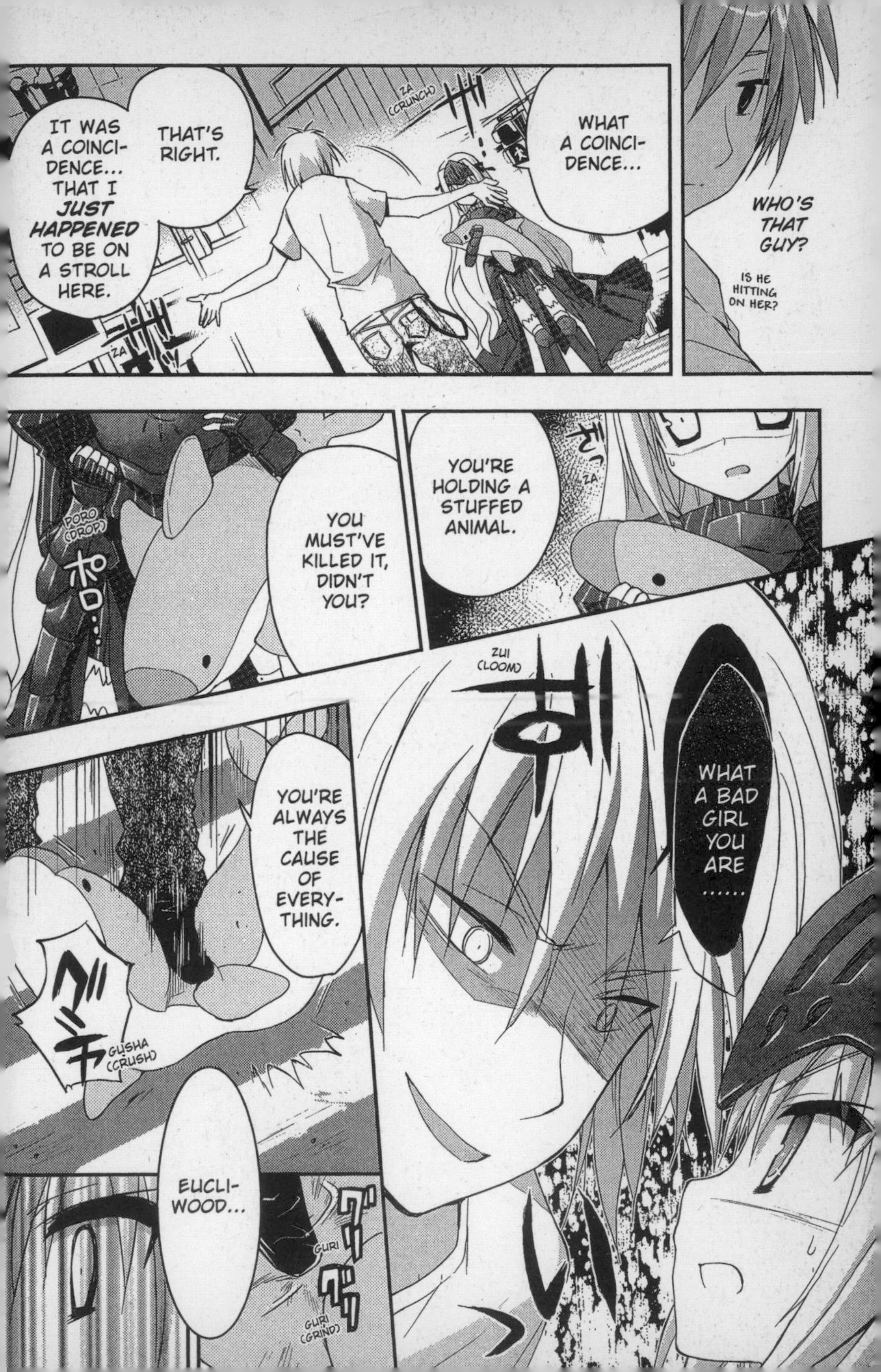
WHO'S THAT GUY?
IS HE HITTING ON HER?
WHAT A COINCIDENCE...
ZA (CRUNCH)
THAT'S RIGHT.
IT WAS A COINCIDENCE... THAT I JUST HAPPENED TO BE ON A STROLL HERE.
ZA
YOU'RE HOLDING A STUFFED ANIMAL.
ZA
YOU MUST'VE KILLED IT, DIDN'T YOU?
PORO (DROP)
WHAT A BAD GIRL YOU ARE ......
ZUI (LOOM)
YOU'RE ALWAYS THE CAUSE OF EVERYTHING.
GUSHA (CRUSH)
EUCLIWOOD...
GURI
GURI (GRIND)

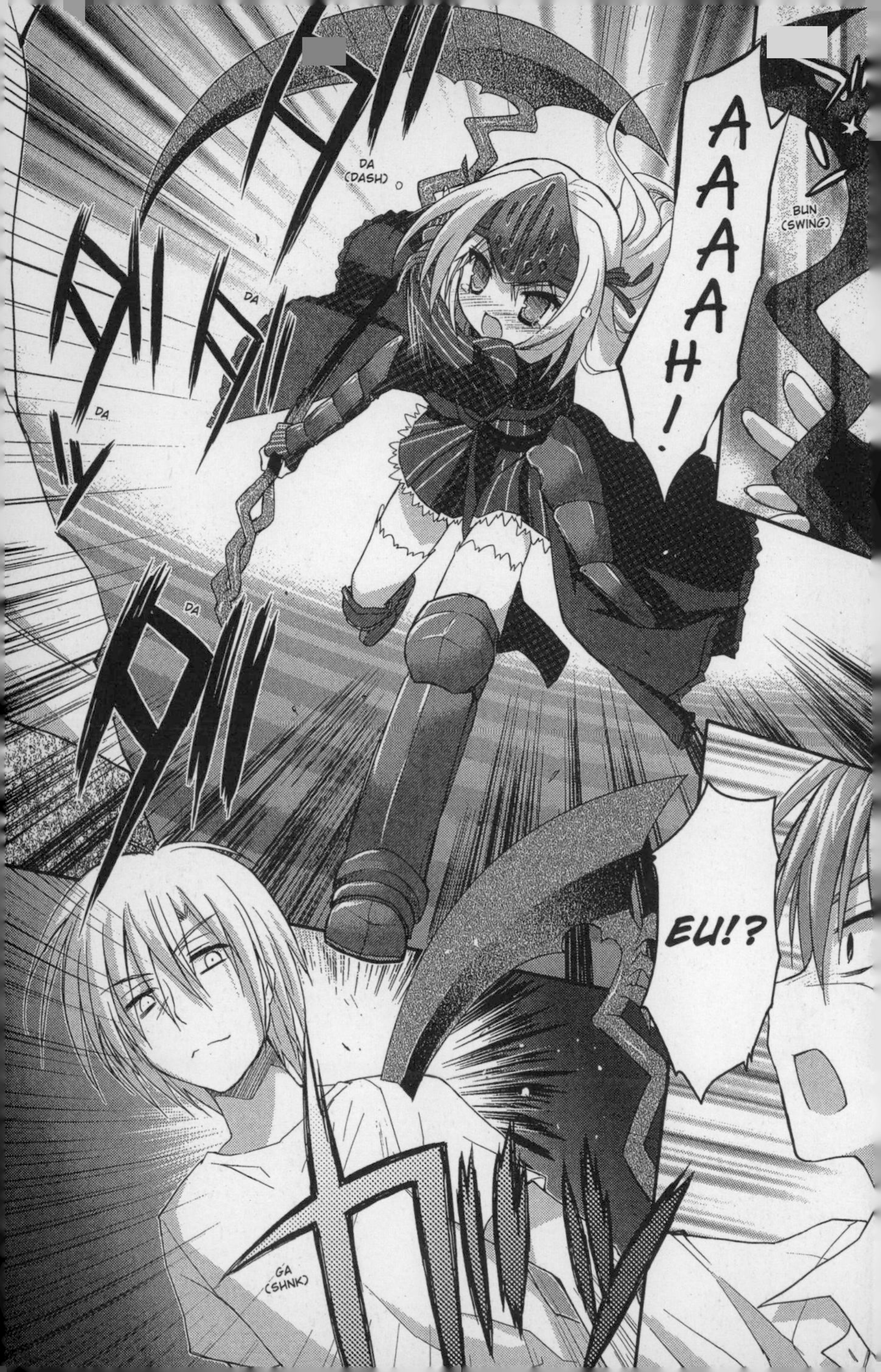
BUN (SWING)
AAAAAH!
DA (DASH)
DA
DA
DA
EU!?
GA (SHNK)

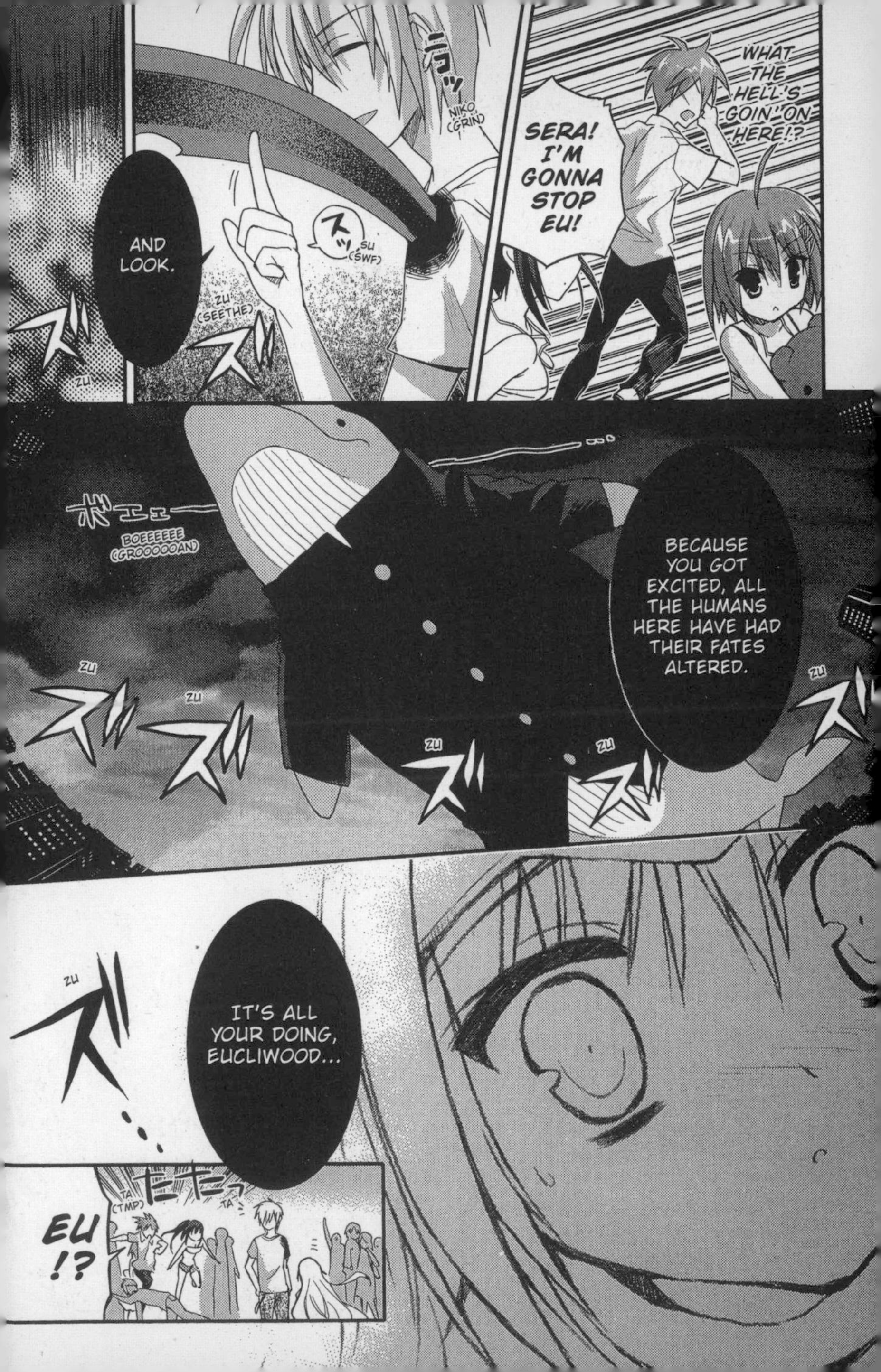

WHAT THE HELL'S GOIN' ON HERE!?
SERA! I'M GONNA STOP EU!
NIKO (GRIN)
AND LOOK.
SU (SWF)
ZU (SEETHE)
ZU
BECAUSE YOU GOT EXCITED, ALL THE HUMANS HERE HAVE HAD THEIR FATES ALTERED.
BOEEEEEE (GROOOOOAN)
ZU
ZU
ZU
ZU
ZU
IT'S ALL YOUR DOING, EUCLIWOOD...
ZU
TA (TMP) TA
EU !?

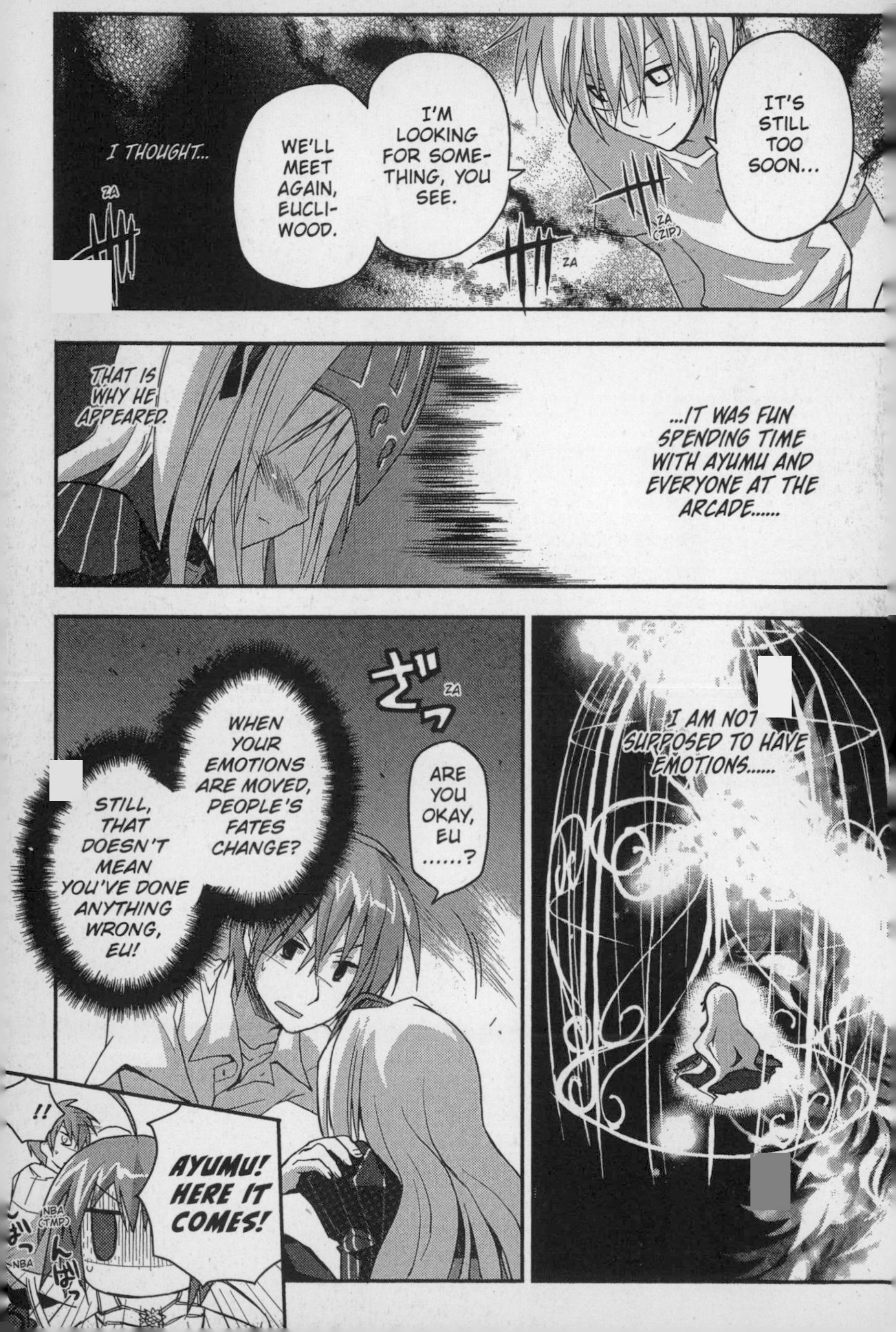
IT'S STILL TOO SOON...
ZA (ZIP)
ZA
I'M LOOKING FOR SOME-THING, YOU SEE.
WE'LL MEET AGAIN, EUCLI-WOOD.
I THOUGHT...
ZA
...IT WAS FUN SPENDING TIME WITH AYUMU AND EVERYONE AT THE ARCADE......
THAT IS WHY HE APPEARED.
I AM NOT SUPPOSED TO HAVE EMOTIONS......
ざっ
ZA
ARE YOU OKAY, EU ......?
WHEN YOUR EMOTIONS ARE MOVED, PEOPLE'S FATES CHANGE?
STILL, THAT DOESN'T MEAN YOU'VE DONE ANYTHING WRONG, EU!
!!
AYUMU! HERE IT COMES!
NBA (TMP)
NBA

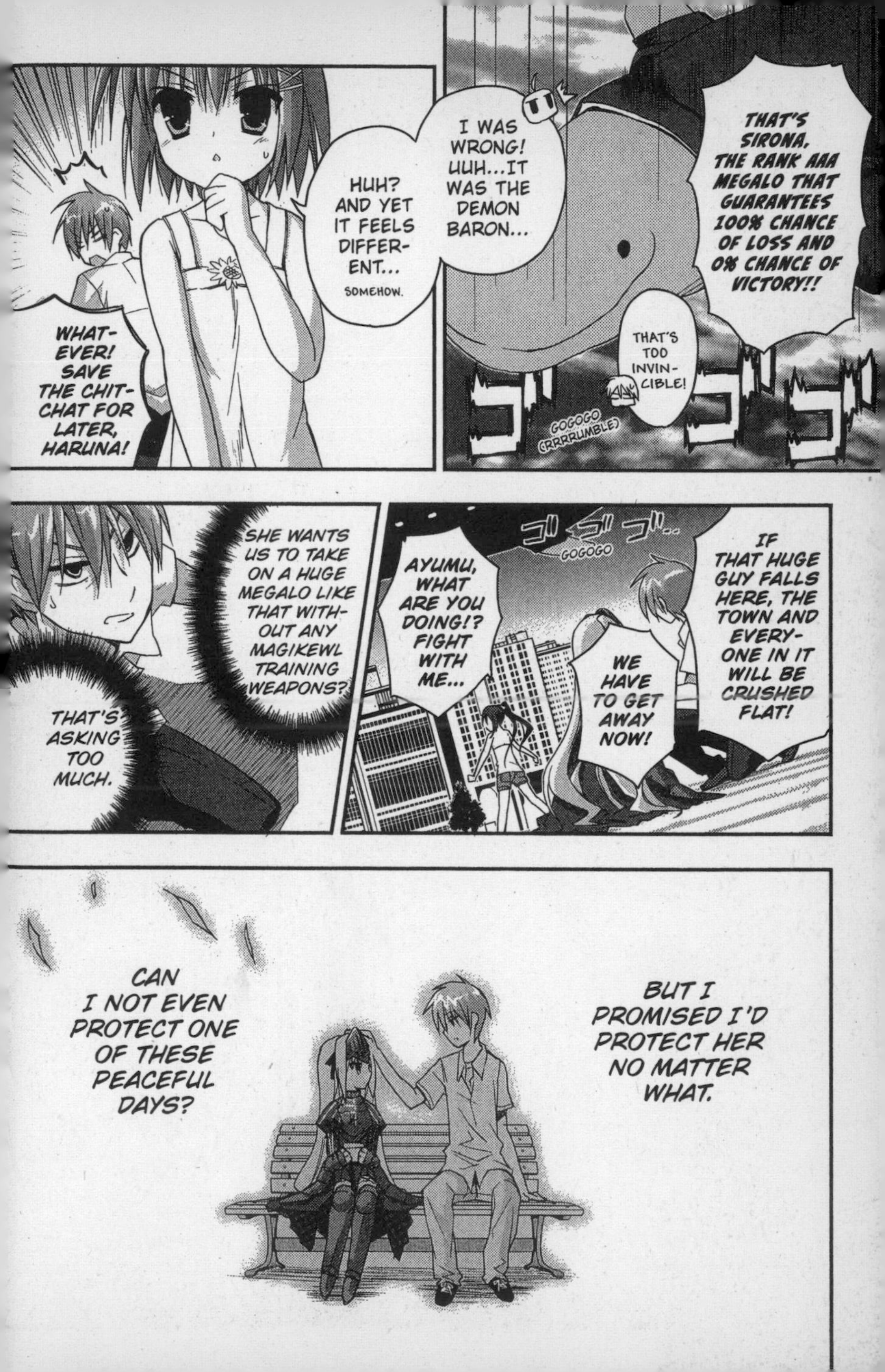
THAT'S SIRONA, THE RANK AAA MEGALO THAT GUARANTEES 100% CHANCE OF LOSS AND 0% CHANCE OF VICTORY!!
THAT'S TOO INVINCIBLE!
GOGOGO (RRRRUMBLE)
I WAS WRONG! UUH...IT WAS THE DEMON BARON...
HUH? AND YET IT FEELS DIFFERENT... SOMEHOW.
WHATEVER! SAVE THE CHIT-CHAT FOR LATER, HARUNA!
IF THAT HUGE GUY FALLS HERE, THE TOWN AND EVERYONE IN IT WILL BE CRUSHED FLAT!
WE HAVE TO GET AWAY NOW!
GOGOGO
AYUMU, WHAT ARE YOU DOING!? FIGHT WITH ME...
SHE WANTS US TO TAKE ON A HUGE MEGALO LIKE THAT WITHOUT ANY MAGIKEWL TRAINING WEAPONS?
THAT'S ASKING TOO MUCH.
BUT I PROMISED I'D PROTECT HER NO MATTER WHAT.
CAN I NOT EVEN PROTECT ONE OF THESE PEACEFUL DAYS?

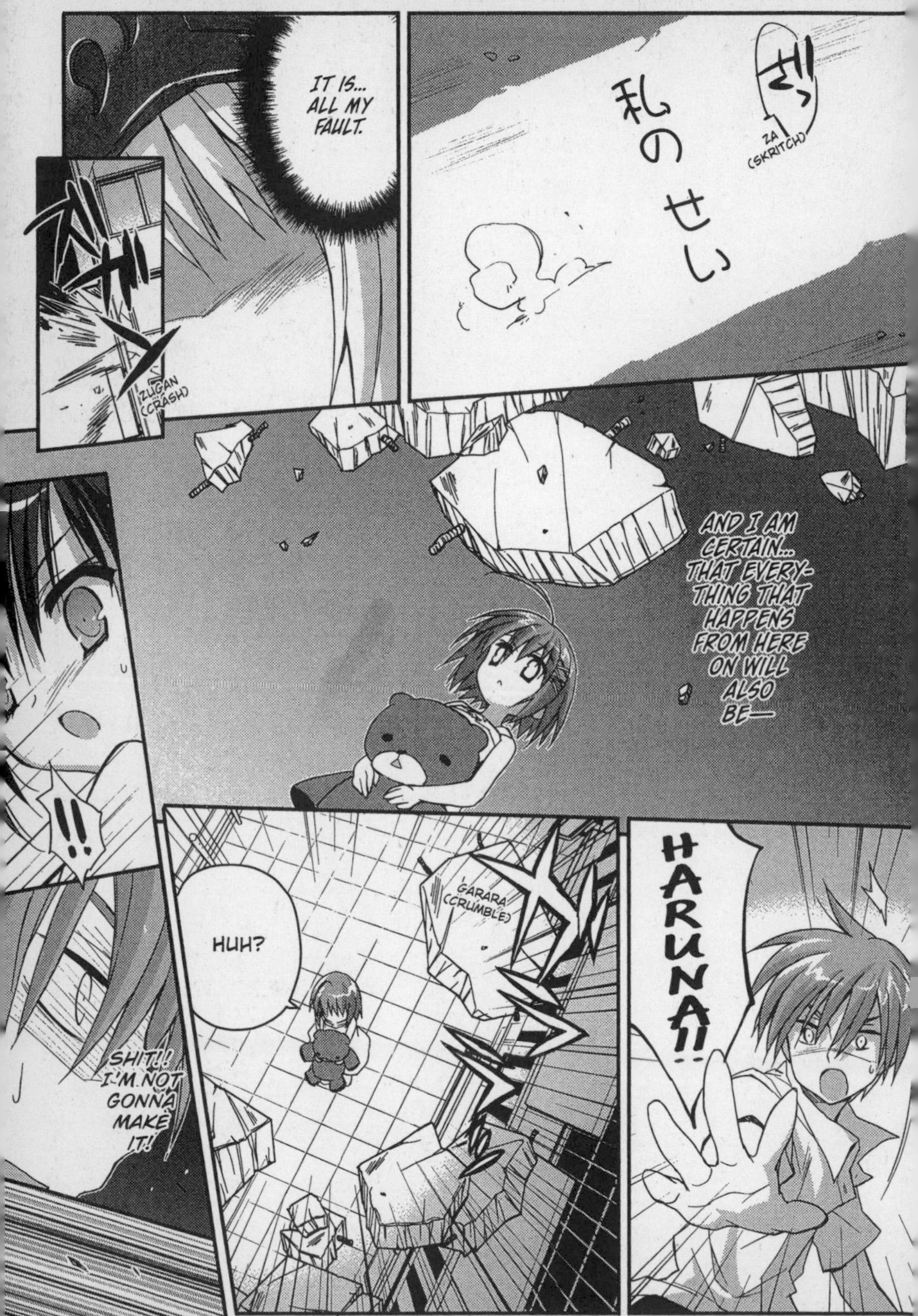

ざっ
ZA (SKRITCH)
私のせい
IT IS... ALL MY FAULT.
ZUGAN (CRASH)
AND I AM CERTAIN... THAT EVERYTHING THAT HAPPENS FROM HERE ON WILL ALSO BE—
!!
HARUNA!!
GARARA (CRUMBLE)
HUH?
SHIT!! I'M NOT GONNA MAKE IT!

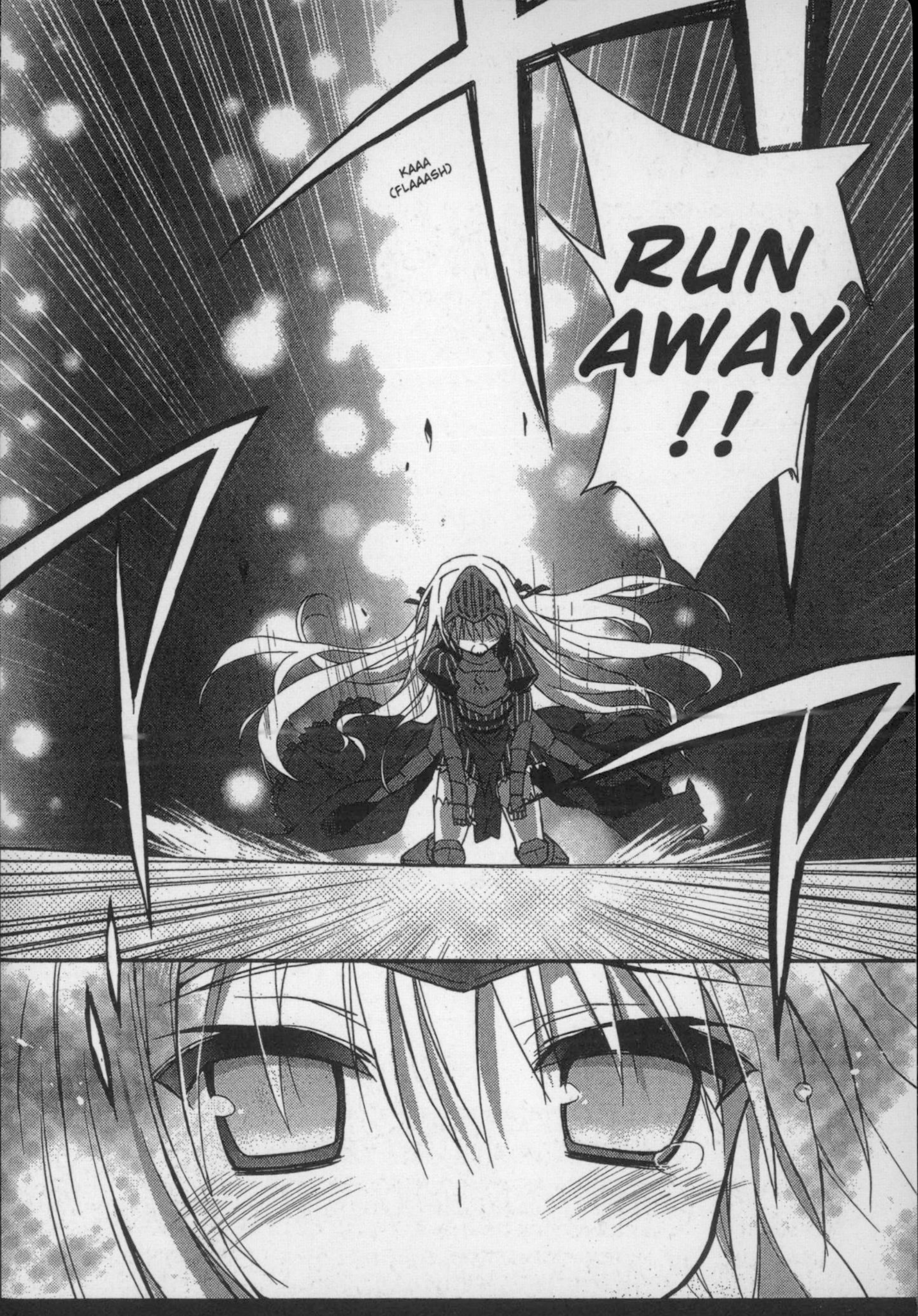
KAAA
(FLAAASH)
RUN AWAY!!

THE VOICE WITH WHICH SHE SAID THOSE WORDS WAS......LOUD AND CLEAR—

TO BE CONTINUED

SHADY NECROMANCER LEVEL CHECKLIST

- [ ] You strain to hear any conversation within a twenty-meter radius.
- [ ] You simply adore the smell of underground passageways.
- [ ] Your recent obsession is becoming popular with the opposite sex.
- [ ] You savor salmon roe by crushing each egg in your mouth one at a time.
- [ ] On trains, you enjoy the sounds, vibrations, and schoolgirls.
- [ ] You can recite the name of every classmate of yours from third grade.
- [ ] Even small, orange fluorescent lights hurt your eyes.
- [ ] You've never once had caramel corn with peanuts.
- [ ] Your kneecaps are a little salty.
- [ ] You tend to suffer from slight gastroptosis.
- [ ] You remove the shiitake mushrooms from meat buns.
- [ ] Party games are always played solo!
- [x] The roots of the cactus in your room rot right away.
- [ ] Small animals tend to gather around you without your knowing. But the minute you notice, they flee.
- [ ] You dream of protecting everyone from nuclear war and of having white hair.

Score	Results
15	Eu - "Simply lovely"
8~	Sera - "You are way too lukewarm. Sitting with your legs drawn to your chest suits you."
1~	Haruna - "You should be more like me! A super-quiet person!"
0	Tomonori - "Do people go up to you just to let you know how loud you're being!?"

BLUE MAGIC EXTRA EDITION YES, IT IS A FOUR-PANEL COMIC.

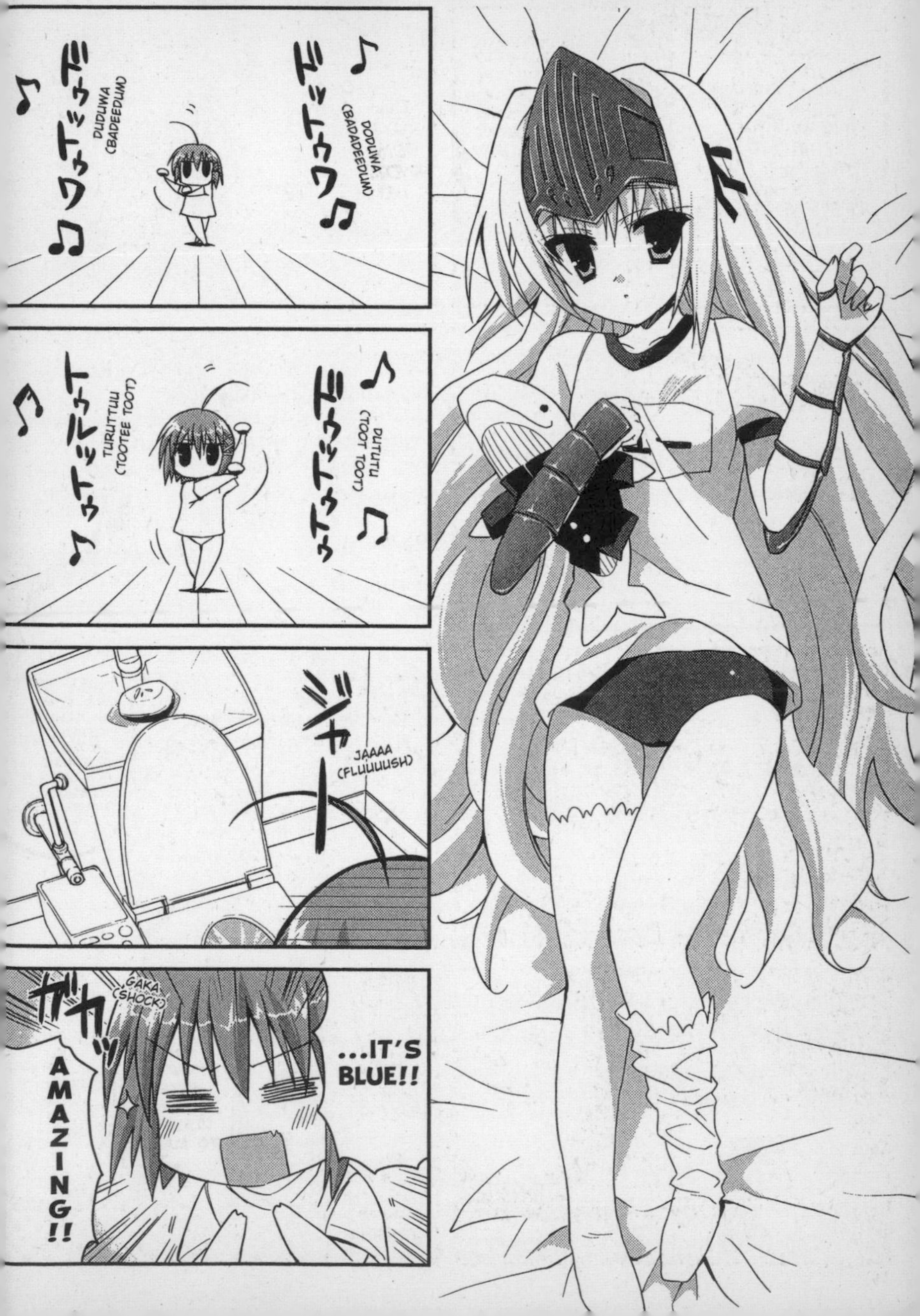
DODUWA (BADAPEEDUM)
DUDUWA (BADEEDUM)
DUTUTU (TOOT TOOT)
TURUTTUU (TOOTEE TOOT)
JAAAA (FLUUUUSH)
GAKA (SHOCK)
...IT'S BLUE!!
AMAZING!!

GYOZA KING

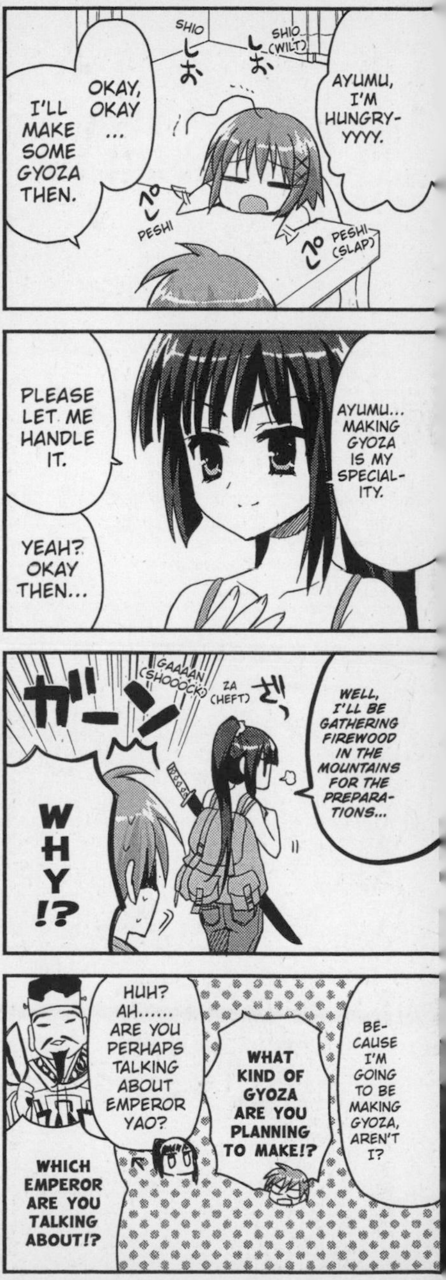
AYUMU, I'M HUNGRY-YYYY.
SHIO (WILT) しお
SHIO しお
PESHI (SLAP) ぺし
PESHI ぺし
OKAY, OKAY ... I'LL MAKE SOME GYOZA THEN.
AYUMU... MAKING GYOZA IS MY SPECIALITY.
PLEASE LET ME HANDLE IT.
YEAH? OKAY THEN...
WELL, I'LL BE GATHERING FIREWOOD IN THE MOUNTAINS FOR THE PREPARATIONS...
ZA (HEFT) ざ
GAAAAN (SHOOOCK) ガーン
WHY!?
BECAUSE I'M GOING TO BE MAKING GYOZA, AREN'T I?
WHAT KIND OF GYOZA ARE YOU PLANNING TO MAKE!?
HUH? AH...... ARE YOU PERHAPS TALKING ABOUT EMPEROR YAO?
WHICH EMPEROR ARE YOU TALKING ABOUT!?

3-D

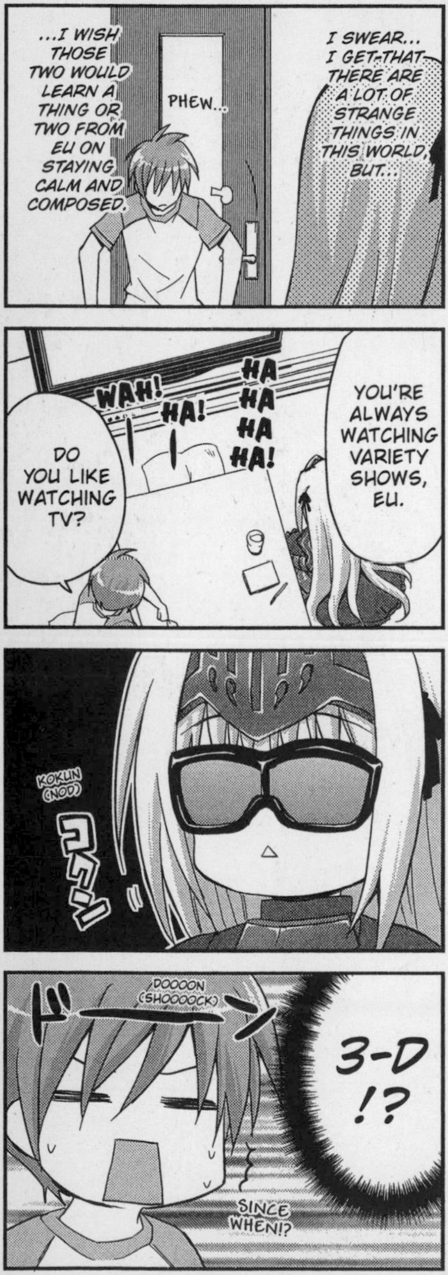
I SWEAR... I GET THAT THERE ARE A LOT OF STRANGE THINGS IN THIS WORLD, BUT...
PHEW...
...I WISH THOSE TWO WOULD LEARN A THING OR TWO FROM EU ON STAYING CALM AND COMPOSED.
YOU'RE ALWAYS WATCHING VARIETY SHOWS, EU.
HA HA HA HA HA!
WAH! HA!
DO YOU LIKE WATCHING TV?
KOKUN (NOD) コクン
DOOOON (SHOOOOCK) ドーン
3-D !?
SINCE WHEN!?

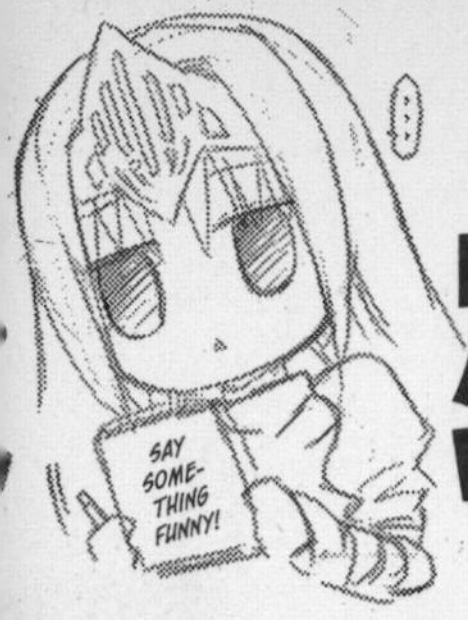
...
SAY SOME-THING FUNNY!

IS THIS AN AFTER-WORD?

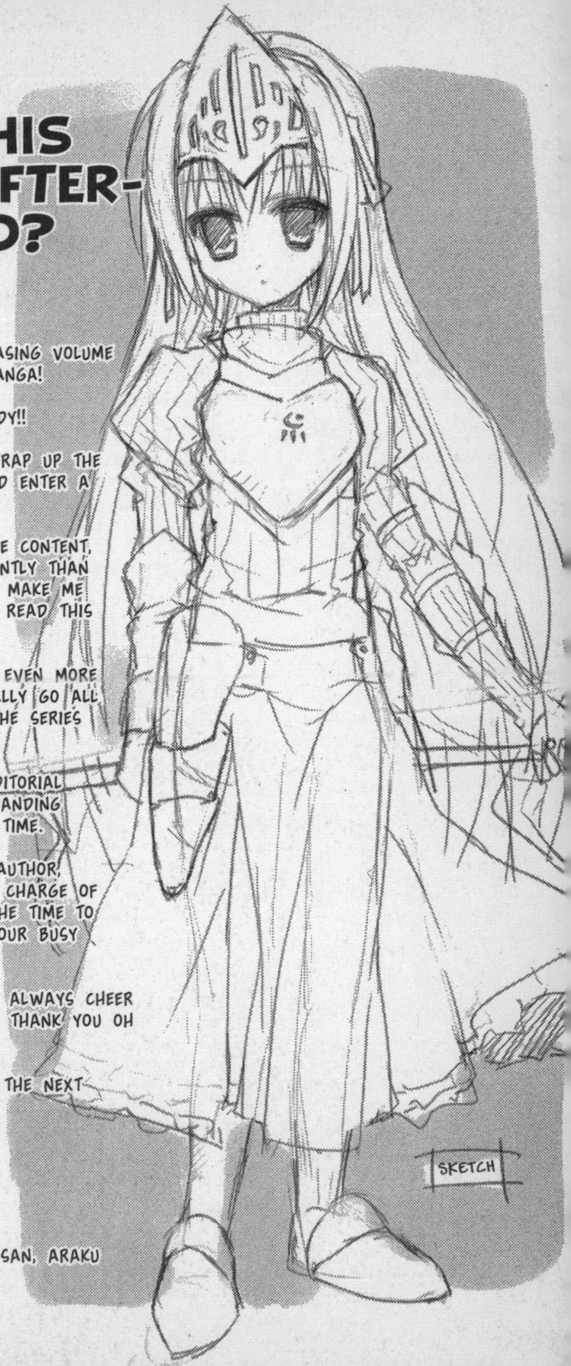
SKETCH

THANK YOU VERY MUCH FOR PURCHASING VOLUME TWO OF THE *IS THIS A ZOMBIE?* MANGA!

IT'S A BATTLE—I MEAN, LOVE COMEDY!!

IN THIS VOLUME, WE COMPLETELY WRAP UP THE KYOUKO ARC FROM VOLUME ONE AND ENTER A WHOLE NEW TURN OF EVENTS.

HAVING TO JUGGLE SO MUCH OF THE CONTENT, PARTS OF THE STORY FLOW DIFFERENTLY THAN THE ORIGINAL SCRIPT, SO IT WOULD MAKE ME VERY HAPPY IF YOU WOULD PLEASE READ THIS AS WELL AS THE NOVEL.

IN VOLUME THREE, I GET TO DRAW EVEN MORE OF THIS ZOMBIE WORLD, AND I REALLY GO ALL OUT IN THIS CHANCE TO PORTRAY THE SERIES IN ITS MANGA FORM.

TO MY EDITORS AND THE WHOLE EDITORIAL DEPARTMENT, SORRY FOR ALWAYS HANDING THINGS IN BARELY IN THE NICK OF TIME.

AND THANK YOU TO THE ORIGINAL AUTHOR, KIMURA-SENSEI, AND THE EDITOR IN CHARGE OF THE ORIGINAL SERIES FOR TAKING THE TIME TO CHECK OVER THE MANGA DESPITE YOUR BUSY SCHEDULES.

AND TO ALL OF YOU READERS WHO ALWAYS CHEER ME ON, I GREATLY APPRECIATE YOU! THANK YOU OH SO VERY MUCH!!

I HOPE YOU WILL CHEER ME ON IN THE NEXT VOLUME TOO.

BEST REGARDS!

SACCHI

★ASSISTANTS★
MIMIZU-SAN, TOMITA-SAN, EKAKIBITO-SAN, ARAKU NISHIKI-SAN, ANZU-SAN

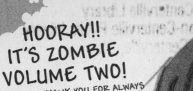

HOORAY!! IT'S ZOMBIE VOLUME TWO!

SACCHI-SAN, THANK YOU FOR ALWAYS DRAWING EVERYONE SO CUTELY!!

KOBUICHI

I'M LOOKING FORWARD TO VOLUME THREE!!!!!

HUH? IT'S ALREADY VOLUME TWO? ISN'T IT A LITTLE SOON? CONGRATULATIONS! AND AT LONG LAST, YUKI MAKES HER DEBUT. WHEN I GOT TO LOOK OVER THE LAYOUTS, I NOTICED THAT EVERY PANEL WITH YUKI IN IT MENTIONS SOME "PERKINESS" OR "JIGGLING." ALL THESE SOUND EFFECTS TO DESCRIBE HER TITS. YOU SURE ARE BOOB OBSESSED, AREN'T YOU!? BUT I'M WITH YOU ALL THE WAY ON THIS. BEST REGARDS HERE-AFTER TOO!

SHINICHI KIMURA

CONGRATULATIONS ON THE RELEASE OF VOLUME TWO!

EU'S CUTENESS IS REACHING MACH LEVELS!

MURI

IS THIS A ZOMBIE? 2 ✻

SACCHI
SHINICHI KIMURA
KOBUICHI • MURIRIN

Translation: Christine Dashiell

Lettering: AndWorld Design

This book is a work of fiction. Names, characters, places, and incidents are the product of the author's imagination or are used fictitiously. Any resemblance to actual events, locales, or persons, living or dead, is coincidental.

KOREHA ZOMBIE DESUKA? Volume 2
© 2011 SACCHI © 2011 SHINICHI KIMURA • KOBUICHI • MURIRIN.
First published in Japan in 2011 by FUJIMISHOBO CO., LTD., Tokyo.
English translation rights arranged with KADOKAWA SHOTEN Co., Ltd., Tokyo through TUTTLE-MORI AGENCY, INC., Tokyo.

Translation © 2012 Hachette Book Group, Inc.

Yen Press
Hachette Book Group
237 Park Avenue, New York, NY 10017

www.HachetteBookGroup.com
www.YenPress.com

Yen Press is an imprint of Hachette Book Group, Inc. The Yen Press name and logo are trademarks of Hachette Book Group, Inc.

First Yen Press Edition: July 2012

ISBN: 978-0-316-21037-9

10 9 8 7 6 5 4

BVG

Printed in the United States of America